ST. GEORGE'S PARISH REGISTERS

[HARFORD COUNTY, MARYLAND]

1689-1793

By
Bill AND *Martha Reamy*

HERITAGE BOOKS
2010

HERITAGE BOOKS
AN IMPRINT OF HERITAGE BOOKS, INC.

Books, CDs, and more—Worldwide

For our listing of thousands of titles see our website at
www.HeritageBooks.com

Published 2010 by
HERITAGE BOOKS, INC.
Publishing Division
100 Railroad Ave. #104
Westminster, Maryland 21157

Copyright © 1988 Bill and Martha Reamy

All rights reserved. No part of this book may be reproduced or transmitted in any form or by any means, electronic or mechanical, including photocopying, recording or by any information storage and retrieval system without written permission from the author, except for the inclusion of brief quotations in a review.

International Standard Book Numbers
Paperbound: 978-1-58549-058-5
Clothbound: 978-0-7884-8578-7

TABLE OF CONTENTS

```
Introduction . . . . . . . . . . . . . . . . . . . . . v
Parish Register . . . . . . . . . . . . . . . . . . . 1
Wardens, Vestrymen & Registrars . . . . . . . . . . . 99
Abstracts of Vestry Proceedings . . . . . . . . . . . 102
Pew Distribution . . . . . . . . . . . . . . . . . . . 114
Member List 1800 . . . . . . . . . . . . . . . . . . . 115
Oaths . . . . . . . . . . . . . . . . . . . . . . . . 116
Index . . . . . . . . . . . . . . . . . . . . . . . . 117
```

The Parishes of St. Paul's, St. John's and St. George's
of Baltimore and Harford Counties

Established in 1692

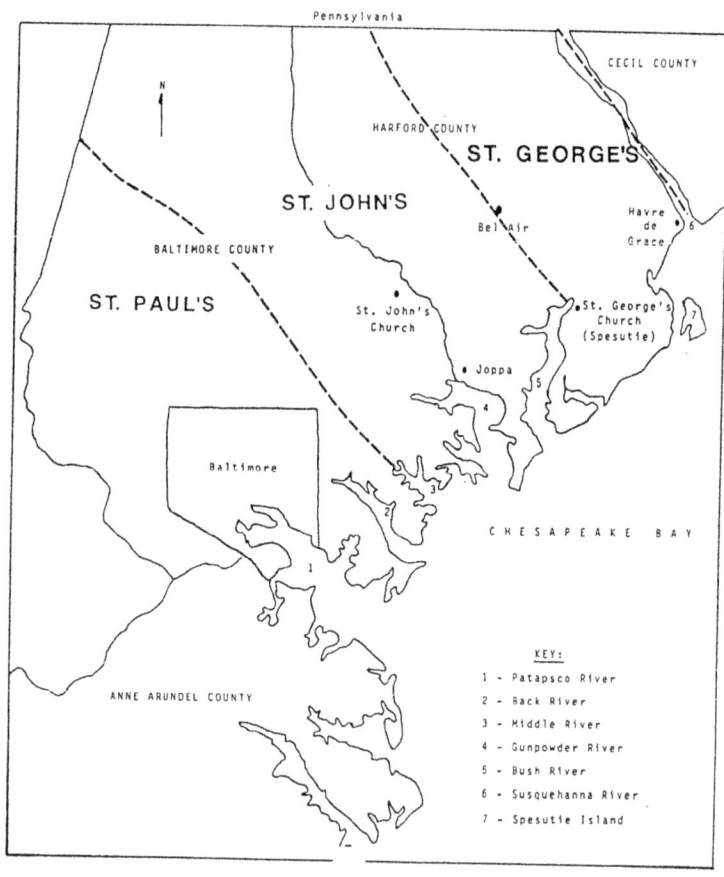

INTRODUCTION

In June of 1692 the Assembly of Maryland passed an "Act for the Service of Almighty God and the Establishment of the Protestant Religion within the Province." This Act gave the Church of England the same "Rights, Liberties, and Franchises," within the colony of Maryland as might be established by law. One of the provisions gave the Justices and the Commissioners of the several counties the power to call together the Principal freeholders to lay out the various parishes and to establish vestries to administer the affairs of the parish.[1]

Accordingly, Baltimore County (which included present day Harford County and parts of Carroll County) was divided into three parishes--St. Paul's, St. John's, and St. George's. The 18th century would see the establishment of two more Anglican (or Protestant Episcopal) Parishes: St. James' and St. Thomas'. Each of the three parishes was given definite boundaries. Those of St. George's Parish were: the Susquehanna River on the east, the Chesapeake Bay on the south, the headwaters of the Bush River on the west, and the Pennsylvania Line on the north. The boundaries of these three parishes remained the same until the 19th century when three parishes were established from parts of St. George's Parish: Havre de Grace in 1809, Deer Creek in 1859, and Churchville in 1869.[2]

The first vestry of St. George's Parish was comprised of Messrs. William Hollis, Laurence Taylor, John Parker, George Smith, Roger Matthews, and Thomas Cord.[3]

The first church to be located in what is now Harford County predated the 1692 Act of Establishment and may have been erected as early as 1671. It appears to have been in use definitely by 1681 when the children of John Cooke were "baptized in Bush River Neck." C. Milton Wright states that the first church was located somewhere on the Aberdeen Proving Ground, and no trace of the church or first graveyard now remains.[4]

In 1718 James Phillips, Esq., "for the live of the Protestant religion," conveyed 2 acres of James' Park to the vestry of St. George's Parish for the purpose of building a church. This church was located on the present site of St. George's (Spesutia) Church, at Perryman, between Pulaski Highway and Perryman Road.[5]

By the mid 1750's the wooden building was in such poor condition that the Assembly of Maryland was petitioned for 75,000 pounds of tobacco to build a new church. The new building was finished in 1758 and was 57' by 35' in size, with brick walls three feet thick. From first to last the building cost about $3500.00 to build and finish. It boasted floors paved with flagstone imported from England, velvet cushions, and linen surplices. This building lasted until the 1830's. The vestry house was originally a frame structure built about 1720; it was replaced about 1766.[6]

From 1692 until 1718 St. George's and St. John's Parishes shared the same pastor. The pastors were: Rev. John Yeo, 1683-1686; John Edwards, 1702-1711; George Irwin, 1716-1718; Evan Evans, 1718-1721 (graduate of Oxford University; later moved to Philadelphia); Robert Wayman, 1722-1724 (also a graduate of Oxford; later served parishes in Pennsylvania and New Jersey); John Humphreys, 1724-1729 (the subject of a glowing obituary in the Vestry Proceedings); John Holbrooke, 1725-1726 (later moved to Virginia); Charles Smith, 1726 (dismissed by the Governor almost as soon as he was installed); Stephen Wilkinson, May 1726-

May 1744; Hugh Carlisle, May 1744-Aug. 1749; Rev. Andrew Lensrum, Sept. 1749-1769 (not too popular with Governor Sharpe, but described as a "worthy minister" by Rev. Thomas Cradock of St. Thomas'); John Porter, 1769; William Edmiston, 1770-1772; William West, 1772-1779 (one of the few clergymen who sided with the American cause); James Wilmer, 1783-1786 (later served as Chaplain, U.S. Senate, 1812, and an Army Chaplain, 1814); John Allen (until 1814).[7]

The records of the parish fall into three categories. The first is made up of the Registers of Births, Deaths, and Marriages. The first original register, started in 1692, was maintained until about May 1745. The second volume contains a copy of the original register, and was continued until about the year 1799. (It was no doubt this second volume that Miss Lucy H. Harrison used when she made her transcript of St. George's Parish Records). The third volume begins in the 1830's. The gap between the second and third volumes may be filled by the private register of Reverend John Allen who served both St. George's and St. John's. All of the original registers, including Rev. John Allen's, are deposited at the Maryland State Archives, Annapolis. Miss Harrison's transcript is at the Maryland Historical Society, Baltimore.

The second group of records is found in two volumes of vestry proceedings: Book A for the years 1718-1772, and Book B, for the years following 1772. Abstracts from these proceedings have been included in this volume. The originals are at the Maryland State Archives in Annapolis.

The third category of records are the cemetery inscriptions, not included in this volume. These tombstone inscriptions have been copied, typed, and indexed by the Governor William Paca Chapter, Daughters of the American Revolution, as part of a multi-volume series of Harford County Bible, Family, and Tombstone Records. These typescripts are at both the Maryland Historical Society Library in Baltimore, and the Daughters of the American Revolution Library in Washington, D.C.

Users of this volume should be aware that following each entry of a birth, marriage, or burial, in the Registers section, the following designations have been used preceding page numbers: {OR xx} is used to designate the Original First Register; {2R xx} refers to the second original register started in the year 1745. {H xx} is used to designate the Harrison Transcript.

In addition to the Protestant Episcopal parishes of St. George's, St. James (My Lady's Manor) and St. John's, Harford County had a number of other churches whose congregations predated 1800. The churches with their of organization in parentheses include: Old School Baptist Meeting (1754), Dublin Methodist (1790), Thomas Run or Watters Methodist (1782), Bethel Presbyterian (1769), Churchville Presbyterian (1738), Slate Ridge Presbyterian (1750), Deer Creek Society of Friends (1736), Priest's Ford Roman Catholic (1747), and St. Ignatius Roman Catholic (1779). All provided the inhabitants of Harford County with places to worship. Unfortunately only the records of Deer Creek Friends Meeting have survived.

This is the fourth volume of church registers published by Family Line Publications. St. John's (called St. John's and St. George's) Registers were transcribed by Henry Peden. In his book some records of St. George's are included which are not included in this volume. St. Thomas' and St. James' Parish Registers were transcribed by Bill and Martha Reamy. Other volumes to be published in this series include: St. Paul's Protestant Episcopal (which includes Baltimore City), First Presbyterian (Baltimore City), and Gunpowder Society of Friends (Baltimore County).

Following this Introduction is a list of surnames with frequently used variations in spelling.

NOTES AND REFERENCES

¹ Archives of Maryland. Volume XIII: Proceedings and Acts of the General Assembly of Maryland, April 1684 - June 1692. William Hand Browne, ed. Baltimore: Maryland Historical Society, 1894. pp. 425-430.

² Percy G. Skirven. The First Parishes of the Province of Maryland. Baltimore: The Norman, Remington Co., c.r.1923. p. 142; Nelson Waite Rightmeyer. Parishes of the Diocese of Maryland. Reisterstown: 1960. pp. 25-26.

³ Rightmeyer, op. cit., lic. cit.

⁴ C. Milton Wright. Our Harford Heritage. c.r.1967. p. 193.

⁵ Baltimore County Land Records. Liber TR # RA. f. 484. Hall of Records.

⁶ Nelson Waite Rightmeyer. Maryland's Established Church. Baltimore: 1956. pp. 144-146.

⁷ Ibid., pp. 304-306.

VARIOUS SURNAME SPELLINGS

Amoss/Amos
Arnold/Arnal
Ashford/Aishford
Balch/Baulick/Baulch
Barn/Barns
Bayley/Bailey
Boice/Bois
Braysher/Brashier/Basysher
Brierly/Bryerley
Burchfield/Birchfield
Cambell/Camble/Campbel/Cample
Collins/Collings
Colson/Colston
Crawford/Crawfoot
Daugherty/Dockarty
Deaver/Dever
Donahue/Dunahue
Donavin/Dunawin
Eliot/Elliot
Freezland/Freeland
Fuller/Fullar
Gallam/Gallham/Galhampton
Garrettson/Garretson/Garrison
Gervace/Jarvis
Giles/Gyles
Ginkins/Genkins/Jenkins
Gilbert/Gilbird
Goodwin/Godwin
Hamilton/Hambleton
Hamby/Hambey
Hargnes/Hargus
Henry/Henery
Kean/Keene
Kimble/Kimball/Kembal
Lauracy/Larrifsee
Leigh/Lee
Litten/Litton
Lisbuy/Lisby
Little/Lyttle
Maccan/Mackan
Mccartney/Maccarty/Mccarty
Marphew/Murphew/Morphew
Maxwell/Masewell
Mitchel/Michel
Newson/Masam
Norvil/Norvell/Norrvel
Osborn/Osbourn/Ozbourn/Ozburn
Paca/Peca
Pogne/Poge
Poteet/Putteet
Prebble/Pribble
Pritchard/Prichard
Ranshaw/Renshaw
Rees/Reece
Rhoades/Rhodes
Rigdon/Rigden
Ruark/Reward
Shepard/Sheppard/
    Sheperd/Shepherd
Sincler/Sinkler
Stewart/Steuart
Taylor/Tayler
Tompson/Tomson/Thompson
Urquhart/Urghvart
Wescomb/Westcomb
Whiteaker/Whitacre
Wilborn/Wilbourn
Wilkisson/Wilkinson

ST. GEORGE'S PARISH REGISTER

Mary HARTSHORN d/o George HARTSHORN(E) b. at Bush River 13 May 1695. {H-176, OR-1}
William SMITH s/o George SMITH b. at Bush River 1 May 1695.
Ruth JOHNSON d/o John JOHNSON b. at Swan Creek 16 September 1695.
Benjamin OSBORN s/o William OSBORN was b. at Swan Creek 17 June 1695.
Mary BEVON d/o Thomas BEVON b. at Bush River 27 May 1695.
Thomas HANNES s/o Miles HANNES b. at Rumly Creek 22 September 1695.
Ann PREBBELL d/o Thomas PREBBELL b. at Swan Creek 8 November 1689.
Thomas PREBBELL s/o Thomas b. at Musketa Creek 27 July 1691.
Mary PREBBELL d/o Thomas b. at Musketa Creek 6 June 1696(5).
John NEWSUM s/o Thomas NEWSUM b. at Delfe the 28 September 1694.
John JACKSON s/o Simeon JACKSON b. at Middle River, Baltimore County 10th December 1689.
Simeon JACKSON s/o Simeon JACKSON b. at Bush River 9 September 1691. {H-177}
Judith JACKSON d/o Simeon JACKSON b. at the head of Musketa Creek 19 December 1693.
Thomas JACKSON s/o Simeon JACKSON b. at the head of Musketa Creek 10th October 1695.
Ketturah COMBEST d/o John COMBEST b. at Swan Creek 10 October 1695.
Sarah COMBEST d/o John COMBEST b. at Swan Creek 17 January 1693.
Samuel TREELL b. 3 March 1688; Bethena TREELL b. the 10 July 1690.
Thomas HOWARD s/o John HOWARD b. 7 October 1683.
John COOK s/o John COOK b. at Bush River 5 December 1681.
William COOK s/o John COOK b. at The Head of Swan Creek 8 November 1684.
Thomas KININGTON and Hannah TREGO m. 15 June 1695.
William CANNON and Mary WILLING m. 18 February 1695. {OR-2}
John JONES & Martha LOVEILL Living on Swan Creek m. 8 July 1695.
Thomas BUTLERS and Mary BURTHEL Living near the head of Rumley Creek m. 23 January 1696.
John HALL and Martha GOULDSMITH Living on the North Branch of the head of Bush River m. 18 July 1693.
William JEFF and Ruth MARTHEWS Living on the Head of Swan Creek m. 12 August 1697.
John HALL and Anne HOLLIS Living at Bush River m. 6 May 1697.
John SHEELD and Elizabeth BUNN Living on the head of Collets Creek m. 16th January 1696.
Martin DEPOST and Tammeson HOLT (HOFF) m. 16th January 1697.
Edmund GRADDE and Jellen DUNAWIN living on the Bay Side m. 10 March 1697.
Thomas MORRIS and Elizabeth JACKSON living upon the Level; Banns published June & July, m. 14th July 1698.
Thomas CORD and Hannah MATHEWS, both of this parish; Banns published July 1698, m. the 4th of August 1698.
John FURAT s/o Peter FURAT b. at the head of Musketa Creek 27 February 1689. {H-178}
Ann FURAT d/o Peter FURAT b. at Spesutia Creek 14 March 1692.
Charles MILES s/o Evan MILES b. at Bush River 21 March 1694.
Elizabeth DEFORGE d/o Knowell DEFORGE b. near to Col. George WELLS 28 December 1691. {H-179}
Samuel BROWN s/o Samuel BROWN b. at Bush River 17 August 1690.
Blanch BROWN s/o Samuel BROWN b. at Bush River 23 April 1695.
Thomas BEVON s/o Thomas BEVON b. at Bush River 25 November 1691.
William BEVON s/o Thomas BEVON b. at Bush River 18 November 1693.

ST. GEORGE'S PARISH REGISTER

Thomas MORRIS and Elizabeth Living on the Level; Bans published June and July 1698.
The Bans of Matrimony Published Between Thomas CORD and Hannah MATTHEWS both of this Parish in July 1698.
Jacob JOHNSON s/o John JOHNSON b. 23 April 1682.
Aron JOHNSON s/o John JOHNSON b. 15th July 1684.
Richard PERKINS s/o Richard PERKINS b. at the head of Musketa Creek the 9 July 1689.
William PERKINS s/o Richard PERKINS b. at the head of Musketa Creek 15 March 1692.
Mary PERKINS d/o Richard PERKINS b. at the head of Swan Creek 2 April 1695. {OR-3}
Elisha PERKINS s/o Richard PERKINS b. at the head of Swan Creek 9th June 1697. {H-180}
John HALL s/o Capt. John HALL b. at Spesusia Creek 13 Jan. 1694.
Edward HALL s/o Capt. John HALL b. at the North Branch of the head of Bush River 15 July at 11 or 12 a Clock at night, 1697.
John BEVON s/o Thomas BEVON b. at Bush River 13 February 1697.
William PRICHAT s/o William PRICHAT b. at Rumley Creek 23 May 1697.
Thomas SIMSON s/o Richard SIMSON b. near to Susquehanna River 5 November 1691.
Susanna SIMSON d/o Richard SIMSON b. near to Susquehanna River 5 April 1693.
William SIMSON s/o Richard SIMSON b. near to the mouth of Susquehana River 14 February 1695.
Elizabeth SIMSON d/o Richard SIMSON b. near Susquehanna River 5 April 1697.
Jane GRENFIELD d/o Thomas GRENFIELD b. at the head of Collats Creek 8 September 1697.
Elizabeth RAMSEY d/o Charles RAMSEY b. at the head of Bush River 17 December 1697.
Frances BUTTERS d/o Thomas BUTTERS b. near to the head of Delf Creek 5 January 1697/8.
Sara HALL d/o John HALL b. at Bush River 1 May 1698.
Abiezer Francis WHITEHEAD s/o Francis WHITEHEAD b. at Spesusia Creek 20 March 1689. {H-181}
Sara MORGAN d/o John MORGAN b. at Spesusia Creek 20 March 1689.
Mary MORGAN daugher of John MORGAN b. at Spesusia Creek 20 February 1691.
Moses JOHNSON s/o John JOHNSON b. at the head of Swan Creek 19 March 1692.
Susanna DREW d/o Anthony DREW b. at the mouth of Rumley Creek 3 January 1695.
Lodowick MARTIN s/o Lodowick MARTIN b. at the Level 30 Dec. 1695.
Mary GREENFIELD d/o Thomas GREENFIELD b. 25 July 1684.
Sarah GREENFIELD d/o Thomas GREENFIELD b. at the head of Collets Creek the Last Day of December 1691. {OR-4}
John GREENFIELD s/o Thomas GREENFIELD b. at the head of Collets Creek 24 January 1695/6.
Susanna UTIE d/o George UTIE b. at the Level 24 September 1695.
Sarah GILLUM daugher of Ralph GILLUM b. at the mouth of Swan Creek 27 February 1695/6.
James BROWN s/o Samuel BROWN b. at Bush River 22 December 1697.
Thomas RAMSEY s/o Charles RAMSEY b. 4 February 1692. {H-182}
Mary RAMSEY d/o Charles RAMSEY b. 17 August 1695.
Susanna NEWSUM d/o Thomas NEWSUM b. at Delf 7 May 1696.
John HOWARD s/o John HOWARD b. at Swan Creek 6 July 1696.

ST. GEORGE'S PARISH REGISTER

Ann LOFTON d/o William LOFTON b. at the head of Swan Creek 10 August 1696.
Thomas LOFTON s/o William LOFTON b. at the head of Swan Creek 25 November 1691.
Isabell LOFTON d/o Wiliam LOFTON b. Musketa Creek 19 Dec. 1693.
Rebecca GAMBELL d/o Giddeon GAMBELL b. at the head of Swan Creek 21 February 1693.
Abraham GAMBELL s/o Giddeon GAMBELL b. at the head of Swan Creek 19 March 1694.
Margaret MILES d/o Evan b. at Rumly Creek 21 December 1696.
James COSLE s/o James COSLE living at Delf b. 8 September 1684.
William COSLE s/o James COSLE living at Delf b. 15 Sept. 1686.
Margaret COSLE d/o James COSLE living at Delf b. 12 April 1691.
Mary COSLE d/o James COSLE living at Delf b. 20 February 1692.
Michael HANNES s/o Miles HANNES b. at Rumly Creek 20 Dec. 1696.
David HULL s/o Joseph HULL living at the Water Mill at Bush River b. 27 March 1696. {H-183}
Dannelana WHITHEAD d/o Francis WHITHEAD b. at Swan Creek 20/25 January 1696/7.
John MILES s/o John MILES b. at Bush River 16 March 1696/7.
Sarah PERRERILL d/o Daniel PERRERILL b. at Bush River 7 August 1691.
William HOLLIS s/o William HOLLIS b. at Bush River 10 March 1696 at 8 at night. {OR-5}
John PREBBELL s/o Thomas PREBBELL b. at Musketa Creek 21 June 1697.
Simeon JACKSON bur. at the Level 20 February 1695/6.
George UTIE bur. at the Level 16 October 1695.
Col. George WELLS bur. on his own plantation upon the Bay Side 19th July 1696.
John GREENFIELD s/o Thomas GREENFIELD bur. at the head of Collats Creek 10 September 1696.
Susanna NEWSUM d/o Thomas NEWSUM bur. at Delf 29 November 1696.
Michael HANNES s/o Miles HANNES bur. at Rumly Creek 28 Dec. 1696.
John CHERN s/o Wilks CHERN bur. at Swan Creek 18 February 1696.
John MILES s/o John MILES bur. at the head of Bush River 3 May 1697.
Mary UTIE bur. at the Level the Last Day of April 1697.
Elizabeth HANNES wife to Miles HANNES bur. at Swan Creek 4 August 1697.
Judith JACKSON d/o Simeon JACKSON buried at the Levil 4 September 1697.
Lewis JARMAN bur. at Rumly Creek first Day of June 1695/6.
William HASEELWOOD bur. at Rumly Creek 15 June 1698.
Semmelua FISHER bur. at the head of Musketa Creek 2 July 1698.
Mary WEND b. 20 December 1697. {H-184}
Mary COMBEST d/o John COMBEST b. at Swan Creek 20 April 1698.
Mary OSBORN and Thomas OSBORN twins dau. & s/o William OSBORN b. at Swan Creek 13 August 1698.
Elizabeth BEVON wife of Thomas BEVON bur. at the head of Rumly Creek 25 June 1698.
Even MILES s/o Even MILES b. at Rumly Creek 7 October 1698.
Banns of Matrimony Between Miles HANNES and Elizabeth KELLE both of Spesutia Island in George's Parish Pub. Nov. 1698.
Banns of Matrimony Between Samuel JACKSON and Sarah MATHEWS both of George's Parish Published in November 1698.
Two Irish Servants the one Named Dennis the other named Mary, bur. at Mr. Marks RICHARDSON at the mouth of Rumly Creek in Georges Parish August 1698.

ST. GEORGE'S PARISH REGISTER

Elizabeth COTTREL d/o John COTTREL b. at the head of Swan Creek 8 August 1698. {H-185}
Mr. Edward BOOTHBY d. upon Spesutia Island 12 December 1698; bur. 23 December 1698.
Anthony DREW s/o Mr. Anthony DREW b. at the Bay Side near the mouth of Rumly Creek 26 December 1697(1?). {OR-6}
Samuel JACKSON of Musketa Creek and Sara MATHEWS of Rumly Creek mar. 11 December 1698.
Bans of Matrimony Published Between Thomas TEMPLE and Elenor LORESON both of our Parish January 1698/9.
Charles BOORIN s/o William BOORIN of Swan Creek bur. at Swan Creek 7 January 1698/9.
William BOORIN of Swan Creek bur. at Swan Creek 21 January 1698/9.
Elizabeth SIMSON d/o Richard SIMSON of Swan Creek bur. at the head of Swan Creek the Last Day of September 1698.
Martha SMITH d/o Emanuell SMITH of the Bay Side near to the mouth of Susquehanna River b. 16 January 1698/9.
Clemensi PARKER w/o John PARKER of Bush River d. 5 December 1698.
Elizabeth HARTSHORN the d/o John PARKER and Clemensy d. at Bush River 20 December 1698.
William PARKER s/o John PARKER and Clemensy PARKER of Bush River d. 27 December 1698.
Edward HARPLE of Bush River d. 20 January 1698/9. {H-186}
Elizabeth CHEETAM d/o Francis CHEETAM and Joan b. at the Bay Side near to the mouth of Rumly Creek 13 October 1693.
Sara MORRIS d/o Thomas MORRIS b. at the Level 17 January 1698/9.
Miles HANNES and Elizabeth KELLY Both of Spesutia Island m. 24 November 1698.
Samuel PARKER s/o John PARKER and Clemensy PARKER of Bush River d. 7 March 1698/9.
Francis CHEETAM of the Bay Side near the mouth of Rumly Creek bur. 29th March 1699.
John HASEELWOOD of the head of Musketa Creek bur. at the mouth of Rumly Creek 2 April 1699.
Thomas TEMPLE and Elinor LORRESON Living at Bush River m. 17 April 1699.
Henry HASELWOOD of the head of Musketa Creek bur. upon his own Plantation 9 June 1699.
Mary BOORIN Widow of Swan Creek bur. at Swan Creek 20 May 1699.
Sara BOORIN d/o William BOORIN and Mary BOORIN of Swan Creek bur. 20 May 1699.
Gilbert PERREIR of the Level bur. 25 March 1699. {OR-7}
Nathaniel ANDREWS of the head of Musketa Creek bur. 24 June 1699.
Banns of Matrimony Published Between John SAVERY and Ann REVES both of this Parish in June 1699; m. 27 June 1699.
Banns of Matrimony Published Between William WHITE and Ann BAKER Widow Both of this Parish in June & July 1699. {H-187}
John JACKSON s/o Simeon JACKSON of the Land bap. 4 July 1699.
Simeon JACKSON s/o Simeon of the Level bap. 4 July 1699.
Thomas JACKSON s/o Simeon of the Levil bap. 4 July 1699.
Sarah MORRIS d/o Thomas MORRIS of the Levil bap. 4 July 1699.
John PREBBELL s/o Thomas PREBBELL of the head of Musketa Creek bap. 2 July 1699. {H-188}
Lawrrant TAYLOR of the head of Collats Creek was bur. at the head of Collats Creek 23 July 1699.
Aquila HALL s/o Mr. John HALL & Martha HALL b. at Cranbury Hall at Bush River 27 June at one of the Clock in morning 1699.

ST. GEORGE'S PARISH REGISTER

Mrs. Elizabeth BOOTHBY widow Spesutia Island bur. at Mr. John HALL's Plantation on this side the Creek over against the Island 4 August 1699.
Robert JACKSON of Bush River and Isabel HOOPER of Cranbury Hall their Banns Published 30 July 1699; and also same Published the first and second Sundays in August 1699; m. 24 August 1699.
Banns of Matrimony Published Between Edward CANTWELL and Joan CHATTUM both of our Parish the 3rd Sunday August 1699, last Sunday in August, and first Sunday in September.
William WHITE and Ann BAKER Widow Both of our Parish m. 12 August 1699. {H-189, OR-8}
Susanna TEMPLE d/o Thomas TEMPLE b. at Rumly Creek 21 Aug. 1699.
Sarah CORD d/o Thomas CORD and Hannah CORD b. at the head of Collets Creek 1 September 1699.
John PARKER, Senr. of Bush River and Isabella SMITH of Gunpowder River Widow m. 12 September 1699.
Aquila PACA and Martha PHILLIPS Both of Bush River m. 11 September 1699.
John WALSTONE s/o John WALSTONE and Margaret WALSTONE b. at Swan Creek 12 March 1687/8.
Arabella WALSTONE d/o John WALSTONE and Margaret WALSTONE b. at Swan Creek 2 June 1690.
Sarah WALSTONE d/o John WALSTONE and Margaret WALSTONE b. at Swan Creek 4 September 1694.
William PRECHAT s/o William PRECHAT of Rumly Creek bur. at Rumly Rumly Creek 6 October 1699.
Edward CANTWELL and John CHATTUM [sic] both of our Parish m. 5 December 1699.
William GREENFIELD s/o Thomas GREENFIELD and Rachell GREENFIELD b. at Spesutia Creek 5 December 1699.
Elizabeth PREBBLE d/o Thomas PREBBLE and Mary PREBBLE b. at the head of Duck Creek 27 December 1699. {H-190}
Mary BOORIN d/o William BOORIN of Swan Creek b. 15 June 1695.
Banns of Matrimony Published Between George MORGAN and Elizabeth SMITH Last Day December 1699/10 [sic]. and again 7 & 14 January 1699/10.
Banns of Matrimony Published Between Larranc TAYLOR and Mary MILES 14 January 1699/10, last Sunday in January; Larranc TAYLOR & Mary MILES were m. 5 February 1699/10.[sic]
George SMITH s/o George SMITH of Bush River bur. 27 Jan. 1699/10.
Jonathan SIMSON s/o Richard SIMSON b. at the Bay Side near to the mouth of Susquehanna River 12 November 1699.
William LOFTON s/o William LOFTON b. at the head of Swan Creek 12 December 1699.
Banns of Matrimony Between Phillip BRANNAN and Susanna THOMAS Published the 1st, 2nd, & 3rd third Sundays of February 1699/10.[sic] {OR-9}
Joshua FOWLER s/o Joshua FOWLER of Bush River b. 2 March 1698/9.
Mary PEACA mother of John HALL and Aquila PEACA Departed this Life in the 67th year of her age 24 December 1699, who was one of the Daughters of Mr. William PARKER Late of Calvert County merchant, which was one of the H Hambroh Company & died in London.
Clark HOLLIS s/o William HOLLIS of Bush River was b. at Bush River 16 January 1699/10.[sic] {H-191}
Sarah PERKINS d/o Richard PERKINS b. at the head of Swan Creek 15 December 1699/10.[sic]
Sarah PERKINS d/o Richard PERKINS of the head of Swan Creek bur. at the head of Swan Creek 15 December 1699/10.[sic]

ST. GEORGE'S PARISH REGISTER

George MORGAN and Elizabeth SMITH m. 10 February 1699/10.[sic]
Daniel JOHNSON s/o Daniel JOHNSON of Spesutia Island b. at Spesutia Island 28 February 1699/10.[sic]
Banns of Matrimony Between William BASHTEEN and Lidia ALGOOD Published in March 1699/00.
Rebecca MILES d/o Evan MILES of Rumly Creek b. at Rumly Creek Creek the 1st March 1699/10.[sic]
Banns of Matrimony Between Thomas GILBERT and Sarah BEDFORD both of this Parish were Published the Last Sunday in April and the first and Second Sunday in May 1700.
Banns of Matrimony Between Henry HEDGE and Mary PARKER both of this Parrish were Published Whit Sunday and Monday and Tuesday in Whitson week 1700.
Thomas GIBBERD and Sarah BEDFORD Both of this Parrish m. the 27th of May 1700.
Joshua WOOD s/o Joshua WOOD of Delf b. 1 October 1694. {H-192}
Isaac WOOD son of Joshua WOOD b. at Delf 2 June 1700.
Jane GREENFIELD d/o Thomas GREENFIELD and Rachel GREENFIELD of Sepsutia Creek bap. 9 June 1700.
William GREENFIELD s/o Thomas GREENFIELD and Rachel GREENFIELD of Sepsutia Creek bap. 9 June 1700. {OR-10}
William JEFF living at the head of Swan Creek bap. last day of June 1700.
Isaac WOOD s/o Joshua WOOD living at the mouth of Rumly Creek bap. last day of June 1700.
Henry HEDG and Mary PARKER both of this parish m. 25 May 1700.
George DREW s/o Anthony DREW of the mouth of Rumly Creek b. 1 April 1700.
Ann RAMSEY d/o Charly RAMSEY of the head of Bush River b. 9 April 1700.
Jonathan HOLLINS servant to Thomas GREENFIELD of Spesutia Creek bur. 22 July 1700.
Shellina SMITH d/o George SMITH and Hannah SMITH of Bush River b. 8 June 1700.
Daniel JOHNSON s/o Daniel JOHNSON of Spesutia Island bur. 29 August 1700.
Abraham JACKSON s/o Robert JACKSON b. at Bush River 12 July about 12 of the clock in the day 1700.
Daniel RILLE(?) of Spesutia Creek servant to Mr. John HALL of Cranbury Hall bur. at Spesutia Creek 13 November 1700.
John SHELDS of Musketa Creek bur. 7 November 1700.
James DRUNKCOORD and Mary GREENFIELD both of this parish m. by banns 22 December 1700.
Samuel TWEEL(WEEL?) s/o Abigell COMBEST living near the head of Collots bur. 5 January 1700.
Mary BASTEENE d/o William BASTEENE b. at the Bayside near to Susquahanna River 28 April 1700.
William BRANACAN s/o Phillip BRANACAN b. near mouth of Musketa Creeke 10 December 1699.
William BRASYEAR s/o William BRASYEAR of Swan Creeke b. 26 May 1696.
Thomas BEVINGS was m. July 8 1700. {OR-11}
John BRASYEAR s/o William BRASYEAR of Swan Creek b. 13 June 1699.
Joseph PARKER s/o John PARKER and Isabella PARKER of Bush River b. 4 March 1700/1.
William CARLIEL servant to William HOLLIS of Bush River bur. 18 June 1700.
John HALL s/o John HALL of Cranbury Hall bur. 24 April 1701.

ST. GEORGE'S PARISH REGISTER

William JEFF and Elizabeth AISHLEYS of Swan Creek Banns published May 1701; m. 29 May 1701.
Thomas LEE and Elizabeth SHELDS both of this parish m. 8 May 1701.
Banns of Matrimony published between John CHEAPMAN of Bush Creek near Susquhannah River and Hannah MARKUM of this parish in June 1701.
Mary PRECHAT d/o William PRECHAT of Rumly Creek b. at Rumly Creek 9 May 1701.
Thomas GILBERT s/o Thomas GILBERT, Junr. of the Bay Side near Susquehanna River b. 6 February 1700.
Nem/Nern GIBBERD [sic] d/o Thomas GIBBERD [sic] b. at the Bayside near Susquehanna River 6 February 1700.
Sarah GIBBERD wife of Thomas GIBBERD, Junr. bur. the 15th of February 1700/1.
Thomas GIBBERD s/o Thomas GIBBERD of the Bayside near Susquehanna River bur. 20 February 1700/1.
Nem/Nern GIBBERD d/o Thomas GIBBERD, Junr. of the Bay Side near Susquehanna River bap. the next Sunday after Easter 1701.
Luce/Lucy CANTWELL d/o Edward CANTWELL b. at the head of Rumly Creek 17 January 1700/1.
Martha COMBEST d/o John COMBEST b. at the head of Collats Creek 9 September 1700.
The Banns of Matrimony Between Thomas BUCKNAL and Elizabeth GRIFFIS Both of Georges Parish Published at Georges Parish Church according to Law in July 1701. {OR-12}
Mary SMITH d/o Emanuel SMITH of the Bay Side near the mouth of Susquehanna River b. the first of June 1701.
Nem/Nern GIBBERD d/o Thomas GIBBERD of the Bay side near Susquehanna River bur. 13 August 1701.
Martha PERKINS d/o Richard PERKINS of the head of Swan Creek b. the Last Day of March 1701.
Hannah JACKSON d/o Samuel JACKSON and Sarah JACKSON was b. at the Level 7 September 1701. {H-193}
John SAVERY s/o John SAVERY of Rumly Creek was b. at Rumly Creek 12 September 1701.
Sara JOHNSON d/o Daniel JOHNSON of Spesutia Island b. 18 September 1701.
Thomas GREENFIELD s/o Thomas GREENFIELD and Rachel GREENFIELD Living at Collats Creek b. at Collats Creek 18 November 1701.
Rachel AISHFORD bur. at John KIMBLES at the mouth of Spesutia Creek 13 December 1701.
Owen SWILLEVANT and Dorothy TAYLOR Widow Living at the head of Collats Creek m. 27 September 1701.
Thomas FENICK bur. at William OSBORN's at Bush River 18 Nov. 1701.
Abraham CORD s/o Thomas CORD Living at the head of Collats Creek b. 3 March 1700; bap. 27 September 1701.
Elizabeth AISHLE Living near to the head of Swan Creek b. 20 June 1693.
William AISHLE Living near the head of Swan Creek b. 27 July 1694. {H-194}
John AISHLE Living near the head of Swan Creek b. 25 July 1697.
Margaret JEFF d/o William JEFF of the head of Swan Creek b. 6 January 1701/2.
Jane FENN of Susquehanna River d/o Thomas FENN b. 2 February 1688/9.
Henry FENN s/o Thomas FENN of Susquehanna River b. 10 August 1692. {OR-13}
Sara PREBBELL d/o Thomas PREBBELL of Duck Creek b. at the head of Duck Creek 12 August 1702.

ST. GEORGE'S PARISH REGISTER

Elizabeth LOFTON d/o William LOFTON and Elizabeth LOFTON of the head of Swan Creek b. 12 July 1702.
Lucian CANTWELL d/o Edward CANTWELL and Joan his wife bap. 31 May 1702.
Sarah DREW d/o Anthony DREW & Maryanne his wife was b. April 30 1702; bapt. 23 August 1702.
Edward DEATH s/o Randal DEATH was bap. July 12th, 1702.
Thomas GREENFIELD s/o Thomas GREENFIELD and Rachel his wife was bap. May 31 1702.
Benjamin WELLS s/o George and Blanch his wife d. 16 April 1702; bur. 19 April 1702.
Elizabeth SMITH the wife of Francis SMITH d. 10 August 1702; bur. 15 August 1702.
George FREEZLAND s/o Stephen FREEZLAND and Sarah his wife b. 7 October 1659. {H-195}
Sarah FREEZLAND d/o Stephen FREEZLAND and Sarah his wife b. 8 August 1664.
Mary HALL d/o John HALL and Amy his wife b. 21 July 1702; bap. 1 October 1702.
William MILES s/o Evan MILES & Rebecca his wife b. 16 Sept. 1702.
William MILES, Rebecca MILES and Evan MILES the s/o & d/o Evan Evan MILES & Rebecca his wife were all three bap. 1 Oct. 1702.
Bethiah PHILLIPS d/o Mr. James PHILLIPS and Bethiah his wife b. 25 August 1702. {OR-14}
Mary PACA d/o Aquila PACA and Martha his wife b. 4 Sept. 1701.
PRITCHET Maryan d/o William PRITCHET and Elizabeth his wife bap. 30 November 1706.
Rebecca TANSEY d/o Alexander TANSEY and Rebecca his wife bap. 12 July 1702.
John SAVORY s/o John SAVORY & Anne his wife bap. 30 November 1702.
Isaac WOOD s/o Joshua WOOD and Mary his wife was bap. 8 July 1700. {H-196}
Benjamin COLSON Servant to Thomas BROWN d. 12 October; bur. 14 October 1702.
Selina SMITH bap. 14 July 1700.
Richard SMITHERS of Baltimore County was Joyned to Mrs. Blanch WELLS Spinster 14 February 1700/1.
Blanch SMITHERS d/o Richard SMITHERS and Blanch his wife b. 28th February 1702.
Jonathan MARCY of Baltimore County was Joyned in Holy Matrimony to Mrs. Ann COLLYER Spinster of Spesutia Parrish 25 Nov. 1701.
Charles RAMSEY s/o Charles RAMSEY and Elizabeth his wife b. 10 May 1702.
Thomas FAUKNER Servant to Charles RAMSEY Departed this Life 24 December 1702; bur. 27 December 1702.
Mary BROWN d/o Samuel BROWN & Mary his wife was b. 9 October 1700; bap. 15 November 1700.
Cadwallady JONES of Baltimore County Planter was Joyned in Holy Matrimony unto Mary ELLIS Spinster 23 April 1702.
Elizabeth WHITTECAR the d/o John WHITTECAR and Katharine his wife b. 12 January 1687. {OR-15}
Ruth WHITTECAR d/o John WHITTECAR and Katharine his wife b. 27 March 1690.
John WHITTECAR s/o John WHITTECAR & Catharine his wife b. 23 April 1691. {H-197}
Charles WHITTECAR s/o John WHITTECAR and Catharine his wife b. 12/10? October 1693.
Sarah WHITTECAR d/o John WHITTECAR and Catharine his wife b. 10 November 1699.

ST. GEORGE'S PARISH REGISTER

Abraham WHITTECAR s/o John WHITTECAR and Catharine his wife b. 19 September 1702.
Robert WATERS was m. unto Ann ALLEN of Baltimore County 13 December 1701.
Tho. RUSSEL Baltimore County Planter was Joyned unto Mary CAHELL Spinster in holy Matrimony 27 July 1702.
John FREEZLAND s/o Stephen FREEZLAND and Sarah his wife b. 10 March 1668.
Tho. GLOVER d. August 22d at Mrs. WELLS's & was bur. 23 August 1702.
James FOWLER the s/o Joshua FOWLER and Mary his wife b. 22 July 1702.
Edward CANTWELL the s/o Edward CANTWELL and Joan his wife was b. 11 January 1702/3.
Mr. Robert GIBSON of Spesutia hundred in George's Parish Gent. was Joyned in the Holy Estate of Matrimony unto Mrs. Mary GOLDSMITH Spinster of the same Parish 15 December 1702.
Mr. Garret GARRISON of George's Parish in Baltimore County Gent.; was Joyned in the Holy Estate of Matrimony unto Mrs. Elizabeth FREEBOURN Spinster 5 December 1702.
George GARRISON s/o Garrett GARRISON and Elizabeth his wife was b. 26 November 1703. {H-198, OR-16}
John HALL s/o John HALL of Cranbury Hall Esqr. and Martha his wife was b. 3 December 1701.
John HALL the s/o John HALL of the Cranbury Hall Esqr. & Martha his wife was bap. 30 March 1703.
Sarah HOLLICE the d/o William HOLLIS and Mary his wife was b. 1 March 1690.
Avarilla HOLLIS the d/o William HOLLICE and Mary his wife was b. 20 September 1693.
William HOLLIS the s/o William HOLLICE and Mary his wife was b. 10 March 1696.
Clark HOLLIS the s/o William HOLLIS and Mary his wife was b. 16 January 1699.
Mary HOLLIS the d/o WIlliam HOLLIS and Mary his wife was b. 20 February 1703.
Sarah PREBBLE the d/o Thomas PREBBLE & Mary his wife was bap. 4 October 1702.
George GARRISON the s/o Garrett GARRISON & Elizabeth his wife bap. 16 May 1703.
Elizabeth BRANICAN the d/o BRANICAN Phillip and Susannah his wife was b. 17 December 1701.
Absolom BROWN the s/o Samuel BROWN & Mary his wife was b. 22 June 1703 & bap. August 8th 1703. {H-199, OR-17}
Gregory FARMER and Sarah HEWS were Published August 8 1703.
Gregory FARMER and Sarah HEWS were Joyned in the Holy Estate of Matrimony 27 August 1703.
Banns of Matrimony Between Joseph CRAMPTON and Mary CASTLY (COSTLY?) were Published in Pesusie 20 August 1703 & they were m. 19 October 1703.
Thomas JACKSON and Mary KEMBAL were joyned in the Holy Estate of Matrimony 25 July 1703.
Maryan MOTTS the d/o ___ MOTTS and ___ his wife was b. 27 August 1702; bap. 7br the 8th 1703.
Charles JONES the s/o Cadwalladar JONES & Mary his wife was b. 25 June 1703; bap. 8th August 1703.
Mary JONES the wife of Cadwalladar JONES Departed this Life the 25 June 1703 and was bur. 27 June 1703.

ST. GEORGE'S PARISH REGISTER

Elizabeth VINER Servant to William OSBORN d. March 28th & was bur. March 30th 1703.
Mary HOLLIS the d/o William HOLLIS and Mary his wife d. 9 July 1703 and was bur. 11 July 1703.
John PARKER's wife Junio d. August 20th; bur. August 22d 1703.
Mary RUSSEL the wife of Thomas RUSSEL d. 26 Aug. ; bur 27th 1703.
Thomas CORD the s/o Thomas CORD and Hannah his wife was b. 28 July 1703 & was bap. 28 December 1703. {H-200}
Mary HOLLIS the wife of William HOLLIS d. January 11th and was bur. January 15 1703/4.
Daniel BRYAN and Ann VEARES were Published the 17 October 1703.
Daniel BRYAN and Ann VEARES were Joyned in the holy Estate of Matrimony 28 November 1703.
Daniel MACKARTE were Published and WOOLSHER (?) December 25 & were m. January 23 1703/4.
Thomas GUILBER(?) was m. in the Holy State of Matrimony unto Hannah ASHFORD 1 April 1703.
John KEMBAL Junr. m. to Elizabeth GUILBERT April 16 1703.
Banns of Matrimony Between Edward SWAN and Elizabeth GRIFFITH were Published 21 December 1703 and they were married 24 January 1703/4. {OR-18}
William PERKINS was Joined In the Holy State of Marriage unto Martha MILES 3 February 1703/4.
Lawrence TAYLOR was Joyned in the Holy State of Marriage unto Agnus MOUNTEGUE 7 February 1703/4.
Thomas NICHOLS s/o John NICHOLS d. & was bur. 12 July 1704.
Henry JACKSON d. & was bur. September 15th 1705.
Liddia CROMPTON the d/o Joseph CROMPTON and Margaret his wife was b. 19 March 1706 & was bap. April 28 1706.
Elizabeth LOFTON wife of William LOFTON d. 20 & was bur. October 24 1703/4.
William LOFTON d. and was bur. April 13th 1704.
Rachel GREENFIELD the wife of Thomas GREENFIELD was bur. January 5 1704/5.
Thomas GREENFIELD the husband of Rachel GREENFIELD bur. January 11, 1704/5.
Edward HALL Servant to John HALL Esqr. was bur. July 22 1704.
Thomas CAPLE Husband to Mary CAPLE was bur. & d. 27 April 1704.
Mary CAPLE the wife of Thomas CAPLE was bur.
Mr. Henry JACKSON d. and was bur. September 15 1705.
Abraham WATSON and Margaret GINKINS were Published February 3 1705/6 & m. February 14.
Thomas MASTERS and Margaret JONES Published April 28 1706.
Thomas SKY & Elizabeth MARYFIELD Published June 5; m. 23 July 1706.
Henry BURK & Easter PINE Published January 1 & m. 6 Jan. 1796/7.
John BELCHER & the Widow PERKINS Published February & March 16 1706.
John DEBRULER & Mary DRUNKARD m. April 12th 1704.
Mr. John WINWRIGHT & Mrs. Ann RICHARDSON were m. 1705.
William LOVE & Arrabella WALSTON were m. April 27 1706.
Mr. George CHANCY and Mrs. SMITH were m. June 22 1706.
Mr. Robert ROBERTS & Mrs. PARKER were m. October 15 1706. {OR-19}
Mary PARKS the d/o Edward PARKS & Dorothy his wife b. 12 August August & bap. 20 April 1706. {H-202}
Isaac BUTTERWORTH the s/o Isaac BUTTERWORTH and Esther his wife was b. 4 November 1704.
Maryan PRITCHARD the d/o William PRITCHARD and Elizabeth his wife was b. 9 April 1702.

ST. GEORGE'S PARISH REGISTER

Micajah GREENFIELD the s/o Thomas GREENFIELD & Rachel his wife b. 23 March 1703/4 & was bap. 23 July 1704.
John HALL the s/o John HALL and Amy his wife was b. August 4 1706.
Mary HODGE the d/o Henry HODGE & Mary his wife was b. 5 November 1706 & bap. July 20th 1707.
Mary TAYLOR the d/o Lawrence & Agnus his wife was b. 1 February 1706 and bap. March 2nd 1706.
Mary EDMUNDS d/o Elizabeth ELLIS b. 16 February 1705.
Elias CRAFFORD the s/o James CRAFFORD and Elizabeth his wife was b. 8 November 1706.
Solomon WESTREY the s/o Michael WESTREY & Jean his wife was b. & bap. 26 November 1706.
Elizabeth BRANNICAN the d/o Phillip BRANNICAN and Susanna his wife was b. December 17th 1701.
Christopher SHEPHARD the s/o Rowland SHEPHARD and Bridget his wife was b. March 10th 1696.
Rowland SHEPHARD s/o Rowland & Bridget b. 28 March 1696.
Elizabeth SHEPHARD b. March 4th 1700; George SHEPHARD b. January 4th 1702; Mary SHEPHEARD d/o Rowland & Bridget his wife.
Thomas EDMONS d. December 23rd and was bur. the 29th 1705.
Benjamin SMITH d. April the 5th and was bur. the 8th, 1705.
James OSBOURN was bur. November 15th 1705/6.   {OR-20}
Mary CAPLE d. October the 21st and was bur. October 24 1706.
Blanch BROWN the d/o Samuel BROWN d. December 9 & was bur. December 13th 1706.
William PERKINS d. January the 8th and was buried the 9th 1706.
Hannah MATHEWS the wife of Roger MATHEWS d. and was bur. the 6th of February 1706/7.
Mr. Thomas WAINWRIGHT of Prince Georges County and Mrs. Susanna RICHARDSON of Baltimore were Joyned in the Holy State of Matrimony by Mr. John Edwardson January the 21st 1705/6.
Clemency HEDGE the d/o Henry HEDGE and Mary his wife was b. 14 August 1704 and bap. 7br 17 1704.   [II-203]
Francis RUSSEL the s/o Thomas RUSSEL and Mary his wife was b. 25 September 1703; bap. 2br 25th 1703/4.
Diane SAVORY d/o John and Anne b. 21 January 1703/4.
Joshua WOODS s/o Moses and Aaron [sic] b. March 29th 1704, bap. April 2d, 1704.
Mary NORRIS the d/o William NORRIS and Sarah his wife b. 31 March 1704 & bap. May 28th 1704.
Sarah FOWLER b. March 31st 1704 and was bap. (?) June 4, 1704.
Micais GREENFIELD the s/o Thomas GREENFIELD and Rachel his wife was b. March 23d, 1703/4; bap. July 23, 1704.   {H-204}
Sarah WEST d/o Robert WEST and Sara his wife was b. 24 October 1701; bap. 12 May 1704.
Constania WEST was b. 14 April 1703 & bap. 12 May 1704.
Mary COLEMAN d/o Elizabeth COLMAN [sic] b. July 5th, 1699.
David CROMPTON the s/o Joseph CROMPTON and Margaret his wife was b. August 27th 1704; bap. 15th 8br 1704.
Giles KEMBAL the s/o John KEMBAL and Elizabeth his wife was b. 24 February 1703/4; bap. June 5th, 1704.   {OR-21}
Francis BROWN the d/o Samuel BROWN and Mary his wife b. 6 June 1705; bap. June 30th 1705.
Sarah MOLTON the d/o Mathew MOLTON and Ann his wife was b. 3 May 1705; bap. July 8th, 1705.
Archabel BUCHANNAN the s/o Archabel BUCHANNAN and Mary his wife was b. April 12th 1705; bap. June 12th 1705.

ST. GEORGE'S PARISH REGISTER

Mary JACKSON the d/o Samuel JACKSON and Sarah his wife b. 28 April 1704; bap. May 28th, 1704.
Sara WOOD d/o Joshua and Elizabeth WOOD b. 8br 21 1706.
Thomas CORD s/o Thomas CORD and Hannah his wife was b. 28 July 1703.
Mary ELLIS the wife of Caldwall JONES was bur. 27 June 1703.
Elizabeth YORK the wife of William YORK d. November 24th and was bur. November 27th, 1703.
Mary HOLLIS the wife of William HOLLIS d. January 8th 1703/4; bur. January 15th 1703/4.
George SMITH the husband of Hannah SMITH d. April 20th 1704; bur. April 22nd, 1704.
Mrs. Blanch WELLS, the wife of George WELLS, d. April 21st; bur. April 25th, 1704.
Emanuel SMITH d. April 20th; bur. April 24th 1704.
TREBBLE Thomas d. June 12; bur. June 14 1704.
Tho. BURROWS d. July 30; bur. July 31 1704.
OSBORN William Senior d. January 7; bur. 9 1704.
PARKER John Senior d. January 12 & bur. 20 1704/5.
James DRUNKARD d. February 1 & bur. February 5 1704/5.
Mr. Mark RICHARDSON d. February 19; bur. 24 February 1704/5.
John WALSTON d. December 7 & bur. December 12 1704.
Jean LONE wife of William LONE d. March 12 & bur. 13 March 1704/5. {OR-22}
William WABLINGTON d. October 19 & bur. October 21 1795.
Robert GIBSON husband of Mary GIBSON d. & bur. 10 June 1704.
John KEMBAL Senr. d. & bur. April 4 1705.
James OSBOURN d. & bur. 13 December 1705.
Lewis NOEL and Mary FERRIL published 8br 25 & m. November 25 1704.
Jacob JOHNSON and Alice MORE published November 12 1704 & m. January 11 1704.
Tobias EMMERSON and Mary BUR were published December 10 1704 & m. January 15 1704/5.
Archibel BUCHANNON and Mary TREBBLE m. 9 April 1705.
Mark WHITTACAR and Katherine TEAG published May 13 1705 & m. June 10 1705.
John DAVIS and Easther FUGAT published Oct. 14 & m. 9br 12 1702.
William WISE and Margaret OSBOURN published September 30 & m. October 15 1705.
Richard TREADWAY and _____ PARKER published November 7 1705 & m. December 17 1705.
Micael WESTRY and Jean SOLOMON published November 11 1705 & m. December 10 1705.
Edward SWAN and Elizabeth GRIFFITH m. January 24 1703/4.
Tho. BUCKNEL and Elizabeth BURK published November 9 1794 & m. December 13, 1704.
Cadd. JONES and Mary POOL m. May 7 1704.
John ROBERTS and Mary JACKSON m. 11 April 1705.
Joshua WOOD m. Elizabeth PITTCOCK December 15 1704.
Benjamin SMITH m. Sarah HOLLIS 25 February 1704/5.
George CHANEY m. 22 June 1706.
Elizabeth MORRIS d/o Thomas MORRIS and Elizabeth his wife b. October 1 1701. {OR-23}
Mary MORRIS d/o Thomas MORRIS and Elizabeth b. July 10 1702.
Susanna MORRIS d/o Thomas MORRIS and Elizabeth his wife b. 2 April 1705.
Thomas MORRIS s/o Thomas MORRIS and Elizabeth his wife b. August 1 1701(7?). {H-205}

12

ST. GEORGE'S PARISH REGISTER

William TAYLOR s/o Lawrence TAYLOR and Agnus b. 26 November 1705.
William PHENIX, the s/o William and Bridget his wife was b. 26 September 1705; bap. June 4 1706.
William PHENIX the s/o William PHENIX and Bridget his wife d. 26 September; bur. 28 September 1707.
Parker HALL the s/o John HALL Esqr. and Martha his wife was b. 13 September 1707 and was bap.
Francis BUCKNALL the s/o Thomas and Mary his wife was b. 25 April 1705.
Thomas BUCKNALL the s/o Thomas BUCK[sic] and Mary his wife was b. 5 March 1707.
Roger CORD the s/o Thomas CORD and Hannah his wife was b. 25 August 1707; bap. October 12th 1707.
David & Henry THOMAS the Sons of David THOMAS and Hannah his wife were b. 8 April 1708; bap. 11 April 1708.   {H-206}
Elizabeth BROWN the d/o Richard BROWN and Mary his wife b. 26 July 1708; bap. 15 August 1708.
Richard TREDAWAY b. s/o Richard TREDAWAY December 8th 1706.
Anthony DEMASTERS the s/o Anthony DEMASTERS and Catharine his wife was b. 7 November 1706.
Thomas SIMPSON 17 years old November 5 1707; Susan SIMPSON 15 years old April 2d 1707; William SIMPSON 14 years old February 14th 1707; Jonathan SIMPSON b. 12 November 1707; Mathew SIMPSON was 6 years old August 27 1708; Ann SIMPSON was 3 years old January 25 1708; Elizabeth SIMPSON was 7 months old February 27 1708.   {OR-24}
Mr. John BROWN the s/o Thomas BROWN was Joined in the Holy state of Marriage unto Elizabeth SICKLEMORE the 18 November 1705.
Thomas BROWN the s/o John BROWN and Elizabeth his wife was b. 18 September 1708; bap. September 29th 1708.
Phillip BRANNICAN the s/o Phillip BRANNICAN and Susan his wife was b. 27 August 1707.
Sarah SHYE the d/o Thomas SHYE and Elizabeth his wife b. 31 December 1707.
William TAYLOR d. and was bur. 27 November 1707.
Mary TAYLOR the d/o Law TAYLOR d. and was bur. June 19 1708.
Edward BRANNICAN, Sam BROWN's man was bur. the 28 November 1707.
Sarah JACKSON the d/o Sarah JACKSON b. June 20 1707.
Mr. BALE d. and was bur. February 5th 1708.
Thomas GUILBERT the s/o Thomas GUILBERT and Hannah his wife was b. 1 July 1705.   {H-207}
Elizabeth GUILBERT the d/o Thomas GUILBERT and Hannah his wife wife was b. 27 June 1708.
Roger DUDNEY and Jane LEAK were Pub. August 10 and m. September 10 1708.
Robert PARKS the s/o Edward PARKS and Dorothy his wife was b. 12 September; bap. November 10 1707.
John CHAMBLEY's Banns Pubd. to Margery CHEEK October 1 1708, m.
John MASTERS the s/o Anthony MASTERS was b. December 6 1709.
Thomas TRIBLE d. May the 4th in 1709.   {OR-25}
James PRESBURY and Martha GOLDSMITH m. February 26 1708.
William FENIX d. in the year 1708.
Mary FENIX was b. February 2nd 1708.
Mary DUDNEY, at Owens BRIGHT's Child b. May 10th 1703.
Elizabeth DAY[,] Bridget's other Child b. March 31, 1707.
Mary WILLIAMS d/o John WILLIAMS b. February 11th, 1706.
Mrs. ARNOLD d. February 21st 1708.
Emanuel SEALY d. January the 14th 1708.
Henry RELPH d. January the 1st 1708.

ST. GEORGE'S PARISH REGISTER

George SMITHS s/o Richard SMITHS b. January 29 1708. {H-208}
Tobias EMMERSON girl b. December the 29th in 1708.
John SMITHS s/o Richard SMITHS b. August 3d, 1704.
Henry HEDGE d. February 25th, 1708/9.
Charles RIGDON s/o George RIGDON b. January the Last 1705.
Elizabeth RIGDON b. the 7th February 1708.
Stephen FRELAND d. in the year 1708.
Stephen FRELAND's wife & Daughter d. February in the year 1708.
Hugh BRANDIGAN d. in the year 1708.
Blanch SMITHS d. March the 19th 1708.
Mrs. BALE bur. March the 18th 1708.
Thomas TRIBLE d. in the year 1709.
James TOD was Drowned May the 9th, 1709.
Samuel BROWNs Wife d. April the Last 1709. {OR-26}
Timothy KEENE and Mary MOONE m. May 14 1709.
Anthony DREW & Margaret BROWN m. May 17 1709.
Richard GARRETT d. in May 1709.
Sarah SEALY d. in May 1709.
Thomas BURCHFIELD and Mary WILSON m. June the Last 1709.
Richard SMITHES and Philixana MAXWELL m. August 18 1709.
William COMPTON s/o Joseph COMPTON b. May 15th 1709.
Geenet CRAFOOT d/o James CRAFOOT b. July 27 1709.
James COBB and Rebecca ERNSTON m. October 30 1709.
John STEELE and Mary CLARK m. November 11 1709.
Solomon(?) GILBERT s/o Jarvis GILBERT b. May 22d 1709.
Thomas GALLION s/o John GALLION b. May 29 1709.
Patrick HALE m. to _____ December 17 1709.
William COSLEY and Mary ELLIS m. December 26 1709.
Roger MATHEWS d. December 1709.
Samuel BROWN and Mark [sic] SKELTON m. January 2 1709/10.
John SMITH and Mary HEDGE m. February 2 1709/10.
Joshua MERRIKEN and Elizabeth EWINS m. February 16 1709/10.
Mathew MOATON s/o Mathew MOATON b. August 24 1709. {H-209}
Henry HEDGE s/o Henry HEDGE b. January 18th 1708/9.
Ewrah BALE d. in the year 1709.
Thomas TEMPLE d. in May, his wife in April 1710. {OR-27}
Elizabeth RAMSEY Wife of Charles RAMSEY d. May 1710.
Edward WILDAY d. May 1710.
Peter CARROLL and Mary RENSHAW m. May 4th 1710.
Mary FREELAND d/o Stephen FREELAND b. December 25 1710.
John HANSON s/o Thomas HANSON d. April 1710.
William LOUGH and Temperance PICKETT m. July 6 1710.
Robert BURCHFIELD s/o Thomas and Mary BURCHFIELD b. February 27th 1710.
Stephen FREELAND s/o George and Mary FRELAND [sic] b. October 14th 1710.
Elizabeth NORRIS Wife of Thomas NORRIS d. in December 1710.
Samuel PRICHETT s/o Obediah and Margett PRICHETT b. March 6 1710.
Robert KINSBY and Mary WOOD m. August 1st, 1710.
Hannah TOMMAS [sic] d/o Daniel & Hannah THOMAS b. April 30 1710.
Richard RUFF s/o Richard and Sarah RUFF b. September 28 1710.
Christopher SHEPARD s/o Rowland and Bridget SHEPARD, b. November 19 1710.
Mary SMITHS d/o Richard and Philizana SMITHS b. 15 October 1710.
Sophia HALL d/o John and Martha HALL b. the 4 February 1709.
George, s/o George and Sarah CHANCY was b. 12 May 1708; bap. 12 May 1709.
James CHANCY s/o George and Sarah was b. 2 April 1712.

ST. GEORGE'S PARISH REGISTER

James s/o William and Avarilla OSBORN was b. 6 January 1711; bap. 5 April 1712. {H-210}
Frances HALL d/o John and Amy HALL was b. 10 June 1711.
John s/o John and Amy HALL was b. 6 October 1706.
Frances SWAN wife of Edward SWAN Departed this Life 8 December 1711. {OR-28}
Edward SWAN departed this Life 18 March 1711.
Margaret d/o William and Arabella LONY b. 15 July 1708.
John s/o William and Arrabella LONEY was b. 22 April 1711.
Susanna d/o Phillip and Susanna BRANNAGHAN b. 11 December 1704.
Hugh s/o Phillip and Susannah BRANNAGHAN b. 12 September 1711.
Frances d/o John and Susannah Maria STOKES b. 4 January 1705.
John s/o John and Susanna Maria STOKES was b. 3 November 1707.
Humphrey Wells s/o John and Susanna Maria STOKES was b. the 27th of March 1709.
Mary d/o John and Susannah Maria STOKES was b. 9 June 1712.
Judith d/o Thomas and Sarah ELLET was b. 19 March 1708.
Thomas s/o Thomas and Mary [sic] ELLET b. 19 November 1711.
Isaac s/o Thomas and Hannah CORD was b. 15 September 1710. {H-211}
William GARLAND s/o Henry and Lydia GARLAND b. 26 January 1712.
Sarah GARLAND d/o Henry and Lydia GARLAND was b. 2 August 1709.
Elizabeth d/o Henry GARLAND was b. 19 January 1710.
Daniel OBRYAN s/o Terence and Margaret OBRYAN in Cecil County 9 September 1709. {OR-29}
Charles s/o Daniel and Mary OBRYAN b. in Cecil County 5 May 1708.
Elizabeth DAUGH d/o Bridget DAGUH was b. 31 March 1701.
Owen s/o Bridget DAUGH was b. 11 December 1710.
George s/o George and Elizabeth RIGDON was b. 5 April 1710.
Daniel the Third s/o Richard and Sarah RUFF b. 27 January 1712.
Humphrey Wells STOKES s/o John and Susanna Maria STOKES was bap. 1 May 1713. {H-212}
Thomas FRISBY, George WELLS, Frances FRISBY - Sureties.
Hannah MATHEWS was b. at Rumly Creek 24 September 1711, d/o Roger and Mary MATHEWS.
Thomas CHISNAL s/o John and Elinor CHISNALL b. 2 September 1704.
Samuel COLIT s/o Samuel and Catharine COLIT b. 1 October 1704.
Anne COLIT was b. 6 March 1706.
John COLLET was b. 19 July 1709.
Ells NORRIS the d/o William and Sarah NORRIS b. 16 April 1713.
Susanna CORD d/o Thomas CORD and Hannah CORD b. 16 April 1713.
William LONEY the s/o William & Arrabella LONEY b. 18 Jan. 1713.
James TAYLOR s/o Lawrence and Agnes TAYLOR b. 11 January 1713.
Edward DANIEL Departed this Life 9 August 1713. {OR-30}
Capt. Lawrence DREPER Departed this Life 12 April 1713.
Richard MITCHEL was b. 26 August 1710.
Thomas BURCHFIELD was b. 8 August 1712.
Samuel BROWN Departed this Life 5 October 1712.
John MILS Departed this Life 5 February, 1712.
William COOCK and Sarah GARRETT was m. 27 August 1713.
Joseph JOHNSON and Ann TOD was m. 5 July 1713.
Mary BROWN Departed this Life 6 March 1712.
Mary ROGERS was b. 26 September 1712. {H-213}
Elizabeth GILLBART was b. 12 July 1711.
John CLARK and Elizabeth DREPER was m. 16 October 1713.
William PRICHET Departed this Life 25 October 1713.
Thomas GILLBART Departed this Life 24 October 1713.
Thomas HANSON Departed this Life 1 November 1713.
Edgar LIPER(?) and Elizabeth PRICHET was m. 30 October 1713.
Charles TALBOT and Elizabeth WOOD was m. 4 June 1713.

ST. GEORGE'S PARISH REGISTER

Mary CROW Departed this life 16 November 1713.
Mary TREDAWAY was b. 12 January 1709.
Thomas TREDAWAY was b. 6 March 1711.
Martha LESTER was b. 30 July 1713. {OR-31}
John WHITEAKER Departed this Life 25 November 1713.
Lawrence DREPER and Mary DREW was m. 24 December 1713.
William WOODCOK and Mary AMBOY was m. 24 December 1713.
John SMITH Departed this Life 21 December 1713.
Mary SMITH Departed this Life 20 December 1713.
William ROBINSON and Sarah COMBEST was m. 8 December 1713.
James CROW was b. 11 November 1713.
Philip PARKS was b. 29 December 1712.
Mary KEEN was b. 5 May 1710.
Hannah HARDEMAN was b. 24 July 1711.
John TOMSON was b. 2 April 1705.
Henry HELL (HALL?) was b. 11 October 1710. {H-214}
Peter LESTER was m. 8 May 1713.
Michael COLIT was b. 7 August 1713.
John MURFFY was b. 11 March 1710.
Edward MURFFY was b. 20 December 1712.
Darcas MURFFY departed this life 5 February 1711.
James PRITCHARD was b. 17 May 1713.
Ruth BELCHER b. 6 October 1708.
Jarvis GILBERT was b. 20 November 1713. {OR-32}
Robert WEST was b. 5 November 1706.
John WEST was b. 29 December 1711.
Precilla WEST was b. 28 March 1709.
Richard PERKINS was b. 18 December 1713.
Ford BARNS was b. 12 April 1698.
Joseph BARNS was b. 20 December 1701.
James BARNS was b. 26 March 1704.
Elizabeth CLARK was b. 15 November 1707.
Martha CLARK was b. 15 October 1713.
Augustus BROWN was b. 25 September 1710.
Gabriel BROWN was b. 1 May 1712.
Obediah PRITCHARD was b. 25 March 1711.
Grigory FARMER b. 2 August 1704; Margarit FARMER b. 2
  September 1706; Hannah FARMER b. 1 March 1707/8; Sarah FARMER
  b. 21 April 1710; John FARMER b. 21 February 1712.
Mary WARD b. 11 February 1711; Stephen WARD b. 5 Nov. 1712/13.(?)
Mary WARD d. 15 February 1712.
Stephen WARD d. 12 November 1713.
Sibil WESTERLY d. 19 February 1713.
Ralph DANDE and Mary FOX was m. 23 September 1714.
Bethiah PHILLIPS the wife of James PHILLIPS Departed this Life 13
  December 1714.
Elizabeth WHITEAKER d/o Mark WHITEAKER b. 25 February 1704.{H-215}
Thomas WHITEAKER s/o Mark WHITEAKER was b. 13 June 1712.
George EAVES and Mary COSTLEY was m. 1 September 1714.
John CHISNALD Departed this Life 1 April 1714.
Elizabeth COSTLEY wife of James COSTLEY Departed this Life 15
  April 1714.
James COSTLEY and Elinor CHISNALD was m. 2 August 1714.
John WEBSTER Junr. and Mary MAC DANIEL was m. 28 February 1714.
James HOLLINGSWORTH and Ann CHITCHING was m. 27 February 1714.
Samuel HUGHS and Jane WATKINS was m. 4 November 1714.
Elizabeth DEAVER d/o John DEAVER and Hannah his wife was b.
  August 1st 1703. {OR-33}

ST. GEORGE'S PARISH REGISTER

Samuel DEAVER b. 20 August 1705; Mary DEAVER b. 29 March 1708; Hannah DEAVER b. 2 July 1710; Thomas DEAVER b. 16 January 1713; s/o & d/o John DEAVER and Hannah his wife.
Thomas RUSSEL and Mary BORING was m. 7 November 1714.
Jonathan s/o Robert and Sarah WEST was b. 28 June 1714.
Elizabeth d/o Gregory and Sarah FARMER was b. 14 December 1714.
Roger MATHEWS and Mary CARVIL was m. November 14 1710.
John MATHEWS s/o Roger and Mary was b. June 26 1714 and was bap. May 20 1715. {H-216}
Anthoney BALE and Ann PLUMMER was m. June 18 1715.
John RUFF s/o Richard RUFF and Sarah his wife was b. June 23 1714.
John COWING and Susanna TEAGUE was m. 25 September 1712.
Sarah COWING d/o John and Susanna his wife was b. 18 July 1713.
John COWING s/o of John and Susanna his wife was b. 21 May 1715.
Thomas GALLION s/o John and Mary his wife was 6 years old 29 May 1715.
Solomon GALLION s/o John and Mary his wife was 3 years old 6 February 1715.
Samuel GALLION s/o John GALLION and Mary his wife was b. 27 July 1714.
Plisannah WEBSTER d/o John and Hannah WEBSTER was b. 21 January 1715.
William HAMBY s/so Francis and Elizabeth HAMBY was 12 years old 24 August 1715.
Francis HAMBY s/o Francis and Elizabeth HAMBY was 8 years old 1 April 1715.
Mary HAMBY d/o Francis and Elizabeth HAMBY was 6 years old 2 August 1715.
Samuel HAMBY s/o Francis and Elizabeth b. 5 August 1711.
Jane DANDE d/o Ralph and Mary his wife b. 18 May 1715.
Lawrence TAYLOR s/o Lawrence and Agnus b. 12 June and was bur. the 13th of the same. [no year]
John CLARK and Elizabeth DRAPER was m. 16 October 1714.
Ann KEAN d/o Timothy and Mary KEAN his wife b. 23 January 1714.
Thomas JOHNSON s/o Thomas and Mary JOHNSON his wife d. 30 April 1714. {H-217}
Rachel JOHNSON d/o Thomas and Mary JOHNSON his wife b. 20 July 1714.
John Miles YOUNGBLOOD s/o Thomas and Mary YOUNGBLOOD his wife was b. 31 October 1708.
Robert HAWKINS and Ann TREBLE (PREBLE?) was m. 15 November 1709.
Thomas HAWKINS s/o Robert & Ann HAWKINS his wife b. 25 Nov. 1712.
Elizabeth and Sarah GARLAND d/o Henry and Lidia GARLAND his wife d. in August 1714.
Samuel JACKSON s/o John and Katherine JACKSON b. 13 January 1713.
Daniel MACCARTY and Sarah MORRIS was m. 20 January 1714.
____ BROWN d/o of John and Elizabeth his wife was b. 15 February and d. 15 March 1714.
Elizabeth LITTON d/o of Thomas and Ann LITTON his wife b. 6 April 1715. {OR-34}
Elizabeth GARRETTSON b. 30 April 1704; John GARRETTSON b. 17 February 1706; Sarah GARRETTSON b. 30 December 1708; James GARRETTSON b. 15 October 1709; Sophia GARRETTSON b. 15 November 1711; Freeborne GARRETTSON b. 15 February 1713. All sons & daughters of Garrett & Elizabeth GARRETTSON his wife.
Peregrine BROWN s/o Samuel and Mary his wife b. 9 September 1715.
Jacob CORD s/o Thomas and Hannah CORD his wife b. 13 June 1715.

ST. GEORGE'S PARISH REGISTER

John RUPH(RUSH?) s/o Richard and Sarah RUPH(RUSH?) his wife was bap. 9 October 1715.
John COMBEST s/o Annah Lury COMBEST b. 4 December 1715.
Margaret GILBERT the wife of Jarvis GILBERT Departed this Life 16 January 1715. {H-218}
Thomas THURSTON Departed this Life 11 January 1715.
John CRAWFORD s/o James and Francis CRAWFORD his wife b. 11 March 1703.
Katherine CRAWFORD d/o James and Francis b. 15 February 1712.
Peter FARMER s/o Grigory FARMER and Sarah his wife b. 8 February 1715/6.
Richard POWEL Departed this Life 6 February 1715/6.
Sarah FREELAND was 2 years old August 15, 1715 d/o George and Mary his wife.
Perdine FREELAND d/o George and Mary his wife b. 1 March 1715.
Stephen FREELAND s/o George and Mary his wife Departed this Life 20 December 1714.
Mary MACCOMUS d/o John and Ann MACCOMUS his wife b. 3 Feb. 1713.
John MACCOMUS s/o John and Ann MACCOMUS his wife b. 2 Nov. 1715.
Rachel EMSON d/o James and Rebecca EMSON his wife b. 7 June 1708.
Rebecca COBB was b. 26 March 1710; Charity COBB was b. 15 April 1712; Margaret COBB was b. 15 May 1714; the d/o James and Rebecca COBB his wife.
Frances JOHNSON was b. 1 November 1703; Hannah JOHNSON was b. 6 June 1705; Rachel JOHNSON d/o was b. 5 June 1707; Sophia JOHNSON was b. 22 November 1709; Charity JOHNSON was b. 17 February 1712. All daughters of Daniel and Frances JOHNSON his wife.
Daniel JOHNSON Departed this Life 14 September 1715. {H-219}
Daniel JOHNSON s/o Daniel and Frances JOHNSON his wife was b. 2 October 1715.
Elizabeth EVES d/o George & Mary EVES his wife b. 23 April 1716.
Frances CRAWFORD the wife of James CRAWFORD Departed this Life 25 October 1715.
George HOLLINGSWORTH the s/o James and Ann HOLLINGSWORTH his wife was b. 17 November 1715.
John HAWKINS s/o Robert and Ann HAWKINS his wife b. 25 February 1715/16.
Mary WEST d/o Robert and Sarah WEST his wife b. 28 April 1716.
Robert CLARK and Sillinah SMITH was m. 18 February 1717/18.
James PHILLIPS Gentleman and Johannah KEMP Widow Both of this parish was m. by the Rev. William TIBBS, Minister of St. Pauls Parish in 1716.
Mark WHITEAKER s/o Mark and Catharine WHITEAKER his wife b. 15 February 1715/6. {OR-35}
Susanna CORD d/o Thomas and Hannah CORD his wife Departed this Life 4 August 1716.
Ann LESTER mother of Peter LESTER Departed this Life 17 August 1716.
Thomas GASH and Hannah GILBERT was m. 22 December 1715.
Johanna GASH d/o Thomas and Hannah GASH his wife b. 8 Nov. 1716.
Michael GILBERT s/o Thomas and Johanna GILBERT his wife Departed this Life 3 September 1716. {H-220}
Sarah Collins SIMPSON d/o Susanna SIMPSON b. 27 February 1715.
Hannah MITCHEL d/o Thomas and Ann MITCHEL his wife b. upon Easter Monday 1716.
William DOWLEY s/o John and Elizabeth DOWLEY his wife b. 6 September 1703.

ST. GEORGE'S PARISH REGISTER

Mary FREELAND d/o Stephen and Sarah FREELAND his wife b. 25 December 1708.
John DRAPER s/o John and Abigle DRAPER his wife b. 27 Nov. 1709.
Susanna DRAPER d/o John and Abigle b. 25 December 1713.
Mary GARRETTSON d/o Garrett and Elizabeth GARRETTSON his wife b. 28 February 1715.
James LOW b. 29 June 1702; Thomas LOW b. 5 February 1706; Samuel LOW b. 16 January 1707/8; Abraham LOW b. 19 January 1709/10; sons of William and Rebecca wife.
Catherine WHITEAKER wife to Mark WHITEAKER Departed this Life 15 November 1717.
John WEBSTER s/o John and Mary his wife b. 24 June 1717.
Sarah RUFF d/o Richard and Sarah his wife b. 12 October 1717.
John NEWSOM and Mary FINCHECOME (STINCHCOMB?) was m. __ February 1715.
Thomas NEWSOM s/o John and Mary NEWSOM his wife b. 16 Dec. 1715.
Mark WHITEAKER and Elizabeth EMSON was m. 13 February 1717.
Hannah THOMAS wife of David THOMAS Departed 12 April 1718.
George LESTER s/o Peter and Ann LESTER his wife b. 25 Dec. 1717.
James COBB s/o James COBB and Rebecca his wife b. 16 Sept. 1716.
James COBB Departed this Life 12 March 1718.   {H-221}
James PHILLIPS s/o James PHILLIPS and Johannah his wife b. 13 December 1716.   {OR-36}
Hester BUTTERWORTH b. 28 March 1711; Mary BUTTERWORTH b. 10 June 1712/3; Hannah BUTTERWORTH b. 27 April 1714; Francis BUTTERWORTH b. 26 November 1716; d/o Isaac and Hesther BUTTERWORTH his wife.
William KEMBALL Departed this Life 5 December 1717.
Charles WHITEAKER and Mary KEMBALL was m. 30 January 1717/8.
Kesiah DEAVER d/o John and Hannah DEAVER d. 15 August 1716.
John PERKINS s/o William & Elizabeth PERKINS b. 13 February 1717.
Roger MATHEWS s/o Roger & Mary MATHEWS his wife b. 26 April 1718.
Mary CORD d/o Thomas and Hannah CORD his wife b. 16 October 1717.
George WELLS d. 28 December 1716.
William MARSHALL and Mrs. Mary WELLS was m. 19 June 1718.
Hellen NEWSOM d/o John and Mary NEWSOM was b. 14 August 1718.
Sarah HOW d/o Christopher and Rebecca HOW was b. 15 July 1716.
Martha FARMER d/o Gregory and Sarah FARMER his wife b. 7 January 1717/8.   {H-222}
James BROWN s/o Samuel and Mary BROWN his wife b. 8 April 1718.
Charity WHITEAKER d/o Mark and Elizabeth WHITEAKER b 8 Dec. 1718.
Martha LITTON d/o Sarah LITTON & Thomas MILES the father b. 27 April 1718.
Jonathan WARD and Sarah WALSTON was m. 28 September 1712.
George WARD s/o Jonathan and Sarah WARD his wife was b. 3 March and Sarah his wife d. the same day 1715/6.
Jonathan WARD and Ann HALL was m. 8 January 1717/8.
Susanna PHILLIPS d/o James & Johannah his wife b. 5 Sept. 1718.
Avarilla OSBORN d/o William and Avarilla his wife b. 6 Oct. 1718.
Henry MORRIS s/o Thomas and Mary MORRIS his wife b. 20 Oct. 1713.
Thomas DONOWIN s/o Timothy and Mary DONOWIN his wife was b. 29 June 1706.
Lawrence DRAPER s/o Lawrence and Mary DRAPER his wife b. 6 September 1715.
Anthony and Mary DRAPER, twins, s/o & d/o Lawrence and Mary DRAPER his wife b. 29 July 1717.
John HAWKINS and Rebecca EMSON was m. 23 December 1718.
Thomas KNIGHT and Susanna SIMPSON was m. 28 November 1718. {OR-37}
Light KNIGHT s/o Thomas and Susanna was b. 8 June 1719.

ST. GEORGE'S PARISH REGISTER

Charles GILBERT s/o Jarvis and Mary GILBERT his wife b. 29 September 1717.
Rowland KEMBAL and Hannah JACKSON was m. 15 May 17??
Robert KEMBAL s/o Rowland and Hannah KEMBEL his wife was b. 16 January 1717. {H-223}
Frances CLARK d/o Robert and Sillinah CLARK his wife b. 1 April 1719.
Elizabeth BURROUGH d/o Richard and Elizabeth BURROUGH his wife b. 16 October 1717.
Sarah GASH d/o Thomas and Hannah GASH his wife b. 16 July 1719.
Thomas FARMER s/o Grigory & Sarah FARMER his wife b. 18 ?? 1719.
Christopher BELLROES and Annah THOMPSON was joined together in matrimony 25 September 1719.
Elizabeth COWING d/o John and Susanna COWING his wife b. 2 February 1715.
Martha COWING d/o John and Susanna was b. 2 January 1718/9.
Elizabeth DURBIN d/o of John and Avarilla DURBIN his wife b. 25 October 1718.
Margaret HUGHS d/o Samuel & Jane HUGHS his wife b. 18 Oct. 1716.
John HUGHS s/o Samuel & Jane HUGHS his wife b. 15 March 1719.
James EMSON Junr. Departed this Life 21 February 1719/20.
Semelia GARRETTSON d/o Garrett and Elizabeth GARRETTSON was b. 1 June 1718.
James HOLLINGSWORTH s/o James and Ann HOLLINGSWORTH his wife was b. 28 February 1718.
Francis HOLLAND s/o Francis and Susanna HOLLAND his wife was b. 13 August 1719.
Sarah RUFF d/o Richard & Sarah RUFF d. 28 March 1720. {H-224}
Hannah RUFF d/o Richard & Sarah RUFF his wife b. 29 March 1720.
Elizabeth CLARK the wife of John CLARK d. 4 April 1720.
Alexander HOUSTEN Departed this Life 18 November 1719.
Catherine NEWSOM wife of Thomas NEWSOM d. 23 March 1720.
John NEWSOM s/o Thomas NEWSOM Departed 19 April 1720.
Thomas BURCHFIELD s/o Adam & Mary his wife b. 21 February 1710/1.
Elizabeth BURCHFIELD d/o Adam & Mary was b. 13 May 1714.
Mary BURCHFIELD d/o Adam & Mary was b. 26 October 1716.
Richard MORRIS s/o Thomas MORRIS and Elizabeth his wife was b. 1 February 1709.
Mary MATHEWS the wife of Roger MATHEWS d. 4 August 1718.
Elizabeth KNIGHT d/o Thomas KNIGHT and Susannah his wife was b. 23 February 1720.
Peter BONNEY Departed this Life 16 January 1719.
Thomas NEWSOM Departed this Life 5 February 1720. {H-225}
James WEBSTER s/o John & Hannah WEBSTER his wife d. 15 Mar. 1719.
Madam Martha HALL Departed this Life 4 February 1720 Aged 52 years 4 months and 4 days; Being d/o Mr. Edward BRADALL and Mary his wife and was m. to her husband John HALL Esq. 27 years 6 months and 19 days.
Luraney WHITEAKER d/o Charles and Mary WHITEAKER his wife Departed 27 March 1720.
John OLEE the servant of John DURBIN Departed 10 September 1720.
James BROWN Departed 24 December 1720.
William NORRIS Departed this Life 2 May 1720.
Henry MILLEN m. Mary NORRIS 5 July 1720.
Ann LESTER d/o Peter and Ann LESTER his wife b. 5 September and d. 14 September 1720.
Mary BURCHFIELD b. 6 July 1716; Adam BURCHFIELD b. 17 December 1719 and d. 17 July 1720. Children of Thomas BURCHFIELD and Mary his wife; Mary wife of Thomas d. 3 April 1720.

ST. GEORGE'S PARISH REGISTER

John JACKSON was b. the August last - 1710; Margaret JACKSON was b. 21 February 1719 and d. 12 July 1720; Juleon JACKSON was b. 24 August 1720. The children John and Catharine his wife.
Blanch ROBINSON d/o William and Sarah ROBINSON his wife was b. 5 October and d. 18 December 1720.
Jacob COMBEST s/o Martha COMBEST was b. 10 November 1718.
Susanna WEST d/o Robert and Sarah WEST his wife b. 6 March 1717.
Obediah PRITCHET s/o Obediah & Margaret his wife b. 25 May 1713.
Sarah PRITCHET d/o of Obediah & Margaret b. 12 February 1716/7.
John HUGHS s/o William & Elizabeth HUGHS his wife was b. 20 September 1719. {H-226}
Esther HUGHS d/o William & Elizabeth his wife b. 21 April 1717.
Sarah COOK d/o William and Sarah COOK his wife was b. 1 March and d. 15 May 1720.
James WHITEAKER s/o Mark and Elizabeth WHITEAKER was b. 8 February 1720/1.
Sophia SEAMER d/o Elizabeth SEAMER was b. 26 September 1720.
Joshua COCKEY d. 1 December 1720.
Mary BROWN the d/o Zackariah d. (n.d.)
Miles HANNIS Departed this Life 5 February 1720.
Edward CANTWELL Departed 31 March 1721.
Rachel MACKELROY was b. 7 August 1713; John MACKELROY was b. 5 December 1715; William MACKELROY was b. 23 December 1717; Archabald MACKELROY was b. 13 February 1719. The daughter and sons of John and Francis [sic] MACKELROY his wife. {OR-39}
Moses WEST s/o Sarah WEST Jun. was b. 28 March 1721.
Peter WHITEAKER s/o John & Ann WHITEAKER his wife b. 6 May 1716.
John WHITEAKER s/o John & Ann WHITEAKER was b. 14 September 1718, and d. 4 October 1719.
John WHITEAKER Departed this Life 10 April 1720.
Samuel FARMER s/o Grigory and Sarah FARMER his wife b. 25 April 1721.
Hannah DEAVER d/o Antil DEAVER & Sarah his wife b. 27 May 1720.
Cornelius POULSON and Ann EMSON was m. 23 December 1720.
Edward HALL and Avarilla CARVIL was m. 31 October 1717. {H-227}
John HALL s/o Edward & Avarilla HALL his wife b. 8 June 1719.
Martha HALL d/o Edward & Avarilla HALL his wife was b. 15 January 1720/1.
Sarah TAYLOR d/o Lorance & Agnes b. 3 June 1719.
William BARNS d. 22 May 1720.
John CROW and Margaret COMPTON was m. 6 April 1719.
Sarah COTTERILL (COTRALL) d/o John & Elizabeth COTRALL his wife was b. 6 February 1712.
Mary SIMPSON d/o William and Elizabeth SIMPSON his wife was b. 4 February 1714.
William SIMPSON s/o William and Elizabeth SIMPSON his wife b. 31 March 1721.
Samuel MACCARTY was b. 20 August 1716; Mary MACCARTY was b. 6 January 1718/9; Daniel MACCARTY was b. 18 March 1720/1; the sons and daughter of Daniel and Sarah his wife.
Peter WHITEAKER b. 27 April 1696, s/o John WHITEAKER Senr.
Elizabeth LOFTON was b. 1 January 1714; Sarah LOFTON was b. October the Last, 1716; Mary LOFTON was b. 10 November 1718; Rachel LOFTON was b. 1 October 1720; d/o Thomas and Elinor LOFTON his wife.
Elisha PERKINS and Margaret SHERRIL was m. 1 December 1718.
Elizabeth PERKINS d/o of Elisha and Margaret PERKINS his wife was b. 18 November 1719.
Enock WEST s/o Robert and Sarah WEST his wife b. 17 May 1721.

ST. GEORGE'S PARISH REGISTER

Mary OGLESBY d/o Daniel & Martha OGLESBY his wife b. 26 May 1717.
Elisha OGLESBY s/o Daniel & Martha OGLESBY his wife b. {H-228}
1 September 1718.
Ruth OGLESBY d/o Daniel & Martha OGLESBY was b. 6 January 1720/1.
Simeon JACKSON s/o Simeon JACKSON & Mary his wife b. 18 June 1721.
Elizabeth HAMBY d/o Francis & Elizabeth HAMBY his wife b. 10 September 1715.
Thomas MITCHEL s/o Thomas & Ann MITCHEL his wife b. 7 February 1719/20.
Thomas Baker RIGDON was b. 15 April 1713; John RIGDON was b. 17 September 1716; William RIGDON was b. 17 January 1719; s/o George and Elizabeth RIGDON his wife.
Moses THOMAS s/o John THOMAS and Mary his wife b. 26 June 1721.
Hannah KEEN d/o Timothy & Mary KEEN his wife b. 12 June 1721.
Mary HOLLAND d/o Francis and Susanna HOLLAND was b. 18 June 1721.
John DURBIN s/o John & Avarilla DURBIN his wife b. 15 April 1721.
John WEBSTER Junr. Departed this Life 6 April 1720.
Michael WEBSTER s/o John Junr. and Mary his wife b. 7 February 1719 and d. 17 February 1720.
Jane HUGHS d/o Samuel & Jane HUGHS his wife was b. 20 May 1721.
William STIGINGS and Mary MASTERS was m. 13 July 1721.
Foard BARNS and Margaret FARMER was m. 21 September 1721.
William COTTAM (COTTAIN?) Departed this Life 16 September 1720.
Mary Clark OSBORN d/o William and Avarilla OSBORN his wife was b. 13 August 1721.
William HOLLIS and Ann RHODES was m. 30 March 1720. {H-229}
Clark HOLLIS Departed this Life 15 November 1720.
James HOLLIDAY and Sarah MOTTON was m. 30 October 1721.
Jane TREDWAY Departed this Life 15 January 1720.
John HAWKINS s/o John HAWKINS Junr. and Rebecca his wife was b. 16 July 1721.
Mary WOOD d/o Joshua & Martha WOOD his wife b. 23 September 1720.
Hannah CLARK d/o Robert and _____ CLARK his wife b. 8 June 1721.
Rowland HUGHS s/o William & Elizabeth HUGHS his wife b. 6 February 1721/2. {OR-41}
Robert HOLLIDAY s/o James and Sarah HOLLADAY [sic] his wife b. 6 January 1721/2.
Thomas COWING s/o John & Susanna COWING his wife b. 26 May 1721.
Garrett GARRETTSON s/o Garrett & Elizabeth his wife b. 10 February 1721/0 [sic].
Mary GASH d/o Tho. and Hannah GASH his wife was b. 8 June 1721/2.
Margarett DREW Departed this Life 21 February 1721/2.
Richard BRASHIER s/o William & Jane his wife b. 6 February 1720.
Elizabeth POWLSON d/o Cornelious and Ann POWLSON his wife was b. 6 January 1721/2.
Thomas BYFOOT s/o William & Sarah BYFOOT his wife b. 3 Nov. 1721.
Mary BAYLEY d/o John & Lucy BAYLEY his wife was b. 2 January 1721/20.[sic]
Thomas BURCHFIELD and Johannah CANTWELL was m. 4 August 1721.
Johannah PHILLIPS d/o Col. James PHILLIPS was b. 28 March 1720.
Col. James PHILLIPS Died 30 March 1720. {H-230}
Mr. Aquilla HALL and Johannah PHILLIPS widow of Col. James PHILLIPS was m. 17 December 1720.
Edward HARRIS and Frances JOHNSON was m. 19 June 1719.
Mary LESTER d/o Peter and Ann LESTER his wife b. 19 May 1722.
John HAWKINS s/o John HAWKINS Junr. and Rebecca his wife b. 16 July 1721.
Mary RUFF d/o Richard and Sarah RUFF his wife b. 10 July 1722.

ST. GEORGE'S PARISH REGISTER

Joseph HUNTER s/o William & Mary HUNTER his wife b. 25 Feb. 1722.
Job BARNS and Constant WEST was m. 11 Ocotober 1722.
John COOPER and Alce GILL was m. 23 October 1722.
Sarah BRASHIER d/o William and Jane BRASHIER b. 18 June 1722.
James HOLLIDAY Departed this Life 19 January 1722/3.
John MOLTON s/o Mathew & Ann MOLTON his wife b. 19 February 1715.
Mary PERKINS b. 17 June 1720; Ruben PERKINS b. 12 February 1721/2; children of William & Elizabeth PERKINS his wife.
Sarah FARMER d/o Grigory & Sarah FARMER his wife Departed this Life 16 February 172?/?. {OR-42}
Peter WHITEAKER and Francis BROWN was m. 8 January 1722/3.
Isaac WOOD s/o Joshua and Martha WOOD his wife b. 18 Jan. 1722/3.
Mary LITTON was b. 1 April 1717; Hannah LITTON was b. 10 March 1719; Thomas LITTON was b. 30 January 1721; d/o and s/o Thomas LITTON and Ann his wife.
William HAMBY and Martha SIMPSON were m. 25 December 1722.
Elizabeth HAMBY d/o William and Martha (SIMPSON) his wife was b. 21 July 1723. {H-231}
Gregory FARMER and Rachel EMSON was m. 14 June 1723.
Joseph GALLION s/o John & Mary GALLION his wife b. 9 Nov. 1722.
John WARD and Susanna GOBY was m. 26 December 1721.
Mary WARD d/o John & Susanna WARD his wife was b. 21 May 1723.
Thomas KNIGHT s/o Thomas and Susanna KNIGHT b. 12 September 1723.
Ruth CORD d/o Abraham and Rebecca CORD his wife b. 11 June 1723.
Mary JACKSON d/o John and Katharine JACKSON his wife b. 14 November 1723.
Amoss GARRETT s/o Bennett and Arrabella GARRETT his wife was b. 10 June 1723.
William HUNTER s/o William & Mary HUNTER his wife b. 2 Dec. 1723.
Martha WEBSTER d/o John WEBSTER Jurn. and Mary his wife was b. 15 August 1714.
John WHITEAKER s/o Charles and Mary WHITEAKER his wife b. 2 July 1722.
Charles WHITEAKER s/o Charles & Mary was b. 11 January 1723/4.
Daniel WEST s/o Sarah WEST Junr. was b. 17 December 1723.
Thomas JOHNSON s/o Joseph and Martha JOHNSON his wife was b. 12 June 1723.
Job BARNS s/o Job and Constant BARNS his wife b. 20 Dec. 1723.
Thomas DURBIN s/o John and Avarilla DURBIN his wife was b. 18 December 1723. {OR-43, H-232}
Sarah FARMER d/o Gregory and Sarah FARMER his wife b. 18 March 1723/4.
John BAYLEY s/o John and Lucy BAYLEY his wife was b. 13 March 1724/3[sic].
William OSBORN s/o William OSBORN and Avarilla his wife b. 26 March 1724.
Avarilla OSBORN wife of William OSBORN Departed 26 March 1724.
Jemima ENGLAND d/o Joseph ENGLAND and Margaret his wife was b. 11 September 1723.
Sarah HUGHS d/o Samuel HUGHS and Jane his wife b. 15 Oct. 1723.
William COWING s/o John COWING and Susanna his wife was b. 14 April 1723.
Joshua WOOD s/o Isaac WOOD & Elizabeth his wife b. 17 April 1722.
Sarah BRASHIER d/o William BRASHIER and Jane his wife was b. 26 January 1723.
Hannah BRAGG d/o Sarah BRAGG was b. 15 January 1724/3. [sic]
Ford BARNS s/o Ford & Margaret BARNS his wife b. 26 June 1724.
Elizabeth WEBSTER d/o Michael and Elizabeth WEBSTER his wife b. 1 November 1723.

ST. GEORGE'S PARISH REGISTER

Hannah WEBSTER d/o Isaac WEBSTER & Margaret his wife was b. 28 March 1724.
Augustus BROWN was b. 28 September 1710; Gabril BROWN was b. 1 May 1712; s/o John BROWN and Elizabeth his wife.
Sarah BURROUGH d/o Richard and Elizabeth BURROUGH his wife was b. 8 January 1721.   {H-233}
Sarah ROBINSON d/o William & Sarah his wife b. 15 December 1722.
Hannah SIMPSON d/o William & Elizabeth his wife b. 31 Jan. 1722.
Mary DRAPER d/o John & Abigal DRAPER his wife b. 6 October 1718.
Thomas DRAPER s/o John & Abigal DRAPER his wife b. 26 Sept. 1724.
Priscilla COOPER d/o John & Alce COOPER his wife b. 7 Oct. 1724.
Mary HAWKINS d/o Robert & Ann HAWKINS his wife was b. November (? 1721.   {OR-44}
Elizabeth HAWKINS d/o Robert & Ann HAWKINS was b. 19 April 1724.
Prisilla COOPER d/o John & Alce COOPER his wife Departed this Life 29 December 1724.
Empson WHITEAKER s/o Mark and Elizabeth WHITEAKER his wife was b. September the Last Day 1724.
Henry WISEMAN s/o Elizabeth Voss BEECH was b. 26 August 1719.
Hannah WEBSTER d/o Michael and Elizabeth WEBSTER b. 8 March 1724.
Margaret BARNS d/o Job & Constant BARNS his wife b. 30 July 1725.
John BAUCHAM s/o Nicholas & Mary BAUCHAM his wife b. 1 July 1725.
Alexander MACCOMUS s/o John & Ann MACCOMUS his wife was b. 27 August 1721.
Mary MACCOUMUS d/o John and Ann was b. 2 April 1724.
Anthony GILBERT s/o John & Rebecca GILBERT his wife was b. 19 May 1723.
Isaac WOOD s/o Isaac & Elizabeth WOOD his wife b. 28 May 1725.
Richard SIMPSON s/o Thomas SIMPSON & Elianor his wife b. 26 December 1714.   {H-234}
William SIMPSON s/o Thomas SIMPSON & Mary his wife was b. 28 January 1718.
Elianor SIMPSON d/o Thomas SIMPSON & Mary his wife was b. 11 July 1721.
Sarah PREBLE d/o John PREBLE & Ann his wife b. 22 December 1719.
Thomas PREBLE s/o John PREBLE & Ann his wife b. 25 March 1724.
Thomas JOHNSON s/o Thomas JOHNSON and Mary his wife of Deer Creek was b. 22 March 1716/17.
Keren JOHNSON d/o Thomas JOHNSON & Mary his wife b. 5 Nov. 1724.
Sarah CRAWFORD d/o James CRAWFORD and Sarah his wife was b. 23 November 1724.   {OR-45}
Mary GASH d/o Thomas GASH & Hannah his wife b. 10 December 1725.
John LITTON s/o Thomas LITTON and Ann his wife b. 10 March 1723/2 [sic].
Isaac LITTON s/o Thomas & Ann LITTON his wife b. 13 Feb. 1725/4 [sic].
Rebecca POULSON d/o Cornelious and Ann POULSON his wife was b. 5 October 1724.
Flower SWIFT and Elizabeth WHITEAKER was m. 13 May 1725.
James BALCH s/o Hezekiah BALCH & Martha his wife b. 5 Dec. 1714.
Thomas BALCH s/o Hezekiah BALCH and Dorothy his wife b. 15 November 1717.
Hezekiah BALCH s/o Hezekiah BALCH and Dorothy his wife b. 6 March 1721.   {H-235}
Daniel DURBIN s/o John DURBIN & Avarilla his wife b. 2 July 1725.
Mary BALCH d/o Hezekiah BALCH & Dorothy his wife b. 2 Oct. 1725.
Francis HAMBY s/o William HAMBY and Martha his wife b. 15 March 1724.
Mary HUGHS d/o Samuel HUGHS and Jane his wife b. 4 July 1725.

ST. GEORGE'S PARISH REGISTER

Thomas SWIFT s/o Flower SWIFT and Elizabeth his wife b. 19 January 1725/26.
Thomas ARNOLD s/o William ARNOLD and Elizabeth his wife was b. 10 December 1723.
Edmund LINDSEY and Elizabeth BEASLEY was m. 20 February 1725.
Thomas BURCHFIELD and Elizabeth MACARLEY Widow was m. 21 February 1725.
Digbey DRAPER s/o Lawrence DRAPER & Mary his wife b. 8 January 1719.
Frances DRAPER d/o Lawrence & Mary his wife b. 21 August 1723.
Edward COWING s/o John COWING & Susanna his wife b. 5 June 1725.
Matthew MOLTON Departed this Life 15 April 1725.
Silence COLLINS d/o Francis COLLINS and Ann his wife was b. 13 November 1725.
Mary GASH d/o Thomas GASH and Hannah his wife Departed this Life November 1724.   {H-236-OR-46}
Blanch GASH d/o Thomas GASH departed this Life 29 January 1724.
Kent MITCHEL s/o Thomas MITCHEL & Ann his wife b. 2 Jan. 1724/5.
John PACA s/o Aquila PACA & Frances his wife b. 14 April 1725.
Joseph POGNE s/o John POGNE & Sarah his wife b 22 November 1724.
Mary POGNE d/o John POGNE & Sarah his wife b. 7 February 1725.
Gilbert SIMPSON s/o Thomas SIMPSON & Mary his wife b. 21 July 1724 and Departed this Life 22 July 1725.
Thomas SIMPSON and Mary SMITH was m. 13 February 1717.
David KNIGHT s/o Thomas KNIGHT & Susanna his wife b. 6 May 1726.
Robert WEST and Sarah SPINKS was m. 10 November 1695.
Edward EVANS was m. to Rachel JOHNSON 3 December 1724.
Margaret ALLEN d/o Joseph ALLEN and Elizabeth his wife b. 8 November 1718.
Sarah GALLION d/o John GALLION & Mary his wife b. 14 March 1725.
John BALCH s/o Hezekiah BALCH and Martha his wife was b. 23 January 1715/6.
Susanna MITCHEL d/o Thomas MITCHEL and Susanna his wife Departed this Life 30 August 1725.
Hannah EVANS d/o Edward EVANS & Rachel his wife b. 17 Sept. 1725.
Elizabeth HUGHS d/o William HUGHS and Elizabeth his wife d/o John CRAWLEY was b. 12 February 1723.
Jacob HERRINGTON was m. to Hannah JOHNSON 26 October 1720.
Hannah HERRINGTON d/o Jacob HERRINGTON and Hannah his wife was b. 31 March 1723.   {H-237}
Mary HERRINGTON d/o Jacob HERRINGTON and Hannah his wife the 30 November 1725.
Abraham HERRINGTON s/o Jacob HERRINGTON and Hannah his wife b. 7 April 1726.
Hannah JOHNSON d/o Joseph JOHNSON & Martha his wife b. 3 October 1725.
Frances BURCHFIELD d/o Adam BURCHFIELD and Mary his wife was b. 13 March 1723/4.
Thomas HOLLINGSWORTH s/o James HOLLINGSWORTH and Ann his wife was b. 3 December 1721.   {OR-47}
Frances WELLS d/o Richard WELLS and Elizabeth his wife b. 20 December 1720.
Elizabeth WELLS d/o Richard WELLS & Elizabeth b. 10 May 1722.
Mary WELLS d/o Richard WELLS & Elizabeth b. 23 April 1724.
Cassandra WELLS d/o Richard WELLS and Elizabeth b. 14 January 1725/6.
William DULEY was m. to Blanch JONES 15 October 1725.
William OSBORN s/o Benjamin OSBORN and Sarah his wife b. 17 July 1719.   {H-238}

ST. GEORGE'S PARISH REGISTER

Susanna OSBORN d/o Benjamin OSBORN and Sarah b. 6 January 1716.
Margaret OSBORN d/o Benjamin OSBORN and Sarah b. 10 March 1717 and said Margaret Departed this Life 15 October 1719.
Hannah OSBORN d/o Benjamin OSBORN and Sarah b. 14 October 1721.
Henry BEAVER s/o William BEAVER & Mary his wife b. 24 March 1710.
William BEAVER s/o William BEAVER & Mary was b. 29 July 1713.
John BEAVER s/o William BEAVER & Mary was b. 14 August 1721.
Michael BEAVER s/o William BEAVER & Mary was b. 12 July 1724.
Sarah DEAVER d/o Antil DEAVER & Sarah his wife b. 18 August 1725.
Peter WHITEAKER was m. to Frances BROWN 10 January 1722.
John BEDDOE was m. to Sarah LITTEN 3 December 1724.
Enock RIGDON s/o George RIGDON and Elizabeth his wife was b. 4 January 1725/6.
Blanch JACKSON d/o Simeon JACKSON and Mary his wife b. 26 July 1723.
James BULLOCK was m. to Mary JOB 4 January 1724.
Mary BOYCE d/o John BOYCE & Elizabeth his wife b. 21 January 1722/3.
Hannah BOYCE d/o John BOYCE and Elizabeth his wife b. 18 January 1724/5. {H-239}
Michael GILBERT was b. 15 June 1707; Mary GILBERT was b. 14 December, 1719; son & daughter of Garvis GILBERT and Mary his wife. {OR-48}
Charles GILBERT s/o Garvis GILBERT and Mary his wife Departed this Life 25 March 1720.
Hannah GILBERT d/o Garvis GILBERT and Mary his wife b. 28 October 1721.
Mary GILBERT d/o Garvis GILBERT and Mary his wife Departed this Life 20 May 1720.
Mary CLARK d/o Robert CLARK and Silvana his wife b. 25 Oct. 1723.
Robert CLARK s/o Robert CLARK & Silvana was b. 1 May 1726.
James PARKER was b. 4 March 1723 & he Departed this Life 31 May 1726.
James WHITEAKER s/o Charles WHITEAKER and Mary his wife was b. 22 December 1726.
Mary JONES wife of Humphry JONES Departed this Life 7 Dec. 1725.
John GALLION was m. to Elizabeth EVANS 29 May 1726.
Thomas LYALL s/o John LYALL & Ann his wife was b. 15 April 1721.
Ann LYALL d/o John LYALL & Ann his wife was b. 22 May 1724.
Jane BRASHIER d/o William BRASHIER and Jane his wife b. 31 March 1726. {H-240}
Sarah COLLINS was bap. 20 April 1720.
Light KNIGHT was bap. 20 April 1720; Elizabeth KNIGHT bap. 22 July 1722; Thomas KNIGHT bap. 3 December 1724.
Daniel COLLET s/o Daniel COLLET & Ruth his wife b. 13 February 1724.
Daniel COLLET Departed this Life 13 February 1725/6.
Benjamin OSBORN s/o Benjamin OSBORN and Sarah his wife b. 10 June 1726.
William ARNOLD s/o William ARNOLD and Elizabeth his wife was b. 5 July 1726.
Arthur MACURAHON m. Rachel GILBERT 29 June 1726.
Ann HAWKINS d/o John HAWKINS Junr. and Rebecca his wife b. 29 March 1724; John HAWKINS s/o above b. 23 May 1726.
Sarah RUSSEL d/o Frances[sic] RUSSEL and Elizabeth his wife was b. 29 October 1725.
Joseph JACKSON s/o Simeon JACKSON & Mary his wife b. 13 September 1726. {OR-49}
Sarah KEMBAL d/o Rowland KEMBAL & Hannah his wife b. 7 Dec. 1722;

ST. GEORGE'S PARISH REGISTER

Samuel KEMBAL s/o Rowland KEMBAL & Hannah was b. 27 June 1725.
Joanna BAYLEY d/o John BAYLEY & Lucy his wife b. 1 March 1725/6.
Aquilla GILBERT s/o Garvis GILBERT & Mary his wife b. 23 February 1726/7.
Mary SIMPSON d/o Thomas SIMPSON and Mary his wife b. 7 March 1726/7.
Samuel SMITH was m. to Anne SIMPSON 28 August 1726.
Sarah SMITH d/o Samuel SMITH & Ann his wife was b. 10 Oct. 1726.
James BARNS s/o Ford BARNS and Margaret his wife b. 7 June 1726.
Kezia HOLLIS d/o William HOLLIS & Ann his wife b. 17 August 1723.
William HOLLIS s/o William HOLLIS & Ann b. 10 October 1726.
Phillip DEE s/o Phillip DEE & Elinor his wife b. 31 October 1726.
Thomas HARGUES s/o Thomas HARGUES & Elizabeth his wife b. 30 October 1724.
Mary HARGUES d/o Thomas HARGUES & Elizabeth b. 7 February 1725/6.
Mary PREBLE[sic] d/o John PREBBLE and Ann his wife b. 3 October 1726.
Richard COOK s/o William COOK & Sarah his wife b. 21 May 1715.
Richard COOK s/o William COOK & Sarah Departed this Life the 31 March 1722.
Jeremiah COOK s/o William COOK & Sarah his wife was b. 1 January 1717/18.
John COOK s/o William COOK & Sarah his wife b. 28 February 1721/2.
Elizabeth COOK d/o William COOK & Sarah his wife b. 5 April 1725.
William PERRY s/o William PERRY & Sarah his wife b. 14 September 1726.   {H-242}
Johnson BOYCE s/o John BOYCE & Elizabeth his wife b. 27 February 1726.
Hannah CRAWFORD d/o James CRAWFORD & Sarah his wife b. 10 December 1726.
Elioaanah POWELL d/o John POWEL[sic] & Philis his wife was b. 3 November 1726.
Elias COWING s/o John COWING & Susanna his wife b. 14 February 1726/7.
Bethiah DRAPER d/o Lawrence DRAPER & Mary his wife b. 14 October 1726.
Hannah WILLIAMSON d/o Thomas WILLIAMSON & Sarah his wife b. 15 September 1725.
Eleanor HUGHS d/o William HUGHS & Elizabeth his wife b. 8 August 1726.
Sarah BULLOCK d/o James BULLOCK & Sarah his wife b. 12 Nov. 1726.
Robert DERUMPLE s/o Robert DERUMPLE & Middleton his wife was b. 16 November 1721.   {OR-50}
Hezakiah WILSON s/o Jane WILSON was b. 18 November 1723.
Sarah WILSON d/o Jane WILSON was b. 12 May 1725.
Mary RUFF d/o Richard RUFF & Sarah his wife b. 10 July 1722.
Sarah RUFF d/o Richard RUFF & Sarah his wife b. 6 July 1726.
Joseph THOMAS s/o John THOMAS & Mary his wife b. 9 October 1723.
Elizabeth WOOD d/o Isaac WOOD & Elizabeth his wife b. 6 March 1726/7.
Rachel MORGAN was b. 10 December 1719; Charles MORGAN was b. 2 February, 1721/2; children of George MORGAN & Johanna his wife.
John COOK m. to Sarah WEST 30 December 1726.   {H-243}
Mary COOK d/o John COOK & Sarah his wife b. 13 March 1726/7.
Margaret JACKSON d/o John JACKSON & Catharine his wife was b. 17 September 1726.
Edward MITCHEL s/o Thomas MITCHEL & Ann his wife b. 21 Apr. 1727.
Elizabeth WOOD d/o Isaac WOOD and Elizabeth his wife was b. 5 April 1726.

ST. GEORGE'S PARISH REGISTER

Thomas BURCHFIELD m. to Mary JOHNSON 10 August 1727.
Mary CANTWELL d/o Edward CANTWELL & Sarah his wife b. 18 February 1725/26.
William JAMES s/o Michael JAMES & Elizabeth his wife was b. 18 March 1725/26.
Henry BAYLEY s/o John & Lucy BAYLEY b. 28 February 1727/8.
Jacob HANSON & Rebecca MILES entered into the Holy Estate of Matrimony 8 January 1723/24.
Sibbel HANSON b. 15 February 1723/4; Thomas HANSON b. 7 October 1725; Jacob HANSON b. 10 October 1727; s/o & d/o Jacob HANSON & Rebecca his wife.
Elizabeth FIELDS Departed this Life 28 October 1727.
Susannah _____ Departed this Life 20 August 1727.
Stephen ROBERTS Departed this Life 3 April 1723.
Edward DENHAM was m. to Middleton DERUMPLE 20 April 1726.
Elizabeth MURRY b. 4 October 1720; James MURRY b. 11 February 1722/3; Rachel MURRY b. 11 April 1725; George MURRY b. 29 July 1727; s/o & d/o George MURRY and Mary his wife. {H-244-OR-51}
Middleton DENHAM Departed this Life 8 June 1726.
Stephen GERISH s/o Mary GERISH was b. 13 April 1727 and d. 5 March 1727/8.
John WELCH was m. to Ann HOLLANDSWORTH 4 July 1724.
John WELCH s/o John WELCH & Ann his wife b. 14 August 1725.
William SMITH b. 8 January 1722/3; George SMITH b. 27 July 1725; Nathaniel SMITH b. 2 April 1728; s/o William SMITH and Mary his wife.
Roger MATHEWS m. to Elizabeth GARRETT 23 May 1726.
James MATHEWS s/o Roger & Elizabeth his wife b. 7 September 1727.
Joseph YATES m. to Mary COWDERY 5 November 1712.
Susanna YATES b. 4 February 1714/15; Robert YATES b. 2 February 1717/18; William YATES b. 1 May 1720; Joseph YATES b. 4 May 1725; Mary YATES b. 4 May 1725 and d. 15 November 1727; s/o & d/o Joseph YATES and Mary his wife.
Mary YATES wife of Joseph YATES d. 15 November 1727.
John EVANS b. 28 February 1725/6 & d. 1 July 1726; James EVANS b. 2 February 1726/7; sons of Mary EVANS.
James HOLLANDSWORTH d. 14 November 1721.
Rowland SHEPARD was m. to Jane TAYLOR 22 June 1727; Rowland SHEPARD d. 21 April 1728.
Abraham SNELSON d. 6 January 1722/3.
Elizabeth TIPPER/LIPPER d. 17 January 1724/5.
Benjamin DAVIS s/o Elizabeth DAVIS b. 20 January 1724/5.
Evan MILES m. to Elizabeth DAVIS 24 July 1726.
Hollis HANDSON s/o Benjamin HANDSON & Sarah his wife b. 4 June 1726. {OR-52}
Caturinah OGG d/o Francis & Caturinah his wife b. 31 Dec. 1721.
William GARLAND m. to Bethiah OGG 10 June 1728. {H-245}
William OSBORN m. to Cathurinah RHOADES 1 March 1727/8.
Nathaniel FRENCH s/o Michael FRENCH and Elizabeth his wife b. 1 October 1727.
Samuel BROWN b. 23 January 1720/1 and d. 4 May 1724; Samuel BROWN b. 18 March 1723/4; Absolam BROWN b. 12 April 1727; s/o Samuel BROWN and Mary his wife.
John MORPHEW m. to Mary ELIOT 7 March 1707.
Darkas MURPHEW b. 20 Jan. 1709 and d. 15 Feb. 1711; Cathurinah MORPHEW b. 28 Sept. 1719; Rachel MORPHEW b. 27 Dec. 1723 and d. 3 Jan. 1723/4; Timothy MORPHEW b. 17 June 1721; William MORPHEW b. 16 Aug. 1725; Honour b. 13 Sept. 1728; sons and daughters of John MORPHEW and Mary his wife.

ST. GEORGE'S PARISH REGISTER

John BURCHFIELD s/o Thomas BURCHFIELD and Mary his wife was b. 15 December 1728.
Margaret WEBSTER b. 21 January 1725/26; Mary WEBSTER b. 6 April 1728; d/o Isaac WEBSTER and Margaret his wife.
Daniel VEAL m. to Christian SPENCER 15 August 1726.
Elizabeth VEAL b. 7 November 1726; Hannah VEAL b. 17 January 1728/29; d/o Daniel and Christian VEAL.
One female child b. to Michael TAYLOR 20 August 1725.
Ann TAYLOR wife of Michael TAYLOR d. 7 May 1726.
Thomas TAYLOR s/o Michael TAYLOR and Margaret his wife b. 27 May 1728.
Isaac CORD b. 18 August 1725; Stinchcomb CORD b. 14 April 1728; s/o & d/o Abraham CORD and Rebecca his wife. {OR-53}
Sarah CANTWELL d/o Edward CANTWELL and Sarah his wife b. 16 March 1728. {H-246}
William YATES b. 29 October 1728; Elizabeth YATES b. 18 August 1720; Thomas YATES b. 26 August 1723; John YATES b. 26 March 1728; s/o & d/o Thomas YATES and Elizabeth his wife.
Bradberry HUNTER s/o William HUNTER and Mary his wife b. 17 February 1723.
George DREW m. to Hannah LISBY 26 July 1722.
Mary Ann DREW b. 21 November 1723; Anthony DREW b. 29 April 1726; Francis DREW b. 11 January 1727; s/o & d/o George DREW and Hannah his wife.
Adam BURCHFIELD s/o Adam BURCHFIELD & Mary his wife b. 26 May 1726.
Edward DENHAM m. to Mary GERISH 28 February 1728.
Susanna ALLEN d/o William ALLEN & Mary his wife b. 19 Oct. 1726.
Absolam BROWN m. to Sarah SHEPARD 19 January 1728/9.
Mary ARNOLD d. 3 January 1726.
William COSTLY s/o Alce COSTLY b. 16 August 1727; d. 22 January 1727.
John MUTRAN s/o Ann MUTRAN b. 13 December 1716.
Martin BROWN s/o Richard BROWN and Elizabeth his wife b. 12 April 1719.
William COSTLY d. 12 December 1728.
John ROACH m. to Rozannah DENNIS 2 February 1726.
William ROACH s/o John ROACH & Rozannah his wife b. 2 Aug. 1728.
Marcy PRICE b. 26 September 1723; Mary PRICE b. 7 July 1725; d/o Griffin PRICE and Mariah his wife.
William COSTLY b. 29 June 1714; Thomas COSTLY b. 13 March 1715; James COSTLY b. 15 October 1720; Mary COSTLY b. 15 October, 1720; John COSTLY b. 30 May 1723; Susanna COSTLY b. 27 February 1724; Margaret COSTLY b. 28 November 1727; s/o & d/o William COSTLY and Mary his wife. {H-247-OR-54}
Henry GARRETT m. to Mary BUTTERWORTH 19 December 1728.
Isaac BUTTERWORTH Senr. d. 27 February 1728.
Isaac BUTTERWORTH Junr. m. to Jane WHEELER 18 December 1728.
Thomas CRISUP m. to Hannah JOHNSON 30 April 1727.
Daniel CRISUP s/o Thomas CRISUP & Hannah his wife b. 27 February 1727.
Ann FOSTER b. 25 January 1723; William FOSTER b. 28 February 1726; James FOSTER b. 20 October 1728; s/o & d/o William FOSTER and Mary his wife.
Isabel JOHNSON d. 14 June 1728.
Joshua WOOD s/o Joshua WOOD & Martha his wife b. 18 December 1727. Martha WOOD d. 20 April 1728.
Edward GARRETTSON s/o Garrett GARRETTSON and Elizabeth his wife b. 5 February 1726.

ST. GEORGE'S PARISH REGISTER

Mary DEAVER d/o Antil DEAVER & Sarah his wife b. 3 May 1728.
Martha SPENCER d/o Martha SPENCER b. 28 February 1723.
Charles MILES s/o Evan MILES & Elizabeth his wife b. 8 Nov. 1728.
Thomas PRICE m. to Martha SPENCER 29 January 1726.
Mary PRICE d/o Thomas PRICE & Martha his wife b. 9 November 1728.
John MORPHEW d. 1 April 1729. {OR-55}
John HALL b. 9 October 1722; Aquilla HALL b. 7 October 1724 and d. 1 December 1724; Martha HALL b. 6 July 1725; Aquilla HALL b. 1 September 1726 and d. 1727; Aquilla HALL b. 10 January 1727; s/o and d/o Aquila HALL & Johannah his wife. {H-248}
Mr. Aquila HALL d. 25 December 1728.
Henry RUFF s/o Richard RUFF & Sarah his wife b. 2 April 1729.
John ADKINS d. 1 October 1728.
John ADKINSON d. 2 March 1728.
Henry BICARD b. 7 July 1723; Anna Mary BICARD b. 15 July 1725; Elizabeth BICARD b. 6 July 1728; s/o & d/o Henry BICARD and Christanah his wife.
Henry BENNINGTON m. to Sarah HARRIS 26 December 1726.
Moses BENNINGTON b. 2 January 1722; Thomas BENNINGTON b. 5 February 1723; Henry BENNINGTON b. 5 May 1727; s/o Henry BENNINGTON and Sarah his wife.
Elizabeth DULY d/o William DULY & Blanch his wife b. 10 May 1728.
Obediah PRITCHARD d. 9 October 1727.
Sarah ANDERSON d/o Charles ANDERSON and Grace his wife b. 7 June 1728.
Charles ANDERSON m. to Grace PRESTON 2 November 1726. {OR-56}
William OSBORN m. to Avarilla HOLLIS 24 January 1710.
James OSBORN b. 6 January 1711; Mary OSBORN b. 6 October 1713 and d. October 1715; Mary OSBORN b. 6 August 1721 and d. August 1723; William OSBORN b. 26 March 1724; s/o & d/o William OSBORN & Avarilla his wife.
Avarilla OSBORN wife of William OSBORN d. 26 March 1724.
William SNELSON s/o Abraham SNELSON & Rachel his wife b. June (?) 1709.
James ROBERTS s/o Elizabeth ROBERTS b. 13 September 1726.
Hannah Peninah Winnifred POWEL d/o John POWEL and Phillis his wife b. 7 March 1722.
Mary WHITEAKER d/o Charles WHITEAKER and Mary his wife b. 3 August 1728. {H-249}
Blanch WHITEAKER d/o Peter WHITEAKER & Frances his wife b. 10 April 1728.
Edward SANDERS m. to Christian BEARDY 29 October 1728.
Mary SANDERS d/o Edward SANDERS and Christian his wife b. 11 April 1729.
Ruth CORD d/o Abraham CORD & Rebecca his wife d. November 1724.
Susanna MARSHALL d/o Mrs. Mary MARSHALL b. 25 November 1726.
Hannah BARNS d/o Ford BARNS & Margaret his wife b. 26 Sept. 1728.
Joshua WOOD m. to Prisilla WEST 15 April 1729. {OR-57}
Rowland SHEPARD s/o Rowland SHEPARD & Jane his wife b. 9 August 1728.
Jonathan HUGHS m. to Jane SHEPARD 10 December 1728.
William ALLEN s/o William ALLEN and Mary his wife b. 11 March 1728/9.
Thomas JACKSON m. to Elizabeth DEBRULAR September 1724.
Mary DEBRULAR b. 28 January 1720; John DEBRULAR b. 25 January 1724; d/o & s/o Anthony DEBRULAR and Elizabeth his wife.
Simeon JACKSON b. 18 November 1727; Hannah JACKSON b. 29 November 1726, d. 26 December 1727; s/o & d/o Thomas JACKSON and Elizabeth his wife.

ST. GEORGE'S PARISH REGISTER

William BENINGTON s/o Henry BENINGTON & Sarah his wife b. 12 June 1729.
Benjamin OSBORN s/o William OSBORN and Catharine his wife b. 13 June 1729.
Francis CHATHAM s/o Henry CHATHAM and Mary his wife b. 17 October 1729.
Prisilla WOOD d. 22 September 1729.
Frances LITTLE b. 18 September 1725; Rosanna LITTLE b. 2 February 1727; d/o James LITTLE and Elizabeth his wife.
Lawrence TAYLOR d. 11 November 1727. {H-250}
Joseph YATES m. to Mary EVANS 30 June 1729. {OR-58}
John YATES s/o Joseph YATES & Mary his wife b. 19 August 1729.
Elizabeth JOHNSON d/o Joseph JOHNSON & Ann his wife was b. about the last of October 1719, being Sunday.
Henry JOHNSON s/o Joseph JOHNSON & Ann his wife b. 22 March 1715/16 and d. 1720.
Ann JOHNSON wife of Joseph JOHNSON d. February 1719.
Mary BROWN wife of Samuel BROWN d. 16 October 1729.
William KEMBAL b. 24 June 1729; James KEMBAL b. 24 June 1729; s/o Rowland KEMBAL and Hannah his wife.
Simeon JACKSON s/o Simeon JACKSON & Mary his wife b. 24 August 1729.
Thomas SINKIN servant to Joseph JOHNSON d. 5 December 1729.
Thomas SEAMORE s/o Elizabeth SEAMORE d. 1723.
Ann JOHNSON d/o Joseph JOHNSON & Ann his wife b. and d. 1728.
Henry HEDGE d. 1720; Mary HEDGE d. 1720.
Thomas HANSON d. 1720.
HORSEMAN, a female child d. 1720.
Wilborn William MORRIS s/o Mary MORRIS b. 24 March 1727/8.
James JACKSON s/o Jno. & Catharine JACKSON b. 31 Jan 1729/30.
Presilla DEPOST d. 1 November 1729.
Martin DEPOST m. to Martha ANDERSON December 1729.
Archibald BUCKANNA Senr. d. 2 March 1728/9.
Archibald BUCKANNA Jr. m. Anne ROBERT 28 April 1729.
Ruth GARRETT d/o Bennet GARRETT and Arrabella his wife b. 21 May 1729.
Edward DENHAM d. 16 January 1729/30. {OR-59}
Emelia MATHEWS d/o Roger MATHEWS & Elizabeth his wife b. 7 September 1729. {H-251}
Avinton PHELPS m. to Rachel MUCKLEDUROY 23 April 1730.
Hannah CRAWFORD b. 15 December 1725; Mordica CRAWFORD b. 24 June 1729; s/o & d/o James & Sarah his wife.
Elizabeth BROWN b. 17 December 1728 d/o Thomas & Sarah his wife.
Isaac WEBSTER s/o Isaac WEBSTER and Margaret his wife was b. 23 December 1720.
Ann MACCOMUS d/o John MACCOMUS & Ann his wife b. 6 July 1730.
Mary BUTTERWORTH d/o Isaac BUTTERWORTH and Jane his wife b. 25 March 1730.
Margaret OSBORN b. 15 March 1727; James OSBORN b. 25 March 1730; d/o & s/o Benjamin OSBORN and Sarah his wife.
Zachriah BROWN b. 20 September 1728; John BROWN b. 8 March 1729; s/o John BROWN & Mary his wife.
Isaac HERRINGTON b. 30 November 1727; Ann HERRINGTON b. 13 May 1729; Jacob HERRINGTON b. 20 August 1730; s/o & d/o Jacob HERRINGTON & Hannah his wife.
Margarett SWIFT b. 19 February 1728 d/o Flower SWIFT and Elizabeth his wife.
Mary JONES b. 17 February 1728 d/o Thomas JONES & Mary his wife.
Isaac JOHNSON Departed this Life 20 April 1729.

ST. GEORGE'S PARISH REGISTER

Benjamin GILBERT s/o Garvis GILBERT and Mary his wife b. 14 June 1729. {OR-60}
James HUNTER s/o William HUNTER & Mary his wife b. 6 March 1729.
William CLARK b. 18 June 1728; Sarah CLARK b. 30 July 1730; s/o & d/o Robert and Sillinah his wife. {H-252}
Leonard WHEELER b. 18 September 1722; Ann WHEELER b. 30 April 1725; s/o & d/o Benjamin WHEELER and Elizabeth his wife.
Elizabeth WHEELER d/o Thomas WHEELER and Sarah his wife b. 8 December 1729.
Isaac GARRETT s/o Henry GARRETT & Mary his wife b. 14 Sept. 1729.
Clark HOLLIS b. 6 June 1729 s/o William HOLLIS & Ann his wife.
John DEAVER s/o Antil and Sarah his wife was b. 1 May 1731.
Martha WOOD d/o Joshua WOOD & Martha his wife b. 14 Feb. 1724.
Hannah WOOD d/o Isaac WOOD & Elizabeth his wife b. 15 Nov. 1731.
Thomas CORD m. to Mary WILLIAMS 10 February 1730.
William GREENFIELD s/o William and Elizabeth his wife b. 24 October 1730.
Edward SANDERS s/o Edward & Christian his wife b. 23 Aug. 1731.
Owen SWILLAWIN m. to Ann MILLINER 30 November 1723.
Mary SWILLAWIN b. 13 December 1724; John SWILLAWIN b. ?
Ruth CORD b. 13 December 1730 and d. 3 December 1731.
John FIELD m. to Catharine HOGG 23 December 1729. {OR-61}
James ALLEN d. 22 January 1728.
John CAWTHREY m. to Isabel ALLEN 27 August 1731.
Thomas JOHNSON m. to Alis BOND 17 October 1724.
Thomas JOHNSON b. 14 November 1726; William JOHNSON b. 9 September 1729; s/o Thomas JOHNSON and Alis his wife.
James TOMSON m. to Elizabeth GILBERT 30 October 1727.
Aquila TOMSON b. 28 March 1728; Margaret TOMSON b. 30 October 1730; s/o & d/o James & Elizabeth his wife. {H-253}
Jane WILLIAMS b. 13 May 1725; David WILLIAMS b. 13 October 1727; Daniel WILLIAMS b. 13 August 1730; s/o & d/o Paul WILLIAMS and Mary his wife.
Edward HENSON s/o Jacob HANSON [sic] & Rebecca his wife b. 7 January 1731.
Ann RIGDON d/o George RIGDON & Elizabeth his wife b. 4 July 1731.
Precilla NELSON d/o John NELSON & Francis [sic] his wife b. 28 February 1729.
William BRASHIER b. 18 November 1727; Elizabeth BRASHIER b. 15 May 1729 and d. 18 May 1730; Thomas BRASHIER b. 18 June 1731; s/o & d/o Thomas BRASHIER and Sarah his wife.
John HAYS m. to Mary CRABTREE 31 October 1727.
Mary HAYS b. 7 December 1728; Elizabeth HAYS b. 30 April 1731; d/o John HAYS and Grace [sic] his wife.
Mary ARMSTRONG d. 12 February 1739; Sarah ARMSTRONG b. 14 November 1729; Joshua ARMSTRONG b. 16 May 1731; s/o & d/o Soloman and Mary his wife.
Margaret ALLEN d. 20 March 1731.
Sarah COOK d/o William & Sarah his wife b. 12 March 1727.
William COOK d. 26 September 1731.
Pine? DEMOSE b. 25 October 1723; Thomas DEMOSE b. 5 September 1726; James DEMOSE b. 8 September 1728; Charles DEMOSE b. 2 November 1731; s/o & d/o Lewis DEMOSE and Catherine his wife.
John GILES s/o Jacob GILES & Hannah his wife b. 20 October 1729.
John BOTTS m. to Sarah WOOD 9 December 1730. {OR-62}
George BOTTS s/o John BOTTS & Sarah his wife b. 10 December 1731.
Elizabeth WHITEAKER d/o Mark & Elizabeth his wife b. 28 Aug.1726.
Mark WHITEAKER d. 1 May 1729. {H-256}

ST. GEORGE'S PARISH REGISTER

Francis TAYLOR m. to Elizabeth WHITEAKER 6 October 1729.
Grace TAYLOR d/o Francis & Elizabeth his wife b. 5 August 1730.
Robert ELSTON m. to Elizabeth PARKER 1 August 1731.
Francis FREEMAN m. to Elizabeth PIKE 17 June 1724.
Mary FREEMAN b. 5 January 1727; Elizabeth FREEMAN b. 9 February 1729; d/o Francis & Elizabeth his wife.
Sherwood LEE m. Eliner TEMPLE 3 November 1729.
John LEE s/o Sheerwood LEE and Eliner his wife b. 6 June 1731.
Thomas RYCRAFT m. to Sarah PRESTON 6 February 1730.
Alexander HILL m. to Mary REDMAN 15 July 1731.
Ann SMITH b. 12 Feb. 1723; Abraham SMITH b. 13 March 1727; Isaac SMITH b. 4 July 1729; s/o & d/o John SMITH and Mary his wife.
Michael GILBERT m. to Sarah PRESTON 17 December 1728.
Martha GILBERT d/o Michael GILBERT and Sarah his wife b. 20 November 1729. {OR-63}
James GIBSON s/o Francis GIBSON was b. 2? October 1731.
George THURSTON m. to Frances GIBSON 30 January 1730.
John Miles YOUNGBLOOD m. to Mary COAL 21 January 1729.
Henry Miles YOUNGBLOOD s/o John & Mary his wife b. 17 January 1730.
Elizabeth WALKER b. 20 May 1723; John WALKER b. 6 March 1725; William WALKER b. 20 June 1727; Mary WALKER b. 1 August 1730; s/o & d/o William WALKER and Elizabeth his wife.
William WALKER d. 14 January 1731.
Rachel DAWLEY d/o William DAWLEY & Blanch his wife b 7 May 1730.
William HAWKINS & Sarah HAWKINS b. 20 January 1726; s/o & d/o Robert HAWKINS and Ann his wife.
James MORGAN m. to Jane BRASHIER 14 December 1728. {H-255}
Mary MORGAN d/o James MORGAN & Jane his wife b 17 August 1729.
James BARNS d. 27 March 1729.
James BARNS s/o Ford BARNS & Margaret his wife was b. 5 January 1730.
John BARNS b. 2 February 1727; Elizabeth BARNS b. 2 May 1730; s/o & d/o Job BARNS and Constant his wife.
William JENKINS m. to Rachel BALLS 14 August 1726. {OR-64}
Rachel JENKINS b. 13 October 1729; Elizabeth JENKINS b. 11 November 1727; d/o William JENKINS and Rachel his wife.
Joseph WILSON m. to Hannah FARMER 4 February 1729.
John WILSON b. 12 February 1730; Joseph WILSON b. 20 April 1731; s/o Joseph and Hannah his wife.
Presilla COOK d/o John COOK & Sarah his wife b. 27 March 1730.
Samuel COOPER s/o Samuel COOPER & Sarah his wife b. 1 Feb. 1730.
Joseph GALLION d. 7 January 1730.
James GALLION m. to Pheby JOHNSON 15 August 1731.
Thomas OSBORN s/o Benjamin OSBORN & Sarah his wife b. 10 April 1732.
George BIDDER b. 27 August 1727; Joseph BIDDER b. 10 November 1729; s/o John and Sarah BIDDER.
John KIMBEL s/o Rowland KEMBEL[sic] and Hannah his wife was b. 12 April 1732.
Lawrence TAYLOR s/o James TAYLOR & Mary his wife b. 1 Feb. 1731.
James GALLION s/o John & Elizabeth his wife was b. 12 May 1731.
Zackariah SPENCER m. to Christian COOB 2 February 1728.
Thomas SIMPSON s/o Thomas SIMPSON & Mary his wife b. 3 Feb. 1729.
Sarah SIMPSON d/o William SIMPSON and Elizabeth his wife was b. 16 February 1729. {H-356, OR-65}
Richard TUCHSTONE m. to Sarah JOHNSON 25 February 1717.
William ROBINSON m. to Sarah COMBEST 11 December 1703.
Sarah LAWRASSEY d/o Mary LAWRASSEY b. 13 August 1728.

ST. GEORGE'S PARISH REGISTER

Elizabeth HARGESS b. 15 November 1726; William HARGESS b. 14 June 1728; children of Thomas & Eliza his wife.
William WILBORN m. to Ann CRABTREE 21 January 1731.
Thomas CULLINGS d. 17 October 1731.
Elizabeth MOOR d. 3 September 1721.
Michael LITTON s/o Thomas LITTON & Ann his wife b. 14 APril 1730.
Bennett GARRETT s/o Henry & Mary his wife b. __ December 1731.
Sarah PYCRAFT d/o Thomas PYCRAFT & Sarah his wife b. 25 December 1731.
Gabriel BROWN m. to Mary KEAN 10 February 1730.
James TAYLOR m. to Mary FOSTER 26 November 1731.
Francis CHATTAM b. 1 October 1726; Edmund CHATTAM b. 23 June 1729; s/o Henry CHATTAM and Mary his wife.
Simeon JACKSON s/o Simeon JACKSON & Mary his wife b. 24 August 1729.
Moses b. ditto 26 December 1731.(probably son of Simeon JACKSON)
Adam BURCHFIELD s/o Adam BURCHFIELD & Mary his wife b. 26 May 1726.
Samuel JACKSON b. 8 November 1736; Sarah JACKSON b. 15 December 1731; children of Thomas and Elizabeth his wife.
Frances OSBORN d/o William OSBORN and Catharine his wife b. 10 December 1731.
Julon ? JACKSON d. 10 May 1731; Sarah JACKSON b. 3 April 1731; children of John JACKSON and Catherine his wife. {OR-66}
Sarah CANTWELL b. 15 March 1728; Hannah CANTWELL b. 28 February 1729; d/o Edward CANTWELL and Sarah his wife.
Evan MILES b. 14 December 1731; Charles MILES b. 8 November 1728; s/o Evan MILES and Elizabeth his wife. {H-257}
Thomas DUNNAWAY m. to Frances HALL 6 March 1731.
James GARLAND s/o William GARLAND & Bethia his wife b. 6 November 1730.
Sarah HUGHS d/o Jonathan & Jane HUGHS his wife b. 14 Dec. 1730.
Thomas LITTLE m. to Mary SHEPARD 27 June 1731.
Joseph BURCHFIELD s/o Thomas BURCHFIELD & Mary his wife was b. 16 April 1731.
Arthur MONDAY m. to Elizabeth HAMBY 26 December 1730.
Samuel ROSS m. to Rebecca WOOD 30 November 1729.
John WOOD s/o Rebecca WOOD b. 25 December 1727.
Thomas ROSS b. 30 Sept. 1730 s/o Samuel ROSS & Rebecca his wife.
Seborn TUCKER m. to Margaret COB 2 April 1730.
Jacob TUCKER s/o Seborn TUCKER & Margaret his wife b. 22 May 1731.
John WHITE m. to Presilla COBB 18 May 1726.
John WHITE b. 2 September 1728; James WHITE b. 7 December 1730; s/o John WHITE and Presilla his wife.
Joseph HAWKINS b. 23 April 1728; Rebecca HAWKINS b. 23 February 1729; s/o & d/o John HAWKINS Junr. and Rebecca his wife.
Charles JONES m. to Frances COBB 26 December 1727.
Benjamin JONES b. 4 October 1728; Charles JONES b. 12 November 1731; s/o Charles JONES and Frances his wife.
James CANNON m. to Mary BOREN 24 December 1724. {OR-67}
Ann CANNON b. 28 August 1722; James CANNON b. 8 December 1725; John CANNON b. 16 February 1727; Sarah CANNON b. May 25th 1739 d. ??; children of James CANNON and Mary his wife. {H-258}
Ann CLARK b. 24 February 1715; Margaret CLARK b. 16 February 1720; children of Matthew CLARK and Elizabeth his wife.
James BARNS m. to Bethiah LONEY 27 May 1726.
John BARNS b. 24 November 1727; Jemimah BARNS b. 5 May 1729; s/o James and Bethiah his wife.

ST. GEORGE'S PARISH REGISTER

Daniel ANDERSON b. 4 December 1728; Margaret ANDERSON b. 22 February 1730; d. 12 March 1730; children of Charles ANDERSON and Grace his wife.
Thomas BUCKNAL d. 28 June 1719.
Francis HAMBY m. to Alce MONDAY 20 June 1729.
Mary HAMBY d/o Francis HAMBY & Alce his wife b. 21 December 1730.
Jane GRAY b. 15 April 1725; Henry GRAY b. 27 February 1729; children of Henry GRAY and Judith his wife.
Barthia DENSON b. 10 April 1731; William DENSON d. 7 May 1730; children of William DENSON and Margaret his wife.
John LYAL m. to Ann MUTURE 2 February 1717.
Thomas LYAL d. 27 December 1726
Robert CANNON m. to Sophia JOHNSON 8 July 1725.
Rachel CANNON b. 1 November 1726, d. the December 3rd; Sarah CANNON b. 28 February 1728, d. 13 July 1729; Elizabeth CANNON b. 22 June 1730; children of Robert CANNON & Sophia his wife.
Thomas FRETWELL m. to Ann PALMER 22 October 1727.
Daniel GORDEN m. to Mary WEST 23 November 1729.   {OR-68}
Peter WHITEAKER s/o Peter and Frances his wife b. 1 Dec. 1729.
Francis BUCKNAL m. Blanch BROWN 11 November 1729.
Judith BUCKNAL d/o Francis and Blanch his wife b. 11 April 1730.
William PERRY m. to Sarah MACCARTY 12 December 1726.
William MITCHEL s/o Thomas MITCHAL and Ann his wife b. 10 August 1730.   {H-259}
Mary ARNOLD d/o William ARNOLD and Elizabeth his wife b. ?? December 1730.
William ARNOLD m. to Elizabeth GILBERT 23 November 1722.
Michael GASH b. 19 May 1728; Thomas GASH b. 13 October 1730; s/o Thomas GASH and Johannah his wife.
Joseph FORESIGHT m. to Mary MARSHALL 19 August 1731.
Mary FORESIGHT d/o Joseph & Mary his wife b. 8 August 1727.
Mary FORESIGHT d. 8 May 1730.
William RICE m. to Elizabeth BUTTUM? 15 August 1731.
John CANNADAY m. to Mary ARNOLD 2 December 1729.
Rachel CANNADAY d/o John & Mary his wife b. 7 March 1727.
Patrick RUARK(?) m. to Ann CARLISS 6 January 1731.
Edward THORP (THARP?) m. to Catherine CULLINGS 6 January 1731.
Thomas MORRISS m. to Mary MURPHY 19 January 1731.
Michael TEMPLE s/o Susanna TEMPLE was b. 11 July 1724.
Henry MUNDAY m. to Susanna TEMPLE 25 November 1725.   {OR-69}
John MUNDAY b. 25 October 1726; Henry MUNDAY b. 28 April 1729; Thomas MUNDAY b. 7 October 1730; s/o Henry MUNDAY and Susanna his wife.
William DEWLEY m. to Blanch JONES 21 October 1725.
Elizabeth DEWLEY b. 22 November 1726 and d. 6 August 1727; Elizabeth DEWLEY b. 10 May 1728; Rachel DEWLEY b. 7 May 1730; d/o William DEWLEY and Blanch his wife.
Cadwalladay JONES m. to Mary POWEL(?) 30 April 1704.
Blanch JONES b. 28 January 1706; Thomas JONES b. 14 February 1708; Apa.(?) JONES b. 22 April 1710; Mary JONES b. 13 January 1716 and d. 7 June 1720; Avarilla JONES b. 7 June 1721; Frances JONES b. 7 May 1722; children of Cadwallady JONES and Mary his wife.
Sarah SHEPPARD b. 28 August 1725; Elizabeth SHEPPARD d. 13 October 1728; Rachel SHEPPARD b. 5 September 1731; Ann SHEPPARD d. 5 April 1729; Mary SHEPPARD d. 15 August 1731; d/o John SHEPPARD and Sarah his wife.
Robert WEST Junr. m. to Johannah _____ 22 January 1730.

ST. GEORGE'S PARISH REGISTER

Hannah PERKINS b. 24 May 1731; Rachel PERKINS b. 6 January 1725; Mary PERKINS b. 20 December 1728; children of Joseph & Mary his wife.
James LYNCH m. to Mary LEE 23 November 1728.
Margaret LYNCH d/o James LYNCH & Mary his wife b. 10 March 1730.
Thomas DRAPER b. 16 September 1725; Jonathan DRAPER b. 29 November 1727 and d. 12 March 1728; Martha DRAPER b. 28 December 1728; children of John DRAPER & Abigal his wife.
January 22nd 1732 then was Robert WEST Junr. m. to Johannah GASH.
William CANNON m. to Frances JOHNSON 28 December 1721.
Mary CANNON b. 22 December 1722; William CANNON b. 20 March 1725; Charity CANNON b. 18 December 1729; Hannah CANNON b. 5 November and d. 15 September 1731; children of Wiliam CANNON and Frances his wife.
Jeremiah JOHNSON b. 1 May 1728; Joseph JOHNSON b. 17 November 1730; s/o Joseph JOHNSON and Martha his wife.
William DUNN b. 27 December 1731; Jenit DUNN b. 19 November 1729; s/o & d/o John DUNN and Christian his wife.
Edmond LINZEY m. to Elizabeth BEEZLEY 28 February 1725.
John LINZEY s/o Edmond & Elizabeth his wife b. 28 January ????
Hannah MILLER d/o William MILLER & Hannah his wife b. 8 September 1731.
Robert STOKES s/o Humphry Wells STOKES and Mary his wife was b. 8 December 1731. {H-261}
Garvis GILBERT s/o Michael GILBERT & Sarah his wife b. 25 January 1731.
Stephen RIGDEN s/o George RIGDEN & Elizabeth his wife was b. 30 July 1729.
John ALLEN s/o William ALLEN & Mary his wife b. 21 January 1731.
Isaac JOHNSON died 19 April 1730.
Thomas JOHNSON died 12 October 1730.
May 8 1731 then was b. Sophia WHITE d/o Thomas WHITE & Sophia his wife.
Owen HUNTER s/o William HUNTER & Mary his wife b. 11 August 1732.
William SNELSON and Margaret HOGG m. 4 February 1732. {OR-70}
George COLE and Martha LITTEN m. 2 March 1732.
Elizabeth b. 11 November 1723; Hannah b. 24 March 1724; John b. 25 May 1727; Michael b. 12 July 1729; Mary b. 12 August 1731; s/o & d/o Michael WEBSTER and Elizabeth his wife.
James WEBSTER was b. 20 January 1733 s/o Michael WEBSTER & Elizabeth his wife.
Mary LYNCH d/o James LYNCH & Mary his wife was b. 27 June 1732.
February 24th 1731 then was b. Elizabeth BUTTERWORTH d/o Isaac BUTTERWORTH and Jane his wife.
November 5th 1732 then was b. Barnett JOHNSON s/o Thomas JOHNSON and Alce his wife.
July 20th 1733 then was b. John BROWN s/o Gabriel BROWN & Mary his wife.
December the 22nd 1731 then was b. William LOVE s/o Robert LOVE and Sarah his wife. {H-262}
November 10th 1732 then was b. Tamar LOVE d/o Robert LOVE and Sarah his wife.
November 11th 1732 then was b. James THOMPSON s/o James THOMPSON and Elizabeth his wife.
August the 6th 1732 then was b. William RICE s/o William RICE and Elizabeth his wife.
January the 16th 1732 then was b. Elizabeth WALLOX d/o John WALLOX and Elizabeth his wife.

ST. GEORGE'S PARISH REGISTER

December 12th 1732 then was b. John MASON s/o John MASON and Elizabeth his wife.
June 17th 1733 then was b. William JACKSON s/o Thomas JACKSON and Elizabeth his wife.
January 28th 1732 then was b. Jo. FIELD s/o John FIELD and Catharine his wife.
November 15th 1721 then d. William JENKINS.
August 16th 1722 then was m. Edward LOWRY and Sarah JENKINS.
April 28th 1723 then d. Edward LOWRY.
February 21st 1729 then was m. William GLASPIN and Sarah LOWRY.
December 21 1730 then was William RAMSEY m. to Elizabeth DEW(?).
June 2d 1731 then was b. Charles RAMSEY s/o William RAMSEY & Elizabeth his wife. {OR-72}
April 26th 1733 then was Samuel GILBERT m. to Martha WEBSTER.
July 29th 1733 then was b. Elizabeth DEAVER d/o Antil DEAVER and Sarah his wife.
May 28th 1733 then d. Richard RUFF.
October 13th 1726 then was Thomas BRAYSHER m. to Sarah CONSTANCE.
William BRAYSHER b. 18 November 1727; Elizabeth BRAYSHER b. 15 May 1729 & d. 22 May 1720; Thomas BRAYSHER b. 18 June 1731; children of Thomas BRAYSHER and Sarah his wife. {H-263}
Mary URGHVART b. 30 November 1719; Ann URGHVART b. 1 September 1721; John URGHVART b. 21 March 1724; Hannah URGHVART b. 30 January 1725; Elizabeth URGHVART b. 27 September 1727; Sarah URGHVART b. 28 July 1729; Rachel URGHVART b. 5 December 1731; children of Alexander URGHVART and Elizabeth his wife.
November 4th 1729 then was b. Sarah WELLS d/o Richard WELLS and Elizabeth his wife.
November 17th 1731 then was b. Susannah WELLS d/o of Richard WELLS and Elizabeth his wife.
February 17th 1729 then was b. Rachel EVANS d/o Edward EVANS and Rachel his wife.
August 20th 1731 then was b. Edward EVANS s/o Edward EVANS and Rachel his wife.
November 13th 1728 then was b. Thomas BADHAM s/o Richard BADHAM and Sarah his wife.
Margaret CONSTANTE [sic]b. 30 March 1722; Susanah CONSTANTE [sic] b. 3 May 1724; John CONSTANT b. 14 August 1725; William CONSTANT b. 23 May 1727; children of John CONSTANT and Susannah his wife.
Jacob JONES b. 20 July 1720; William JONES b. 10 January 1723; Stephen JONES b. 11 December 1726; Benjamin JONES b. 27 March 1728; children of Jacob JONES and Elisabeth his wife.
April 28th 1739 then d. Jacob JONES.
August 5th 1731 then was John WALLOX m. to Elizabeth JONES.
March 25th 1733 then was b. Sophia PRIBBLE d/o John PRIBBLE and Anne his wife. {OR-73}
November 8th 1732 then was b. Mary LEE d/o Elizabeth LEE.
March 1st 1732 then was Richard DEAVER Junr. m. to Sarah PRITCHARD.
August 6th 1732 then was b. John BENNINGTON s/o Henry BENNINGTON and Sarah his wife. {H-264}
April 4th 1733 then was b. Hannah PRITCHARD d/o Henry PRITCHARD and Christina his wife.
March 26th 1733 then was William FLOOD m. to Jane FRENCH??
June 3d 1733 then was b. Mary FLOOD d/o William FLOOD and Jane his wife.
September 7th 1732 then was b. Mary YOUNGBLOOD d/o John Miles YOUNGBLOOD and Mary his wife.

ST. GEORGE'S PARISH REGISTER

March 26th 1733 then was b. Margaret WILSON d/o John WILSON and Mary his wife.
May 20 1728 then was b. Moses COLLINGS s/o Francis COLLINGS and Ann his wife.
Thomas HAMBY b. 15 March 1728; William HAMBY b. 14 October 1727; the two s/o William HAMBY and Martha his wife.
John WILLIAMS was m. to Mary WHEELER 6 December 1706.
Mary WILLIAMS b. 11 January 1707; John WILLIAMS b. 10 August 1709; Elisabeth WILLIAMS b. 11 September 1711; Ann WILLIAMS b. 18 April 1713; Morriss WILLIAMS b. 10 October 1720; William WILLIAMS b. 12 October 1720; Thomas WILLIAMS b. 12 Sept. 1725 & d. 4 May 1726; children of John WILLIAMS & Mary his wife.
Thomas GALHAMPTON was m. to Elizabeth HILL 10 November 1720.
Elizabeth GALHAMPTON b. 3 June 1721; John GALHAMPTON b. 26 May 1725; Catherine GALHAMPTON b. 15 October 1728; Mary GALHAMPTON b. 17 August 1732; children of Thomas GILHAMPTON and Elizabeth his wife.
Thomas WILBOURN s/o Thomas WILBOURN & Margaret his wife b. 18 January 1730.
Edward WILBOURN d. 24 June 1731. {H-265}
Sarah DURBIN b. 15 April 1728; William DURBIN b. 26 January 1730; children of John DURBIN and Avarilla his wife.
Catharine GRAVES d/o William GRAVES & Catharine his wife was b. 25 August 1729.
Joseph LEE was m. to Elizabeth ASHMORE 12 June 1733.
John CANTWELL was m. to Mary BURCHFIELD 4 February 1732. {OR-74}
Daniel OGLESBY b. 20 June 1722; Subrid OGLESBY b. 17 June 1724; Margaret OGLESBY b. 3 April 1726; Elisha OGLESBY b. 17 August 1727; William OGLESBY b. 18 June 1729; Richard OGLESBY b. 13 October 1731; children of David OGLESBY & Martha his wife.
William GWIN was m. to Sarah GINKINS 28 June 1721.
Thomas GWIN b. 3 April 1722 & d. 13 February 1723.
Sarah GWIN b. 25 April 1727; Rachel GWIN b. 6 February 1729; Mary GWIN b. 27 June 1731;children of William GWIN & Sarah his wife.
Peter LESTER d. 4 May 1733.
Charles STORY was m. to Ann BRITTAIN 15 May 1733.
Sarah HAWKINS d/o Thomas HAWKINS & Elizabeth his wife b. 10 January 1732.
Lucy CANTWELL d/o Edward CANTWELL & Sarah his wife was b. 21 March 1731.
John BAYLEY d. 29 October 1732.
Ruth & Sarah REWARK twins, children of Patrick REWARK and Ann his wife b. 30 April 1732.
Patrick REWARK d. 25 February 1732. {H-266}
Richard MANING was m. to Elizabeth SMITH 7 April 1733.
Zackariah SPENCER s/o Zackariah SPENCER & Christian his wife was b. 13 March 1732.
Adam MILLER s/o William MILLER & Hannah his wife b. 13 March 1732.
Elizabeth PERKINS b. 30 September 1726; Isabel PERKINS b. 30 October 1728; Stephen John PERKINS b. 9 January 1730; children of William PERKINS and Elizabeth his wife.
Thomas WEST s/o Robert WEST Junr. & Johanna his wife b. 13 June 1732.
Thomas HAWKINS was m. to Elizabeth FARMER 24th January 1731.
George BROWN s/o Absolam BROWN and Sarah his wife b. 9 Nov. 1732.
Sarah BROWN wife of Absolam BROWN d. 5 December 1732.
Bridget SHEPERD d. 1 April 1731.
Rowland SHEPERD d. 10 February 1731.

ST. GEORGE'S PARISH REGISTER

Mary RHODES d/o Henry RHODES & Ann his wife b. 6 September 1733.
January 9th 1732 then was b. George CLARK s/o Robert CLARK and
   Sillina his wife.   {OR-75}
January 30th 1731 then d. Mr. William SMITH, Gentleman.
July 2d 1733 then was John STRINGER m. to Mary COLLIER.
January 4th 1731 then d. John DEAVER.
October 2d 1731 then was b. William JOHNS, s/o Mary DEAVER.
May 13th 1731 then was Andrew TOMPSON m. to Elizabeth SHAW.
March 14th 1731 then d. John MILES.
May 9th 1732 then was b. Cassandra JONES d/o Thomas JONES & Mary
   his wife.
April 4th 1733 then was John LEE m. to Alice NORRIS.
August 15th 1732 then was b. Robert COOK s/o John COOK & Sarah
   his wife.   {H-267}
January 26th 1732 then was b. Elizabeth BARNS d/o Ford BARNS and
   Margaret his wife.
January 1st 1732 then was m. Francis WHITE to Ann WILKINSON.
January 1st 1724 then was b. John STANLEY s/o Richard STANLEY &
   Ann his wife.
June 15th 1732 then was Francis GINKINS m. to Mary DOWNS.
September 27, 1732 then was b. Sarah GINKINS d/o Francis GINKINS
   and Mary his wife.
Johannah BEESLEY d/o William BEESLEY & Alce CARRINGTON was b. 2
   September 1731.
March 4th 1732 then was b. William GINKINS s/o William GINKINS &
   Rachel his wife.
January 29th 1732 then was b. Mary BRIERLY d/o John BRIERLY and
   Catharine his wife.
December 31st 1731 then was b. William JOHNSON s/o Joseph JOHNSON
   and Martha his wife.
August 17th 1732 then was b. Mary GALHAMPTON d/o Thomas
   GALHAMPTON & Elizabeth his wife.
October 20th 1731 then was b. Joshua FOWLER s/o James FOWLER and
   Margaret his wife.
Timothy KEEN d. 10 March 1733.
Timothy KEEN posthume of Timothy KEEN & Mary his wife b. 15
   April 1730.
Ann VEAL d/o Daniel VEAL & Christian his wife b. 15 Nov. 1731.
December 4th 1732 b. Elizabeth LITTEN d/o Thomas LITTEN & Ann
   his wife.
John HAWKINS d. 22d July 1733.
April 17th 1733 then was Solomon GALLION m. to Martha JOHNSON.
December 10th 1733 b. Catharine WHITACRE d/o Charles WHITACRE
   and Mary his wife.
March 6th 1732/3 b. John WEBSTER s/o Isaac WEBSTER & Margaret his
   wife.   {OR-76}
July 31st 1733 b. James HAWKINS s/o John HAWKINS & Rebecca his
   wife.
November 16th 1732 b. Rachel TAYLOR d/o Francis TAYLOR &
   Elizabeth his wife.
Sarah WILSON b. 14 April 1728; Samuel WILSON b. 13 April 1731;
   s/o & d/o Samuel WILSON and Rebecca his wife.
May 15th 1733 then was James PRESTON m. to Sarah PUTTEET.
June 12th 1733 then was William PUTTEET m. to Joan STEWART.
February ___ 1732/3 then was David THOMAS m. to Elizabeth WHEELAR.
May 18th 1733 b. Hannah BAKER d/o Morris BAKER & Christen his
   wife.
July 7th 1733 b. Thomas CRABTREE s/o Thomas CRABTREE & Mary his
   wife.

ST. GEORGE'S PARISH REGISTER

July 20th 1733 b. John FREEMAN s/o Francis FREEMAN & Elizabeth his wife.
October 20th 1733 then was Henry MORE m. to Agnus TAYLOR.
December 24th 1733 then d. Joseph GALLION s/o John GALLION.
January 14th 1733 then d. James CAVE.
May 14th 1733 b. John GALLION s/o John GALLION & Elizabeth his wife.
December 10th 1733 then d. John GALLION.
March 31st 1733 b. Francis MIDDLEMORE s/o Mr. Josias & Frances MIDDLEMORE his wife.
September 19th 1733 b. Mary CROOK d/o Ann CROOK.
October 29th 1731 b. Benjamin WHEELAR; July 6th 1733 b. Sarah WHEELAR s/o Thomas WHEELAR & Sarah his wife.
August 29th 1733 b. John GARRETT s/o Henry GARRETT & Mary his wife. {H-269}
September 27th 1717 b. Robert & Ann HAWKINS twins of Robert HAWKINS and Ann his wife.
February 7th 1733 then was Obediah PRITCHARD m. to Elizabeth LITTEN.
October 7th 1733 then d. George BROWN s/o Absolam BROWN.
February 5th 1732/3 then d. James LYNCH.
April 22d 1729 then was Augustus BROWN m. to Ann CUTCHEN. {OR-77}
Feb. 1st 1732/3 then was William NORTON m. to Elizabeth CLARK.
Feb. 10th 1733/4 then was Richard DAWKINS m. to Jane THORNTON.
February 2d 1733/4 then was Richard LOADER m. to Sarah ELLIOT.
January 22d 1733 b. Hannah GALLION d/o Solomon GALLION & Martha his wife.
March 16th 1733/4 then d. Mary MILES.
Decemnber 20th 1733 b. James CRAWFOOT s/o James CRAWFOOT & Sarah his wife.
March 11th 1733/4 then d. John THOMPSON.
March 7th 1733/4 b. Mary DEAVER d/o Richard DEAVER & Sarah his wife.
March 4th 1731/2 b. Thomas WILKISSON; August 13th 1733 b. John WILKISSON; s/o The Revd. Stephen WILKISSON & Ruth his wife.
March 5th 1733/4 then d. Thomas NASAM.
January 25th 1732/3 b. Martha PECA(PACA) d/o Mr. Aquila PECA (PACA) and Rachel his wife.
July 27th 1731 b. Ann MATHEWS d/o Mr. Roger MATHEWS & Elizabeth his wife.
August 22d 1733 b. Avarilla DURBIN d/o John DURBIN & Avarilla his wife.
April 14th 1734 then was Thomas BAKER m. to Mary CRAWFORD.
April 1st 1731 then was b. John BROWN s/o Thomas BROWN and Sarah his wife. {H-270}
January 5th 1731 than was b. James SYLBY s/o John SYLBY and Ann his wife.
June 16th 1731 then was b. John LEE s/o Sheerwood LEE and Eleanor his wife.
April 23d 1734 then d. Rail JOHNSON aged about twenty years.
May 25th 1732 then was b. William Minor COOK [sic] d/o William COOK and Sarah his wife.
January 1st 1732/3 then was b. Francis HAMBY s/o William HAMBY and Martha his wife.
March 31st 1734 then was b. Mary GILBIRD d/o Samuel GILBIRD and Martha his wife.
August 18th 1725 then was b. Isaac CORD; October 25th 1732 then was b. James CORD; s/o Abraham CORD and Rebeccah his wife.

ST. GEORGE'S PARISH REGISTER

March 4th 1733/4 then was b. James BIRCHFIELD s/o Thomas
BIRCHFIELD and Mary his wife. {OR-78}
January 1733/4 then d. Joseph PRITCHARD.
February 19th 1733/4 then was Abraham CORD m. to Mary PRITCHARD.
September __ 1732 then was Joshua WOOD m. to Mary GARRETT.
January 13th 1733/4 then was b. Stephen WOOD s/o Joshua WOOD and
Mary his wife.
March 2d 1731/2 then was b. Phebe CORD d/o Thomas CORD and Mary his
wife.
February 17th 1733/4 then was b. Luranah TAYLER d/o James TAYLER
and Mary his wife.
May 2d 1734 then was b. Sarah MONDAY d/o Henry MONDAY and Susanna
his wife.
January 28th 1733 then was b. Elizabeth WHITE d/o Mr. Thomas
WHITE and Sophia his wife.
February 26th 1733 then was b. Aquila MATHEWS s/o Mr. Roger
MATHEWS and Elizabeth his wife. {H-271}
September 5th 1733 then was Christopher SHEPARD m. to Sarah DREW.
June 18th 1733 then was b. Samuel SUTTON s/o Robert SUTTON and
Mary his wife.
June 9th 1734 then was Richard NOAH m. to Martha MEADS.
February 10th 1733 then was b. Mary NOAH d/o Richard NOAH and
Martha MEADS.
May 8th 1733 then was Blanch GASH d/o Thomas GASH and Johannah
his wife born.
December 26th 1733 then d. Francis OGG.
December 28th 1733 then d. Stockett OGG s/o Francis OGG.
November 14th 1733 then was b. Jacob GILES s/o Jacob GILES and
Hannah his wife.
January 6th 1733 then was b. Benjamin PERKINS s/o Richard PERKINS
and Mary his wife.
Then was John CROW m. to Judith MAGEE on the Monday before Ash
Wednesday.
January 28th 1732 then was b. Jane WILBOURN d/o William WILBOURN
and Ann his wife.
December 16th 1733 then was b. Martha WILBOURN d/o Thomas
WILBOURN and Margaret his wife.
January 1st 1733 then was John JOHNSON m. to Hannah MITCHEL.
Jan. 1st 1733 then was Richard MITCHEL m. to Elizabeth WILLIAMS.
February 4th 1731/2 then was b. Samuel SYMPSON s/o Thomas SYMPSON
and Mary his wife.
May 12th 1734 then was b. Augustus BROWN s/o Augustus BROWN and
Ann his wife. {OR-79}
June 3d 1734 then was b. Joseph ALLEN s/o William ALLEN and Mary
his wife.
May 2d 1734 then was b. Rowland COURTNEY s/o Robert COURTNEY
and Abigail his wife. {H-272}
April 19th 1734 then was b. Ann SYMPSON d/o William SYMPSON and
Elizabeth his wife.
April 28th 1734 then was b. Elizabeth POAG d/o John POAG and
Sarah his wife.
April 4th 1732 then was b. James BARNS; June 4th 1734 was b.
Rachel BARNS; s/o & d/o James BARNS and Bethyah his wife.
February 3rd 1733 then was William FULLAR m. to Jane JOHNSON in
Cecil County.
April 1st 1721 then was b. John THOMAS, August 29th 1723 b.
Joseph THOMAS; April 1st 1726 b. Nathan THOMAS; s/o John THOMAS
and Sarah his wife.
Samuel WESTCOMBE was m. to Sarah THOMAS 19 January 1732.

ST. GEORGE'S PARISH REGISTER

April 6th 1732 then was b. Hannah WESTCOMBE d/o Samuel WESTCOMBE and Sarah his wife.
February 24th 1734 then was b. Sarah PRESTON d/o James PRESTON and Sarah his wife.
April 14th 1734 then was b. William RICE s/o William RICE and Elizabeth his wife.
Robert CLARK was m. to Elizabeth SMITHSON 5 December 1729.
April 3d 1730 then was b. Sarah CLARK; Sept. 5th 1733 then was b. Elizabeth CLARK; d/o Robert CLARK and Elizabeth his wife.
July 12th 1734 then d. Mary YATES wife of Joseph YATES.
October 7th 1733 then was b. Sarah THOMPSON d/o Andrew THOMPSON and Elizabeth his wife. {H-273}
September 24th 1732 then was b. Sophia WOOD d/o Isaac WOOD and Elizabeth his wife.
March 27th 1734 then was b. Charles ANDERSON s/o Charles ANDERSON and Grace his wife. {OR-80}
January 29th 1733/4 then was b. Mary GILBIRD d/o Garvis GILBIRD and Mary his wife.
October 1st 1732 then was Thomas GALLION m. to Mary YOUNG in Cecil County.
December 11th 1733 then was b. Jacob GALLION s/o Thomas GALLION and Mary his wife.
May 17th 1734 then was b. Micah GILBERT s/o Michael GILBERT and Sarah his wife.
July 8th 1726 then was b. Alice COOPER; Nov. 29th 1728 b. John COOPER; March 23rd 1731 was b. Thomas COOPER; May 13th 1733 was b. Stephen COOPER; s/o & d/o John COOPER and Alice his wife.
February 10th 1734 then was b. Rachel GALLION d/o James GALLION and Phebe his wife.
August 16th 1728 then was b. John SUTTON; June 24th 1732 b. Jeremiah SUTTON; s/o Jeremiah SUTTON and Ann his wife.
March 26th 1734 then d. Ann SMITH wife of Samuel SMITH.
January 29th 1733 then was b. Nathan SMITH s/o Samuel SMITH and Anne his wife.
June 18th 1734 then was Samuel SMITH m. to Elizabeth GALLION.
June 25th 1730 then was Amos PILGRIM m. to Rachel MACMAHON.
April 27th 1732 then was b. Mary PILGRIM and Rachel PILGRIM, twins; August 21st 1734 b. Amos PILGRIM; s/o & d/o Amos PILGRIM and Rachel his wife. {H-274, OR-80}
September 12th 1733 then was b. Ann HAYS d/o John HAYS and Grace his wife.
May 29th 1734 then was b. John PUTTEET [sic] s/o William POTEET and Joan his wife.
October 12th 1733 then was b. Thomas WHITE s/o Francis WHITE and Ann his wife.
December 22d 1732 then was b. Johannah ARNAL d/o William ARNAL and Elizabeth his wife.
October 1st 1734 then was b. Jane GALHAMPTON d/o Thomas GALHAMPTON and Elizabeth his wife. {H-275, OR-81}
February 18th 1718 then was Robert CLARK m. to Sillinah SMITH.
April 1st 1719 then was b. Frances CLARK; June 8th 1721 b. Hannah CLARK; October 25th 1723 b. Mary CLARK; May 1st 1726 b. Robert CLARK; January 18th 1728 b. William CLARK; July 30th 1730 b. Sarah CLARK; June 9th 1732 b. George CLARK; June 24th 1734 b. Hester CLARK; June 2d 1736 b. Elizabeth CLARK; March 21st 1737 b. David CLARK; d/o & s/o Robert CLARK and Syllina his wife.
January 29th 1739 then was Thomas RANSHAW m. unto Frances CLARK.
January 29th 1739 then was James AMOS m. unto Hannah CLARK.

ST. GEORGE'S PARISH REGISTER

December 6th 1740 then was b. Jane RANSHAW d/o Thomas RANSHAW and Frances his wife.
May 31st 1741 then was b. Robert AMOS s/o James AMOSS [sic] and Hannah his wife.
September 8th 1733 then was b. Thomas FEELER s/o Thomas STREET and Sarah FEELER. {OR-82}
Thomas STREET was m. to Sarah FEELER ___ 1733.
June 11th 1734 then was b. Martha SYLBY d/o John SYLBY and Anne his wife.
May 7th 1733 then was b. James EAGAN s/o Richard EAGAN and Elizabeth his wife.
September 3d 1729 then was b. Grace HUGHS; September 3d 1732 b. Gwain HUGHS; d/o William HUGHS & Elizabeth his wife the d/o John CRAWLEY.
September 15th 1734 then d. Josiah SMITH s/o Samuel SMITH.
July 24th 1733 b. Micajah GREENFIELD s/o William GREENFIELD & Elizabeth his wife.
November 25th 1733 then was b. Elizabeth BAYSHER d/o Thomas BAYSHER and Sarah his wife.
September 8th 1726 then was b. Cormack alias Charles FLANAGAN; April ___ 1731 b. John FLANAGAN; November 13th 1733 b. Katherine FLANAGAN; s/o & d/o Edward FLANAGAN and Mary his wife.
July 3rd 1734 then was b. James BROWN s/o Thomas BROWN and Sarah his wife.
December 6th 1734 then d. Mrs. Elizabeth SMITH Senr. {H-276}
December 11th 1734 then was b. Isaac BUTTERWORTH s/o Isaac BUTTERWORTH and Jean his wife.
September 29th 1734 then d. John MONDAY s/o Henry MONDAY.
December 18th 1733 then was John LEWIS m. to Margaret DEWLEY.
August 1st 1734 then was b. Sarah OZBOURN d/o Benjamin OZBOURN and Sarah his wife.
September 28th 1734 then d. Sheerwood LEE s/o Sheerwood LEE.
August 29th 1734 then was John SAVORY m. to Mary BUCKNAL.
October 25th 1710 then was b. Benjamin DEVER s/o Richard DEVER and Mary his wife.
October 25th 1734 then was b. William WILBOURN s/o William WILBOURN and Ann his wife.
Geres COLLINS b. April 1731 d/o Francis COLLINS and Ann his wife. (Entry marked out in original register.)
Grace LEEK was b. April ___ 1731 d/o Abraham LEEK & Sarah his wife.
Martha CORD b. 7 August 1734 d/o Mary CORD. {OR-83}
July 3d 1734 then was b. Mary JACKSON d/o Simon JACKSON and Mary his wife.
August 15th 1734 then was b. Stephen KIMBALL s/o of Rowland KIMBALL and Hannah his wife.
November 1st 1733 then was b. John THOMAS s/o John THOMAS and Mary his wife.
Mary CARROLL b. 30 January 1729; Mordicai CARROLL b. 18 June 1731; Catharine CARROLL b. 10 June 1734; children of Edward CARROLL and Katharine his wife.
February 9th 1733 then was b. Mary Ann OZBURN d/o William OZBURN and Katharine his wife.
November 28th 1734 then was George CHAUNCY m. to Susannah OGG.
December 18th 1734 then was b. Thomas MILES s/o Evan MILES and Elizabeth his wife.
December 4th 1734 then was b. James CASSADY s/o James CASSADY and Mary his wife. {H-277}
October 16th 1734 then was John GILES m. to Sarah BUTTERWORTH.

ST. GEORGE'S PARISH REGISTER

August 7th 1734 then was b. Susanna SHEPHERD d/o Christopher SHEPHERD and Sarah his wife.
March 21st 1733 then was b. Avarilla HANSON d/o Benjamin HANSON and Sarah his wife.
December 25th 1734 then was Richard MORRISS m. to Mary MURPHY.
November 17th 1734 then was b. Catharine RHODES d/o Henry RHODES and Ann his wife.
Hester HICKSON b. August __ 1727; Hannah HICKSON b. 2 September 1729; d/o Joseph HICKSON and Jane his wife (viz. Jane WILSON).
November 6th 1733 then was b. Johannah CANTWELL; April 27th 1734 b. John CANTWELL; s/o & d/o John CANTWELL and Mary his wife.
September 11th 1734 then was b. Sarah GRIFFITH d/o Samuel GRIFFITH and Mary his wife.
January 21st 1733 then was b. Margaret HANSON d/o Jacob HANSON and Rebecca his wife.
January 14th 1733 then was b. Rachel SNELSON d/o William SNELSON and Margaret his wife.
September 5th 1734 then was b. William GARLAND s/o William GARLAND and Bethyah his wife.
December 26th 1734 then was William ANNUS m. to Ruth KERSEY.
John KIMBLE s/o Rowland KIMBLE and Hannah his wife b. April __ 1732.
November 19th 1734 then was b. Sarah WILSON d/o John WILSON and Mary his wife.
October 4th 1734 then was b. Sarah COLLINS d/o Francis COLLINS and Ann his wife.
January 31st 1725 then was b. Mary LEEK d/o Abraham LEEK and Sarah his wife. {H-278, OR-84}
Immanuel JONES b. 13 March 1737; Cordelia JONES b. 7 November 1728; children of Immanuel JONES and Sarah LEEK.
John WALKER b. on Shrove Tuesday February -- 1731.
January 1st 1734 then was John CAMMEL m. to Ann JOHNSON.
February 12th 1733 then d. John WILLIAMS.
Abigal DENSON d/o William and Mary DENSON d. October __ 1734.
December 11th 1734 then was b. Joseph SUTTON s/o Jeremiah SUTTON and Ann his wife.
August 31st then was b. Elisha PERKINS s/o Elisha PERKINS and Margery his wife.
February 18th 1733 then was b. John BOTTS s/o John BOTTS and Sarah his wife.
March 6th 1730 then was b. Michael HARVEY; July 8th 1733 then was b. Evans HARVEY; s/o William HARVEY and Sarah his wife.
January 20th 1732 then was b. Jane HAMBY d/o Francis HAMBY, Junr. and Alice his wife.
Oct. 27th 1732 then was b. Daniel HOSSEY; July 15th 1734 then was b. Rachel HOSSEY; s/o & d/o Isaac HOSSEY & Elizabeth his wife.
November the 10th 1734 then was b. Cotteril BAYLEY s/o Charles BAYLEY and Sarah his wife.
Richard JENKINS d. the __ day of December 1734.
September 15th 1734 then was b. Thomas JOHNSON of John JOHNSON and Rachel his wife.
November 24th 1724 then was b. James COLE s/o Thomas COLE and Elizabeth his wife. {H-279}
December 25th 1727 then was Thomas GILBERT m. to Elizabeth COLE.
Ruth GILBERT b. 13 October 1728; Thomas GILBERT b. 11 June 1732; d/o & s/o Thomas GILBERT and Elizabeth his wife.
June 30th 1729 then was Michael YESTWOOD m. to Elizabeth.

ST. GEORGE'S PARISH REGISTER

James YESTWOOD b. 7 June 1730; Hannah YESTWOOD b. 3 February 1732; Mary YESTWOOD b. 12 June 1734; children of Michael YESTWOOD and Elizabeth his wife.
January 16th 1734 was Roger DUNAHUE m. to Elizabeth THOMPSON.
October 27th 1732 then was b. Cassiah BARNS d/o Job BARNS and Constance his wife. {OR-85}
December 8th 1720 then was Samuel HOWEL m. to Priscilla FREEBORN.
September 15th 1721 then was b. Daniel HOWEL; January 11th 1722 then was b. Samuel HOWEL; June 10th 1725 then was b. Mordica HOWEL; November 3d 1726 then was b. Phebe HOWEL; September 3d 1728 then was b. Aquila HOWEL; [no date] then was b. Frenetta HOWEL; March 10th 1733 then was b. Job HOWEL; s/o & d/o Samuel HOWEL and Priscilla his wife.
December 23d 1731 then was b. Elizabeth BULLOCK; August 17th 1734 then was b. James BULLOCK; d/o & s/o James BULLOCK and Mary his wife.
January 11th 1734 then was b. Gregory Farmer HAWKINS s/o Thomas HAWKINS and Elizabeth his wife. {H-280}
August 31st 1733 then was b. William URGHVART s/o Alexander URGHVART and Elizabeth his wife.
February 4th 1734 then d. Elizabeth URGHVART wife of Alexander.
December 1st 1734 then was b. James WOOD s/o Isaac WOOD and Elizabeth his wife.
January 6th 1734 then was Beven SPAIN m. to Elizabeth RIGDON.
October 12th 1734 then d. Ann FRETWELL wife of Thomas FRETWELL.
February 9th 1734 then was John DRAPER Junr. m. to Mary REES.
May 1st 1734 then was b. Ann WALKER d/o Elizabeth WALKER.
September 3d 1734 then d. Joseph ALLEN s/o William & Mary ALLEN.
May 1st 1733 then was b. Elizabeth CONSTANCE d/o John CONSTANCE and Susanna his wife.
March 5th 1734 then was b. Robert WEST s/o Robert WEST Junr. and Johannah his wife.
February 1st 1734 then was b. Francis GENKINS s/o Francis GENKINS and Mary his wife.
March 15th 1734 then was b. Hannah GARRETT d/o Henry GARRETT and Mary his wife.
April 15th 1734 then d. Hannah MILLER wife of William MILLER
April 7th 1735 then was John FLEEHARTEE m. to Hannah PENICK.
March 26th 1735 then d. Sarah MONDAY d/o Henry MONDAY and Susanna his wife. {OR-86}
March 26th 1729 then was b. Jane TREDWAY; Aug. 15th 1732 then was b. Thomas TREDWAY; d/o & s/o Richard TREDWAY & Martha his wife.
March 31st 1735 then was b. Sarah WESCOMB d/o Samuel WESCOMB and Sarah his wife.
February 10th 1734 then was b. James BUCKNAL s/o Francis BUCKNAL and Blanch his wife.
February 4th 1734 then was b. Mary MITCHELL d/o Richard MITCHELL and Elisabeth his wife.
January 30th 1734 then was b. Ann JONES d/o Immanuel JONES and Sarah his wife.
December 5th 1734 then was b. Sarah GORDON d/o Richard GORDON and Mary his wife.
March 27th 1735 then was John RENSHAW m. to Mary LITTEN.
December 8th 1734 then was b. John COOK s/o John COOK and Sarah his wife.
January 21st 1734 then was b. Gregory Farmer BARNES s/o Ford BARNES and Margaret his wife.
December 27th 1734 then was Thomas TREDWAY m. to Mary BULL.

ST. GEORGE'S PARISH REGISTER

January 25th 1734 then was b. John TREDWAY s/o Thomas TREDWAY and Mary his wife.
John STEPHENS d. in the month of February 1734.
January 24th 1734 then was b. Samuel GOODWIN s/o William GOODWIN and Elizabeth his wife.
October 17th 1734 then was b. John YOUNGBLOOD s/o John Miles YOUNGBLOOD and Mary his wife.
February 27th 1734 then was b. Mary GINKINS d/o William GINKINS & Rachel his wife.
April 9th 1735 then was Roger BISHOP m. to Avis GINKINS.
February 11th 1734 then was John ADKINSON m. to Ann SHEPHERD.
April 20th 1735 then was Peter BLACK m. to Elizabeth WILSON.
March 9th 1734 then was b. Frances WHITACRE d/o Peter WHITACRE and Frances his wife.
May 12th 1734 then was b. Elizabeth DAWKINS d/o Richard DAWKINS and Joan his wife.
April 20th 1735 then was b. Martha MORGAN d/o Edward MORGAN and Sarah his wife.
December 13th 1734 then was b. Mary JOHNSON d/o Joseph JOHNSON and Martha his wife.
February 15th 1733 then was b. Robert BRYERLEY s/o John BRYERLEY and Catharine his wife.
November 24th 1734 then was Samuel DENNIS m. to Alice CARRAGAN.
February 25th 1734 then was b. Elisha DENNIS d/o Samuel Dennis and Alice his wife. {H-282}
June 20th 1734 then was b. Robert DUNN s/o John DUNN and Christian his wife.
February 4th 1734 then was b. Elianor SYMMONS d/o Samuel SYMMONS and Mary his wife.
April 16th 1734 then was b. Mary ARMSTRONG d/o Solomon ARMSTRONG and Mary his wife.
February 14th 1731 then was b. Mary BAKER; April 21st 1733 then was b. Elizabeth BAKER; d/o Thomas BAKER and Mary his wife.
February 10th 1734 then was b. Thomas WHEELER s/o Thomas WHEELER and Sarah his wife.
February 16th 1734 then d. Katharine RHODES d/o Henry RHODES.
January 18th 1734 then was Absolam BROWN m. to Mary CORD.
February 8th 1734 then was Thomas FARLOW m. to Elizabeth LYTTLE.
May 5th 1735 then was b. Isaac WHITAKER s/o Charles WHITAKER and Mary his wife.
April ___ 1735 then was Alexander URGHVART m. to Mary REESE.
May 22d 1735 then was William WILLIAMS m. to Lucy Ann BAYLEY.
June 9th 1730 then was Thomas DEAVER m. to Deborah HARTLEY.
June 25th 1731 then was b. Thomas DEAVER; November 6th 1733 then was b. Stephen DEAVER; s/o Thomas DEAVER and Deborah his wife.
June 15th 1735 then was William GRAVES m. to Sarah BEVER.
January 4th 1731 then was b. Katharine MONDAY d/o Arthur MONDAY and Elizabeth his wife.
Then was b. Ann WILKINSON d/o The Rev. Stephen WILKINSON and Ruth his wife [no date given]. {H-283}
June 15th 1735 then d. Lawrence TAYLER s/o James and Mary TAYLER.
May 19th 1735 then was John Cole SPEGLE m. to Deborah COTRALL.
April 26th 1734 then was b. Ruth HARGUS d/o Elizabeth HARGUS & d. June 20th 1735. {OR-88}
July 13th 1735 then was Samuel PRITCHARD m. to Isabella COTRALL.
May 1st 1735 then was James PRITCHARD m. to Elizabeth DURBIN.
April 14th 1735 then was b. William SAVORY s/o John SAVORY and Mary his wife.

ST. GEORGE'S PARISH REGISTER

July 14th 1735 then was b. Sheerwood LEE s/o Sheerwood LEE and Elianor his wife.
June 10th 1735 then was Gervace GILBERT m. to Elisabeth PRESTON.
January 9th 1734 then was b. Margaret CROW d/o John CROW and Judith his wife.
February 8th 1734 then was b. Bethyah THORNBURY d/o Elizabeth THORNBURY.
June 28th 1735 then was Richard SCOTT m. to Mary KEAN.
July 16th 1735 then was b. Luhannah CORD d/o Thomas CORD and Mary his wife.
March 1st 1725 then was b. Elizabeth Vois HENISSEE d/o Elizabeth Vois HENISSEE.
John COOLEY b. 22 September 1729; Edward COOLEY b. 23 March 1731; Alice COOLEY b. February 2, 1734; children of Edward COOLEY and Elizabeth his wife.
March 1st 1733 b. James LEE s/o James LEE & Elizabeth his wife.
March 20th 1734 then was b. William HILL s/o Alexander HILL and Mary his wife.
November 25th 1733 then was b. Elizabeth GWIN d/o William GWIN and Sarah his wife. {H-284}
Mary BRADLEY b. 24 November 1723; Jane BRADLEY and Elizabeth BRADLEY, twins, b. 28 September 1730; Ann BRADLEY b. 3 November 1733; children of Thomas BRADLEY and Ann his wife.
February 18th 1734 then was b. Andrew POLSON s/o Cornelius POLSON and Ann his wife.
February 18th 1732 then was b. Jacob SMITH s/o John SMITH and Mary his wife.
April 15th 1734 then was b. Susannah TUCKER d/o Seaborn TUCKER and Margaret his wife.
July 2d 1735 then was b. Ann DEAVER d/o Antil DEAVER and Sarah his wife.
Susanna YATES d/o Joseph YATES d. in the month of May 1735.
September 15th 1735 was Joseph YATES m. to Catharine HERRITT.
October 2d 1735 then was b. Aquila DULEY s/o William DULEY and Blanch his wife.
April 13th 1735 then was b. Susannah WEBSTER d/o Isaac WEBSTER and Margaret his wife. {OR-89}
January 2d 1734 then was b. Samuel PRITCHARD s/o Obadiah PRITCHARD and Elizabeth his wife.
April 27th 1735 then was b. Thomas JONES s/o Thomas JONES and Mary his wife.
February 18th 1732 then was b. Thomas HERRINGTON; April 2d 1735 then was b. Sarah HERRINGTON; s/o & d/o Jacob HERRINGTON and Johannah his wife.
August 19th 1735 then was William COLE m. to Sarah GILES.
November 15th 1733 was Robert HAMBLETON m. to Rebecca BIGNALL.
March 26th 1734 then was b. Ann HAMBLETON d/o Robert HAMBLETON and Rebecca his wife.
August 23rd 1734 then d. Elisabeth BARNS d/o Job BARNS.
August 23rd 1735 then was b. Elizabeth BARNS d/o Job BARNS and Constance his wife.
June 1st 1735 then was Thomas AISHFORD m. to Mary COX.
December 21st 1734 then was b. Parker WELLS s/o Richard WELLS and Elizabeth his wife.
June 3d 1735 then was John FARMER m. to Sophia JONES.
January 6th 1734 then was b. David DAVIS s/o Henry DAVIS and Sarah his wife.
August 10th 1735 then was b. Samuel LITTEN s/o Thomas LITTEN and Ann his wife.

ST. GEORGE'S PARISH REGISTER

June 1st 1735 then was b. Sarah JOHNSON d/o Thomas JOHNSON and Alice his wife.
March 5th 1734 then was b. Sarah LOVE d/o Robert LOVE and Sarah his wife.
July 17th 1735 then was b. Elizabeth JACKSON d/o Thomas JACKSON and Elizabeth his wife.
October 16th 1735 then was b. James LEE s/o James LEE and Elizabeth his wife.
September 25th 1735 then was b. James PRESTON s/o James PRESTON and Sarah his wife.
June 10th 1735 then was John LEE m. to Jane HICKSON.
August 26th 1735 then was b. Zacharias ALLEN s/o William ALLEN and Mary his wife.
October 11th 1735 then was b. Sarah HANSON d/o Jacob HANSON and Rebecca his wife.
October 14th 1735 then d. Mrs. Johannah HALL.
October 24th 1735 then was b. Mary FARLOW d/o Thomas FARLOW and Elizabeth his wife.
June 20th 1735 then was b. Sarah ARNOLD d/o William ARNOLD and Elizabeth his wife.
August 18th 1735 then was b. Margaret EAGAN d/o Richard EAGAN and Katharine his wife.   {H-286, OR-90}
October 23d 1735 then was b. Thomas SPAIN s/o Bever SPAIN and Elizabeth his wife.
April 30th 1734 then was Alexander THOMPSON m. to Sarah SMITHSON.
November 7th 1735 then d. John JOHNSON s/o Joseph JOHNSON.
December 4th 1735 then Robert BIRCHFIELD m. Ann CLARK.
April 25th 1735 then Owen MACKAN m. Elizabeth CULLEN.
September 16th 1735 then John BEECHAM m. Ann BURTON.
December 23d 1735 b. Elizabeth STOKES d/o Elizabeth STOKES.
July 29th 1731 then was b. John SHEPHERD s/o Constance SHEPHERD.
January 13th 1735 then d. Richard KEMP.
November 26th 1734 was Mr. John HALL Jr. m. to Mrs. Hannah JOHNS.
September 21st 1735 then was b. Martha HALL d/o John HALL Junr. and Hannah his wife.
January 7th 1734 then d. Martha HALL d/o Aquila HALL and Johanna HALL his wife.
January 8th 1735 then was b. Margaret BARTLE d/o Mary BARTLE.
December 30th 1735 d. Abigale CORTNEY d/o Rowland CORTNEY, aged about 16 years.
August 1st 1733 then d. Amey DUNAWIN d/o Thomas DUNAWIN.
December 22d 1735 then was b. Johannah CANTWELL d/o Edward CANTWELL and ____ his wife.
March 18th 1728 then was b. Thomas WATKINS; March 15th 1731 then was b. John WATKINS; s/o John WATKINS and Margaret his wife.
November 20th 1735 then was b. Hannah SMITH d/o William SMITH and Mary his wife.   {H-287}
November 14th 1734 then d. Utee HOLLAND s/o Mr. Francis HOLLAND.
May 4th 1731 was b. Ann RUARK d/o Patrick RUARK and his wife.
October 17th 1735 was b. Hannah HERRINGTON d/o Sarah HERRINGTON.
November 26th 1735 then was b. Sarah CHANCY d/o George CHANCY and Susannah his wife.   {OR-91}
January 26th 1735 then was John WEST m. to Susannah OZBOURN.
February 2d 1735 then was John NORVELL m. to Mary BAYLEY.
December 14th 1734 then was b. John PEACOCK s/o John PEACOCK and Frances his wife.
August 6th 1733 then was b. Drusilla DREW d/o George DREW and Hannah his wife.
November 15th 1733 d. Mrs. Hannah DREW wife of Mr. George DREW.

ST. GEORGE'S PARISH REGISTER

Then was George DREW m. to Johannah PHILLIPS [no date].
January 9th 1735 then d. Mr. George DREW.
March 14th 1733 then was b. Hannah JACKSON d/o John JACKSON and Katharine his wife.
March 9th 1734 then was b. Cordelia STOKES d/o George STOKES and Susannah his wife.
February 7th 1735 then was b. Joannah LEE d/o John LEE and Jane his wife.
February 18th 1735 then d. Stephen John PERKINS s/o William PERKINS of Susquehanna River.
February 20th 1735 then d. Mary BELCHER wife of John BELCHER.
January 14th 1735 then was b. Moses WILLIAMS s/o William WILLIAMS and Lucy his wife.
March 6th 1735 then d. Francis CANTWELL s/o John CANTWELL.
March 21st 1735 then Francis ARPIN m. Ann MACFARLOE.
December 12th 1734 was George RIGDON Junr. m. to Sarah THOMPSON.
June 10th 1735 then was b. Ann RIGDON d/o George RIGDON and Sarah his wife. {H-288}
April 16th 1736 then d. Elizabeth CLARK near Susquehannah River.
March 22d 1735 then was b. Alice Hannah RENSHAW d/o John RENSHAW and Mary his wife.
April 22d 1736 then was b. John RICE s/o of William RICE and Elizabeth his wife.
February 6th 1736 then was b. Thomas THOMPSON s/o Alexander THOMPSON and Sarah his wife.
January 15th 1735 then was b. Mary JOHNSON d/o Henry JOHNSON and Jane his wife.
January 31st 1735 then was b. Rachel SPENCER d/o Zackariah SPENCER and Charity his wife.
February 19th 1735 then was b. John HAYS s/o John HAYS and Grace his wife.
February 6th 1735 then was b. Elizabeth HAWKINS d/o John HAWKINS and Rebecca his wife.
January 15th 1735 then was b. James CAMBELL s/o John CAMBELL and Ann his wife.
March 4th 1735 then was b. Elisabeth FARMER d/o John FARMER and Sophia his wife.
Thomas GRIFFITH s/o Lewes GRIFFITH and Alice his wife b. in the month of February 1731.
March 10th 1733 then d. Alce GRIFFITH wife of Lewis GRIFFITH.
July 5th 1733 then was b. Godfrey VINE s/o Godfred VINE and Sarah his wife.
May 4th 1736 then d. Mr. Thomas WARREN near Susquehannah River.
January 5th 1735 then was Richard PERKINS Junr. m. to Elizabeth CUTCHEN. {OR-92}
March 25th 1736 then was b. Henry COLE s/o George COLE and Martha his wife. {H-289}
November 11th 1732 b. James SINKLER; November 16th 1735 then was b. William SINKLER s/o William SINKLER and Elisabeth his wife.
March 24th 1735 then was b. Margaret WEST d/o John WEST and Susannah his wife.
March 24th 1735 then was John BAULCH m. to Mary CANNON.
March 3d 1735 then was b. Robert HAMBLETON s/o Robert HAMBLETON and Rebecca his wife.
May 1st 1736 then was b. Martha RHODES d/o Henry RHODES and Ann his wife.
October 28th 1735 was b. William WALKER s/o Elizabeth WALKER.
March 24th 1735 then was b. Aquilla HARGAS s/o Elizabeth HARGAS.

ST. GEORGE'S PARISH REGISTER

February 17th 1735 then was b. Edward HALL s/o Mr. Parker HALL and Blanch his wife.
October 30th 1735 then was b. Hannah WOOD d/o Joshua WOOD and Mary his wife.
Hannah CLARK b. 25 September 1734; Mary CLARK b. 7 February 1735; d/o John CLARK and Hannah his wife.
Frances Utie HOLLAND d/o Francis HOLLAND and Susanna his wife b. 2 March 1735.
Ann POGE d/o John POGE and Sarah his wife b. 29 January 1735.
June 25th 1735 then was b. Elizabeth SMITH d/o Samuel SMITH and Elizabeth his wife.
April 22d 1736 then was b. Caleb SYLBY s/o Ann SYLBY the wife of John SYLBY.
July 25th 1736 then was William WALTERS m. to Mary JONES.
November 29th 1735 then was b. William WESTWOOD s/o Elijah WESTWOOD and Mary his wife.   {H-209, OR-92"B"}
September 28th 1736 then was Zachariah ROUSE m. to Ann ADKISSON.
July 25th 1736 then was William WALTERS m. to Mary JONES.
July 8th 1737 then James MORGAN m. Elisabeth WALKER.
September 16th 1737 was William BAKER m. to Elizabeth CANNON.
June 20th 1738 then was b. William BAKER s/o William BAKER and Elizabeth his wife.
June 10th 1737 then was b. Alice STAPLETON d/o Edward STAPLETON and Rachel his wife.
March 3d 1737 then was b. John COLSTON s/o John COLSTON and Rebecca his wife.
June 15th 1738 Abraham RENSHAW m. Anna HAWKINS.
October 29th 1737 then was John FARLEY (HARLEY?) m. to Mary WEEKS.
July 2d 1737 then was b. Rebecca ASHMORE d/o Walter ASHMORE and Magaret his wife.
January 5th 1737 then was Daniel PRESTON m. to Ann GRAFTON.
January 19th 1737 then was James BAULICK m. to Ann GOODWIN.
July 30th 1738 then was William BENTLEY m. to Elizabeth BUTTER (BUTLER?).
October 24th 1738 d. Mr. Garrett GARRETTSON & bur. 2 November.
December 2d 1736 then was John WILLIAMS m. to Margaret CLARK.
January 21 1737 then was b. Peter WILLIAMS s/o John WILLIAMS and Margaret his wife.
April 20th 1738 then was b. Agnus Mountaine TAYLER d/o James TAYLER and Mary his wife.
August 25th 1738 then was b. Martha MACKENNEY d/o Jane MACKENNEY.
October 12th 1738 then Robert KIMBLE m. Sarah TAYLER.
December 22d 1738 then was b. Hannah KIMBLE d/o Robert KIMBLE and Sarah his wife.
August 14th 1738 then James LYLEY m. Margaret PAINTER.
August 18th 1738 then Samuel HAMBY m. Mary SYMPSON.
November 26th 1738 then John LARRIFSEE m. Mary DENSON.
December 14th then was b. Christopher MONDAY; September 22d 1738 then was b. Arthur MONDAY; s/o Arthur MONDAY and Elizabeth his wife.   {H-291}
January 19th 1738 then d. John WELCH.
January 17th 1738 then d. George LUMBARD.
December 26th 1726(?) then was Lewis TUCKER m. unto Katharine PARTRIDGE.   {OR-93}
January 21st 1730 b. William TUCKER s/o Lewis TUCKER & Katharine his wife.
August 26th 1735 then was b. Zackariah ALLEN s/o William ALLEN and Mary his wife.

ST. GEORGE'S CHURCH REGISTER

November 12th 1737 then was b. Martha COOK d/o James COOK and Ann his wife and she d. 24 November 1737.
November 7th 1738 then was b. Martha COOK d/o James COOK and Ann his wife.
November 27th 1738 then d. William SMITH.
July 1st 1738 then was b. James SHEPHERD s/o Christopher SHEPHERD and Sarah his wife.
March 3d 1738 then d. Sarah WESTCOMBE.
March 7th 1736 then was b. Samuel GILBERT s/o Samuel GILBERT and Martha his wife.
December 27th 1738 then was b. John Webster GILBERT s/o Samuel GILBERT and Martha his wife.
July 9th 1738 then was b. Hester GILES d/o John GILES and Sarah his wife.
August 22d 1738 then was b. Mary WEBSTER d/o Michael WEBSTER and Elizabeth his wife.
October 23d 1738 then was b. William TREDWAY s/o Thomas TREDWAY and Mary his wife.
October 22d 1737 then was b. William WATKINS s/o John WATKINS and Margaret his wife.
February 4th 1738 then was b. William GOODIN s/o John GOODIN and Margaret his wife.
December 22d 1738 then d. John COOK.
October 2d 1735 then was b. Nathaniel GYLES s/o Jacob GYLES and Hannah his wife.
February 25th 1735 then was b. Richard TREDWAY s/o Richard TREDWAY and Martha his wife. {OR-93B}
May 23d 1736 then was b. John BRAYSHER s/o Thomas BRAYSHER and Sarah his wife.
August 18th 1736 then was b. James WILBOURN s/o William WILBOURN and Ann his wife.
Amos HOLLIS s/o William HOLLIS and Anna his wife was b. 15 November 1735.
Catharine HOLLIS d/o of William and Ann b. 20 December 1731.
October 15th 1736 then was Edmund MORRISS m. to Mary DEBRULER.
Mary DURBIN d/o John DURBIN & Avarilla his wife b. 22 Feb. 1735.
October 3d 1736 then was b. Elizabeth ROUSE d/o Zachariah ROUSE and Elizabeth his wife.
May 8th 1736 then was b. Mariana SHEPHERD d/o Christopher SHEPHERD and Sarah his wife.
October 17th 1736 then was b. Margaret DEVER d/o Richard DEVER and Sarah his wife.
August 16th 1736 then d. Thomas BURNETT.
August 10th 1736 then was b. Thomas Cole SPEGLE s/o John Cole SPEGLE and Rebecca his wife.
June 11th 1736 then was b. Elizabeth THOMPSON d/o Andrew THOMPSON Junr. and Elizabeth his wife.
August 24th 1736 then was b. Richard EAGAN s/o Richard EAGAN and Katharine his wife.
July 13th 1736 then was Thomas BURCHFIELD Junr. m. to Sarah GASH.
August 15th 1736 b. Stephen PRIBBLE s/o John PRIBBLE & Anna his wife.
June 18th 1736 then was b. Kezia GALLION d/o Solomon GALLION & Martha his wife.
May 9th 1736 b. James GALLION s/o James GALLION and Phebe his wife.
August 6th 1736 then was b. Elizabeth MORRISS d/o Richard MORRISS and Mary his wife. {H-293, OR-94}

ST. GEORGE'S CHURCH REGISTER

February 6th 1735 then was b. Margaret PRICHARD d/o James PRICHARD and Elizabeth his wife.
July 4th 1736 then was b. Susannah DREW d/o George DREW and Joannah his wife.
October 12th 1736 then was b. Isaac CORD s/o Hannah CORD.
June 24th 1734 then was b. Edward MILES s/o Evan MILES and Elisabeth his wife.
December 13th 1736 then was b. James LEWIS s/o John LEWIS and Margaret his wife.
March 22d 1735 then was b. Thomas BROWN s/o Thomas BROWN and Sarah his wife.
March 14th 1735 then was b. Sarah GIBBINS d/o Thomas GIBBINS and Mary his wife.
November 24th 1736 then d. Thomas WHINERY.
November 18th 1736 then was b. William WOOD s/o Isaac WOOD and Elizabeth his wife.
September 13th 1736 then was b. Margaret GILBERT s/o Gervace GILBERT Junr. and Elizabeth his wife.
August 29th 1736 then was b. Nathaniel GYLES s/o John GYLES and Sarah his wife.
January 16th 1736 then d. Benjamin HANSON.
July 12th 1736 then was b. Purify GREENFIELD d/o William GREENFIELD and Elizabeth his wife.
February 17th 1736 was Edward MERRIARTER(?) m. to Sarah HANSON.
December 23d 1736 then was b. Sarah NORVELL d/o John NORVELL and Mary his wife.
September 17th 1736 then was b. John GOODIN s/o John GOODIN and Margaret his wife.
November 17th 1736 then was b. William BARNS s/o James BARNS & Bethyah his wife. {H-294}
September 3d 1736 then was b. Jacob OZBOURN s/o Benjamin OZBOURN and Sarah his wife.
June 3d 1736 then was Samuel FOWLER m. to Sarah MACCARTY.
June 19th 1736 then was b. Chrispin TREDWAY s/o Thomas TREDWAY and Mary his wife.
November 19th 1736 then was Daniel JUDD m. to Sarah FOWLER.
October 26th 1736 then was b. John JOHNSON s/o Thomas JOHNSON and Mary his wife.
January 4th 1736 then was b. Margaret ANDERSON d/o Charles ANDERSON and Grace his wife. {OR-95}
June 6th 1736 then was b. James WELLS s/o Richard WELLS and Elisabeth his wife.
January 10th 1736 then was b. Elizabeth BAILEY d/o Charles BAILEY and Sarah his wife.
October 26th 1736 then was b. Alice HAMBY d/o Samuel HAMBY and Alice his wife.
November 10th 1736 then was Jonathan JONES m. to Martha FARMER.
April 4th 1736 then was b. Hannah WILSON d/o Joseph WILSON and Hannah his wife.
December 2d 1736 then was b. Elizabeth YESTWOOD d/o Michael YESTWOOD and Elizabeth his wife.
December 10th 1736 then was b. Josiah COMBEST s/o Thomas COMBEST and Elisabeth his wife.
September 4th 1736 then was b. Rachel GREGORY d/o Edmund GREGORY and Rachel his wife.
March 16th 1736 then was b. Robert Biggin PERKINS s/o Richard PERKINS Junr. and Elisabeth his wife.
January 6th 1736 then was Samuel ROSS m. to Elizabeth LEE.

ST. GEORGE'S CHURCH REGISTER

December 7th 1736 then was b. Martha SYMPSON d/o Thomas SYMPSON and Mary his wife. {H-295}
March 23d 1736 then was b. Sarah WEST d/o Robert WEST Junr. and Joannah his wife.
February 1st 1737 then was Alexander PARRISH m. to Jane CHATTO.
February 28th 1737 then was Thomas LITTLE m. to Avarilla OZBOURN.
April 18th 1737 then was John MATHEWS m. to Anna MASEWELL.
January 10th 1736 then was b. Thomas PILGRIM s/o Amos PILGRIM and Rachel his wife.
December 7th 1736 then was b. Margaret BROWN d/o Augustus BROWN and Ann his wife.
July 2d 1736 then was b. James TAYLOR s/o James TAYLOR and Mary his wife.
March 31st 1737 then was b. Anna BARNS d/o Ford BARNS and Margaret his wife.
February 22d 1736 then was b. John CROW s/o John CROW and Judith his wife.
April 10th 1737 then was b. Hester BROWN d/o Samuel BROWN and Mary his wife.
March 4th 1738 then was Oliver VERNUM (?) m. unto Mary BROWN.
January 16th 1736 then was b. Margaret ARMSTRONG d/o Solomon ARMSTRONG and Mary his wife. {OR-96}
May 5th 1737 then was b. Sarah FOWLER d/o Samuel FOWLER and Mary his wife.
December 11th 1736 then was b. Jacob BROWN s/o Gabriel BROWN and Mary his wife.
March 26th 1737 then was b. John WEST s/o John WEST and Susannah his wife.
April 17th 1737 then was Alexander SPENCER m. to Elizabeth LEE.
Theophilus JONES & Elizabeth JONES twins of Charles JONES and Frances his wife b. 15 June 1736.
Cadwalder JONES s/o Charles JONES and Frances his wife b. 11 May 1734.
September 7th 1736 then was b. William GWIN s/o William GWIN and Sarah his wife. {H-296}
March 24th 1736 then was b. Hannah COLLINS d/o Francis COLLINS and Ann his wife.
September 5th 1736 then was b. John BRIERLY s/o John BRIERLY and Catherine his wife.
March 14th 1736 then was b. James Isham JOHNSON s/o Joseph JOHNSON and Martha his wife.
January 31st 1736 then was b. Roger BISHOP s/o Roger BISHOP and Avis his wife.
May 1st 1736 then was Edward MOURN m. to Elizabeth LAMBETH.
July 8th 1736 then was b. Phillip COLE s/o William COLE and Sarah his wife.
January 5th 1730 then was b. James BARNS s/o Ford BARNS and Margaret his wife.
August 27th 1736 then was b. Jane BOND d/o John BOND and Elianor his wife.
August 28th 1736 then was b. Margaret WALTERS d/o William VATOR alias WALTERS and Mary his wife.
August 28th 1736 then was b. Margaret TUCKER d/o Seaborn TUCKER and Margaret his wife.
October 30th 1735 then was b. James BLACK s/o Peter BLACK and Elizabeth his wife.
June 16th 1736 then was b. Rachel DRAPER d/o John DRAPER Junr. and Mary his wife.
June 3rd 1737 then was Christopher REDMAN m. to Ann BELL.

ST. GEORGE'S CHURCH REGISTER

July 13th 1736 then was b. John PRITCHARD s/o Samuel PRITCHARD and Isabella his wife.
May 10th 1735 then was b. Mary FOWLER d/o James FOWLER and Margaret his wife.
September 10th 1736 then was b. Leven MATHEWS s/o Roger MATHEWS and Elizabeth his wife.
May 8th 1737 then d. Joseph ALLEN at Swan Creek. {H-297}
June 20th 1737 then d. Arrabella GARRETT wife of Bennett GARRETT.
April 30th 1737 then was b. Joshua SPAIN s/o Beaver SPAIN and Elizabeth his wife.
September 26th 1737 b. Mary JONES d/o Jonathan JONES and Martha his wife.
December 1st 1736 then was b. Isabella WILKINSON d/o The Rev. Stephen WILKINSON and Ruth his wife.
February 14th 1736 then was b. John WOOD s/o Joshua WOOD and Mary his wife.
September 1st 1737 then was Lawrence ANCHER m. to Alice BATTS.
June 29th 1737 then was b. John SYMPSON s/o William SYMPSON and Elizabeth his wife.
September 11th 1737 then d. William WILLIAMS.
July 11th 1737 then was b. Martha OSBOURN d/o William OSBOURN and Katharine his wife.
June 24th 1737 then Benjamin TAYLER m. Ann HAWKINS.
June 14th 1737 then was b. Abraham SNELSON s/o William SNELSON and Margaret his wife.
August 19th 1737 then d. Ann ROUSE wife of Zachary ROUSE.
August 18th 1737 then was b. James JACKSON s/o John JACKSON and Katharine his wife.
September 27th 1737 Mr. James PHILLIPS m. to Mrs. Sarah KNIGHT.
May 28th 1737 then was b. Sarah GALHAMPTON d/o Thomas GALHAMPTON and Elizabeth his wife.
May 12th 1737 then was b. Martha WHEELER d/o Thomas WHEELER and Sarah his wife.
August 20th 1737 then was b. Thomas STREET s/o Thomas STREET and Sarah his wife.
March 9th 1735 then was b. Rebecca CRAWFORD d/o James CRAWFORD and Sarah his wife.
September 18th 1737 then William MAC CLOUD m. Ruth CRAWFORD.
June 23rd 1737 then was b. John JOHNSON s/o John JOHNSON and Hannah his wife. {H-298}
November 26th 1736 then d. John MACCOMUS Junr.
October 14th 1736 then was b. Ann MICHEL d/o Richard MICHEL and Elizabeth his wife. {OR-98}
January 14th 1736 then was b. Mary HAWKINS d/o Thomas HAWKINS and Elizabeth his wife.
January 31st 1735 then was b. Abraham BOTTS s/o John BOTTS and Sarah his wife.
March 27th 1735 then was b. Susanna COWEN d/o John COWEN and Susanna his wife.
January 27th 1736 b. Elisabeth JOHNSON d/o Alexander JOHNSON & Jane his wife.
March 22d 1736 then d. Susannah CONSTANCE.
December 22d 1736 then was b. Isabel PUTTEET d/o William PUTTEET and Jane his wife.
July 25th 1736 then was b. Samuel WAIT s/o Samuel WAIT and Mary his wife.
October 23d 1736 then was b. Richard DAWKINS s/o Richard DAWKINS and Jane his wife.
October 6th then d. Jane DAWKINS.

ST. GEORGE'S CHURCH REGISTER

May 28th 1724 then was b. John MAC DANIEL s/o Elinor MAC DANIEL.
September 30th 1737 then was b. William FOWLER s/o James FOWLER and Margaret his wife.
September 8th 1737 then was b. William LITTLE s/o Thomas LITTLE and Avarilla his wife.
September 27th 1737 then was b. Thomas BARNS s/o Job BARNS and Constance his wife.
October 2d 1737 then was b. Martha DEAVER d/o Antil DEAVER and Sarah his wife.
April 28th 1737 then d. Edward PAINTER. {H-299}
August 1st 1737 then ws b. Abraham WHITAKER s/o Charles WHITAKER and Mary his wife.
December 22d 1737 then was John LONEY m. to Sarah DENSON.
December 22d 1737 then was John DENSON m. to Elizabeth COWEN.
November 22d 1737 then was Peter FARMER m. to Mary WOOD.
November 6th 1737 then was Solomon REECE m. to Mary DRAPER.
December 12th 1737 then was b. Sarah FARMER d/o John FARMER and Sophia his wife.
Ann LYAL d. in the month of May 1736.
August 16th 1736 then was John LYAL m. to Elisabeth FARMER.
June 11th 1737 then was b. Thomas SYMPSON s/o Sarah SYMPSON.
August 8th 1737 then was Robert COLLINGS m. to Jemima JOY.
December 5th 1737 then was Abraham BOYD m. to Hester BUTTERWORTH.
December 14th 1734 then was b. John LOW; January 26th 1725 b. Abraham LOW; s/o Ralph LOW and Ruth his wife.
Ann VEAL b. 10 November 1733; Mary VEAL b. 25 February 1734; Rachel VEAL b. 17 November 1736; children of Daniel VEAL and Christian his wife. {OR-99}
December 27th 1737 then was b. William JUDD s/o Daniel JUDD and Sarah his wife.
February 7th 1737 then was Thomas HILLIARD m. to Susanna WEST.
Dec. 1st 1737 then was George HOLLANDSWORTH m. to Hannah NELSON.
December 8th 1737 then was George LESTER m. unto Alce LEE.
February 7th 1737 then d. Henry MILLIN.
February 1st 1735 then was b. Mary DEVER d/o Mary DEVER.
December 10th 1737 then was b. Ruth CANTWELL d/o Edward CANTWELL and Sarah his wife. {H-300}
March 31st 1738 then was b. Warner COOLEY s/o Edward COOLEY and Elizabeth his wife.
September 12th 1737 then d. William WILLIAMS. (Shows in entry above as having d. September 11th 1737.)
February 23d 1737 then was b. James WAIT s/o Samuel WAIT and Mary his wife.
March 10th 1737 then was b. George RIGDON s/o George RIDGON Junr. and Sarah his wife.
John HAYS b. 18 June 1731; Mary HAYS b. 5 April 1733; Elizabeth HAYS b. 18 June 1735; Martha HAYS b. 9 December 1737; children of Edmund HAYS Junr. and Elizabeth his wife.
December 19th 1737 then Samuel LEWIS m. Sarah MARSHALL.
April 18th 1734 then was b. Prudence FORESIGHT d/o Joseph FORESIGHT and Mary his wife.
January 25th 1737 then Daniel POGE m. Jane ANTIL.
June 30th 1737 then was b. John Giles CROMWELL s/o Oliver CROMWELL and Anna Maria his wife.
December 15th 1737 then was Bennet GARRETT m. to Martha PRESBURY.
John DEVER was b. 25 October 1735; Mary DEVER was b. 21 ___ 1737; children of Thomas DEVER and Deborah his wife.
Alexander NICHOLA was b. 12 June 1735; Phebe NICHOLA was b. 12 September 1732; children of Ann NICHOLA.

ST. GEORGE'S CHURCH REGISTER

March 17th then was b. Amellia BROWN d/o Thomas BROWN and Sarah his wife.
March 12th 1737 then d. Richard DAWKINS s/o Richard DAWKINS.
April 7th 1737 then was b. Samuel GRIFFITH s/o Sam GRIFFITH and Mary his wife. {OR-100}
Samuel RICHARDS b. 3 November 1731; Jeremiah RICHARDS b. 25 August 17??; children of William RICHARDS and Mary his wife.
May 20th 1738 then was b. Rachel COOLEY d/o Edward COOLEY and Elizabeth his wife. {H-301}
March 8th 1737 then was b. Samuel MORGAN s/o Edward MORGAN and Sarah his wife.
January 27th 1737 then was b. William GENKINS s/o Francis GENKINS and Mary his wife.
March 21st 1737 then was b. Rachel HAWKINS d/o John HAWKINS and Rebecca his wife.
April 16th 1738 then was b. John TAYLER s/o Benjamin TAYLER and Ann his wife.
May 30th 1738 then was b. Thomas HAMBLETON son Robert HAMBLETON and Rebecca his wife.
October 25th 1737 then was b. Sarah GENKINS d/o William GENKINS and Rachel his wife.
Moses WILSON s/o John WILSON and Mary his wife was b. on Whitsunday being the __ day of __ 1738.
March 2d 1724 b. Peter BLACK alias Tassey; July 7th 1737 b. Thomas BLACK; s/o Peter BLACK and Elizabeth his wife.
April 16th 1738 then was b. George POGE s/o John POGE and Sarah his wife.
September 26th 1737 then was b. Sarah BISHOP d/o Roger BISHOP and Eviss his wife.
December 11th 1737 then was b. Elanor GOODWIN d/o William GOODWIN and Elizabeth his wife.
August 28th 1738 then was b. Tryal WESTCOMBE s/o Samuel WESTCOMBE and Sarah his wife.
March 4th 1737 then was b. Elizabeth ARNAL d/o William ARNAL and Elizabeth his wife.
August 9th 1738 then was b. Aquila BURCHFIELD s/o Thomas BURCHFIELD and Sarah his wife.
August 11th 1738 then was b. Joseph ALLEN s/o William ALLEN and Mary his wife.
John CLARK s/o John CLARK of the Level and Hannah his wife was b. 23 February 1737. {H-302,OR-101}
October 21st 1736 then was b. Sarah Charlotta WHITE d/o Major Thomas WHITE and Sophia his wife.
September 2d 1737 then was b. Edward CANTWELL s/o John CANTWELL and Mary his wife.
September 30th 1738 then was b. Mary NORVEL d/o John NORVEL and Mary his wife.
October 15th 1738 d. Sarah WILLIAMSON wife of Thomas WILLIAMSON.
September 12th 1738 was b. Stephen HARGAS s/o Elizabeth HARGAS.
September 21st __ then was b. Obediah PRITCHARD s/o Samuel PRITCHARD and Isabella his wife.
September 17th 1738 then was b. Michael TAYLER s/o Abraham TAYLER and Hannah his wife.
July 11th 1737 then d. Stephen KEMBLE s/o Rowland KEMBLE.
September 13th 1738 then was b. Stephen KEMBLE s/o Rowland KEMBLE and Hannah his wife.
March 14th 1737 then was b. Amos CORD s/o Thomas CORD and Mary his wife.

ST. GEORGE'S CHURCH REGISTER

August 26th 1738 then was b. Ann MAC CLOUD d/o William MAC CLOUD and Ruth his wife.
September 10th 1738 then was b. Anne SMITH d/o Samuel SMITH and Elisabeth his wife.
June 16th 1738 then was b. Sarah DENSON d/o John DENSON and Elizabeth his wife.
May 20th 1738 then was b. William LONEY s/o John LONEY and Sarah his wife.
Nov. 28 1738 then was b. Mary LEE d/o John LEE and Jane his wife.
January 6th 1737 then was b. Joshua SYMPSON s/o Thomas SYMPSON and Mary his wife.
August 8th 1737 then was b. Martha GILBERT d/o Gervace GILBERT and Mary his wife. {H-303}
August 22d 1738 then was b. Sarah PHILLIPS d/o James PHILLIPS and Sarah his wife.
Hannah BROWN d/o Absolam BROWN and Mary his wife b. 15 November 1737 and d. 16th August 1738.
December 22d 1738 then was b. Martha FARMER d/o Peter FARMER and Mary his wife.
January 22d 1737 then Henry THOMAS was m. to Jane PUTTEET.
May 12th 1732 then was b. John WALLIS s/o Samuel WALLIS and Cassandra his wife.
August 28th 1738 then was b. Gervace GILBERT s/o Gervace GILBERT Junr. and Elisabeth his wife.
November 24th 1734 then was b. Mary WALLIS; April 21st 1736 b. Samuel WALLIS; d/o & s/o Samuel WALLIS & Cassandra his wife.
January 2d 1730 then was b. Henry DAVIS; June 3d 1733 then was b. Jane DAVIS; October 13th 1737 then was b. Mary DAVIS; s/o & d/o Henry DAVIS and Sarah his wife.
January 19th 1738 then was b. Elizabeth ASHMORE d/o Walter ASHMORE and Margaret his wife.
November 30th 1738 Jonathan WILD was m. to Sarah PRIBBLE.
November 23d 1738 then was Michael GILBERT m. to Mary TAYLER.
June 5th 1739 then d. Gervace GILBERT.
March 5th 1738 then was Francis RYLEY m. to Elizabeth ENGLAND.
March 18th 1738 then was b. Benjamin WOOD s/o Isaac WOOD and Elizabeth his wife.
January 10th 1738 then was b. Margaret JONES and Hannah JONES, twins of Jonathan JONES and Martha his wife.
May 8th 1738 then d. Thomas TIPPINS (LIPPINS?).
May 15th 1738 then was b. Rachel CRAWFOOT d/o James CRAWFOOT and Sarah his wife. {H-304}
January 18th 1738 then was b. Avarilla PRITCHARD d/o James PRITCHARD and Elizabeth his wife.
January 18th 1738 then was b. Michael YESTWOOD s/o Michael YESTWOOD and Elizabeth his wife.
January 15th 1738 then was Jonas COURTNEY m. to Comfort COLE.
May 26th 1739 then d. Michael YESTWOOD.
March 3d 1738 then was b. Sarah REECE d/o Solomon REECE Junr. & Mary his wife. {OR-103}
March 9th 1738 then was b. Thomas Symmons DRAPER s/o John DRAPER Junr. and Mary his wife.
February 26th 1738 then was b. Keziah COMBEST d/o Thomas COMBEST and Elizabeth his wife.
November 16th 1738 then was James CROW m. to Hannah ????
June 8th 1739 then was b. Edward JAMES s/o Michael JAMES and Constance his wife.
September 15th 1738 then was b. Margaret LEWIS d/o Samuel LEWIS and Sarah his wife.

ST. GEORGE'S CHURCH REGISTER

June 6th 1739 then was b. Samuel FOWLER s/o Samuel FOWLER and Mary his wife.
February 18th 1735 then was b. Henry William KEEN s/o Henry KEEN and Emelia his wife.
November 5th 1738 then was b. John JOHNSON s/o Thomas JOHNSON and Alce his wife.
March 14th 1738 then d. Robert LOVE.
May 11th 1739 then was b. Ruth LOVE d/o Posthumus of Robert LOVE and Sarah his wife.
April 25th 1739 then was b. Johannah OCHISSON d/o Joseph OCHISSON and Elizabeth his wife.
April 7th 1731 then was b. Jacob BUTTERAM s/o John BUTTERAM and Jane his wife.
May 30th 1738 then was b. Isaac BOTTS s/o John BOTTS and Sarah his wife. {H-305}
May 28th 1738 then was b. John MORRISS s/o Richard MORRISS and Mary his wife.
February 26th 1736 then was b. Sarah MURPHEY d/o Dorcass MURPHY.
October 17 1738 then was Joseph HODSKEN m. to Catherine CARROLL.
January 13th 1738 then was b. James PRICHARD s/o Obediah PRICHARD and Elizabeth his wife.
December 1st 1738 then was b. Hannah THOMPSON d/o Andrew THOMPSON and Elizabeth his wife.
March 29th 1738 then was b. Matthew THOMPSON s/o Alexander THOMPSON and Sarah his wife.
June 8th 1740 then was John HOLLAND m. to Sarah WILABEE.
November 13th 1738 then was b. Sarah RHODES d/o Henry RHODES and Ann his wife. {OR-104}
November 12th 1738 then was b. George CHANCY s/o George CHANCY and Susanna his wife.
February 19th 1738 then was b. Edward Bedle GARRETT s/o Bennett GARRETT and Martha his wife, and the said Edward Bedle GARRETT d. 26 April 1739.
August 16th 1739 then was John COURTNEY m. to Frances GREENFIELD.
June 8th 1739 then was b. John VERNUEL s/o Oliver VERMIEL and Mary his wife.
Isaac PERKINS m. Mary LEE in the month of Mary 1739.
January 16th 1731 then was b. Comfort PAWMER d/o John PAWMER and Elizabeth his wife.
October 2d 1738 then was b. Sarah BROWN; d/o John BROWN and Mary his wife.
February 27th 1738 then d. Mary BROWN wife of John BROWN.
November 7th 1737 then was b. John ENNIS s/o William ENNIS and Ruth his wife. {H-306}
January 1st 1738 then was Andrew RIDDLE m. to Ann NICHOLAS.
March 27th 1739 then d. Abigal COURTNEY wife of Robert COURTNEY.
March 2nd 1738 then was b. James MONDAY s/o Henry MONDAY and Susanna his wife.
July 30th 1739 Then was b. Margaret PRESTON d/o Daniel PRESTON and Ann his wife.
August 30th 1739 d. Mary WHITAKER wife of Charles WHITAKER.
August 4th 1739 then was b. Sarah DEVER d/o Richard DEVER Junr. and Sarah his wife.
September 30th 1739 then was b. Constance BARNS d/o Job BARNS and Constance his wife.
August 15th 1738 then was Thomas DOWNS m. unto Gulielmus GOODEN.
June 1st 1739 then James MACDANIEL m. Sarah JONES.
August 20th 1739 then was b. Ann MACDANIEL d/o James MACDANIEL and Sarah his wife.

ST. GEORGE'S CHURCH REGISTER

May 22nd 1739 then d. John MACCOMUS.
July 15th 1739 then was b. John OZBORN s/o Benjamin OZBORN and Sarah his wife.
January 15th 1739 then d. John PRITON.
January 15th 1739 then d. Benjamin DEVER.
January 18th 1737 then was b. James Maxwell MATHEWS; October 8th 1739 then was b. Cassandra MATHEWS; s/o & d/o John MATHEWS and Ann his wife.
October 2d 1737 then was William DOCKARTY m. unto Mary BARTLE.
October 11th 1737 then was b. George DOCKARTY; March 28th 1739 then was b. Mary DOCKARTY s/o & d/o William DOCKARTY and Mary his wife.
October 15th 1739 then was b. Hannah FARMER d/o John FARMER and Sophia his wife. {H-307}
September 10th 1739 then was b. Sarah LESTER d/o George LESTER and Alce his wife.
January 28th 1737 then d. John BOIS.
August 14th 1739 was Thomas WILLIAMSON m. unto Elizabeth BOIS.
January 26th 1738 then was Capt. Peregrine FRISBY m. to Mrs. Mary HOLLAND.
October 20th 1739 then was b. Thomas RANSHAW s/o Abraham RANSHAW and Anna his wife.
December 31st 1739 then d. Ann RIGDON d/o George RIGDON and Elizabeth his wife.
December 22nd 1739 then d. Sarah JOHNSON d/o Thomas JOHNSON and Alice his wife.
August 31st 1739 then was b. Mary PUTTEET d/o William PUTTEET and Joan his wife.
May 31st 1739 then was b. Mary WHEELER d/o Thomas WHEELER and Sarah his wife.
September 25th 1739 then was b. Mary GRIFFITH d/o Samuel GRIFFITH and Elizabeth his wife.
September 15th 1739 then was b. Daniel JUDD s/o Daniel JUDD and Sarah his wife. {OR-106}
December 27th 1739 d. Mary BUCHER wife of James BUCHER.
November 12th 1739 then was William SYMPSON m. to Mary LARRISSEE.
February 2nd 1739 then was b. Anna SYMPSON; September 23d 1739 then was b. Thomas SYMPSON; d/o & s/o William SYMPSON and Mary his wife.
February 26th 1738 then was b. Margaret BARNS d/o Ford BARNS and Margaret his wife.
August 9th 1739 then was b. Sinai GALLION d/o Thomas GALLION and Mary his wife.
May 5th 1739 then d. Benjamin MURPHY. {H-308}
Martin Tayler GILBERT b. 9 September 1739.
February 23d 1739 then d. Jacob JOHNSON.
January 21st 1739 then was b. James PRIBBLE s/o John PRIBBLE & Ann his wife.
August 5th 1739 then was Lewis GRIFFITH m. unto Mary JOHNSON.
September 18th 1739 then d. John JOHNSON.
March ___ 1739 then James ROE(?) m. Mary DOYLE.
March 13th 1735 then was b. Rachel PERKINS d/o William PERKINS and Elizabeth his wife.
William PERKINS s/o William PERKINS and Elizabeth his wife d. in the month of September 1739.
December 14th 1739 then was b. Margaret PERKINS d/o William PERKINS and Elizabeth his wife.
April 7th 1740 then was Stephen SCARLET m. to Ruth BELSHER.
October 18th 1738 then d. John HIGGINSON.

ST. GEORGE'S CHURCH REGISTER

July 4th 1739 then was Charles BOULTON m. to Ann HIGGINSON.
June 19th 1739 then was Thomas BROWN m. to Susanna HIGGINSON.
April 3d 1740 then was b. William BROWN s/o Thomas BROWN and Susanna his wife.
December 11th 1736 then was b. Jeremiah HAMBEY s/o William HAMBEY and Martha his wife.
October 24th 1739 then was John LOCKARD m. to Christian TIPPINS.
October 25th 1738 then was b. Hannah DURBIN d/o John DURBIN and Avarilla his wife.
March 15th 1739 then d. Charles ANDERSON.
April 7th 1740 then d. Margaret DENSON wife of William DENSON.
April 2d 1740 then d. John DENSON.
November 15th 1739 then was b. Mary WILES d/o Jonathan WILES and Sarah his wife. {H-309}
February 19th 1739 then was b. John LONEY s/o John LONEY and Sarah his wife.
Rebecca HANSON wife of Jacob HANSON d. in the month of Jan. 1737.
January 23d 1738 then was Jacob HANSON m. unto Margaret HUGHES.
December 3d 1739 then was b. Mary HANSON d/o Jacob HANSON and Margaret his wife. {OR-107}
April 10th 1740 then d. Michael JAMES.
February 20th 1739 then d. Andrew THOMPSON.
Sarah GARRETT d/o Henry GARRETT & Mary his wife b. 9 August 1736.
Elizabeth GARRETT d/o Henry & Mary his wife b. 20 September 1738.
Sarah BROWN b. 14 April 1740 d/o Absolam BROWN & Mary his wife.
Thomas BROWN s/o Augustus BROWN & Ann his wife b. 1 April 1739.
Samuel MAC CARTHY was m. to Sarah ROBINSON 16 November 1739.
Ann LITTLE d/o Thomas LITTLE & Avarilla his wife b. 15 Mar. 1738.
March 25th 1740 then d. Margaret DEVER d/o Richard DEVER Junr.
April 25th 1740 d. Anna LITTEN d/o Thomas LITTEN & Anna his wife.
May 14th 1740 then d. James PRICHARD s/o Obediah and Elizabeth PRICHARD.
April 14th 1740 then was b. Thomas CROW s/o John CROW and Judith his wife.
John WORTHINGTON s/o b. 5 October 1732; Elizabeth WORTHINGTON b. on Tuesday about two of the clock in the afternoon the 22 July 1735, and d. Sunday night 3 August 1735. {H-310}
Charles WORTHINGTON s/o Mr. Charles WORTHINGTON and Sarah his wife b. Tuesday about 11 o'clock in the afternoon 6 July 1736.
Anna WORTHINGTON d/o Mr. Charles WORTHINGTON and Sarah his wife b. Saturday in the forenoon 10 June 1738.
Elizabeth BAULCH d/o James BAULCH & Ann his wife b. 7 March 1738.
Charles DAVIS s/o Henry DAVIS and Sarah his wife b. about one o'clock in the forenoon 23 January 1739. {OR-108}
Mary LEE d/o James LEE & Elizabeth his wife b. 13 November 1739.
John WOODY m. to Mary LYNSEY 27 December 1738.
Elianor WOODY d/o John WOODY and Mary his wife b. 23 May 1739.
Mary PERKINS d/o Richard PERKINS Senr. and Mary his wife and Grand Daughter to William SHEERWILL Senr. b. 1 December 1739.
John RHODES s/o William RHODES & Mary his wife b. 20 Sept. 1738.
John Permenta MORGAN s/o James MORGAN and Elizabeth his wife b. 12 February 1738.
Sarah VINEY d/o Godfrey VINEY and Sarah his wife b. 6 Sept. 1736.
John VINEY s/o Godfrey VINEY & Sarah his wife b. 7 March 1738.
Stephen ROW s/o James ROW and Lydia his wife b. 13 April 1739.
William DENSON d. 9 April 1740. {H-311}
Richard BAYLEY d. 9 April 1740.
Martha DUN d/o John DUN & Christen his wife b. 6 November 1736.
Mary DUN d/o John DUN & Christen his wife b. 6 May 1739.

ST. GEORGE'S PARISH REGISTER

Mary CROCKET d/o Joseph CROCKET & Jane his wife b. 2 March 1739.
Sarah JOHNSON d/o Joseph JOHNSON & Martha his wife b. 10 January 1739.
May 6th 1740 then d. Jeremiah JOHNSON s/o Joseph JOHNSON and Martha his wife.
May 26th 1739 then d. Thomas DEAVER.
Thomas DEAVER s/o Thomas DEAVER and Deborah his wife b. 28 December 1739.
Susanna BOND d/o Charles BOND & Elianer his wife b. 1 Sept. 1737.
Charles BOND s/o Charles BOND & Elianer his wife b. 21 Nov. 1739.
Samuel CROCKETT s/o Samuel CROCKETT and Esther his wife b. 11 February 1739.
Anna HILL d/o Alexander HILL and Mary his wife b. 15 October 1738.
Elianor WARD d/o Jane WARD was b. in the month of May 1738.
Bridget AYRES d/o Abraham AYRES and Bridget his wife b. 23 October 1738.
William GRAYDON m. Mary AYRES 4 December 1739.
William MAC CARTNEY was m. unto Jane SMITH 23 March 1739.
Elizabeth PRESTON d/o James PRESTON and Sarah his wife was b. 15 October 1739.
Sarah PATTERSON d/o Robert PATTERSON and Jane his wife b. 12 November 1739. {H-312}
Mary DOWNS d/o Thomas DOWNS & Guilielmus his wife b. 7 June 1740.
Charles WILLIAMS m. Judith JONES 13 July 1739.
Martha WILSON d/o Joseph WILSON and Hannah his wife b. 10 November 1739.
Jonathan JONES s/o Thomas JONES & Mary his wife b. 16 Feb. 1739.
Gilbert DUNAHUE s/o Roger DUNAHUE and Elizabeth his wife b. 29 February 1739.
Thomas BIRCHFIELD s/o Thomas BIRCHFIELD Junr. and Sarah his wife b. 13 January 1739, and the said Thomas d. 5 April 1740.
Mary COWIN d/o Sarah COWIN b. 20 March 1738.
Sarah COWIN d/o John COWEN [sic] d. 27 April 1739.
January 27th 1739 then d. Mary COSLEY.
Lucy CANTWELL d/o Edward CANTWELL and Sarah his wife d. 27 January 1739. {OR-110}
Edward CANTWELL s/o Edward CANTWELL and Sarah his wife b. 28 February 1739.
January 27th 1739 then d. Jane NORVELL.
Mary RICE d/o William RICE & Elizabeth his wife b. 14 April 1738.
Jonathan BOYTON m. Elizabeth GENKINS 15 July 1740.
John HUGHS m. Elizabeth NORRIS 11 September 1740. {H-313}
John THOMPSON was m. unto Mary PUTTEE 13 November 1740.
Faithey ELIOT d/o John ELIOT & Unity his wife b. 5 January 1739.
Susannah GARLAND d/o William GARLAND and Bethyah his wife b. 29 November 1737.
Sarah CROSS d/o John CROSS and Sarah his wife b. 25 March 1740.
Moses WILSON s/o John WILSON and Mary his wife b. 27 April 1740.
Mathew GENKINS s/o William GENKINS and Rachel his wife b. 3 August 1740.
Robert TAYLOR s/o George TAYLOR and Ann his wife b. 15 Oct. 1740.
William DALLAM b. 13 November 1735; Samuel DALLAM b. 13 October 1737; Ann DALLAM b. 10 December 1739; children of Richard DALLAM and Frances his wife.
July 2d 1740 then was Henry STONE m. to Constance JAMES.
William JAMES d. 26 June 1740.
John JAMES d. in the month of July 1740.
Elizabeth RICE wife of William RICE d. 12 May 1740.
Henry KEEN s/o Henry KEEN and Emilla his wife b. 4 July 1740.

ST. GEORGE'S PARISH REGISTER

Charles WHITAKER d. 3 October 1739. {OR-111}
Arabella GILBERT d/o Garvace GILBERT and Mary his wife b. 13 February 1739 (Posthumus).
June 26th 1739 John WEBSTER Junr. m. Hannah GILBERT. {H-314}
Mary FARMER d/o Peter FARMER & Mary his wife b. 27 November 1740.
John GILES s/o John GILES & Sarah his wife b. 14 January 1740/1.
James PRICHARD s/o Obediah PRICHARD and Elizabeth his wife b. 9 February 1740/1.
Henry WISEMAN Alias BEECH was m. unto Jane GARVIN 29 April 1740.
Daniel PRICHARD s/o James PRICHARD and Elizabeth his wife b. 24 November 1740.
John HOLLAND s/o John HOLLAND and Sarah his wife b. 24 November 1740.
February 15th 1739 then d. Phebe CAMPBEL d/o John CAMPBEL and Ann his wife.
January 2d 1740 then was b. Phebe CAMPBEL d/o John CAMPBEL and Ann his wife.
James LITTEN s/o Thomas LITTEN & Ann his wife b. 5 February 1740.
September 12th 1738 then d. Elizabeth YESTWOOD d/o Michl. and Elizabeth YESTWOOD.
September 18th 1738 then d. Michael YESTWOOD d/o [sic] Michl. and Elizabeth YESTWOOD.
October 1st 1738 then d. Mary YESTWOOD d/o Michl. and Elizabeth YESTWOOD.
John DURBAN Junr. was m. to Mary HAWKINS 16 October 1740.
Reuben PRICHARD s/o Samuel PRICHARD and Isabella his wife b. 7 January 1740.
Mary HALL d/o Mr. Parker HALL & Blanch his wife b. 25 Oct. 1739.
John BAYLEY s/o Charles BAYLEY and Sarah his wife b. 6 Oct. 1740.
April 30th 1740 then d. James HOLLINGSWORTH.
October 2d 1740 then Robert COURTNEY was m. to Hannah COOK.
Sarah JOHNSON d/o Joseph & Martha JOHNSON d. 12 June 1740.{H-315}
Daniel RUFF was m. unto Elizabeth WEBSTER 11 May 1740. {OR-112}
Sarah BROWN d/o Mr. Thomas BROWN and Sarah his wife b. 14 September 1740.
Charity BUTTERWORTH d/o Isaac BUTTERWORTH and Jane his wife b. 11 March 1739.
James PHILLIPS s/o James PHILLIPS and Sarah his wife b. 9 February 1740.
Annaple CLARK d/o John CLARK & Hannah his wife b. 27 Dec. 1739.
February 4th 1740 then d. Elizabeth BROWN d/o John and Mary BROWN his wife.
Sarah DUNAVIN d/o Thomas DUNAVIN & Frances his wife b. 24 June 1738.
Anna HOLLIS d/o William HOLLIS and Anna his wife b. 22 April 1739.
Margaret SNELSON wife of William SNELSON d. 1 February 1739.
March 9th 1739 then d. William SNELSON.
Susanna HILLIARD d/o Thomas HILLIARD and Susanna his wife b. 14 October 1740.
January 24th 1739 then Samuel BRICE m. Elizabeth ANHOUSIN.
May 13th 1740 then d. Samuel BRICE.
Elizabeth DAVIDG d/o Hudson DAVIDG and Susannah his wife b. 29 August 1740?. {H-316}
William BROWN m. Margaret CONSTANCE 31 December 1740.
John COMBEST s/o Thomas COMBEST and Elizabeth his wife b. 18 March 1740.
October 20th 1740 then was b. William BUCKNALL s/o Francis BUCKNALL and Blanch his wife.
April 2d 1740 then d. William MACCLOUD.

ST. GEORGE'S PARISH REGISTER

Mary FLANAGAN d/o Edward FLANAGAN and Mary his wife b. 11 January 1735. {OR-113}
Eleonor FLANAGAN d/o Edward & Mary FLANAGAN b. 2 June 1739.
February 6th 1739 then was b. Elisabeth RIDDLE d/o Andrew RIDDLE and Ann his wife.
April 3d 1741 then d. Susanna COWIN wife of John COWIN.
Thomas SCARLET s/o Stephen SCARLET & Ruth his wife b. 13 February 1740.
John CROW s/o James CROW & Hannah his wife b. 1 January 1740.
Dec. 10th 1739 d. Stephen WOOD s/o Joshua WOOD and Mary his wife.
Sarah WOOD d/o Joshua WOOD & Mary his wife b. 2 February 1738.
May 14th 1740 then d. Joshua WOOD.
Elizabeth GOVER d/o Ephraim GOVER and Elizabeth his wife b. 4 April 1741.
Richard MITCHEL s/o Richard MITCHEL and Elizabeth his wife b. 7 October 1740.
Sarah INGRAM d/o Arthur INGRAM and Ann his wife b. 15 March 1739.
Oct. 1st 1740 b. Thomas AYRS s/o Benjamin AYRS & Mary his wife.
Elizabeth COURTNEY d/o Jonas COURTNEY and Comfort his wife b. 12 January 1740.
Fanny ARNEL d/o William ARNEL & Elizabeth his wife b. 9 April 1740.
February 7th 1740 d. Elizabeth GILBERT wife of Thomas GILBERT.
George Lester RHODES s/o Henry RHODES and Anna his wife b. 2 September 1740.
Sarah RHODES d. 5 October 1739.
Mary Cole SPEGLE d/o John Cole SPEGLE and Rebecca his wife b. 8 May 1738.
John Cole SPEGLE d. 23 April 1741.
William MACCARTY s/o Samuel MCACARTY & Sarah his wife b. 6 March ?
February 3d 1740 then George JONES m. Elizabeth LINLEY.
May 15th 1741 then James BUTCHER m. Elizabeth EASTWOOD. {OR-114}
August 28th 1740 then d. Hannah KIMBLE d/o Robert & Sarah KIMBLE.
Sophia KIMBLE d/o Robert KIMBLE & Sarah his wife b. 22 Sept.1740.
Thomas TAYLOR s/o Abraham TAYLOR and Hannah his wife b. 23 January 1740.
August 19th then Aaron PORTER m. Jane MACKENNY.
Sarah MORRIS d/o Richard MORRIS and Mary his wife b. 3 Jan. 1740.
James NORVEL s/o John NORVEL and Mary his wife b. 26 March 1741.
Adam CANTWELL s/o John CANTWELL & Mary his wife b. 6 Jan. 1740.
John HALL was b. 8 October 1737; Josiah HALL was b. 31 March 1739 and d. 3 October following in the year 1739; Mary HALL was b. 21 May 1740; children of Majr. John HALL and Hannah his wife.
Joseph REYLEY s/o Francis REYLEY and Elizabeth his wife was b. 26 December 1740. {H-318}
George LITTLE s/o Thomas LITTLE and Avarilla his wife b. 19 March 1740, and the same day d. Avarilla LITTLE wife of Thomas.
Rachel COURTNEY d/o John COURTNEY & Frances his wife b. 18 June 1740.
Barnett EAGAN and Hugh EAGAN twins s/o Richard EAGAN and Katharine his wife b. 20 June 1740.
Margaret ASHMORE d/o Walter ASHMORE and Margaret his wife b. 13 December 1740.
William WELLS s/o Richard WELLS & Elizabeth his wife b. 18 December 1740.
Elianor EAGAN d/o James EAGAN and Rachel his wife b. 22 February 1735.
Robert CREGG d. 4 September 1739.
Job BARNS d. 11 November 1739.

ST. GEORGE'S PARISH REGISTER

May 7th 1741 then was William ELIOT m. to Keren JOHNSON.
Skipwith COLE s/o Skipwith COLE and Margaret his wife b. 16 March 1736. {OR-115}
William COLE s/o Capt. Skipwith COLE and Margaret his wife was b. 5 August 1738.
Phillip COLE s/o Capt. Skipwith COLE and Margaret his wife b. 6 December 1740.
Mr. Francis HOLLAND of Spesutia Island d. 7 August 1738.
Frances HOLLAND d/o Francis HOLLAND and Susanna his wife d. 7 May 1740. {H-319}
Martha PRICE wife of Thomas PRICE d. 22 April 1741.
March 11th 1740 then was John RIGDON m. unto Elizabeth OACHISSON.
Isabella BRIARLY d/o Robert BRIERLY [sic] and Margaret his wife b. 17 February 1740.
John THOMAS s/o Henry THOMAS and Jane his wife b. 26 Jan. 1740.
Elizabeth RIGDON d/o George RIGDON Junr. and Sarah his wife b. 17 December 1740.
Mary GENKINS d/o Francis GENKINS & Mary his wife b. 31 Aug. 1739.
June 9th 1740 then d. Mary SMITH widow of William SMITH of Delph.
Frances FRITZBY d/o Peregrine FRITZBY and Mary his wife b. 4 August 1741.
October 23d 1740 then was Daniel MURDAGH m. to Martha COWEN.
James MURDAGH s/o Daniel MURDAGH and Martha his wife b. 3 July 1741.
Elianor RAMSEY d/o John RAMSEY and Christian his wife b. 27 June 1741.
Joshua JUDD s/o Daniel JUDD & Sarah his wife b. 21 August 1741.
September 10th 1741 then was Henry HAILL m. unto Mary BRADLEY.
October 12th 1741 then d. Mr. Benjamin WHEELER.
February 5th 1740 then was Winstone SMITH m. to Prescilla PACA.
November 4th 1740 then was b. Thomas JONES s/o Jonathan JONES and Martha his wife. {H-320}
William DULY d. in the year 1739. {OR-116}
William BEAVER Junr. was m. unto Blanch DULY in October 1741.
Francis BEAVER b. __ July 1741 s/o William BEAVER and Blanch his wife.
Thomas HUGHS s/o John HUGHS & Elizabeth his wife b. 10 June 1741.
Thomas HAWKINS s/o Thomas HAWKINS and Elizabeth his wife b. 27 January 1740.
Gregory FARMER s/o John FARMER & Sophia his wife b. 29 September 1741.
April 15th 1739 was b. Sarah HERRINGTON d/o Sarah HERRINGTON.
Richard and Mary BARNS twins & children of James BARNS and Bethyah his wife were b. 1 June 1740.
Fanny GALLION d/o James GALLION and Phebe his wife b. 28 August 1738, and d. 26 February 1740.
Mary GALLION d/o James GALLION and Phebe his wife b. 28 April 1739.
October 27th 1741 then was Thomas HORNER m. unto Grace ANDERSON.
William DRAPER s/o John DRAPER Junr. and Mary his wife b. 13 September 1740.
Benjamin WILSON s/o John WILSON & Mary his wife b. 4 April 1739.
Oliver VERNON s/o Oliver VERNON and Mary his wife b. __ May on Whitsun Monday 1740.
Bennett MATHEWS s/o Roger MATHEWS and Elizabeth his wife b. 10 March 1739.
Mr. Roger MATHEWS d. 20 October 1740. {H-321}
William COLE s/o John COLE & Mary his wife b. 24 July 1741.
Thomas HOLLINGSWORTH m. Keziah HOLLIS 14 January 1741.

ST. GEORGE'S PARISH REGISTER

{End of first original register.}
William POGE s/o John POGE & Sarah his wife b. 7 April 1740.
John GALLION s/o John GALLION and Elizabeth his wife b. 9 May 1730.
April 15th 1739 was b. Sarah HERRINGTON d/o Sarah HERRINGTON.
May 15th 1741 then was b. Sarah GILBERT d/o Garvace GILBERT and Elizabeth his wife.
September 14th 1741 then was b. James THOMPSON s/o John THOMPSON and Mary his wife.
April 12th 1734 then was b. Ann FIELD d/o John FIELD and Catharine his wife.
July 28th 1740 then was b. Aquilla BRASHIER s/o Thomas BRASHIER and Sarah his wife.
Mary FOWLER d/o Samuel FOWLER & Mary his wife b. 24 October 1741.
December 1st 1741 then d. Avarilla DURBIN wife of John DURBIN.
February 2d 1739 then was b. Sarah BOTTS d/o John BOTTS and Sarah his wife.
Moses WOOD s/o Isaac WOOD & Elizabeth his wife b. 20 Aug. 1741.
August 26th 1741 d. Joshua WOOD s/o Isaac WOOD.   {OR2-160}
December 1st 1741 then was b. Thomas GALHAMPTON s/o Thomas GALHAMPTON and Elizabeth his wife.
Martin TREDWAY s/o Thomas TREDWAY & Mary his wife b. 7 Oct. 1741.
Hannah BURCHFIELD d/o Thomas BURCHFIELD Junr. and Sarah his wife was b. 3 June 1741.   {H-322}
November 7th 1738 then William MACGOMERY m. Mary BRIERLY.
August 31st 1739 then was b. Elizabeth MACGOMERY d/o William MACGOMERY & Mary his wife.
Daniel DURBIN s/o John DURBIN Junr. and Mary his wife b. 1 December 1741.
September 30th 1741 then d. Martha MACKENNY.
Ashberry CORD s/o Thomas CORD & Mary his wife b. 2 Dec. 1741.
July 7th 1741 then Cornelious KELLY m. Alce LOW.
Sarah PRESTON d/o Daniel PRESTON & Ann his wife b. 17 Nov. 1741.
Mary TAYLOR d/o James TAYLOR & Mary his wife b. 30 March 1741.
October 2d 1737 then was b. Mary FOX d/o Margaret FOX.
May 7th 1741 then Aquila JONES m. Elizabeth BRICE.
Mary JONES d/o Aquila JONES & Elizabeth his wife b. 4 March 1741.
Margaret JOHNSON d/o Abraham JOHNSON & Lydia his wife b. 28 October 1741.
Pearcy ELLIOT s/o William ELLIOT & Keren his wife b. 20 February 1741.
Elizabeth MORGAN d/o Edward MORGAN and Sarah his wife b. 18 September 1740.
James SCOTT m. Ann WHEELER 18 February 1741.
Leonard WHEELER m. Ann BOND 16 February 1741.
Hannah WHEELER d/o Thomas WHEELER and Sarah his wife b. 16 February 1740.
December 2d 1740 then d. Elizabeth WOLLOX wife of John WOLLOX.
December 16th 1741 then was John WOLLOX m. to Elizabeth YATES.
Jean CROCKET d/o Samuel CROCKET & Esther his wife b. 24 February 1741.   {H-323}
Samuel CROCKET s/o Joseph CROCKET & Jean his wife b. 9 March 1740.
May 16th 1740 then James BUTCHER m. Elizabeth ESTWOOD.
November 10th 1741 then was b. Mary BUTCHER d/o James BUTCHER and Elizabeth his wife.
January 5th 1741 then was b. Elizabeth RIGDON d/o John RIGDON and Elizabeth his wife.

ST. GEORGE'S PARISH REGISTER

August 20th 1740 then was b. Alexander Philip GOODWIN s/o John GOODWIN and Margaret his wife.
Hannah PRESTON d/o James PRESTON & Sarah his wife b. 4 Feb. 1741.
Thomas BEECH s/o Henry BEECH & Jane his wife b. 31 August 1741.
John WOOD m. Elizabeth BRADFORD in the month of November 1739.
Alce WOOD d/o John WOOD & Elizabeth his wife b. 2 Feb. 1741.
John HOLLINGSWORTH m. Mary DEAVER in the month of August 1741.
October 22d 1741 then d. Catherine TUCKER wife of Lewis TUCKER.
Terrence BRADY m. Sarah HILLIARD in the month of December 1740.
Catherine JACKSON wife of John JACKSON d. in the month of November 1740.
Margaret JACKSON d/o John JACKSON & Catharine his wife d. in the month of May 1740.
Cynthia PATTERSON d/o Robert PATTERSON & Jane his wife b. 21st day of January 1741. {OR2-162}
Avarilla OSBORN d/o William OSBORN and Catherine his wife was b. 8 February 1741.
Mary HOLLIS d/o William HOLLIS and Ann his wife was b. 26 November 1741. {H-324}
Francis GARLAND s/o William GARLAND and Bethyah his wife b. 1 January 1741.
Elizabeth LYAL d/o John LYAL and Elizabeth his wife b. 23 August 1741.
John WILLIAMS s/o John WILLIAMS and Margaret his wife b. 25 July 1740.
Sarah HORNER d/o Thomas HORNER & Grace his wife b. 26 Dec. 1741.
Casandra MATHEWS d/o John MATHEWS & Ann his wife b. 8 Aug. 1740.
John MATHEWS s/o John MATHEWS & Ann his wife b. 31 July 1741.
Garrald BROWN s/o Thomas BROWN & Sarah his wife b. 21 April 1742.
Jacob GALLION s/o James GALLION & Phebe his wife b. 3 April 1742.
John GARRETTSON was m. to Sarah MERRYARTER 21 April 1742.
April 21st 1740 then d. Mr. Bennett GARRETT.
January 21st 1741 then was Thomas FARMER m. unto Elizabeth ROSS.
July 27th 1742 then was William MACCOMUS m. to Hannah DEAVER.
Ann MACCOMUS wife of John MACCOMUS d. in December 1741.
April 24th 1741 then d. Thomas CROSS. {OR2-163}
Martha JOHNSON s/o Joseph JOHNSON and Martha his wife was b. 6 May 1741.
January 4th 1741 then Nicholas BAKER was m. to Martha WOOD.
February 10th 1741 then was James STEWART m. to Mary WOOD.
Grace SMITH d/o Samuel SMITH and Elizabeth his wife b. 10 October 174?. {H-325}
Walter BILLINGSBY(?) m. Sarah LOVE 27 August 1742.
Aquila MATHEWS s/o Roger MATHEWS and Elizabeth his wife d. 15 August 1742.
Elizabeth WHEELER d. 21 June 1742.
Mrs. Sophia WHITE wife of Majr. Thomas WHITE d. 18 June 1742.
Charles FITSPATRICK m. Jane FAIRBOURN 20 October 1742.
John RENSHAW s/o Abraham RENSHAW & Ann his wife b. 17 June 1741.
Jane WEBB d/o Samuel WEBB & Jane his wife b. 9 March 1741.
Ann TAYLOR d/o Robert TAYLOR & Jane his wife b. 21 November 1741.
John GRIFFITH s/o Samuel GRIFFITH and Elizabeth his wife b. 11 February 1741, and d. 15 October 1742.
Thomas HAIL s/o Henry HAIL & Mary his wife b. 19 October 1742.
John DEAVER m. Perina GREENFIELD 21 October 1742
Sarah WESTCOMB d/o Samuel WESTCOMB and Sarah his wife b. 6 July 1742.
Josias CRAWFORD s/o James CRAWFORD & Sarah his wife b. 2 December 1742.

ST. GEORGE'S PARISH REGISTER

Robert HAWKINS s/o Thomas HAWKINS and Elizabeth his wife b. 16 February 1742.
Avarilla BOTTS and Mary BOTTS twins d/o John BOTTS and Sarah his wife b. 5 August 1742.   {OR2-164, H-326}
Martha HANSON d/o Jacob HANSON and Margaret his wife b. 3 November 1741.
Sarah HANSON d. 25 November 1742.
John HALL m. Susanna MARSHALL 2 June 1742.
December 2d 1742 then d. Mary FARMER d/o Peter FARMER and Mary his wife.
William BAKER s/o Thomas BAKER & Mary his wife b. 13 Sept. 1742.
Martha Pain Norriss LESTER d/o George LESTER and Alce his wife b. 25 April 1742.
Martha JONES d/o Jonathan JONES and Martha his wife b. 25 August 1742.
John FARMER d. 15 September 1742.
Sarah FARMER d/o John FARMER d. 16 September 1742.
John FARMER s/o John FARMER & Sophia his wife b. 10 Nov. 1742.
Robert HAWKINS Junr. m. Lydia CRUTCHLEY 13 January 1742.
Aquila HALL s/o John HALL & Hannah his wife b. 17 June 1742.
James COBB m. Mary POGE 18 March 1741.
Margaret COBB d/o James COBB & Mary his wife b. 25 December 1742.
James ASHMORE s/o Walter ASHMORE and Margaret his wife b. 4 November 1742.   {H-327}
James COBB s/o James COBB and Ruth his wife b. 27 November 1735.
Joseph COBB s/o James COBB and Ruth his wife b. 4 February 1737.
James BRICE m. Mary JOHNSON 6 January 1742.   {OR2-165}
Mary HILL d/o Alexander HILL & Mary his wife b. 16 February 1740.
William JACKSON s/o Mary JACKSON b. 2 June 1742.
Henry COLSTON s/o John COLSTON and Rebecca his wife b. 10 November 1741.
John HAWKINS m. Mary WELLS 1 March 1741.
Ann RENSHAW d/o John RENSHAW & Mary his wife b. 19 February 1741.
Charles HOPKINS s/o William HOPKINS and Rachel his wife b. 1 August 1741.
Joseph MORGAN m. Constance BARNS ___ September 1740.
Joseph MORGAN s/o Joseph MORGAN & Constance his wife b. 3 February 1741.
Nathan RIGBIE s/o James RIGBIE and Elizabeth his wife b. 8 January 1742.
Richard DAWKINS s/o Richard DAWKINS and Mary his wife b. 23 April 1742.
Johannah PHILLIPS d/o James PHILLIPS and Sarah his wife b. 11 October 1742.
Rebecca MATHEWS d/o John MATHEWS & Ann his wife b. 10 March 1742.
February 25th 1741 then John COMBEST m. Mary BOWDEY.   {H-328}
Joseph RENSHAW m. Elizabeth WELLS 28 October 1742.
Thomas COMBEST s/o John COMBEST & Mary his wife b. 13 June 1742.
Elianor DAVIS d/o Henry DAVIS & ___ his wife b. 5 May 1742.
January 28th 1742 then John RYLEY m. Ruth ANSHOR.
William COURTNEY s/o John COURTNEY and Francis [sic] his wife b. 28 October 1742, and d. 21 December 1742.   {OR2-166}
James ALLEN s/o William ALLEN & Mary his wife b. 1 February 1742.
Alexander RIGDON s/o Thomas RIGDON and Ann his wife b. 12 April 1743.
Elizabeth BROWN d/o Martin BROWN & Mary his wife b. 24 September 1742.
Thomas BROWNLEY s/o Arthur BROWNLEY and Margaret his wife b. 2 March 1742.

ST. GEORGE'S PARISH REGISTER

Sarah RULEY d/o Francis RULEY and Elizabeth is wife b. 11 February 1742.
Elianor DAUGHERTY d/o William DAUGHERTY and Mary his wife b. 30 December 1742.
Martha DEAVER d/o Antil DEAVER & Sarah his wife d. 13 May 1743.
John COWEN m. Elizabeth BOND 22 April 1743.
Mary INGRAM d/o Arthur INGRAM & Ann his wife b. 18 October 1742.
Martha ARNOLD d/o William ARNOLD and Elizabeth his wife b. 20 August 1742.
June 7th 1743 then Thomas MIDDLETON m. Jane PERRY. {H-329}
Thomas WALKER s/o Mary WALKER b. 19 April 1742.
Thomas MITCHEL Junr. m. Hannah OSBORN 24 December 1742.
Kent MITCHELL s/o Thomas MITCHEL Junr. and Hannah his wife b. 8 May 1743.
Thomas ARNOLD m. Sarah SMITH 15 September 1742.
William SYMPSON m. Avarilla PERKINS 18 August 1742.
Sarah MACCARTY d/o Samuel MACCARTY and Sarah his wife b. on Easter Monday 24 April 1743.
Sarah MURDAUGH d/o Daniel MURDAUGH and Martha his wife b. 28 March 1743. {OR2-167}
Josiah KIMBLE s/o Robert KEMBLE [sic] and Sarah his wife b. 17 February 1742.
Lawrence TAYLOR s/o Abraham TAYLOR and Hannah his wife b. 9 February 1742.
Thomas PORTER s/o Aaron PORTER & Jane his wife b. 9 January 1742.
February 8th 1742 then was b. Ann GRIFFITH d/o Mary GRIFFITH.
Thomas MITCHEL s/o Richard MITCHEL and Elizabeth his wife b. 8 June 1743.
James SCARLET s/o Stephen SCARLET & Ruth his wife b. 7 Dec. 1742.
John BROWN s/o Thomas BROWN and Susanna his wife b. 11 May 1742.
Mary CROW d/o James CROW & Hannah his wife b. 22 July 1742.
Hannah CROW wife of James CROW d. 1 March 1742. {H-330}
Aventen PERKINS s/o Richard PERKINS and Mary his wife b. 23 March 1742.
Adam PERKINS m. Mary WALTERS 23 May 1743.
William PERKINS s/o Isaac PERKINS & Mary his wife b. 23 October 1740.
November 6th 1739 then Daniel KENLY m. Frances WELLS.
March 17th 1741 then was b. William KENLY s/o Daniel KENLY and Frances his wife.
June 23d 1743 then Thomas RHODES m. Margaret ALLEN.
Elizabeth DOWNS d/o Thomas DOWNS and Guiolmus his wife b. 31 August 1742. {OR2-168}
Mary WILSON d/o Joseph WILSON & Hannah his wife b. 24 May 1743.
Hannah WOODEY d/o John WOODEY & Mary his wife b. 23 Oct. 1740.
Robert WOODEY s/o John WOODEY & Mary his wife b. 8 Nov. 1742.
January 26th 1741 then Stephen FISHER m. Elizabeth GOODWIN.
Elizabeth FISHER d/o Stephen FISHER and Elizabeth his wife b. 13 October 1742.
October 12th 1742 then was b. George COLLINGS s/o Robert COLLINGS and Ann his wife.
Frances JONES d/o Charles JONES & Francis [sic] his wife b. 17 July 1739.
Rebecca JONES d/o Charles JONES & Frances his wife b. 7 February 1741. {H-331}
January 25th 1742 then was b. Jane PORTER d/o John PORTER and Ann his wife.
February 6th 1742 then Benjamin GOODWIN m. Hannah URGHQUART.
January ___ 1742 then d. Thomas JONES.

68

ST. GEORGE'S PARISH REGISTER

Casandra COLE d/o Skipworth COLE & Mary his wife b. 8 Jan. 1742.
Martha BARNS d/o Ford BARNS & Margaret his wife b. 8 June 1742, and d. 12 October 1742.
John HUGHS s/o John HUGHS & Elizabeth his wife b. 29 Dec. 1742.
Stephen LONEY s/o John LONEY & Sarah his wife b. 25 June 1742.
May 4th 1743 then Thomas PRICE m. Sarah CROSS.
June 9th 1742 then was b. Enock HOLLINGSWORTH s/o John HOLLINSWORTH and Mary his wife. {OR2-169}
John RHODES s/o Henry RHODES & Ann his wife b. 20 March 1742.
Charles WHITEAKER s/o John WHITEAKER and Mary his wife b. 11 December 1742.
Elizabeth MORRIS d/o Edmond MORRIS & Mary his wife b. 4 May 1740.
Mary MORRIS d/o Edmond MORRIS & Mary his wife b. 13 August 1742.
June 2d 1743 then Jacob COMBEST m. Mary SOLAVAN.
Mary MORRIS d/o Richard MORRIS & Mary his wife b. 3 March 1742.
Susanna KEMBAL d/o Sarah KEMBAL b. 8 June 1743. {H-332}
Preston GILBERT s/o Jarvace GILBERT and Elizabeth his wife b. 10 April 1743.
Nathan RIGBIE s/o Coll. Nathan RIGBIE and Cassandra his wife b. 18 June 1723.
Michael GILBERT b. 19 April 1741; William GILBERT b. 20 April s/o Samuel GILBERT and Martha his wife.
James SINCLER m. Mary LESTER 25 December 1742.
Elizabeth LEE b. 3 August 1737 d/o Sheerwood LEE & Elianor his wife.
John HANSON m. to Semelia GARRETTSON 4 August 1743.
Samuel HAMBY m. Mary SYMPSON 20 August 1737. {OR2-170}
Elizabeth HAMBY b. 20 Aug. 1738 d/o Samuel HAMBY & Mary his wife.
Sarah HAMBY b. 8 September 1739 d/o Samuel HAMBY & Mary his wife.
Frances HAMBY b. 10 June 1743 d/o Samuel HAMBY & Mary his wife.
Margaret WEBSTER d/o Michael WEBSTER and Elizabeth his wife b. 7 November 1741.
Margaret GALLION d/o Thomas GALLION & Mary his wife b. 15 August 1743.
James OSBORN m. to Jane HUGHS 17 September 1743.
Ann CLEGG departed this life 24 February 1743. {H-333}
Providence BAKER d/o Nicholas BAKER and Martha his wife b. 17 September 1743.
Grigory FARMER s/o Peter FARMER & Mary his wife b. 12 Sept. 1743.
James CROW m. to Grace DENSON 7 February 1743.
John BURTON m. to Mary HARGAS 15 January 1743.
Hannah SMITH b. 29 December 1743 d/o Samuel SMITH and Elizabeth his wife.
James PRITCHARD s/o James PRITCHARD and Elizabeth his wife b. 16 August 1743.
Thomas ARNOLD was m. to Sarah SMITH 15 September 1742.
William ARNOLD b. 13 September 1743 d/o [sic] Thomas ARNOLD and Sarah his wife.
Isaac GRIFFITH s/o Samuel GRIFFITH and Mary his wife b. 4 September 1743, and d. 20 March 1743.
Richard GRIFFITH was m. To Jane REES 22 November 1743.
Henry GARLAND was m. to Sarah HERRINGTON 27 January 1743.
Cassandra HORNER d/o Thomas HORNER and Grace his wife b. 21 March 1743.
Daniel PRESTON s/o Daniel PRESTON and Ann his wife b. 4 December 1743. {OR2-171}
Hannah WOOD d/o Isaac WOOD & Elizabeth his wife b. 20 November 1743. {H-334}

ST. GEORGE'S PARISH REGISTER

Margaret WILLIAMS d/o John WILLIAMS and Margaret his wife was b. 26 December 1742.
Ford BARNS s/o James BARNS & Bethiah his wife b. 11 Sept. 1743.
Ford BARNS was m. to Ruth GARRETT 20 October 1743.
Martha BARNS b. 1 Jan. 1743 d/o Ford BARNS & Margaret his wife.
Francis BURTON s/o William BURTON and Jane his wife b. 20 December 1735.
Mary BURTON d/o William BURTON & Jane his wife b. 29 Jan. 1738.
Sarah HOLLINGSWORTH b. 25 April 1739; Ann HOLLINGSWORTH b. 9 October 1743; d/o George HOLLINGSWORTH and Hannah his wife.
Mary JOHNSON d/o Robert JOHNSON and Elizabeth his wife b. 25 January 1743.
Elianor RICE d/o William RICE & Ann his wife b. 30 Sept. 1743.
Ann LEWIS d/o John LEWIS & Ann his wife b. 18 August 1742.
Soloman REES s/o Soloman REES & Mary his wife b. 21 Oct. 1743.
Elizabeth BEECH d/o Henry BEECH & Jane his wife b. 9 April 1744.
Ruben SIMPSON s/o William SIMPSON and Avarilla his wife b. 6 October 1743. {OR2-172}
Phebe GALLION d/o Solomon GALLION and Martha his wife b. 2 June 1744. {H-335}
Francis RILEY s/o John RILEY & Ruth his wife b. 20 Sept. 1743.
Ann PRITCHARD d/o Obediah PRITCHARD and Elizabeth his wife b. 13 December 1736.
Andrew THOMPSON s/o Andrew THOMPSON and Elizabeth his wife b. 15 February 1744.
Thomas NEWMAN s/o Thomas NEWMAN & Ann his wife b. 16 May 1744.
William RIGDON s/o George RIGDON & Ann his wife b. 15 June 1744.
William GOODWIN s/o Benjamin GOODWIN and Hannah his wife b. 7 January 1744.
John RIGDON s/o John RIGDON & Elizabeth his wife b. 18 June 1744.
Ann CLARK d/o Robert CLARK & Sillina his wife b. 29 May 1743.
William ELLIOT s/o William ELLIOT & Caran his wife b. 13 November 1743.
Elizabeth GILBERT d/o Michael GILBERT and Mary his wife b. 24 March 1744.
The Rev. Mr. Stephen WILKINSON d. 10 March 1743.
Abraham VERNUM s/o Oliver VERNUM & Mary his wife b. 3 May 1741.
Hannah NORVIL b. 4 August 1743 d/o John NORVIL & Mary his wife.
Mary LESTER d/o George LESTER & Alce his wife b. 3 Sept. 1743.
Mary TAYLOR wife of James TAYLOR d. 13 July 1744.
Mary NORVIL wife of John NORVIL d. 9 July 1744.
Mary CHANCY d/o George CHANCY and Susannah his wife b. 3 September 1744.
Elizabeth FARMER d/o Thomas FARMER and Elizabeth his wife b. 16 ?? 1743. {H-336}
Casandra RENSHAW b. 8 September 1743 d/o Joseph RENSHAW and Elizabeth his wife. {OR2-173}
Samuel JOHNSON b. 29 March 1742; Mary JOHNSON b. 23 February 1743; James JOHNSON b. 10 January 1743 [sic]; children of Dann JOHNSON and Levina his wife.
Ralph DURBIN s/o John DURBIN and Elianor his wife b. 18 December 1743.
William ELLIOT s/o John ELLIOT & Unity his wife b. 9 April 1744.
Annes READ d/o John READ & Mary his wife b. 9 May 1744.
Margaret GENKINS d/o William GENKINS and Rachel his wife b. 4 August 1744.
Faithfull WEBB b. 19 Sept. 1743 d/o Samuel WEBB & Jane his wife.
Cassandra RENSHAW d/o John RENSHAW and Mary his wife b. 16 December 1743.

ST. GEORGE'S PARISH REGISTER

June 16th 1744 then was b. Susanna HALL d/o John HALL and Susanna his wife; 26 June 1744 then d. Mrs. Susanna HALL wife of Mr. John HALL.
Hannah GOODING d/o Jacob GOODING & Mary his wife b. 10 June 1744.
Elizabeth COURTNEY d/o John COURTNEY and Frances his wife b. 18 March 1743.
Jane STEWART d/o Charles STEWART & Mary his wife b. 8 __ 1742.
James STEWART s/o Charles STEWART & Mary his wife b. 2 June 1744.
Roger PERRYMAN m. to Martha ARMSTRONG 15 July 1742.   {H-337}
Mary PERRYMAN departed his life 14 May 1742.   {OR2-174}
John DEBRULAR m. to Frances BURIDGE 14 May 1743.
Mary MULAIN d/o Edward MULAIN and Margaret his wife b. 18 April 1743.
Mary DRAPER d/o John DRAPER and Mary his wife b. 26 April 1744.
Edward CANTWELL was m. Blanch JACKSON 5 January 1744.
John PRESTON was m. to Mary GARNET 29 August 1743.
Ann PRESTON d/o John PRESTON & Mary his wife b. 28 Feb. 1744.
Abraham ROBINSON was m. to Sarah SIMPSON 24 September 1744.
Mary JOHNSON d/o Abraham JOHNSON and Lidia his wife b. 16 August 1744.
John ROUSE m. Elizabeth PERRYMAN 8 September 1744.
Francis HOLLAND m. Cordelia NIGHT 7 June 1744.
August 23d 1744 then was Amoss GARRETT m. to Frances DREW.
Mary COOLEY d/o Edward COOLEY and Elizabeth his wife b. 25 March 1740.
Priscilla SMITH d/o Winstone SMITH and Priscilla his wife b. 9 January 1742; 17 January 1742 then d. Mrs. Priscilla SMITH wife of Winstone SMITH.
July 18th 1743 Mr. Winstone SMITH m. to Mrs. Susanna STOKES.
Jane GRIFFITH wife of Richard GRIFFITH d. 31 August 1744.{H-338}
Martha & Israel COMBEST s/o & d/o Jacob and Mary COMBEST his wife was b. 24 May 1744.
John Hall HUGHS s/o Sarah HUGHS b. 10 July 1742.
William GALLION s/o James GALLION and Phebe his wife b. August 10 1744.   {OR2-175}
Benjamin HANSON s/o John HANSON and Semelia his wife b. 11 June 1744.
Aaron TREDWAY s/o Thomas TREDWAY and Elizabeth his wife b. 2 November 1744.
Sarah RAMSEY b. 4 March 1734; Elizabeth RAMSEY b. 18 July 1736; William RAMSEY b. 9 January 1738; Charles RAMSEY b. 11 February 1740; Mary RAMSEY b. 13 November 1742; children of William RAMSEY and Elizabeth his wife.
Ann PRESTON d/o James PRESTON & Sarah his wife b. 4 Sept. 1744.
John JOHNSON s/o Thomas JOHNSON & Sarah his wife b. 25 Jan. 1743.
Charles GILBERT was m. to Elizabeth HAWKINS 27 September 1744.
Margaret BAYLEY d/o Charles BAYLEY and Sarah his wife b. 26 December 1742.
Mrs. Ann MATHEWS d. 30 October 1744 wife of Mr. John MATHEWS.
John BROWN s/o Thomas BROWN & Susanna his wife d. 8 Oct. 1744.
Thomas BROWN s/o Thomas BROWN and Susannah his wife b. 25 December 1744.
Mary SCARLET d/o Stephen SCARLET & Ruth his wife b. 20 Mar. 1744.
Ann HAIL d/o Henry HAIL & Mary his wife b. 13 October 1744.
Samuel WEBSTER m. to Elizabeth DALLAM 2 February 1726. {H-339}
Elizabeth WEBSTER b. 25 November 1727 and d. 10 November 1729; Alizanah WEBSTER b. 15 January 1729; Elizabeth WEBSTER b. 10 March 1731; John WEBSTER b. 19 June 1734; Samuel WEBSTER b. 9 June 1736; Richard Dallam WEBSTER b. 15 April 1738 and d. 28

ST. GEORGE'S PARISH REGISTER

April 1740; Richard WEBSTER b. 7 April 1740; Hannah & Michael WEBSTER b. 25 February 1742; children of Samuel WEBSTER and Elizabeth his wife.
Thomas WHEELER s/o Leonard WHEELER and Ann his wife b. 26 January 1743. {OR2-176}
Daniel REES m. Elizbeth NIGHT 28 December 1743.
Abraham REES s/o Daniel REES and Elizabeth his wife b. 11 June 1744.
Martha GALLION b. 31 January 1738; Sarah GALLION b. 25 October 1741; d/o Soloman GALLION and Martha his wife.
Samuel HARPER m. Sarah MACCRAREE 27 December 1744.
Major Aquila PACA d. 8 February 1743.
John MACCOMUS s/o William MACCOMUS and Hannah his wife b. 7 October 1744.
Avarilla & Prescilla GRIFFITH both twins of Samuel GRIFFITH and Mary his wife b. 23 November 1744.
Felix HUGHS was m. to Catherine NOBLE 1 October 1743. {OR2-177}
Thomas HUGHS s/o Felix HUGHS & Catherine his wife b. 7 July 1744.
Henry GARRETT & Mary his wife was m. 19 December 1728.
Isaac GARRETT b. 14 September 1729; Bennett GARRETT b. 30 December 1731; John GARRETT b. 29 August 1733; Hannah GARRETT b. 15 March 1734; Sarah GARRETT b. 9 August 1736; Elizabeth GARRETT b. 20 September 1738; Richard GARRETT b. 29 March 1740; Amoss GARRETT b. 20 June 1741; Mary GARRETT b. 11 June 1743; s/o & d/o Henry GARRETT and Mary his wife.
Isaac BUTTERWORTH m. Jane WHEELER 18 December 1728.
Mary BUTTERWORTH b. 25 March 1729; Elizabeth BUTTERWORTH b. 24 February 1731; Isaac BUTTERWORTH b. 11 December 1734; Benjamin BUTTERWORTH b. 4 February 1736; Charity BUTTERWORTH b. 11 March 1739; Jane BUTTERWORTH b. 24 June 1742 and d. 27 October 1742; children of Isaac BUTTERWORTH and Jane his wife.
Allen GRAY s/o Catherine NOBLE was b. 7 February 1739.
Thomas CROW b. 14 April 1740; Mansfield CROW b. 23 November 1742; s/o John CROW & Judith his wife.
James OSBORN s/o James OSBORN & Jane his wife b. 16 November 1744.
Josias OSBORN s/o James OSBORN & Jane his wife b. 17 Sept. 1743.
James LEE s/o William LEE and Elizabeth his wife b. 27 Feb. 1741.
Joshua PARIS s/o Elizabeth PARIS b. 16 May 1740. {OR2-178}
Charles JONES s/o Aquila JONES and Elizabeth his wife b. 13 April 1744.
Sarah BRASHIER d/o Thomas BRASHIER and Sarah his wife b. 12 June 1744. {H-341}
Elizabeth RUFF d/o Daniel RUFF and Elizabeth his wife b. 26 December 1744.
Freeborn BROWN s/o Thomas BROWN & Sarah his wife b. 19 Nov. 1743. December 26th 1743 then was Isaac BUTTERAM m. to Ann LYAL.
John BUTTERAM s/o Isaac BUTTERAM & Ann his wife b. 13 March 1744.
Charles Anderson PRITCHARD s/o Samuel PRITCHARD and Isabel his wife b. 10 July 1743.
William BOWEN s/o Edward BOWEN & Mary his wife b. 13 May 1741.
Aquila HALL s/o Coll. John HALL and Hannah his wife departed this life 30 October 1743.
Benedict Edward HALL s/o Coll. John HALL and Hannah his wife b. 20 October 1744.
Blanch HALL d/o Mr. Parker HALL & Blanch his wife b. 27 February 1743. {OR2-179}
August 29th 1745 then was Samuel LEWIS m. to Margaret HUGHS.
March 13th 1744 then was b. John HANSON s/o Jacob HANSON and Margaret his wife.

ST. GEORGE'S PARISH REGISTER

February 11th 1742 then was b. Margaret WEST; 8 June 1745 then was b. David WEST; d/o & s/o John WEST and Susanna his wife.
November 1st 1744 Mr. George GARRETTSON m. to Mrs. Martha TODD.
August 9th 1743 Mr. John HALL m. to Mrs. Barthiah STANSBURY.
August 25th 1744 then was b. Sophia HALL d/o Mr. John HALL and Barthiah his wife. {H-342}
October 2nd 1744 then was b. Joseph BAYLEY s/o Charles BAYLEY and Sarah his wife.
August __ 1737 then d. John HALL Esq. being 79 years.
November 15th 1745 then was b. John PATTERSON s/o Robert PATTERSON and Jane his wife.
April 22d 1745 then was b. William DAUGHERTY s/o William DAUGHERTY and Mary his wife.
October 31st 1745 then was b. Josias ALLEN s/o William ALLEN and Mary his wife. {OR2-180}
July 25th 1745 then was b. Mary HUGHS d/o John HUGHS and Elizabeth his wife.
April 15th 1746 then was James CAIN m. to Ann SPICER.
January 19th 1746 then was b. Frenetah GARRETTSON d/o Mr. George GARRETTSON and Martha his wife.
November 22d 1745 then was Elianor KELLEY d/o John KELLEY and Elizabeth his wife.
June 10th 1744 then was b. Sarah CLARK d/o John CLARK and Hannah his wife.
April 2d 1746 then was James BROWN m. to Sarah JOHNSON.
April 24th 1746 Mr. James GARRETTSON m. to Catherine NELSON.
November 24th 1744 then was b. Daniel MURDAGH [sic] s/o Daniel MURDAUGH and Martha his wife.
October 23d 1745 then was b. John CAMMEL s/o John CAMMEL and Ann his wife.
July 7th 1746 then was b. Josias Carvil HALL s/o Coll. John HALL and Hannah his wife. {OR2-181}
April 8th 1745 then was b. Susanna PHILLIPS d/o Mr. James PHILLIPS and Sarah his wife, & departed this life 17 May 1745.
July 8th 1746 then was b. Cordelia PHILLIPS d/o Mr. James PHILLIPS and Sarah his wife. {H-343}
May 3d 1746 then was b. Elizabeth JONES d/o Aquila JONES and Elizabeth his wife.
March 26th 1746 then was b. Grafton PRESTON s/o Daniel PRESTON and Ann his wife.
March 23d then was b. Garrett GARRETTSON s/o Mr. George GARRETTSON and Martha his wife.
April 11th 1747 then d. Garrett GARRETTSON s/o Mr. George GARRETTSON and Martha his wife.
January 1st 1745 then was b. Catharine MORON d/o of Edward MORON and Elizabeth his wife.
November 30th 1746 then d. Richard DEAVER.
April 13th 1746 then was b. Dennis DUNN; October 12th 1744 then was b. Elizabeth DUNN; s/o & d/o Dennis DUNN and Bridgett his wife. {OR2-182}
January 10th 1746 then was b. Martha HALL d/o Mr. John HALL and Barthiah his wife.
August 20th 1746 then was b. John HANSON s/o John HANSON and Semelia his wife.
February __ 1746 then was b. John BRIERLY s/o Hugh BRIERLY and Rebecca his wife.
January 6th 1743 then was b. Samuel BRICE; August 15th 1746 then was b. Thomas BRICE; s/o James BRICE and Mary his wife.

ST. GEORGE'S PARISH REGISTER

June 7th 1744 then was b. Joseph RENSHAW; September 14th 1746 then was b. Abraham RENSHAW; s/o Abraham RENSHAW and Ann his wife.
July 11th 1745 then was b. Nathaniel SIMPSON s/o Richard SIMPSON and Elizabeth his wife.
April 16th 1747 then was b. Susanna MURDAUGH d/o Daniel MURDAUGH and Martha his wife.
June 1st 1745 then was b. Samuel HAWKINS s/o Thomas HAWKINS and Elizabeth his wife. {H-344}
February 15th 1746 then d. Thomas HAWKINS s/o Thomas HAWKINS and Elizabeth his wife. {OR2-183}
May 3d 1747 then was b. Thomas HAWKINS s/o Thomas HAWKINS and Elizabeth his wife.
January 6th 1744 then was b. John MITCHEL; April 2d 1747 then was b. Avarilla MITCHEL; June 10th 1739 then was b. Elizabeth MITCHEL; s/o Richard MITCHEL and Elizabeth his wife.
January 10th 1740 then was Thomas NEWLAND m. to Frances SMITH.
October 18th 1746 then was b. James CHANCY s/o George CHANCY and Susan his wife.
November 14th 1746 then was b. Patrick CRAYTON s/o John CRAYTON and Martha his wife.
August 15th 1745 then was b. Hannah KIMBAL d/o Robert KIMBAL and Sarah his wife.
November 24th 1745 then was b. Mary MURPHEY d/o Timothy MURPHEY and Elizabeth his wife.
March 5th 1747 then was b. Job BARNS s/o Ford BARNS Senr. and Margaret his wife. {OR2-184}
December 20th 1747 then was Thomas EVERITT m. to Margarett PRICE.
November 15th 1746 then was b. Cassandra COMBEST d/o Jacob COMBEST and Mary his wife.
March 2d 1747 then was b. John MURPHY [sic] s/o Timothy MURPHEY and Elizabeth his wife.
August 1st 1745 then was b. Francis HOLLAND; May 9th 1747 then was b. Frances HOLLAND; s/o & d/o Mr. Francis HOLLAND and Cordelia his wife.
February 20th 1743 then was b. Henry VINER s/o Jane VINER.
May 22d 1748 then was b. George PATTERSON s/o Robert PATTERSON and Jane his wife.
February 22d 1748 then was b. Hollis HANSON s/o John HANSON and Semelia his wife. {H-345}
October 22d then d. Sarah FARMER.
February 7th 1746 then d. Jacob HANSON s/o Jacob HANSON and Rebecca his wife.
October 20th 1746 then was b. Samuel & Jacob HANSON twin sons of Jacob HANSON and Margarett his wife.
March 11th 1747 then was b. George GARRETTSON s/o Mr. George GARRETTSON and Martha his wife. {OR2-185}
December 10th 1748 then was b. Edward HALL s/o Mr. John HALL of Cranbury and Barthia his wife.
November 1st 1746 then was b. Sarah DEBRULAR d/o John DEBRULAR and Frances his wife.
September 1st 1748 then was b. Nicholas BAKER s/o Nicholas BAKER and Martha his wife.
March 9th 1745 then was John COWEN and Elizabeth WOOD m.
January 10th 1746 then was b. Hannah COWEN; February 19th 1747 then was b. William COWEN; d/o & s/o John COWEN & Elizabeth his wife.
February 4th 1748 then Elizabeth GARRETTSON departed this life.
February 6th 1748 then Freebourn GARRETTSON departed this life.

ST. GEORGE'S PARISH REGISTER

November 3d 1748 then was b. Daniel PRESTON s/o Daniel PRESTON and Ann his wife.
July 24th 1744 then was b. Sarah FRISBY; September 15th 1746 then was b. Thomas FRISBY; d/o & s/o Peregrine FRISBY and Mary his wife. {H-346,OR2-186}
August 11th 1746 then was Daniel DURBIN m. to Ann MITCHEL.
October 11th 1746 then was b. Scott DURBIN; March 11th 1747 [sic] b. John DURBIN; s/o Daniel DURBIN and Ann his wife.
November 29th 1748 Thomas JOHNSON Junr. m. to Mary CLARK.
January 29th 1748 then was b. Martha HAWKINS d/o Thomas HAWKINS and Elizabeth his wife.
May 25th 1747 then was b. Garrett GARRETTSON; August 12th 1749 then was b. Elizabeth GARRETTSON; s/o & d/o James GARRETTSON and Catherine his wife.
September 7th 1749 then was b. Ford BARNS s/o Ford BARNS and Ruth his wife.
November 5th 1748 then was Ruben PERKINS m. to Avarilla DURBIN.
December 6th 1749 then was b. Hannah PERKINS d/o Ruben PERKINS and Avarilla his wife.
December 7th 1746 then d. Mr. Francis HOLLAND.
March 2d 1748 then was Mr. John HALL of Swantown m. to Mrs. Cordelia HOLLAND.
November 18th 1749 then was b. William HALL of Swantown s/o John HALL and Cordelia his wife.
Richard DEAVER b. 30 January 1745; David DEAVER b. 30 October 1747; August 3d 1749 then was b. Daniel DEAVER; s/o Daniel DEAVER and Mary his wife.
July 28th 1749 then was b. Garrett GARRETTSON s/o George GARRETTSON and Martha his wife.
August 3d 1749 b. William MURPHEY s/o Timothy MURPHEY and Elizabeth his wife. {H-347}
November 4th 1749 then was b. Mary PHILLIPS d/o Mr. James PHILLIPS and Sarah his wife.
May 2d 1736 then was b. Sarah WEST d/o Robert WEST Junr. and Johanna his wife.
October 15th 1738 then d. Sarah WEST d/o Robert WEST Junr. and Johanna his wife.
July 14th 1740 then was b. Jonathan WEST; March 10th 1741 b. Johannah WEST; April 5th 1743 b. Sarah WEST; s/o & d/o Robert WEST Jurn. and Johanna his wife.
November 10th 1744 then d. Sarah WEST d/o Robert WEST Junr. aned Johanna his wife.
Febuary 18th 1746 then was b. John WEST; May 1st 1749 then was b. Michael WEST; s/o Robert WEST Junr. and Johanna his wife.
March 16th 1750 then was b. Benjamin BAKER s/o Nicholas BAKER and Martha his wife.
April 15th 1751 then was b. James PRESTON s/o Daniel PRESTON and Ann his wife.
July 31st 1745 then d. Sarah PRESTON d/o Daniel PRESTON and Ann his wife.
November 21st 1746 then d. Daniel PRESTON s/o Daniel PRESTON and Ann his wife. {OR2-188}
July 14th 1743 then was b. Mary BURCHFIELD; October 16th 1746 then was b. Sarah BURCHFIELD; May 6th 1749 then was b. Elizabeth BURCHFIELD; d/o Thomas BURCHFIELD and Sarah his wife.
March 31st 1752 then was b. Eleazer BRIARLY s/o Hugh BRIARLY and Rebecca his wife. {H-348}
July 27th 1748 then was Daniel DONAWIN m. to Johanna ARNOLD.

ST. GEORGE'S PARISH REGISTER

July 7th 1749 then was b. Philip DONAWIN; September 19th 1751 then was b. Daniel DONAWIN; s/o Daniel DONAWIN and Johanna his wife.
November 4th 1750 then was b. Mary PHILLIPS; September 25th 1752 then was b. Susanna PHILLIPS; d/o Capt. James PHILLIPS and Sarah his wife.
February 22d 1746 then was b. Moses TREADWAY s/o Thomas TREADWAY and Elizabeth his wife.
March 25th 1752 then was b. Josias HALL s/o Mr. John HALL of Cranberry and Barthia his wife.
October 6th 1749 then was b. John Bedle HALL s/o Mr. John HALL of Cranberry and Barthia his wife.
February 14th 1750 then was Aquila HALL m. to Sophia WHITE.
December 27th 1751 then was b. Thomas HALL s/o Aquila HALL and Sophia his wife.
December 8th 1754 then was b. James White HALL; July 31st 1756 then was b. William HALL; February 11th 1758 then was b. Charlotte HALL; January 25th 1760 then was b. Mary HALL; s/o and d/o Aquila HALL and Sophia his wife.
June 9th 1746 then was b. Mordecai Hanby ALLEN s/o James ALLEN and Mary his wife.   {OR2-189}
May 3d 1748 then was b. William Millin ALLEN s/o James ALLEN and Mary his wife.
August 22d 1748 then was b. Samuel PRITCHARD s/o Samuel PRITCHARD and Elizabeth his wife.
December 27th 1746 then was b. James PRITCHARD s/o Samuel PRITCHARD and Ezibella [sic] his wife.   {H-349}
July 15th 1750 then was b. Thomas PRITCHARD s/o Samuel PRITCHARD and Elizabeth his wife.
August 27th 1752 then was b. Charles PRITCHARD s/o Samuel PRITCHARD and Elizabeth his wife.
February 6th 1752 then was John PACA Junr. m. to Margaret LEE.
March 30th 1753 then was b. Aquila PACA s/o John PACA Junr. and Margaret his wife about 8 o'clock at night.
William SMITH and Elizabeth his wife was joined in Matrimony 23 December 1743 before the Revd. Stephen WILKINSON.
March 12th 1745 b. Elizabeth SMITH; April 6th 1747 b. Cassandra SMITH; March 31st 1749 b. Sarah SMITH; November 8th 1750 b. Winstone SMITH; December 3d 1752 b. William SMITH; September __ 1754 then d. the above Cassandra SMITH; s/o & d/o William SMITH and Elizabeth his wife.
March 1st 1735 then was Ann RIGBEE d/o Nathaniel and Cassandra RIGBEE born.
October 8th 1753 then was Nathan SMITH s/o WIlliam SMITH and Elizabeth his wife born.   {OR2-190}
December 22nd 1751 then was Mr. Walter TOLLEY and Miss Martha HALL joyned together in Holy Matrimony by the Revd. Andrew LENDRUM.
October 14th 1753 then was b. Edward Carvil TOLLEY s/o Mr. Walter TOLLEY and Martha his wife.
October 28th 1753 then was b. Barnett PRESTON s/o Daniel PRESTON and Ann his wife.
June 23d 1748 then d. Ann RHOADES wife of Henry RHOADES.
October 25th 1754 then was b. James PACA s/o John PACA Junr. and Margarett his wife.
November 4th 1750 then was b. Mary Goldsmith GARRETSON d/o Mr. George GARRETSON and Martha his wife.
September 8th 1753 then was b. Goldsmith GARRETSON s/o Mr. George GARRETSON and Martha his wife.   {H-350}

ST. GEORGE'S PARISH REGISTER

July 23d 1754 then Majr. William DALLAM m. Miss Ann MATHEWS.
June 30th 1750 then was Doctr. Benjamin CROCKETT m. to Miss Elizabeth CHEW in Cecil County by the Revd. Jno. HAMBELTON.
May 25th 1751 b. Benjamin CROCKETT; April 19th 1754 b. John CROCKETT; July 26th 1756 b. Gilbert CROCKETT; s/o Benjamin CROCKETT and Elizabeth his wife.
January 30th 1755 then was Majr. David BISIT m. to Mrs. Ann ADKINSON. {OR2-191}
February 23d 1748 then was Capt. John MATHEWS & Miss Milcah LUSBY joined together in Holy Matrimony by the Rev. Hugh CARLILE.
December 26th 1749 was b. Mary MATHEWS d/o the above John MATHEWS and Milcah his wife.
October 26th 1751 b. Hannah MATHEWS d/o John & Milcah MATHEWS.
November 4th 1753 b. Roger MATHEWS s/o John & Milcah MATHEWS.
July 28th 1755 b. Rebecca Knight PHILLIPS d/o Coll. James PHILLIPS and Sarah his wife.
December 21st 1749 was m. Edward GARRETSON and Avarilla HANSON.
November 30th 1750 b. Elizabeth GARRETSON d/o Edward GARRETSON and Avarilla his wife.
April 13th 1752 b. Edward GARRETSON s/o Edward GARRETSON and Avarilla his wife.
November 30th 1753 b. Garrett GARRETSON s/o Edward GARRETSON and Avarilla his wife.
1753 b. Peter BRASHER s/o Thomas BRASHER and Elizabeth his wife who both liv'd with Doctr. Josias MIDDLEMORE.
January 1st 1756 b. Aquila MATHEWS s/o Capt. John MATHEWS and Milcah his wife. {OR2-192, H-351}
August 15th 1756 was Mr. Robert STOKES and Miss Rebecca YOUNG joyned together in holy matrimony by the Revd. Hugh DEAN.
November 15th 1756 then departed this life Mr. Robert STOKES at Coll. William YOUNG's and was bur. in the Church Yard at Joppa Town the 21st day of the same month.
September 22d b. John Stokes PACA s/o John PACA Junr. and Margarett his wife on Wednesday half after three o'clock.
Sarah PRESTON d/o Daniol PRESTON & Ann his wife b. 24 March 1756.
July 22d 1754 was Mr. Charles CHRISTIE & Miss Cordelia STOKES joined together in Holy Matrimony.
November 29th 1756 b. Gabriell Charles CHRISTIE s/o Mr. Charles CHRISTIE & Cordelia his wife.
March 17th 1757 then departed this life Mr. Charles CHRISTIE who was then High Sheriff of Baltimore County & was bur. at Joppa Town in the Church Yard.
August 23d 1744 was Mr. Amos GARRETT and Miss Frances DREW joined in Holy Matrimony by the Rev. Hugh CARLILE.
February 23d 1745/6 b. Bennett GARRETT s/o Amos GARRETT and Frances his wife.
February 1st 1750 was b. Cassandra GARRETT d/o Amos GARRETT and Frances his wife.
October 6th 1756 b. Milcah GARRETT d/o Amos GARRETT and Frances his wife. {OR2-193}
February 13th 1757 b. Thomas DEAVER s/o John and Ann DEAVER.
February 4th 1754 then was b. Elizabeth HALL d/o John HALL of Cranberry and Bothya his wife.
March 6th 1756 then was b. Avarilla HALL; March 20th 1758 then was b. Priscilla HALL; d/o John HALL of Cranberry and Bothya his wife.
From a written manuscript in Doctr. Edward WAKEMAN's own handwriting: {H-352}

ST. GEORGE'S PARISH REGISTER

January 28th 1743/4 b. Elizabeth PRITCHARD; March 17th 1744/5 b. Sarah PRITCHARD; d/o Elizabeth PRITCHARD.
May 11th 1756 then was John DEAVER m. to Ann BOND.
May 13th 1758 then was b. William PRESTON s/o Daniel PRESTON and Ann his wife.
June 6th 1729 then was b. William THOMAS s/o Charles THOMAS and Ann his wife.
January 20th 1756 Richard GARRETSON m. to Priscilla NELLSON.
December 11th 1756 b. Freeborn GARRETSON; May 11, 1758 b. Sophia GARRETSON; s/o & d/o Richard & Priscilla GARRETSON.
February 18th 1750 b. Frances GARRETSON; August 3d 1753 b. Martha GARRETSON; June 22d 1756 b. Mary GARRETSON; d/o James GARRETSON and Catherine his wife.
February 19th 1747 then was Samuel KIMBALL m. to Jamima BARNS.
October 1st 1747 b. Ann KIMBALL; January 9th 1749 b. Rachel KIMBALL; March 22d 1751 b. James KIMBALL; May 4th 1753 b. Bothya KIMBALL; December 11th 1755 b. Hannah KIMBALL; Aug. 9th 1758 b. Jamima KIMBALL; d/o & s/o Samuel KIMBALL & Jamima his wife.
November 22d 1750 b. Charles KELLY s/o Charles KELLY & Prissilla his wife.
March 20th 1756 b. Sarah KELLY; October 31st 1758 b. Rachel KELLY; d/o Charles & Prissilla.
January 15th 1756 b. Isaac COLLINS s/o Selence COLLINS.
February 20th 1757 then was Joshua ARMSTRONG m. to Margaret BARNS.
May 7th 1758 b. Solomon ARMSTRONG s/o Joshua & Margaret his wife. {H-353}
January 13th 1752 b. Jacob WEST; November 4th 1754 b. Martha WEST; August 6th 1756 b. Susanna WEST; October 24th 1757 b. William WEST; s/o & d/o John WEST & Susanna his wife.
March 17th, 1757 then was Francis FULTON m. to Ann MATHEW.
February 2, 1749 then was Job BARNS m. to Mary CRAWFORD.
June 11th 1752 b. Job BARNS; August 13th 1754 b. Rachel BARNS; July 4th 1758 b. Ezekiel BARNS; s/o & d/o Job BARNS and Mary his wife.
August 12th 1751 then was Paul CRONEY m. to Elizabeth CARSON.
August 27th 1752 then was b. William CRONY [sic] s/o Paul and Elizabeth his wife.
February 25th 1749 then was Soloman ARMSTRONG m. to Elizabeth BARNS.
December 13th 1749 then was b. Ruth WEST d/o Jonathan & Elinor his wife.
May 19th 1746 b. John GORDON s/o Daniel GORDON & Mary his wife.
July 10th 1746 then was William REESE m. to Ann O'HERD.{OR2-194}
July 8th 1747 b. Mary REESE; November 6th 1749 b. William REESE; November 19th 1751 b. Elizabeth REESE; December 29th 1753 b. Rachel REESE; February 22d 1755 b. Ann REESE; June 1st 1757 b. Hannah REESE; d/o & s/o William REESE and Ann his wife.
March 31st 1753 b. James VISSAGE s/o Thomas VISSAGE & Hannah.
October 1st 1755 b. Jane VISSAGE; April 1st 1755 b. Jacob VISSAGE; d/o & s/o the above.
March 12th 1758 b. Aquilla JONES s/o Mary JONES.
May 15th 1754 then was George RUMMAGE m. to Mary NOBLE.
June 29th 1754 b. Margaret RUMMAGE; August 7th 1755 b. David RUMMAGE; March 7th 1756 b. Elizabeth RUMMAGE; s/o & d/o George RUMMAGE and Mary his wife. {H-354}

ST. GEORGE'S PARISH REGISTER

August 24th 1755 b. Constant BENNINGTON; July 8th 1756 b. Nehemiah BENNINGTON; February 8th 1758 b. Job BENNINGTON; s/o & d/o Henry BENNINGTON and Elizabeth his wife.
October 13th 1752 then was William ALLEN m. to Elizabeth JONES. April 22d 1753 b. Elizabeth ALLEN; July 6th 1755 b. Joseph ALLEN; March 25th 1757 b. William ALLEN; December 8th 1758 b. Zachariah ALLEN; s/o & d/o William ALLEN and Elizabeth his wife.
December 2d 1756 b. Rachel REA; December 2d 1756 b. William REA; d/o & s/o Hugh REA and Margaret his wife.
August 2d 1755 then was George MICHAEL m. to Barbary RISSARD.
January 1st 1754 then was William KIMBALL m. to Sarah HANSON.
June 5th 1755 b. Martha KIMBALL; June 5th 1756 b. Frances KIMBALL; November 6th 1757 b. Roland KIMBALL; d/o & s/o William KIMBALL and Sarah his wife.
August 2d 1751 then was William MURPHY m. to Sarah GISSARD.
September 12th 1752 b. William MURPHY; November 3d 1755 b. Joab MURPHY; s/o William MURPHY and Sarah his wife.
December 5th 1752 then was Absolem BROWN m. to Margaret HANSON.
January 2d 1754 b. Sarah BROWN; December 11th 1756 b. Rebecca BROWN; November 7th 1758 b. Usan BROWN; d/o Absolem BROWN and Margaret his wife.
February 1st 1753 then was James GRANT m. to Elizabeth MORRIS.
January 31st 1756 b. David GRANT s/o James & Elizabeth his wife.
December 17th 1752 b. Dianah MURPHY; October 15th 1753 b. Timothy MURPHY; s/o & d/o of Timothy MURPHY and Elizabeth his wife.
Dec. 22d 1756 b. Ufan MURPHY d/o Timothy & Elizabeth his wife.
January 15th 1745 b. Thomas MORRIS; March 1st 1749 b. Richard MORRIS; March 1st 1753 b. Edward MORRIS; February 1st 1755 b. Michal MORRIS; June 3d 1758 b. John MORRIS; s/o Richard MORRIS and Mary his wife. {H-355}
August 2 1756 then was Alexander MATHISON m. to Sarah MORRIS.
February 2d 1758 then was b. John MATHESON [sic] s/o Alexander and Sarah his wife.
April 12th 1757 then was John READ m. to Eliza JACKSON. [OR2 195]
June 26th 1756 then was Richard MONK m. to Agnes TAYLOR.
August 8th 1756 b. William MONK; September 5th 1758 b. Mary MONK; s/o & d/o Richard MONK and Agnes his wife.
June 8th 1757 then was b. Elizabeth GALLOWAY d/o Samuel and Rebecca his wife.
August 25th 1757 then was Samuel SUTTON m. to Ruth CANTWELL.
Oct. 4th 1757 then was Mary SUTTON b. d/o Samuel & Ruth his wife.
June 2d 1755 then was John FORD m. to Sarah MURPHY.
November 16th 1755 b. Benjamin FORD; March 3d 1757 b. Darkis FORD; s/o & d/o John FORD and Sarah his wife.
December 15th 1746 b. Micajah DEVER; December 16th 1748 b. John DEVER; January 19th 1750 b. James DEVER; March 10th 1752 b. Ufan DEVER; April 2d 1754 b. Thomas DEAVER [sic]; December 11th 1757 b. Elizabeth DEVER; December 8th 1759 b. William DEVER; s/o & d/o John DEVER and Prianah his wife.
October 9th 1754 then was John WATKINS m. to Purify GREENFIELD.
October 14th 1754 b. Margaret WATKINS; January 24th 1756 b. Elizabeth WATKINS; February 23d 1758 b. Susanna WATKINS; d/o John WATKINS and Purafy [sic] his wife.
July 14th 1746 b. Mary KENDALL; October 30th 1747 b. Elizabeth KENDALL; February 4th 1753 b. Martha KENDALL; d/o Isaac KENDALL and Mary his wife. {H-356}
December 18th 1756 b. Elizabeth REVES d/o Josias REVES and Latisha his wife.

ST. GEORGE'S PARISH REGISTER

December 3d 1750 then was Abraham BRUCEBANKS m. to Mary JACKSON.
November 9th 1743 b. Francis Og. s/o Abraham BRUCEBANKS & Catherine his wife.
May 31st 1749 b. Edward s/o A. BRUCEBANKS & Catherine his wife.
October 10th 1753 b. Abraham BRUCEBANKS; October 27th 1755 b. Blanch BRUCEBANKS; December 22d 1757 b. Mary BRUCEBANKS; s/o & d/o Abraham BRUCEBANKS and Mary his wife.
September 18th 1754 then was Nathaniel ASSEL m. to Sarah JACKSON.
October 19th 1755 b. Michael ASSELL [sic]; March 11th 1758 b. Martha ASSELL; s/o & d/o Nathaniel ASSEL and Sarah his wife.
November 18th 1744 b. Martha RESON; April 9th 1748 b. Sarah REASON [sic]; February 9th 1749 b. Thomas REASIN [sic]; d/o & s/o Richard REASIN and Alice his wife.
February 19th 1758 b. James BARTON s/o Lewis BARTON and Joanna his wife.
July 23d 1747 b. Mary KIMBALL; January 1st 1750 b. Giles KIMBALL; May 5th 1753 b. John KIMBALL; February 13th 1755 b. Sarah KIMBALL; February 24th 1758 b. Susanna KIMBALL; s/o & d/o Robert KIMBALL and Sarah his wife.   {OR2-196}
April 10th 1757 then was Joseph MASON m. to Mariah GROVER.
July 31st 1758 b. Elizabeth MASON d/o Joseph and Maria his wife.
September 30th 1754 b. William DONAVIN; October 25th 1756 b. Jacob DONIVIN [sic]; October 25th 1756 b. Thomas DONNAVIN [sic]; March 25th 1758 b. Margaret DONAVIN; s/o & d/o Daniel DONAVIN and Hannah his wife.   {H-357}
March 24th 1746 b. William ARNOLD; April 3d 1754 b. Joseph ARNOLD; s/o William ARNOLD and Sarah his wife.
September 7th 1749 b. Ford BARNS; February 17th 1751 b. Cassandra BARNS; September 17th 1753 b. Bennett BARNS; January 17th 1755 b. Arrabella BARNS; November 5th 1757 b. Richard BARNS; s/o & d/o Ford BARNS and Ruth his wife.
March 11th 1752 then was Nathaniel SMITH m. to Elizabeth WEBSTER.
November 22d 1754 b. Elizabeth SMITH; April 24th 1756 b. Mary SMITH; January 14th 1759 b. Hannah SMITH; d/o Nathaniel SMITH and Elizabeth his wife.
August 9th 1745 b. Sabra KIMBALL d/o Sarah KIMBALL.
May 9th 1747 then was James TAYLOR m. to Sarah KIMBALL.
July 27th 1748 b. Stephen TAYLOR; January 9th 1749 b. Abraham TAYLOR; August 16th 1751 b. Robert TAYLOR; January 28th 1753 b. Heneritta TAYLOR; September 11th 1754 b. Asa TAYLOR; May 27th 1756 b. Amasa TAYLOR; March 4th 1758 b. Jeremiah TAYLOR; s/o & d/o James TAYLOR and Sarah his wife.
May 1st 1755 then d. Abraham TAYLOR.
September __ 1757 then d. Edward MONDAY.
September __ 1757 then d. Hannah MONDAY.
September __ 1757 then d. Aquilla TAYLOR.   {H-358}
November 26th 1749 b. Sarah HANSON; July 12th 1752 b. Sophia HANSON; February 10th 1756 b. Samelia HANSON; January 11th 1758 b. Elizabeth HANSON; d/o John HANSON and Samilia his wife.
July 15th 1746 b. William OSBORN; July 17th 1750 b. Cyrus OSBORN; November 12, 1752 b. Mary OSBORN; August 10th 1755 b. Benja OSBORN; August 10th 1758 b. Martha OSBORN; s/o & d/o James OSBORN and Jane his wife.
February 24th 1755 then was Jacob GALLION m. to Elizabeth ARNOLD.
May 10th 1755 b. Sophia GALLION; March 17th 1758 b. Thomas GALLION; s/o & d/o Jacob GALLION and Elizabeth his wife.
August 6th 1758 then was Peter HENDLEN m. to Mary LEEK.
August 29th 1756 then was James HARMAN m. to Hannah JACKSON.

ST. GEORGE'S CHURCH REGISTER

October 9th 1756 b. William HANNAN; August 26th 1758 b. Margaret HANNAN; s/o & d/o James HANAN [sic] and Hannah his wife.
March 1st 1756 b. Cathrine CASSIDY d/o Simon(?) CASSIDY and Elinor his wife.
February 24th 1758 then was Jacob OSBORN m. unto Sarah FOWLER. December 18th 1758 b. Mary OSBORN d/o Jacob and Sarah OSBORN. June 18th 1745 then was William OSBORN m. unto Margaret LYALL. October 13th 1746 b. Hannah OSBORN; November 24th 1748 b. Ann OSBORN; February 2d 1750 b. Sarah OSBORN; June 20th 1753 b. Susanna OSBORN; December 27th 1755 b. John OSBORN; April 4th 1758 b. James OSBORN; s/o & d/o William OSBORN and Margaret his wife. {H-359, OR2-197}
January 20th 1757 then was Aquilla NELLSON m. to Sarah CHANCEY. November 19th 1757 b. John NELLSON s/o Aquilla and Sarah NELLSON.
March 20th 1755 then Thomas BURCHFIELD m. to Elizabeth TURNER. April 6th 1756 then d. Elizabeth BURCHFIELD.
Feburary 2d 1758 then was Robert MEGAY m. to Sarah LESTER. January 28th 1759 b. George MEGAY s/o Robert and Sarah MEGAY.
January 4th 1749 b. Kissiah LOW d/o Elizabeth LOW.
September 23d 1753 b. William SAUNDERS; March 20th 1755 b. Frances SAUNDERS; December 27th 1758 b. Sarah SAUNDERS; s/o & d/o James SAUNDERS and Elizabeth his wife.
March 31st 1758 then was Jonathan WEST m. to Sophia KIMBALL. February 3d 1759 b. Robert WEST s/o Jonathan and Sophia WEST.
March 1st 1756 b. Frances BRUCEBANKS d/o Ann BRUCEBANKS. [sic]
November 9th 1758 then was Jeremiah COOK m. to Ann BRUCEBANKS. September 26, 1758 b. Mary d/o Jacob HANSON & Margaret his wife.
March 15th 1748 then was William HOLLIS m. to Sarah GALLION. August 21st 1749 b. William HOLLIS; April 21st 1754 b. Frances HOLLIS; August 21st 1757 b. James HOLLIS; s/o & d/o William HOLLIS and Sarah his wife.
March 18th 1755 b. William ROBINSON s/o Thomas & Cathrine ROBINSON.
December 13th 1752 b. Mary HOLLIS; January 27th 1754 b. Hannah HOLLIS; January 27th 1754 b. Ann HOLLIS; August 17th 1756 b. Rachel HOLLIS; October 2d 1758 b. Cathrine HOLLIS; d/o Clark HOLLIS and Hannah his wife.
February 15th 1752 then was Joseph GORDON m. to Ruth CHANEY. March 17th 1752 b. Mary GORDON; October 16th 1758 b. James GORDON; s/o & d/o James GORDEN [sic] and Ruth his wife.
July 14th 1747 b. John JACKSON; October 31, 1749 b. Ephraim JACKSON; August 24th 1754 b. Cathrine JACKSON; s/o & d/o John JACKSON and Hannah his wife. {H-360}
November 9th 1747 b. Mary BROWN; November 25th 1750 b. Susanna BROWN; January 8th 1752 b. James BROWN; April 31st 1755 b. John BROWN; October 29th 1757 b. Elizabeth BROWN; February 4th 1759 b. Hannah BROWN; s/o & d/o James BROWN and Sarah his wife.
May 28th 1754 b. John DAVIS; May 26th 1757 b. Elizabeth DAVIS; s/o & d/o Benjamin DAVIS and Mary his wife.
September 30th 1757 b. Myhannah LESHODY d/o Francis LESHODY and Susana his wife. {OR2-198}
January 30th 1744 b. Charlotta LESTER; July 20th 1748 b. Sophia LESTER; December 28th 1751 b. Norris LESTER; August 8th 1756 b. William LESTER; d/o & s/o George LESTER and Alice his wife.
September 21st 1747 b. Hannah DREW; November 2d 1749 b. Ann DREW; February 7th 1752 b. George DREW; March 31st 1753 b. James DREW; February 20th 1756 b. Henry DREW; May 5th 1758 b. Mary DREW; s/o & d/o Anthony DREW and Ann his wife.
December 27th 1754 then was Mathew REASIN m. to Mary DICKSON.

ST. GEORGE'S CHURCH REGISTER

March 13th 1758 b. James REASIN s/o Mathew and Mary REASIN.
March 22d 1758 then was Stephen KIMBALL m. to Margaret DAUGHARTY alis BARKEY.
January 22d 1759 b. Mary d/o Stephen KIMBALL & Margaret his wife.
March 3d 1742 b. Ann POLOKE; April 30th 1745 b. Mary POLOKE d/o Daniel POLOKE and Jane his wife.
July 19th 1748 then was James COLE m. to Jane POLOKE.
July 7th 1749 b. Jane COLE; July 29, 1751 b. James COLE; April 7th 1754 b. Ephraim COLE; May 14th 1756 b. Comfort COLE; September 2d 1758 b. Elizabeth COLE; s/o & d/o James COLE and Jane his wife. {H-361}
October 21st 1757 b. Linnah d/o of Charles John ASELWORTHY and Blanch his wife.
July 10th 1747 then was William ARNOLD m. to Comfort COURTNEY.
October 22d 1752 b. Ephraim ARNOLD s/o William ARNOLD and Comfort his wife.
January 15th 1743 b. Thomas COURTNEY s/o Jonas COURTNEY and Comfort his wife.
July 25th 1758 then was Thomas BROWN m. to Elizabeth COURTNEY.
June 14th 1745 then was Thomas GILBERT m. to Mary FOWLER.
November 20th 1746 b. William GILBERT; June 10th 1747 b. Michael GILBERT; January 15th 1749 b. Hannah GILBERT; July 5th 1750 b. Elizabeth GILBERT; June 10th 1755 b. Rachel GILBERT; August 30th 1757 b. James GILBERT; February 16th 1759 b. Susanna GILBERT; s/o & d/o Thomas GILBERT and Mary his wife.
August 12th 1747 b. William MITCHELL; March 5th 1749 b. Sarah MITCHELL; June 5th 1752 b. James MITCHELL; August 12th 1754 b. Susanna MITCHELL; February 20th 1758 b. Sophia MITCHELL; s/o & d/o Kent MITCHELL and Hannah his wife.
December 4th 1751 then was William PERRY m. to Elizabellaw [sic] PERKINS.
August 14th 1751 b. Mary PERRY; October 2d 1756 b. James PERRY; February 12th 1758 b. Rachel PERRY; d/o & s/o William PERRY & Elizalla [sic] his wife.
September 14th 1753 b. James MITCHELL; August 10th 1757 b. Gabriel MITCHELL; s/o Elizabeth MITCHELL.
July 7th 1747 b. Sarah COOK d/o Elizabeth COOK.
March 11th 1751 b. Hannah CORD; December 25th 1753 b. Susanna CORD; May 15th 1756 b. Roger CORD; d/o & s/o Jacob CORD and Elizabeth his wife. {H-361}
June 20th 1750 then was Jacob CORD m. to Elizabeth COOK.
December 27th 1748 then was Joseph BAILEY m. to Margaret OSBORN.
September 28th 1749 b. Josias BALEY [sic]; November 17th 1754 b. Charles BAILEY; November 7th 1756 b. Aquilla BAILEY; Jan. 15th 1759 b. Benedict BAILEY; s/o Joseph BAILEY & Margaret his wife
May 13th 1749 b. Aurther INGRAM; February 13th 1752 b. William INGRAM; February 13th 1755 b. Hannah INGRAM; February 13th 175 b. Margaret INGRAM; s/o & d/o Aurthur INGRAM and Ann his wife.
June 20th 1757 then was Thomas JONES m. to Mary DOOLEY.
March 23d 1758 b. Sarah JONES d/o Thomas JONES and Mary his wife
June 1st 1757 then was Nathan SMITH m. to Blanch DOOLEY.
April 3d 1758 b. William SMITH s/o Nathan SMITH & Blanch his wife.
January 24th 1747 b. James WEST; April 1st 1750 b. Isaac WEST; s/o John WEST and Susanna his wife.
January 1st 1752 b. Sarah JONES; March 3d 1754 b. Cassandra JONES; December 23d 1756 b. Elizabeth JONES; February 7th 1758 b. Prissilla JONES; d/o Jonathan JONES and Martha his wife.

ST. GEORGE'S CHURCH REGISTER

August 12th 1756 b. Thomas M. SWAIN; March 26th 1758 b. Jonathan M. SWAIN; s/o David M. SWAIN and Hannah his wife.
December 4th 1752 then was Thomas THOMPSON m. to Ellinor AGON.
September 29th 1753 b. John THOMPSON; March 16th 1755 b. Thomas THOMPSON; January 8th 1758 b. Rachael THOMPSON; January 10th 1759 b. James THOMPSON; s/o & d/o Thomas THOMPSON and Ellinor his wife.
February 11th 1745/6 b. Bothya BARNS d/o James BARNS and Bothya his wife. {H-363}
July 13th 1757 b. Robert Young STOKES s/o Robert STOKES and Rebecca his wife.
March 25th 1758 then was William JENKINS m. to Mary CLARK.
April 1st 1759 b. Hannah JENKINS d/o William JENKINS and Mary his wife.
September 8th 1757 then was Thomas WEST m. to Ann PRITCHARD.
March 2d 1758 b. Elizabeth WEST d/o Thomas WEST & Ann his wife.
January 16th 1758 then was James BROWN m. to Eliza MORGAN.
July 10th 1750 b. Ann JOHNSTON; March 3d 1753 b. Mary JOHNSTON; March 4th 1755 b. Sarah JOHNSTON; March 4th 1757 b. Jean JOHNSTON; February 20th 1759 b. Cathrine JOHNSON [sic]; d/o Samuel JOHNSTON and Cathrine his wife. {OR2-200}
February 4th 1750 b. Benjamin EVERET; August 19th 1752 b. William EVERET; May 9th 1755 b. John EVERET; February 1st 1758 b. Cassandra EVERET; s/o & d/o Thomas EVERET & Margaret his wife.
January 6th 1750 then was Moses COLLINS m. to Patience POWELL.
March 12th 1751 b. Cassandra COLLINS; October 1st 1754 b. Jacob COLLINS; April 15th 1756 b. Samuel COLLINS; April 8th 1759 b. Sarah Powel COLLINS; s/o & d/o Moses COLLINS & Patience his wife.
December 12th 1755 b. Mary COLLINS d/o Sarah COLLINS.
Nov. 7th 1751 then was William COLLINS m. to Johanna CANTWELL.
May 10th 1752 b. Susanna COLLINS; July 13th 1755 b. Sarah COLLINS; September 12th 1756 b. John COLLINS; Jan. 13th 1759 b. Ephraim COLLINS; s/o & d/o William COLLINS & Johanna his wife.
October 1st 1759 b. George BROWN s/o Absolem BROWN and Margaret his wife about 5 of the clock in the morning. {H-364}
January 14th 1760 b. Martha BRUCEBANKS d/o Abraham BRUCEBANKS and Mary his wife.
July 12th 1748 b. Susannah KEENE; February 4th 1750 b. Elizabeth KEENE; August 22nd 1751 b. Rebecca KEENE; August 2d 1753 b. Sarah KEENE; December 17th 1755 b. Samuel Young KEENE; November 19th 1757 b. Anne KEENE; February 11th 1760; Latitia KEENE; d/o & s/o John KEENE and Elizabeth his wife.
March 10th 1756 Wednesday b. Frances GARRETTSON d/o George GARRETTSON and Martha his wife.
June 30th 1758 b. Cordelia HALL; March 30th 1760 b. Sarah HALL; d/o John HALL of Swan Hall(?) and Cordelia his wife.
September 2d 1756 then was m. Edward HALL to Sarah PHILLIPS.
November 28th 1742 b. Edward MORGAN; March 14th 1744 b. William MORGAN; June 18th 1747 b. Mary MORGAN; May 20th 1750 b. Sarah MORGAN; November 28th 1752 b. James MORGAN; May 24th 1755 b. Robert MORGAN; May 27th 1758 b. Abraham MORGAN; s/o & d/o Mr. Edward MORGAN and Sarah his wife.
November 21st 1749 then was William PRIGG m. to Martha MORGAN.
February 10th 1750/1 b. Edward PRIGG; March 27th 1753 b. William PRIGG; January 24th 1755 b. Mary PRIGG; November 2d b. Sarah PRIGG; s/o & d/o William PRIGG and Martha his wife.
October 29th 1748 b. John RAMSEY s/o William RAMSEY and Elizabeth his wife.

ST. GEORGE'S CHURCH REGISTER

May 10th 1760 b. Aquila GARRETTSON s/o Richard GARRETTSON and Priscilla his wife.
February 5th 1754 b. John BULL; May 25th 1756 b. Ann BULL; April 29th 1758 b. Richard BULL; December 30th 1759 b. Isaac BULL; s/o & d/o John BULL and Elizbeth his wife. {H-365, OR2-201}
January 27th 1749 b. Elizabeth CARLISLE d/o Elizabeth BULL.
July 25th 1757 b. Sarah GARRETTSON; October 2d 1759 b. Cordelia GARRETTSON; d/o Mr. Edward GARRETTSON and Avarilla his wife.
August 20th 1756 then was Moses JACKSON m. to Margaret SUTTON.
August 20th 1759 b. Simeon JACKSON s/o Moses JACKSON and Margaret his wife.
August 7th 1760 then d. Elizabeth HALL; April 30th 1760 then was b. Mary HALL; d/o of Capt. John HALL of Cranberry & Bethia his wife.
January 8th 1742/3 b. Margaret STEWART; May 4th 1745 b. Ann STEWART; February 23d 1746/7 b. James STEWART; December 9th 1749 b. Mary STEWART; December 16th 1751 b. Mitchell STEWART: s/o & d/o James STEWART and Mary his wife.
July 19th 1756 then was m. William ASHMORE s/o Walter ASHMORE & Margaret his wife to Susannah O'NEAL, widow of Daniel O'NEAL.
May 21st 1759 b. William ASHMORE s/o William ASHMORE and Susannah his wife.
April 25th 1745 b. Young KEENE; August 24th 1748 b. Mary KEENE; June 26th 1750 b. Amelia KEENE; April 1st 1752 b. Violetta KEENE; December 24th 1755 b. Charles KEENE; January 21st 1758 b. Edmund Lake KEENE; January 8th 1760 b. Parthenia KEENE; s/o & d/o Pollard KEENE and Mary his wife.
June 25th 1753 b. Ufan DAUGHERTY d/o William DAUGHERTY and Mary his wife.
August 27th 1760 b. George KIMBLE s/o Stephen KIMBEL [sic] and Margaret his wife. {H-366}
April 23d 1760 then was John REDDELL m. to Eleanor DAUGHERTY.
January 10th 1761 b. Sarah REDDELL d/o John REDDELL and Eleanor his wife.
October 9th 1760 b. Mary L'SHODY d/o Francis L'SHODY and Laurana his wife.
July 18th 1747 b. Elizabeth BROWN; January 6th 1749/50 b. John BROWN; s/o & d/o Thomas BROWN and Susanna his wife.
July 5th 1749 then d. Thomas BROWN Senr.
July 18th 1751 then was m. Capt. Daniel ROBINSON to Susannah BROWN.
January 28th 1753 b. Mary ROBINSON; October 22nd 1754 b. Anne ROBINSON; February 21st 1758 b. Susannah ROBINSON; d/o Daniel ROBINSON and Susannah his wife.
December 5th 1758 then d. Capt. Daniel ROBINSON
August 8th 1760 then d. Mary ROBINSON d/o Daniel ROBINSON and Susannah his wife.
December 28th 1749 then was m. Bernard PRESTON to Sarah RUFF.
September 23d 1751 b. Sarah PRESTON; April 29th 1754 b. Bernard PRESTON; March 9th 1757 b. Mary PRESTON; May 17th 1760 b. Anna PRESTON; s/o & d/o Bernard PRESTON and Sarah his wife.
April 1st 1761 then was m. Levin MATHEWS to Mary HEWLINGS.
October 18th 1749 then was m. Rev. Andrew LENDRUM to Jane BURNEY in Newcastle on Delaware, by the Rev. George ROSS, Missionary as by his Certificate appeared. {OR2-202}
August 27th 1750 b. Robert Burney LENDRUM the 1st issue of the above marriage.
June 22d then was b. Lucinda LENDRUM the 2d issue of Ditto.

ST. GEORGE'S CHURCH REGISTER

January 30th 1754 b. James LENDRUM 3d issue and d. February 8th 1754; January 24th 1755 b. Mary LENDRUM 4th issue. {H-367}
March 12th 1754 b. Martha BAKER; July 2d 1756 b. John Wood BAKER; January 23d 1759 b. George BAKER; June 1st 1761 b. Joshua BAKER; d/o & s/o of Nicholas BAKER and Martha his wife.
May 31st 1759 then was m. James RICHARDSON (TAYLOR) to Mary RUFF widow of Richard RUFF.
January 30th 1761 b. James RICHARDSON s/o above said James RICHARDSON and Mary his wife.
January 25th 1758 b. Benjamin M'MAHAN; October 17th 1760 b. Thomas M'MAHAN; s/o Benjamin M'MAHAN and Lucretia his wife.
March 21st 1759 then was m. William HORTON to Elizabeth WAKEMAN or PRITCHARD[sic].
February 22d 1760 b. Edward Wakeman HORTON; January 22d 1762 b. William HORTON; s/o William HORTON and Elizabeth his wife.
April 7th 1761 b. Benjamin GARRETTSON s/o Edward GARRETTSON and Avarilla his wife.
September 7th 1758 then was m. James GALLION Junr. to Rachel MARIARTY.
August 5th 1759 b. Priscilla GALLION d/o James GALLION Junr. and Rachel his wife.
May 9th 1762 then was m. Robert DUNN to Sarah WAKEMAN or PRITCHARD[sic].
July 27th 1761 b. Margaret ASHMORE d/o William ASHMORE and Susannah his wife.
November 9th 1742 b. William RENSHAW; February 19th 1745 b. Thomas RENSHAW; May 17th 1747 b. Elizabeth RENSHAW; November 16th 1749 b. Frances RENSHAW; April 3d 1752 b. Selina RENSHAW; August 28th 1754 b. James RENSHAW; June 18th 1757 b. Robert RENSHAW; January 20th 1760 b. Martin RENSHAW; s/o & d/o Thomas RENSHAW and Frances his wife. {H-368}
April 8th 1746 b. Samuel WEBB; October 19th 1752 b. Margaret WEBB; October 2d 1755 b. Sarah WEBB; s/o & d/o Samuel WEBB and Jane his wife.
July 12th 1758 then was William WEBB m. to Elisabeth LEE.
May 30th 1761 b. Margaret WEBB d/o William WEBB and Elizabeth his wife.
May 23d then was m. Nicholas CANTWELL to Elizabeth M'KIM.
October 12th 1754 b. Martha ORR; July 20th 1756 b. James ORR; April 1st 1758 b. Mary ORR; August 10th 1760 b. Ann ORR; d/o & s/o Hugh ORR and Mary his wife.
January 22d 1760 b. John ASHMORE; December 29th 1761 b. Elizabeth ASHMORE; s/o & d/o Frederick ASHMORE and Bridget his wife.
February 8th 1759 then was m. Frederick ASHMORE to Bridget AYRES.
July 19th 1759 then was Samuel WEBSTER (son of Sam) m. to Margaret STEWART.
January 17th 1750 b. Hollis HANSON; December 25th 1752 b. Benjamin HANSON; September 13th 1755 b. Samuel & Mary HANSON; January 10th 1757 b. John HANSON; November 1st 1760 b. Sarah HANSON; s/o & d/o Benjamin HANSON and Elizabeth his wife.
June 3d 1761 then was Joseph BROWN m. to Avarilla OSBORNE.
May 24th 1760 then was m. Peter DIXON to Margaret PECKOO.{OR2-203}
March 3d 1761 b. Johannah DIXON d/o Peter DIXON and Margaret his wife.
February 3d 1761 then was m. James GARLAND to Jane GADDIS.
April 13th 1762 b. Catherine GARLAND d/o James GARLAND and Jane his wife.
February 18th 1761 then was m. Thomas FISHER to Amelia WHITACRE, widow of Peter WHITACRE. {H-369}

ST. GEORGE'S CHURCH REGISTER

November 21st 1761 b. William Hitchcock FISHER s/o Thomas FISHER and Amelia his wife.
June 30th 1761 then was m. Amos HOLLIS to Martha EVERETT, widow of John EVERETT.
August 12th 1760 b. Clark HOLLIS s/o William HOLLIS and Sarah his wife.
Aug. 2d 1756 b. Mary DORSEY, about 12 o'clock @ night on Monday; September 14th 1758 b. Frisby DORSEY about 12 o'clock Thursday morning; January 15th 1761 b. Benedict DORSEY about 1 o'clock Thursday afternoon; s/o & d/o Greenberry DORSEY Junr. and Frances his wife.
October 25th 1759 Mr. James HEATH m. to Miss Susannah HALL.
January 11th 1760 b. Oliver DINNING s/o John DINNING and Mary his wife.
July 28th 1757 then was m. Henry RUFF to Hannah PRESTON.
November 17th 1758 b. Sarah RUFF; March 2d 1760 b. Hannah & Henry RUFF; d/o & s/o Henry RUFF and Hannah his wife.
January 12th 1761 then departed this life about 2 o'clock morning Hannah wife of Henry RUFF.
September 22d 1749 b. Charles WHITLATCH; March 7th 1751 b. Sarah WHITLATCH; July 6th 1753 b. Rachel WHITLATCH; August 4th 1755 b. John WHITLATCH; March 20th 1759 b. Mary WHITLATCH; April 22d 1761 b. William WHITLATCH; s/o & d/o Charles WHITLATCH and Elizabeth his wife.
July 7th 1761 b. Robert CRESWELL s/o James CRESWELL and Catherine his wife.
August 3d 1762 then was m. William OSBORN to Ann BISSETT widow of David BISSETT. {H-370}
April 5th 1761 then was m. Edward WARD Junr. to Mary GRIFFITH.
March 10th 1762 b. Samuel WARD s/o Edward WARD Junr. and Mary his wife.
March 3d 1761 then was m. John TREDWAY to Elizabeth OSBORN widow of Benjamin OSBORN.
February 18th 1762 b. Milcah TREDWAY d/o John TREDWAY and Elizabeth his wife.
June 4th 1758 then was m. Thomas TAYLOR to Jane HANBY.
September 19th 1759 b. Hannah TAYLOR; March 29th 1761 b. Mary TAYLOR; d/o Thomas TAYLOR and Jane his wife.
June 14th 1758 then was m. John M'CABE to Eleanor GOODWIN.
April 8th 1759 b. Catherine M'CABE; September 25th b. Elizabeth M'CABE; March 10th 1762 b. Barnett M'CABE; d/o & s/o John M'CABE and Eleanor his wife.
September 11th 1747 then was m. Samuel HOWELL to Sarah DURBIN.
January 31st 1748 b. Asenath HOWELL; January 18th 1750 b. Mordecai HOWELL; September 11th 1753 b. Samuel HOWELL; February 1st 1756 b. Avarilla HOWELL; s/o & d/o Samuel HOWELL and Sarah his wife.
October 8th 1761 b. Sarah BAILEY d/o Joseph BAILEY and Margaret his wife.
July 10th 1752 b. William PERKINS; March 26th 1755 b. Rachel PERKINS; April 13th 1757 b. Elizabeth PERKINS; August 14th 1759 b. Richard PERKINS; s/o & d/o Reuben PERKINS and Avarilla his wife.
May 24th 1759 then was m. Michael TAYLOR to Mary MITCHELL.
March 27th 1761 b. Elizabeth TAYLOR; August 15th 1762 b. Aquila TAYLOR; s/o & d/o Michael TAYLOR and Mary his wife.
December 2d 1757 b. Charles James CHRISTIE s/o Charles CHRISTIE and Cordelia his wife. {OR2-204}

ST. GEORGE'S CHURCH REGISTER

June 21st 1761 then was m. Dr. Alexander STENHOUSE to Cordelia CHRISTIE widow. {H-371}
January 19th 1762 b. Thomas STEUART s/o George STEUART and Margaret his wife.
June 7th 1761 then was m. Peter HENLEY to Mary WILD.
October 22nd 1760 b. Corbin PRESTON s/o Daniel PRESTON and Ann his wife.
Nov. 5th 1762 b. Sarah HENLEY d/o Peter HENLEY & Mary his wife.
October 18th 1749 b. Frances BISHOP; January 29th 1751 b. Elizabeth BISHOP; February 1st 1754 b. Samuel BISHOP; s/o & d/o Roger BISHOP and Evas his wife.
October 12th 1752 b. Mary ELLETS; January 30th 1755 b. Samuel ELLETS; February 15th 1757 b. Rachel ELLETS; September 24th 1759 b. Elizabeth ELLETS; s/o & d/o William ELLETS and Kern his wife.
February 7th 1746 b. John GOODWIN; April 28th 1749 b. Elizabeth GOODWIN; November 23d 1752 b. Thomas GOODWIN; March 13th 1755 b. Benjamin GOODWIN; October 16th 1758 b. James GOODWIN; March 8th 1760 b. Ann GOODWIN; March 1st 1762 b. Hannah GOODWIN; s/o & d/o Benjamin GOODWIN and Hannah his wife.
December 19th 1754 b. Gregory GALLION; March 12th 1757 b. John GALLION; October 24th 1759 b. William GALLION; s/o Joseph GALLION and Sarah his wife.
January 21st 1753 then was m. Joseph GALLION to Sarah AUCHARD.
December 26th 1755 then was m. Sam GOODWIN to Rebecca BREEDEN (?)
December 19th 1756 b. Isaac GOODWIN; August 10th 1759 b. Joseph GOODWIN; July 4th 1761 b. Elizabeth GOODWIN; s/o & d/o Samuel GOODWIN and Rebecca his wife.
May 24th 1754 b. Eleanor WALKER d/o Mary WALKER.
March 10th 1761 b. Susannah FOSTER; May 27th 1762 b. Annabell FOSTER; d/o Benedict FOSTER and Margaret his wife. {H-372}
September 16th 1746 b. George REEVES; July 12th 1748 b. John REEVES; April 10th 1750 b. Mary REEVES; April 7th 1754 b. Margaret REEVES; 29 March 1754 b. Ann REEVES; June 15th 1756 b. Eleanor REEVES; s/o & d/o Emanuel REEVES and Eleanor his wife.
April 12th 1762 then was m. Samuel MOORE to Senea FUTT.
February 5th 1742 b. Joseph STAPLETON; May 14th 1744 b. Hannah STAPLETON; June 22d 1746 b. Joshua STAPLETON; August 1st 1749 b. Edward STAPLETON; s/o & d/o Edward STAPLETON and Rachel his wife.
September 9th 1749 b. Xtian BRICE; October 11th 1751 b. James BRICE; March 20th 1753 b. William BRICE; November 14th 1754 b. Ali BRICE; April 16th 1756 b. Barnet BRICE; March 15th 1758 b. Margaret BRICE; July 6th 1760 b. John BRICE; July 31st 1762 b. Mary BRICE; s/o & d/o James BRICE and Mary his wife.
Dec. 16th 1754 then was m. William DEAVER to Susannah BIRCHFIELD.
April 11th 1755 b. John DEAVER; February 3d 1757 b. Mary DEAVER; October 11th 1760 b. Nathan DEAVER; September 9th 1762 b. William DEAVER; s/o & d/o William DEAVER and Susannah his wife.
July 18th 1754 then was m. James MORGAN to Mary DAVIS. {OR2-205}
August 29th 1755 b. Prementer MORGAN; December 7th 1757 b. Sarah MORGAN; April 26th 1760 b. James MORGAN; s/o & d/o James MORGAN and Mary his wife.
January 26th 1739 b. Jacob JONES; January 19th 1741 b. Hannah JONES; November 29th 1746 b. William JONES; July 24th 1751 b. Abraham JONES; June 24th 1754 b. Thomas JONES; March 7th 1760 b. Isaac JONES; s/o & d/o William JONES and Elizabeth his wife.
February 17th 1745 b. Jane WALKER d/o Elizabeth WALKER. {H-373}

ST. GEORGE'S CHURCH REGISTER

July 2d 1755 b. Joseph JOHNSON; June 16th 1757 b. Martha JOHNSON; December 29th 1759 b. Elijah JOHNSON; August 24th 1762 b. Ephraim JOHNSON; s/o & d/o Thomas JOHNSON and Ann his wife.
February 14th 1751 then was m. Thomas JOHNSON to Ann BRADLEY.
September 29th 1755 then was m. Zachariah SPENCER to Ann POGUE.
November 17th 1757 b. Elizabeth SPENCER; February 27th 1758 b. Sarah SPENCER; October 10th 1759 b. Ann SPENCER; February 28th 1761 b. Zachariah SPENCER; d/o & s/o Zachariah SPENCER and Ann his wife.
December 2d 1754 then was m. Danial DULANY to Elizabeth BRADLEY.
April 20th 1762 b. Elizabeth AYRES d/o Abraham AYRES Junr. and Elizabeth his wife.
February 19th 1744 b. Charity SPENCER; April 8 1755 b. William SPENCER; December 28th 1747 b. John SPENCER; January 2d 1751 b. Margaret SPENCER; s/o & d/o Charity SPENCER.
August 2d 1760 b. Elizabeth GLASS d/o Thomas GLASS and Judith his wife.
August 31st 1756 b. James LEE s/o James LEE Junr.
February 3d 1759 b. Elizabeth ALEXANDER; February 28th 1760 b. Lydia ALEXANDER; November 27th 1761 b. Rachel ALEXANDER; d/o James ALEXANDER and Lydia his wife.
December 14th 1757 then was m. James ALEXANDER to Lydia JONES.
January 15th 1756 then was m. Thomas STAPLETON to Sarah CROOK.
May 20th 1756 b. Margaret STAPLETON; September 15th 1758 b. Alice STAPLETON; September 22d 1760 b. Sarah STAPLETON; d/o Thomas STAPLETON and Sarah his wife. {H-374}
April 1st 1762[sic] then was m. Nathaniel BRINDLEY to Rachel SPENCER.
December 12th 1753 b. Mary BRINDLEY; January 12th 1755 b. Sarah BRINDLEY; April 4th 1757 b. Elizabeth BRINDLEY; December 4th 1759 b. Constance BRINDLEY; May 23rd 1762 b. Jane BRINDLEY; d/o Nathaniel BRINDLEY and Rachel his wife.
June 9th 1761 m. John WEBSTER (son of Samuel) to Hannah WOOD.
July 4th 1762 b. Elizabeth WEBSTER d/o John WEBSTER and Hannah his wife.
November 10th 1748 then was m. William RIGDON to Mary PRIBBLE
October 24th 1750 b. Ann RIGDON; April 26th 1753 b. George RIGDON; November 6th 1756 b. Mary RIGDON; September 15th 1759 b. James RIGDON; September 7th 1761 b. William RIGDON Junr.; s/o & d/o William RIGDON and Mary his wife.
December 13th 1757 then was m. Henry WATTERS to Mary RUFF.
November 5th 1758 b. Godfrey WATTERS; June 24th 1762 b. Henry WATERS [sic]; s/o Henry WATTERS and Mary his wife.
June 6th 1759 b. Samuel CASSADAY s/o Mary MURPHEY.
January 27th 1762 b. Catherine MURPHEY d/o William MURPHEY and Mary his wife.
February 16th 1758 then was m. James BROWN Junr. (son of Thomas) to Elizabeth MORGAN.
October 7th 1761 then was b. Thomas BROWN s/o James BROWN Junr. and Elizabeth his wife.
January 23d 1763 then was m. David DAVIS to Elizabeth DOOLEY??
January 14th 1759 b. Parker LEE; December 10th 1760 b. James LEE; September 3d 1762 b. Priscilla LEE; s/o & d/o Samuel LEE and M___ his wife. {OR2-206}
October 19th 1750 b. Martin PRESTON; May 22d 1754 b. Mary PRESTON; August 2d b. Bernard PRESTON; s/o & d/o James PRESTON and Clemency his wife. {H-375}
May 25th 1755 b. William CREIGHTON s/o William CREIGHTON and Mary his wife.

ST. GEORGE'S CHURCH REGISTER

November 14th 1740 then was m. John THOMPSON to Mary POTEE.
November 8th 1743 b. John THOMPSON; December 22d 1745 b. Hannah THOMPSON; December 6th 1747 b. Elizabeth THOMPSON; June 17th 1748 b. Sarah THOMPSON; s/o & d/o John THOMPSON & Mary his wife.
July 16th 1754 then departed this life Mary THOMPSON wife of John THOMPSON.
July 18th 1755 then was m. John THOMPSON to Margaret GILBERT.
January 1st 1758 b. Jarvis THOMPSON; December 13th 1759 b. Ann THOMPSON; September 2d 1762 b. Margaret THOMPSON; d/o John THOMPSON and Margaret his wife.
December 4th 1761 b. Elizabeth BARNES [sic] d/o John BARNS and Elizabeth his wife.
October 16th 1754 b. Elizabeth RALSTONE d/o Gavin and Elizabeth RALSTONE.
December 30th 1755 then was m. Samuel RICHARDSON to Sarah DAVIS.
December 18th 1756 b. Delia RICHARDSON; July 25th 1758 b. Elizabeth RICHARDSON; September 9th 1761 b. Sarah RICHARDSON; d/o Samuel RICHARDSON and Sarah his wife.
July 30th 1752 then was m. Joseph POGUE unto Sarah FARMER.
July 1st 1755 b. Susannah POGUE; December 3d 1756 b. John POGUE; April 10th 1758 b. Hannah POGUE; June 24th 1759 b. Sarah POGUE; September 3d 1762 b. Ann POGUE; s/o & d/o Joseph POGUE and Sarah his wife. {H-376}
January 6th 1746 then was m. Charles MORGAN to Margaret POGUE.
October 29th 1747 b. George MORGAN; April 2d 1749 b. Sarah MORGAN; February 9th 1751 b. Hannah MORGAN; May 20th 1754 b. Joseph MORGAN; December 18th 1757 b. Charles MORGAN; March 2d 1759 b. Rachel MORGAN; July 10th 1761 b. Edward MORGAN; s/o & d/o Charles MORGAN and Margaret his wife.
April 28th 1759 b. Ann PEARSON; September 27th 1761 b. Enoch PEARSON; s/o & d/o Thomas PEARSON and Ann his wife.
November 24th 1741 b. Mary BURGEN; November 23d 1743 b. Dennis BURGEN; June 27th 1747 b. Thomas BURGEN; July 16th 1752 b. Catherine BURGEN; April 5th 1755 b. John BURGEN; January 3d 1758 b. James BURGEN; November 3d 1760 b. Isaac BURGEN; s/o & d/o Thomas BURGEN and Ann his wife.
June 20th 1758 b. John SMITH; May 25th 1762 b. Adam SMITH; s/o John SMITH and Mary his wife.
May 24th 1752 b. Hannah BISHOP; May 23d 1754 b. Rachel BISHOP; November 18th 1756 b. Prudence BISHOP; November 15th 1759 b. Elizabeth BISHOP; d/o Jonathan BISHOP and Rachel his wife.
April 1st 1760 b. William M'CULLOCH; April 7th 1762 b. Janet M'CULLOCH; s/o & d/o John M'COLLOCH and Jane his wife.
August 16th 1762 then was m. John RENSHAW to Mary BISHOP.
October 29th 1756 b. William MURDOCH; March 17th 1759 b. James MURDOCH; May 10th 1761 b. Mary MURDOCH; s/o & d/o James MURDOCH and Christian his wife. {H-377}
September 13th 1751 b. Josias WHEELER; February 16th 1754 b. Elizabeth WHEELER; January 19th 1757 b. Susannah WHEELER; s/o & d/o Thomas WHEELER and Elizabeth his wife. {OR2-207}
October 12th 1743 b. Mary CONNOLLY; September 11th 1745 b. Rosannah CONNOLLY; September 10th 1747 b. Catherine CONNOLLY; January 15th 1752 b. Ann CONNOLLY; March 15th 1755 b. Eleanor CONNOLLY; April 10th 1759 b. Alice CONNOLLY; September 1st 1761 b. Sarah CONNOLLY; d/o Barnaby CONNOLLY and Mary his wife.
August 18th 1745 b. Ann RIGDON; January 25th 1748 b. Mary RIGDON; July 30th 1750 b. Baker RIGDON; January 3d 1753 b. Margaret RIGDON; July 3d 1755 b. Ruth RIGDON; September 11th 1757 b.

ST. GEORGE'S CHURCH REGISTER

John RIGDON; January 3d 1761 b. William RIGDON; s/o & d/o John RIGDON and Elizabeth his wife.
December 4th 1750 b. Sarah LEE; October 26th 1756 b. John LEE; October 31st 1759 b. Seaborn LEE; s/o & d/o Mary LEE.
July 16th 1754 b. John DAVIS; January 26th 1756 b. William DAVIS; February 18th 1762 b. Richard DAVIS; s/o William DAVIS and Elizabeth his wife. {H-378}
October 2d 1753 then was Adam BURCHFIELD m. to Ann NELSON.
June 28th 1754 b. Hannah BURCHFIELD; October 2d 1756 b. Mary BURCHFIELD; March 19th 1759 b. Prissilla BURCHFIELD; Feb. 15th b. Adam BURCHFIELD; s/o & d/o Adam BURCHFIELD and Ann his wife.
April 9th 1759 b. James GARRETTSON; March 3d 1762 b. Bennett GARRETTSON; s/o James GARRETTSON and Catherine his wife.
February ___ 1763 then James GARRETTSON departed this life.
January 2d 1763 b. Avarilla HOLLIS d/o Amoss HOLLIS and Martha his wife.
May 30th 1763 b. Catherine BROWN d/o Joseph BROWN and Avarilla his wife.
August 30th 1754 b. Ann EVERITT; March 3d 1756 b. James EVERITT; September 5th 1758 b. John EVERITT; s/o & d/o John EVERITT and Martha his wife.
November 20th 1757 b. John MATHEWS; June 14th 1759 b. Milcah MATHEWS; October 30th 1761 b. Bennett MATHEWS; s/o & d/o John MATHEWS and Milcah his wife.
December 8th 1762 b. Eliza. HALL d/o Capt. John HALL of Cranberry and Berthia his wife.
June 11th 1761 then was William HOW m. to Mary LESTER.
November 17th 1762 b. Else HOW d/o William HOW and Mary his wife.
March 12th 1763 b. Avarilla HANSON d/o Benjamin HANSON and Elizabeth his wife.
January 13th 1757 then was Luke GRIFFITH joined in Holy Matrimony to Mrs. Blanch HALL widow of Parker HALL by the Revd. Andrew LENDRUM.
March 9th 1763 then d. the above Blanch GRIFFITH.
April 6th 1759 then d. Mrs. Jane STANSBURY.
May 15th 1762 then was Samuel SUTTEN m. to Sarah LAZELL.
May 26th 1762 b. Margaret SUTTEN d/o Samuel SUTTEN and Sarah his wife. {H-379}
August 4th 1761 b. Alizanah SMITH; August 14th 1762 b. William SMITH; s/o & d/o Nathaniel SMITH and Elizabeth his wife.
May 30th 1763 then was John JONES m. to Margaret JACKSON.
February 20th 1761 b. Martha BROWN d/o Absolum BROWN and Margaret his wife. {OR2-208}
June 25th 1761 b. William BROWN; April 26th 1763 b. Martha BROWN; s/o & d/o James BROWN and Sarah his wife.
March 2d 1762 b. Jane BRUSBANKS d/o Abram BRUSBANKS and Mary his wife.
October 2d 1759 b. Joseph MURPHY; March 10th 1763 b. Martha MURPHY; s/o & d/o Timothy MURPHY and Elizabeth his wife.
March 28th 1743 b. George GARRETTSON; December 25th 1747 b. Sarah GARRETTSON; December 20th 1749 b. Eliza. GARRETTSON; October 16th 1751 b. John GARRETTSON; October 17th 1753 b. Freeborn GARRETTSON;; December 5th 1755 b. Richard GARRETTSON; December 12th 1759 b. Thomas GARRETTSON; s/o & d/o John GARRETTSON and Sarah his wife.
October 14th 1762 then was Joshua STORY m. to Margarett BRISCOE.
July 24th 1763 b. Jesper STORY & d. 10th March (no year) s/o Joshua STORY and Margarett his wife.

ST. GEORGE'S PARISH REGISTER

October 1st 1763 b. Mary JINKENS d/o William JINKENS and Mary his wife.
January 14th 1760 b. John WATKINS; November 22d 1762 b. William WATKINS; s/o John WATKINS and Purifie (?) his wife.
February 19th 1763 b. Eliza. GARRETTSON d/o Richard GARRETTSON and Prissila his wife.
November 1st 1759 b. David FORD; March 16th 1762 b. Rachel FORD; s/o John FORD and Sarah his wife.
February 3d 1763 b. James GARRETTSON s/o Edward GARRETTSON and Avarilla his wife. {H-380}
October 16th 1763 then was Josiah LYON m. to Eliza. BROWN.
January 12th 1764 then was John TREDWAY m. to Sarah GRIFFITH.
July 3d 1763 then was George LITTLE m. to Catherine ROBERTSON.
January 9th 1764 b. Ann LITTLE d/o George LITTLE and Catherine his wife.
January 22d 1762 b. John JINKENS s/o William JINKENS and Mary his wife.
February 23d 1764 then was Mr. William Robinson PRESBURY m. to Miss Martha HALL d/o Capt. John HALL of Cranberry by the Revd. Andrew LENDRUM.
November 19th 1763 then Mrs. Mary MATHEWS wife of Mr. Leven MATHEWS departed this life.
December 7th 1759 b. Sarah TAYLOR; November 5th 1761 b. Laama TAYLOR; d/o James TAYLOR and Sarah his wife.
September 19th 1757 then was Thomas Frisby HENDERSON & Hannah HOLLANDSWORTH widow of George HOLLANDSWORTH m. by the Revd. Andrew LENDRUM.
March 17th 1759 b. Francis HENDERSON; January 16th 1761 b. Cordelia HENDERSON; d/o Thomas Frisby HENDERSON and Hannah his wife.
July 26th 1763 b. Sally Frisby DORSEY d/o Greenberry DORSEY and Frances his wife.
March 15th 1764 then was Samuel GRIFFITH & Freenettah GARRETTSON (?) m. by the Revd. Andrew LENDRUM.
September 2d 1763 then Garrett GARRETTSON s/o Mrs. George GARRETTSON departed this life.
August 7th 1761 b. John MC GAY; March 2d 1763 b. Robert MC GAY; s/o Robert MC GAY and Sarah his wife. {OR2-209}
December 1st 1741 b. Daniel DURBIN; June 11th 1743 b. John DURBIN; February 25th 1747 b. William DURBIN; February 11th 1749 b. Samuel DURBIN; September 22d 1752 b. Avarilla DURBIN; s/o & d/o John DURBIN and Mary his wife.
March 12th 1760 then was Mr. Garrett GARRETTSON & Mrs. Susannah ROBINSON widow of Capt. Daniel ROBINSON m. by Rev. Andrew LENDRUM.
February 19th 1761 b. Elizabeth GARRETTSON; November 6th 1763 b. Sarah GARRETTSON; d/o Garrett GARRETTSON and Susannah his wife.
January 12th 1764 then was Daniel DURBIN m. to Mary JOHNS d/o Richard JOHNS and Ann his wife.
June 11th 1751 then was William MITCHEL m. to Sarah OSBORN d/o Benjamin OSBORN.
March 22d 1755 b. Martha MITCHEL; December 6th 1757 b. Mary MITCHEL; January 6th 1759 b. Edward MITCHEL; March 17th 1761 b. Elizabeth MITCHEL; March 16th 1763 b. Ann MITCHEL; s/o & d/o William MITCHEL and Sarah his wife.
August 3d 1751 then was Thomas OSBORN m. to Elizabeth SIMPSON.
September 3d 1751 b. William OSBORN; November 11th 1752 b. Sary OSBORN; June 29th 1755 b. Mary OSBORN; March 15th 1757 b. Benjamin OSBORN; February 2d 1759 b. Francis OSBORN; February

ST. GEORGE'S PARISH REGISTER

8th 1761 b. Bennett OSBORN; s/o & d/o Thomas OSBORN and Elizabeth his wife.
November 10th 1762 b. Frances GILBERT; February 16th 1764 b. Martha GILBERT; d/o Thomas GILBERT and Mary his wife.
February 28th 1754 then was John BONNER m. to Christian INGRAM.
March 3d 1755 b. William BONNER; February 13th 1757 b. Sarah BONNER; January 14th 1759 b. Arthur BONNER; May 9th 1761 b. Martha BONNER; s/o & d/o John BONNER and Christian his wife.
Oct. 12th 1743 then was Light KNIGHT m. to Rachel RUSE. {H-382}
February 9th 1746 b. Thomas KNIGHT; February 10th 1748 b. Mary KNIGHT; July 12th 1751 b. Elizabeth KNIGHT; January 7th 1753 b. Ann KNIGHT; July 29th 1756 b. William KNIGHT; April 8th 1758 b. Sarah KNIGHT; January 28th 1760 b. Rachel KNIGHT; s/o & d/o Light KNIGHT and Rachel his wife.
June 28th 1748 then Morriss WILLIAMS m. Ann DU??
December 28th 1751 b. Edward WILLIAMS; January 17th 1754 b. Mary WILLIAMS; January 8th 1757 b. Martha WILLIAMS; August 29th 1761 b. John WILLIAMS; s/o & d/o Morriss WILLIAMS and Ann his wife.
April 5th 1763 b. Abraham TAYLOR s/o Thomas TAYLOR and Jane his wife. {OR2-210}
Nov. 30th 1758 then was Grigory BARNS m. to Elizabeth MITCHEL.
December 6th 1759 b. Avarilla BARNS; April 4th 1761 b. Ford BARNS; June 25th 1762 b. Richard BARNS; March 23d 1764 b. Rachel BARNS; s/o & d/o Grigory BARNS and Elizabeth his wife.
April 8th 1761 d. Ford BARNS.
November 17th 1759 b. Amos BARNS; June 24th 1761 b. Ford BARNS; June 29th 1761 then d. Ford BARNS; s/o Ford BARNS and R'th. his wife.
August 18th 1751 then was Robert CRUTE m. to RACHEL BARNS.
November 24th 1752 b. Rebecca CRUTE; February 17th 1755 b. Sarah CRUTE; March 19th 1757 b. Richard CRUTE; April 15th 1759 b. Francis CRUTE; April 21st 1761 b. Cordelia CRUTE; s/o & d/o of Robert CRUTE and Rachel his wife. {H-383}
March 31st 1761 then d. Robert CRUTE.
June 21st 1762 then was m. William STEAVENSON and Rachel CRUTE widow of Robert.
March 28th 1763 b. George STEAVENSON s/o William and Rachel his wife.
March 15th 1764 then was Nathan SWAIN & Miss Mary DREW m. by the Revd. Andrew LENDRUM.
March 7th 1762 then was Mr. Nathaniel GILES & Miss Sarah HAMMOND m. by the Revd. Thomas CHACE.
December 6th 1762 b. Hannah GILES d/o Nathaniel GILES and Sarah his wife.
March 6th 1760 then was Samuel HILL & Elizabeth HOPKINS m.
April 1st 1761 b. Agness CRESWELL; May 19th 1763 b. Elizabeth CRESWELL; d/o Samuel CRESWELL and Agness his wife.
August 12th 1764 then was Edward THOMPSON & Jemima GROOM m. by the Revd. Andrew LENDRUM.
November 6th 1760 b. Sarah DREW; September 3d 1762 b. Anthony DREW; children of Anthony DREW and Ann his wife. {H-383}
September 16th 1764 b. John LYON s/o Josiah LYON and Elizabeth his wife.
July 20th 1764 b. Elizabeth GRIFFITH d/o Luke GRIFFITH and Catherine his wife.
March 28th 1765 then was Samuel CROSS m. to Susannah PRESBURY.
February 4th 1765 b. George GRIFFITH s/o Samuel GRIFFITH and Freenettah his wife.

ST. GEORGE'S PARISH REGISTER

August 8th 1747 b. Eliza. GILES; February 2d 1749/50 b. James GILES; May 29th 1751 b. Johannah GILES; March 15th 1753 b. Jacob GILES; December 25th 1754 b. Thomas GILES; August 29th 1757 b. Aquilla GILES; April 24th 1759 b. Edward GILES; s/o & d/o Jacob GILES and Johannah his wife. {H-384}
October 11th 1764 then was Martin Tayler GILBERT & Martha GILBERT m. by the Revd. Andrew LENDRUM. {OR2-211}
July 19th 1765 b. Mary GILBERT d/o Martin Tayler GILBERT & Martha his wife.
January 11th 1763 b. Martha HALL; March 17th 1765 b. Parker HALL d/o & s/o John HALL of Swan Town & Cordelia his wife.
February 14th 1765 b. William STEVENSON s/o William STEVENSON and Rachel his wife.
January 20th 1766 Sarah TREDWAY wife of John TREDWAY d.
February 10th 1764 b. John WARD s/o Edward WARD Junr.
December 9th 1764 b. Ruthen GARRETTSON s/o Edward GARRETTSON and Avarilla his wife.
November 29th 1764 then was m. Leven MATHEWS to Mary DAY d/o John DAY and Philliszana his wife by the Revd. Hugh DEANS.
October 5th 1765 b. John Day MATHEWS s/o Leven MATHEWS and Mary his wife and bap. by Revd. Andrew LENDRUM 7 June 1766.
May 16th 1766 b. Hannah HALL d/o John HALL of Cranberry & Bethia his wife.
September 29th 1766 then d. George GRIFFITH s/o Samuel and Freenettah his wife.
June 1st 1761 b. William JEWELL s/o Mary JEWELL.
March 16th 1766 b. Garrett GARRETTSON s/o Garrett GARRETTSON and Susannah his wife. {H-385}
February 16th 1766 b. Eliza. HANSON d/o of Benjamin HANSON and Elizabeth his wife.
November 21st 1766 b. Samuel GRIFFITH s/o Luke GRIFFITH and Catherine his wife.
September 26th 1766 then came Thomas WEST into Pensilvania from the City of London.
July 31st 1758 then was John WOOD & Sarah DAVIDGE m. by the Rev. Andrew LENDRUM.
October 8th 1759 b. Rebecca WOOD; January 13th 1762 b. Mary WOOD; April 18th 1764 b. Susannah WOOD; April 3d 1766 b. Sarah WOOD; d/o John WOOD and Sarah his wife.
October 23d 1766 b. Martha THOMPSON d/o Edward THOMPSON and Jemimah his wife.
September 29th 1767 then d. Mrs. Martha GARRETTSON.
September 12th 1767 b. Mary GRIFFITH d/o Samuel GRIFFITH and Freenettah his wife.
July 18th 1751 then was Daniel ROBINSON & Susana BROWN m. by Revd. Andrew LENDRUM.
May 29th 1768 b. Charles GILBERT s/o Martin Tayler GILBERT and Martha his wife.
March 7th 1766 b. James CROSS s/o Samuel CROSS and Susanah his wife. {OR2-212}
August 22d 1766 b. Sarah MURPHEY d/o Timothy MURPHEY and Eliza. his wife.
June 25th 1767 then was Mr. James PHILLIPS & Miss Martha PACA d/o Capt. John PACA m. by Revd. Hugh DEANS. {H-386}
May 9th 1768 b. Elizabeth WOOD; November 13th 1768 then d. Sarah WOOD; November 15th 1768 then d. Elizabeth WOOD; d/o John WOOD and Sarah his wife.
March 24th 1768 then was Mr. George GARRETTSON & Miss Martha PRESBURY m. by the Revd. Hugh DEANS.

ST. GEORGE'S PARISH REGISTER

March 9th 1769 b. Martha GARRETTSON d/o George GARRETTSON and Martha his wife.
Dec. 19th 1765 b. Thomas BROWN s/o James BROWN & Sarah his wife.
August 3d 1769 b. Avarilla GARRETTSON d/o Edward GARRETTSON and Avarilla his wife.
October 26th 1769 b. John GRIFFITH s/o Samuel GRIFFITH and Freenettah his wife and was bap. 13 May by the Revd. Andrew LENDRUM.
November 25th 1768 b. Luke HANSON s/o Benjamin HANSON and Elizabeth his wife.
June 20th 1765 b. William MC GAY; February 21st 1767 b. Hugh MC GAY; February 11th 1770 b. James MC GAY; s/o Robert MC GAY and Sarah his wife.
April 4th 1769 then was John CLARK and Sophia LESTER m. by the Rev. Andrew LENDRUM.
Jan. 8th 1770 b. Hannah CLARK d/o John CLARK & Sophia his wife.
August 4th 1769 then John CLARK departed this life.
May 29th 1770 then was Joseph TOY and Francess DALLAM m. by the Rev. Andrew LENDRUM.
March 26th 1769 b. Lewis GRIFFITH s/o Luke GRIFFITH and Catherine his wife.
December 8th 1770 Edward GARRETTSON s/o Edward GARRETTSON and Avarilla his wife departed this life.
January 2d 1765 then was Israel COMBEST & Susannah PERRYMAN m. by the Revd. Andrew LENDRUM. {H-387}
November 13th 1763 then was Amos CORD and Susannah KIMBEL m. by the Rev. Andrew LENDRUM. {OR2-213}
June 9th 1764 b. Hannah CORD; August 21st 1766 b. Greenberry CORD; March 27th 1768 b. Aquila CORD; s/o & d/o Amos CORD and Susannah his wife.
September 27th 1747 then was Samuel BUDD & Milcah YOUNG m. by the Rev. James STERLING, Rector of the lower parish in Kent County.
October 6th 1750 b. George BUDD; April 3d 1756 b. Milcah BUDD; June 18th 1757 b. Samuel BUDD; November 25th 1763 b. Sarah BUDD; January 5th 1765 b. Martha BUDD; s/o & d/o Samuel BUDD and Milcah his wife.
February 20th 1767 b. Hannah SUTTEN; April 5th 1768 b. Robert & Sarah SUTTEN, twins; s/o & d/o Samuel SUTTEN & Sarah his wife.
January 25th 1770 then was Mr. Josias Middlemore DALLAM & Miss Sarah SMITH m. by Revd. Hugh DEANS.
January 27th 1770 b. John Josias Middlemore DALLAM s/o Mr. Richard DALLAM and Frances his wife.
February 14th 1766 then was b. James GALLION s/o John GALLION and Elizabeth his wife.
March 2d 1771 b. Martin Tayler GILBERT s/o Martin Tayler GILBERT and Martha his wife.
January 31st 1771 b. James PHILLIPS s/o Mr. James PHILLIPS and Martha his wife.
March 19th 1771 then was Mr. James MATHEWS and Miss Sophia HALL m. by the Revd. Andrew LENDRUM. {H-388}
January 3d 1772 then d. Mrs. Sophia MATHEWS.
January 10th 1769 then was Jacob GALLION and Mary HANSON m. by the Revd. Andrew LENDRUM.
Oct. 30th 1769 b. John GALLION s/o Jacob GALLION & Mary his wife
September 16th 1771 b. Martha GRIFFITH d/o Samuel GRIFFITH and Freenettah his wife and bap. 17 April 1772 by the Revd. Mr. GODLEY. {OR2-214}
June 19th 1764 then was Jacob FORWARD & Faithfull WEBB m. by the Rev. Andrew LENDRUM.

ST. GEORGE'S PARISH REGISTER

June 2d 1765 b. Constance Elizabeth FORWARD; January 10th 1772 b.
  Jane FORWARD; d/o Jacob FORWARD and Faithfull his wife.
March 19th 1773 then John GRIFFITH s/o Samuel GRIFFITH &
  Frenettah his wife departed this life.
March 12th 1765 b. Mary BAKER; August 5th 1768 b. Susanah BAKER;
  d/o Nicols BAKER and Mary his wife.
November 29th 1772 then was Elijah BLACKISTON and Avarilla
  GARRETTSON m.
March 16th 1773 b. Joshua WOOD s/o John WOOD & Sarah his wife.
June 20th 1773 b. Frances GRIFFITH d/o Samuel GRIFFITH and
  Freenettah his wife and was bap. 19 September by Rev. Mr.
  William WEST.
July 11th 1769 then was Robert YOUNG and Sarah MATHEWS m. by the
  Rev. Andrew LENDRUM.
September 14th 1772 b. Margaret & Sarah YOUNG twins of the above
  Robert YOUNG and Sarah his wife.   {H-389}
On 15 September 1757 departed this life Mr. Robert BIRNEY at the
  Revd. Mr. Andrew LENDRUM's.
On 25 January 1760 departed this life Mrs. Jane LENDRUM, wife of
  the Revd. Mr. Andrew LENDRUM.
On 9 April 1772 departed this life the Revd. Mr. Andrew LENDRUM,
  Rector of this parish.
September 2d 1770 then was Jacob COMBEST & Sarah COLLINS m.
June 22d 1771 b. Casandra COMBEST d/o Jacob COMBEST and Sarah his
  wife.
April 8th 1762 b. Nathaniel SULLIVAN s/o Hanah SULIVAN [sic].
July 28th 1767 then was Ettie COMBEST m. to Elizabeth GILBERT.
May 25th 1769 b. Thomas COMBEST; August 1st 1771 b. John COMBEST;
  s/o Ettie COMBEST and Elizabeth his wife.
May 28th 1770 b. Mary Goldsmith GARRETTSON; March 23d 1772 b.
  Elizabeth GARRETTSON; April 9th 1774 b. George GARRETTSON; d/o
  & s/o George GARRETTSON and Martha his wife.   {OR2-215}
May 15th 1771 p. certificate May 15 1774. b. Charlotte
  GRIFFITH d/o Mr. Luke GRIFFITH and Catherine his wife.
November 19th 1752 then was Edmund BULL & Susana LYEN joined in
  holy Matrimony by the Revd. Andrew LENDRUM.
June 23d 1754 b. Rachel BULL; August 17th 1757 b. Jacob BULL;
  March 17th 1760 b. Esther BULL; January 29th 1762 b. Mary BULL;
  April 26th 1764 b. John BULL; s/o & d/o Edmund BULL and Susana
  his wife.
January 3d 1768 b. Leven MATHEWS; February 6th 1771 b. John &
  James MATHEWS; July 2d 1773 b. Ann MATHEWS; s/o & d/o Mr. Leven
  MATHEWS and Mary his wife.   {H-390}
March 22d 1775 then Eliza. HANSON wife of Benjamin HANSON d.
March 29th 1747 b. William SMITH s/o Mr. Winston SMITH and
  Susannah his wife.
July 26th 1774 then George GARRETTSON s/o Mr. George GARRETTSON
  and Martha his wife departed this life.
June 1st b. Ann SUTTEN d/o Samuel SUTTEN & Sarah his wife.
March 11th 1770 b. Everitt HUGHS; August 21st 1772 b. John HUGHS;
  August 24th 1774 b. Scott HUGHS; s/o Mr. John Hall HUGHS and
  Ann his wife.
January 26th 1769 then was John Hall HUGHS & Ann EVERITT m. by
  the Revd. John PORTER.
March 8th 1762 b. John HALL; December 30th 1763 b. Edward HALL;
  December 6th 1765 b. Sophia HALL; March 8th 1768 b. Martha
  HALL; February 5th 1770 b. Eliza. HALL, 9 May 1771 d. Eliza.
  HALL; December 11th 1771 b. Benedict HALL; September 2d 1753 b.

ST. GEORGE'S PARISH REGISTER

Aquila HALL, 13 September 1754 then d. Aquila HALL; s/o & d/o Capt. Aquila HALL and Sophia his wife.
July 26th 1774 d. George GARRETTSON s/o Mr. George GARRETTSON and Martha his wife. {OR2-216}
August 6th 1775 then Mr. Goldsmith GARRETTSON departed this life.
December 18th 1775 Mr. George GARRETTSON departed this life.
February 11th 1776 b. Frances Goldsmith GARRETTSON d/o the above Mr. George GARRETTSON and Martha his wife. {H-391}
August 28th 1775 b. Sarah GRIFFITH d/o Samuel GRIFFITH and Freenettah his wife.
August 30th 1771 b. Francis Utie HOLLAND; May 4th 1773 b. John HOLLAND s/o Capt. Francis HOLLAND and Hannah his wife.
August 19th 1776 b. John WOOD s/o John WOOD & Sarah his wife.
May 1st 1776 b. Avarillah Mariah GRIFFITH d/o Luke GRIFFITH and Catherine his wife.
January 30th 1777 d. Mrs. Martha GARRETTSON widow of Mr. George GARRETTSON.
September 5th 1777 d. Mrs. Freenettah GRIFFITH wife of Samuel GRIFFITH.
October 24th 1777 d. Frances Goldsmith GARRETTSON d/o Mr. George GARRETTSON and Martha his wife.
September 1st 1777 b. Samuel Goldsmith GRIFFITH s/o Samuel GRIFFITH & Freenettah his wife and bap. 21 December by Rev. William WHITE.
November 17th 1778 then was Mr. Samuel GRIFFITH and Mrs. Martha PRESBURY m. by the Revd. John WORSTLEY.
July 30th 1779 then Capt. John HALL of Cranberry departed this life, in the 60th year of his age.
December 27th 1776 b. John ADAMS; March 27th 1779 b. James ADAMS; s/o John ADAMS and Mary his wife.
December 1st 1779 b. Avarilla GRIFFITH d/o Samuel GRIFFITH and Martha his wife.
August 25th 1780 then Mrs. Sarah BROWNE departed this life being 72 years 7 months and 26 days old. {H-392,OR2-217}
September 20th 1767 b. Ailse CASELTINE; September 20th 1771 b. John CASELTINE; s/o & d/o John CASELTINE and Mary his wife.
February 1st 1781 then Mary GRIFFITH d/o Samuel GRIFFITH & Freenettah his wife departed this life.
March 12th 1781 b. John Hall GRIFFITH s/o Samuel GRIFFITH and Martha his wife.
August 2d 1781 then Avarillah GRIFFITH d/o Samuel GRIFFITH and Martha his wife departed this life.
January 20th 1782 then Mrs. Hannah HALL widow of Coll. John HALL departed this life, being 70 years 4 months and 16 days old.
November 18th 1779 then was Gabriel CHRISTIE and Miss Priscilla HALL d/o of Capt. John HALL of Cranberry joined together in the Holy bands of Matrimony by the Revd. John WORSTLEY.
September 29th 1780 b. Charles CHRISTIE s/o Gabriel CHRISTIE and Pricilla his wife.
May 24th 1781 then was Robert Young STOKES, Esqr. and Miss Sarah BROOKE d/o Mr. Clement BROOKE of Baltimore County joined together in Holy Matrimony by the Rev. William WEST.
April 2d 1782 b. William Young STOKES s/o Robert Young STOKES and Sarah his wife.
October 10th 1775 then was the Rites of m. soleminized between Cyrus OSBURN & Miss Susannah ROBINSON.
March 24th 1762 b. Augustine BAYLES s/o Samuel BAYLES and Abigal his wife.

ST. GEORGE'S PARISH REGISTER

October 12th 1782 b. Cordelia CHRISTIE d/o Gabriel CHRISTIE and Priscilla his wife. {H-393}
(No date ?) b. William Axtel GILES s/o Aquila GILES and Eliza his wife.
September 14th 1772 then was m. Joseph RUTH and Catherine MANSFIELD by the Rev. Mr. WEST.
William SMITH m. to Miss Elizabeth GILES d/o Mr. Jacob GILES 7 December 1769. {OR-218}
Jacob Giles SMITH s/o William & Elizabeth SMITH b. 5 Dec. 1770.
Winston SMITH s/o William & Elizabeth SMITH b. 5 September 1772.
Elizabeth SMITH wife of William SMITH d. 11 February 1774.
William SMITH m. Miss Susanna PACA d/o Capt. John PACA 18 April 1776 by the Rev. William WEST.
Elizabeth SMITH d/o William & Susanna SMITH b. 9 September 1777 and departed this life 2 November 1777.
Paca SMITH s/o William & Susanna SMITH b. 2 December 1779.
Frances SMITH d/o William & Susanna SMITH b. 10 October 1781.
John FORWOOD s/o Jacob FORWOOD and Faithful his wife b. 3 January 1779.
Faithful FORWOOD wife of Jacob FORWOOD d. 7 May 1786.
John Brown BAYLES b. 17 October 1788 s/o Augustine and Elizabeth BAYLES.
February 10th 1789 then was Jacob FORWOOD & Martha JARRITT joined in Holy Matrimony by the Revd. John DAVIS. {H-394}

CHRISTENINGS AND MARRIAGES BY THE REV. J. IRELAND
COMMENCING MARCH 1787
{OR2-219}
August 20th 1787 b. Luke GRIFFITH s/o Samuel & Martha GRIFFITH.
March 18th 1787 Sophia White HALL d/o James White HALL & Sarah his wife b.
July 14th 1788 b. John SPENCER s/o Richard SPENCER and Martha his wife.
April 7th 1786 b. Pamela LANCASTER.
May 22d 1788 b. Charlotte FOWLER d/o Samuel FOWLER and Frances his wife.
September 14th 1788 b. Jessie RIDDELL s/o William RIDDELL and Charlotte his wife.
January 13th 1789 b. Sarah COWLY d/o Thomass & Sarah COWLY.
February 26th 1786 b. Pamelia BENNETT; November 26th 1787 b. Victor BENNETT; s/o & d/o Phillip BENNET [sic] and Amelia his wife.
March 21st 1785 b. Rowland GREENFIELD; November 16th 1787 b. Charrott GREENFIELD; September 6th 1789 b. Harriott GREENFIELD; s/o & d/o Thomas Truman GREENFIELD and Frances his wife.
November 1st 1780 b. Bennett STEWART; February 8th 1775 b. Elizabeth STEWART; October 18th 1771 b. Susanna STEWART; s/o & d/o James STEWART and Elizabeth his wife.
August 22d 1781 James STEWART departed this life.
Thomas Henderson GRAY b. 26 September 1783; Elizabeth GRAY b. 22 April 1789; Mary Ann GRAY b. 10 August 1791, bap. by the Rev. John IRELAND as per certificate 13 September 1792; 1795 February 17 b. John GRAY, bap. 20 March 1795; 1797 December 15th b. George GRAY, bap. 8 January 1798; s/o & d/o James GRAY and Elizabeth his wife. {H-394, OR2-220}
January 20th 1777 then was m. John Beadle HALL unto Sarah HALL.
December 24th 1779 b. Hetty HALL; July 3d 1781 b. Edward HALL; April 17th 1786 b. Cordelia Knight HALL; July 14th 1788 b.

ST. GEORGE'S PARISH REGISTER

Aquilla Beadle HALL; s/o & d/o John Beadle HALL and Sarah his wife.
April 12th 1770 m. James GILES to Anna FELL by the Rev. Mr. CHAN.
October 1st 1771 b. Johanna GILES; March 23d 1774 b. Jacob GILES; July 18th 1775 b. Susanna GILES; January 26th 1776 b. Jacob Washington GILES; December 5th 1778 b. Nathaniel GILES; s/o & d/o James and Ann GILES.
Anna GILES wife of James GILES departed this life 8 April 1786 and was buried in the family burying ground at Fell Point 11 April.
June 28th 1787 then was Josias HALL of Harford County s/o John HALL of Cranberry and Barthia his wife joined in holy matrimony with Martha GARRETTSON d/o George GARRETTSON and Martha his wife by the Revd. John IRELAND.
September 9th 1788 b. Martha Matilda HALL; April 25th 1790 b. Louisa Elizabeth HALL; October 8th 1791 b. Mary Clarissa HALL; May 19th 1793 b. Avarilla Jane HALL; d/o Josias HALL and Martha his wife. {H-396, OR2-221}
January 19th 1792 Josiah MATHEWS and Jane FORWOOD was joined in wedlock by the Revd. John IRELAND.
1792 October 19 b. John MATHEWS; 1794 August 20 b. Jacob Forwood MATHEWS; 1798 July 6th b. Mary MATHEWS; s/o & d/o of Josiah MATHEWS and Jane his wife.
1791 September 29 m. Jacob GREENFIELD and Elizabeth EVERIST. Their children as follow viz. Poly b. 3 September 1792; Joseph b. 1 January 1794; Martha b. 6 October 1795; Henry Austin b. 30 October 1797; Jacob b. 7 September 1799.
1777 January 20 according to memorandum in registry book were m. John B. HALL s/o John HALL of Cranberry to Sarah HALL d/o John HALL of Swantown. Their children as follow: Hetta b. 24 December 1779; Edward b. 3 July 1781; Cordelia Night b. 17 April 1786; Aquila Beadle b. 14 July 1788.

ST. GEORGE PARISH
VESTRYMEN & WARDENS
v=Vestryman w=Warden r=Registrar

ASHMORE, Frederick r1761
BENNETT, William, w1755-56
BILLINGSLY, James G., v1763
BILLINGSLY, Walter, w1746
BOLSTER, William, w1789
BOYCE, Roger, v1789 1796-97
BOYD, Abraham, w1741
BROWN, James s/o Thomas, w1761
BROWN, John, w1787-88
BROWN, Thomas, v1738
BUCHANNAH, Archible, v1723
BULL, Edmund, v1774
BURCHFIELD, Thomas, w1734-35
BUTTERWORTH, Isaac, w1730-31
CARLILE, John, Maj., v1792 1794-97 1799
CARLISLE, John, v1798
CHANCEY, George, v1763
CHANCY, George, w1747
CHAUNCEY, John, v1796-97 1799
CHAUNCY, George, v1790 1794 1799
CHAUNCY, John, w1790 v1798
CHRISTIE, John, v1772
CHUSTEE(?), Gabriel, r1782
CLARK, John, v1718-21 1726 1729 1734
CLARK, John, w1764
CLARK, Robert, v1737
COLE, John B., 1788
COLE, Skipwith, Capt., v1743
COPELAND, George, w1774 v1776
COPELAND, John, w1780
COWLING, Aaron, r1788
CRANE, David, w1788
CULVER, Benjamin, w1750 v1764
CULVERT (CULVER?), Benjamin, v1765
DALLAM, Josias William, w1773
DALLAM, Richard s/o Richard, v1771
DALLAM, Richard, v1740
DALLAM, Richard, v1768 w1770-71
DALLAM, Richard, v1773
DALLAM, William, r1730-31
DALLUM, William, Maj., v1757
DALLUM, William, v1754
DEACON, Frank, r1787
DEVER, Antil, w1728
DEVER, Richard, Jr., w1735
DORSEY, Frisby, w1796 1799
DORSEY, Greenberry, v1776 1779 1784 1787
DORSEY, Greenberry, Jr., w1755 v1756-57
DRAPER, Leorance, w1723-24
DREW, Anthony, w1748 v1763
DREW, George, v1728 1735
DUNN, Robert, w1761

DURBAIN, John, w1722-23 1733
EVERETT, John, v1759
FARMER, Gregory, Jr., w1736
FARMER, Gregory, v1718 1721-22
FARMER, John, v1766-67
FARMER, John, w1766
FARMER, John, w1779-80
FISHER, James, w1771
FISHER, William, w1753-54 w1763-64 v1779
FORWOOD, Jacob, v1788
FORWOOD, Jacob, w1788-89
FRISBY, R. Peregrine, Capt., v1742
FURNIVAL, Richard, r1729
GALLION, John, v1762
GAYLOR, John, v1725
GARRET, Henry, w1742
GARRETT, Amos, v1757 1759
GARRETT, Amos, v1770-72 v1779
GARRETT, Bennett v1725 v1728 v1734
GARRETTSON, Garrett, v1760
GARRETTSON, George, v1745
GARRETTSON, George, v1754-47 (d.1757)
GARRETTSON, George, w1771
GARRETTSON, James A. v1750
GARRETTSON, John, w1775
GARRETTSON, Richard, w1757-58 v1766
GARRISON (GARRETTSON), Richard, v1768
GARRISON (GARRETTSON), James A. v1750 1754 1756-57
GARRISON, Garrett, v1722
GARRISON, George, w1735
GARRISON, John, w1742
GARRITT, Bennett, v1725 1728 1734
GILBERT, Charles, v1762
GILBERT, Jarvis, v1723-24
GILBERT, Michael, v1729 v1736 v1746 v1798
GILBERT, Michael, Jr., w1796 1799
GILBERT, Samuel, w1745
GILBERT, William, w1729 1736 v1746
GILES, James, r1779
GOVER, Ephriam, v1762
GREENFIELD, Micajah, w1767-68
GREENFIELD, Richard, v1765
GRIFFIN, Luke, v1759
GRIFFITH, (?), v1788
GRIFFITH, Samuel, v1784 1789 1796-99
GRIFFITH, Samuel, w1736
HAAS(?), Samuel, w1729
HALL, Aquila, v1723 1725
HALL, Aquila, r1745 w1756
HALL, Aquila, v1769 1772
HALL, Benedict Edward, v1784 1792 1794 1796-99 ?1773-4 1784 1787-88

HALL, Benedict, v1771
HALL, Dr., v1784
HALL, Edward, Col., v1739 v1760
HALL, Edward, v1722 1732 w1760 1770 v1775 1779
HALL, J. W., v1788
HALL, Jacob, v1772 1799
HALL, James W., v1789
HALL, James, w1787 1791
HALL, James, v1791
HALL, John, v1722-24 1729-31 1744 w1790
HALL, John, Col., v1754 1756
HALL, John, Jr., v1731 w1745
HALL, John, Sr., v1750 1753
HALL, John B., v1788
HALL, John Biedle, v1788
HALL, John of Cranberry, v1757
HALL, John of Swantown, w1745 v1757-58
HALL, Jonas C. Col., v1784
HALL, Josiah, w1776
HALL, Josias Carvil, v1782 w1790 v1792 1794 1797-98
HALL, Josias, v1794 1796
HALL, Parker, v1745-46 v1790 w1793 w1797
HALL, Thomas, v1794
HALL, William, Jr., v1784
HALL, William, w1772 v1784 1787-89 v1971 (d. 1792)
HANSON, John, v1761 1767 w1798
HEATH, James, v1760
HENDERSON, Philip, Dr., v1780
HOLLAND, Francis, v1744 w1769 v1779 v1793 1794
HOLLINGSWORTH, George, w1743
HOLLIS, William, w1721-22 1731
HORTON, William, v1761
HOWARD, Samuel, r1760
HOWELL, Samuel, v1726
HUGHES, Samuel, v 1738 1787-89 1791
HUGHS, William, w1739
HUMPHREY, John, v1727
HUNTER, William, r1733
HUSBANDS, William, v1770 1772 (d.1774)
HUSBANDS, William, Jr., v1759
JENKINS, Francis, w1767-68
JENKINS, J. Francis, w1768
JENKINS, Samuel, w1774
JENKINS, William, Jr., w1757-58
JOHNSON, Joseph, v-1718 1721
JOHNSON, Thomas, w1776
JOLLEY, John, w1769 1771
JONES, Jonathan, w1752
KEEN(E), Pollard, v1750 1754
KEMBEL, Rowland s/o Thomas, v1728
KIMBLE, James, w1765-66
KIMBLE, Samuel, w1759

LEE, Corbin, v1760
LESTER, George, w1740 1752
LONEY, John, w1750 v1759
LONEY, William, w1779
LUSBY, Joseph, v1752
MATHEWS, Bennet, w1787
MATHEWS, James, v1745 1757
MATHEWS, John, w1739 v1744 1750 1754 v1774
MATHEWS, Leven, v1766 1768
MATHEWS, Roger, v1718 1721 1728 1733 1739 (d.1740)
MATHEWS, Roger, v1784
MATTHEWS, Carvil, w1788 1793-94
MATTHEWS, Roger, v1796-97
MIFFIAN, Henry, w1726
MILLER, Henry, w1732
MITCHEL, Richard, w1747
MORGAN, Edward, w1737 w1746 1750 v1751 v1759
MORGAN, Robert, w1775-76 v1782 1784
MORGAN, Samuel, w1762
MORGAN, William, v1776
OGG, Francis, v1730
OSBORNE, Cyrus, w1797
OSBORNE, William, w1762-64
OSBORN, James, w1744 v1747
OSBOURN, Benjamin s/o Wm., w1753
OSBOURNE, William, v1765
OZBOURN, William, v1721
PACA, Aquila, v1726 1730
PACA, Aquila, Jr., v1779
PACA, John, Jr., v1751 1754
PATTERSON, George, v1782
PATTERSON, Robert, w1750 v1760-61
PEW(?), Matthew, v1726
PHILLIP, James, v1789
PHILLIPS, (?), v1787-88
PHILLIPS, James, w1740 1750 1760 v1769-70
PRESTON, James, v1747 1754
PRICHARD, James, w1743
PRICHARD, Obadiah, w1740
PRICHARD, Samuel, w1738
PRIGDON, Alexander, v1779
PRITCHETT, Obediah, w1721
PUSHIN, John, v1723
RIGBEY, Nathan, Col., v1736
RUFF, Daniel, v1727 w1741 1746
RUFF, Richard, v1727 1731 w1734 v1740 1742
RUMSEY, John, v1779-80
SHEPHERD, Rowland, w1725
SHEREDINE, Jeremiah, v1773 (d.1775)
SMITH, Alexander L., v1793
SMITH, Jacob, w1794
SMITH, William, v1728 1731 w1732 v1745 v1753 1782 1784
SMITH, Winstone, v1743

STEWART, James, w1757
STEWART, Mitchel, w1798
STOKES, John, v1722 1724 1725
STOKES, William, v1729
TAYLOR, James, w1737
TAYLOR, James, w1755-56
TOLLEY, Edward Carvil, v1776
TOLLY, John, v1774
VANSUCKER (VANSICKLE?), Henry, v1789
WARD, Edward, v1752 1754 1762 1776 v1778
WARREN, Thomas, v1733
WATERS, Henry, v1769 1771
WEBB, Samuel, w1746 v1750 1755
WEBB, Samuel, Jr., w1773 v1775 1780
WEBB, William, w1759 v1760 1764-65 v1767 1775
WELLS, Richard, w1732-33
WELLS, Richard, Jr., w1754 v1767
WELLS, William, w1772
WHITECAR (WHITACRE), Charles, w1731-33
WHITE, Thomas, v1731-33 1741-42
WILLMOTT, Richard, v1766 1768 1773
WITHERINGTON, Charles, v1735-36
WOOD, Isaac, w1738
WOOD, Joshua, w1730-31 v1737 (d.1740)
WORTHINGTON, Charles, v1754

These names are listed here as they appeared in the original Vestry book.

ST. GEORGE'S PARISH
ABSTRACTS FROM VESTRY PROCEEDINGS

The following was abstracted from the vestry records available, starting with 1721 and following them through to the late 1700s, when the register records are no longer available. The registers pick up in the 1830s, but none have been located between the late 1700s and the 1830s. The vestry proceedings are complete and available for the researcher to examine. The following items were selected because of their personal nature, giving us a glimpse into the lives of some of the parishioners. The following information is by no means all that is available in these records.

The original vestry books are at the Hall of Records, Annapolis, Maryland, volumes A and B. Many original signatures of vestry members are revealed in the originals. A typewritten carbon of the vestry proceedings is available at the Maryland Historical Society in Baltimore under St. Johns's and St. George's combined.

1718: Edward HALL, Esq. is high sherrif.

Whitten Monday, 1721: (Rev. Evan EVANS, Rector) Ann WHITEKER made her appearance before the minister and congregation and admitted her fault and Thomas JACKSON he allowed the same. Sarah DEVER and John HOLLINGSWORTH made their appearance and acknowledged their fault of being the chief instruments of forging the banns of matrimony published betwix Henry WILLIAMS and Susannah STEVENS(?) by the name of Susannah NORRIS. Agreed with Benjamin BROWN to do repair work on the vestry house and church.
Order given to Obediah PRICHARD, upon Edward HALL for the sum of 2548 pounds of tobacco.

23 July 1722: It was agreed with Mr. Robert WEYMAN to officiate as a minister of St. George's parrish.

27 April 1723: Thomas KNIGHT's allowance made for sum of 500 pounds per quarter during his time of his officiating as a "reeder."

May 1723: Was given unto Moses GROOM upon Mr. HOLLAND 3000 pounds, signed John HOAKS and John ROBERT.

21 December 1724: The Rev. Mr. John HUMPHREY produced introduction from the governor.

13 September 1725: This vestry agrees with the Rev. John HOLBROKE to accept him if he brings an introduction from the governor.

4 June 1726: Agreed with Antill DEAVER for work on railing and "To clean and grubb" the churchyard and make a gate.

21 July 1726: Agreed with Mr. Aquila HALL to get locust posts for the churchyard.

4 February 1728: An order to Thomas BURCHFIELD, blacksmith, for hinges for churchyard gates.

7 April 1729: They agreed with Richard FURNIVAL to keep the register and enter the vestry proceedings and to making alphabet to the Register of Births & Deaths & Marriages on the parchment . . . and in fair weather the churchyard by grubbing and burning the leaves and to sweep the church duly each week and to wash it as occasion requires.

15 May 1729: Vestry appointed George DREW to employ and agree with a workman to plaster and whitewash the church.

VESTRY PROCEEDINGS

30 June 1730: Samuel WEBB (present) appointed tobacco counter for the year "from Esq. HALL's Rolling House to Binams (?) Run with the Mane Road . . . from thence to Dear Creek and with the said creek to the Coll. HOLLAND's quarter and so with the Rolling Road to Esq. HALL's Rolling House."
"Thomas MITCHELL being present is appointed tobacco counter from Esq. HALL's Rolling House to Coll. HOLLAND's quarter and from from there north as far as parrish expands taking all the inhabitants on the north side of Dear Creek and so along Susquahannah River to the Main Road and along Main Road to aforesaid Rolling House."
"James DREW appointed tobacco counter for Lower Hundred of Spesify."
30 July 1730: The vestry wants to know if George DREW will go on with his former agreement about plastering the church.
29 May 1731: William HUNTER, James LEE, and William SMITH all elected tobacco counters.
22 August 1733: William HUNTER appointed registrar for the year and the register book for births, burials and marriages is delivered unto his care. He also agrees to wash and sweep the church and make fires in the vestry house.
28 August 1733: Agreed with Mr. Roger MATHEWS that he will build a "chimney in the vestry house beneath the present chimney and beat away the end sill and boards as he has the joyce the breadth of the chimney."
3 June 1734: Two vestrymen are to be elected in room of Edward HALL and Henry MILLAN, who are unable to serve.
25 February 1734: Ordered that Abraham CORD for unlawful communication with Elisabeth HARGAS, Thomas COMBEST and James MORGAN be summoned before the vestry.
4 March 1734: Advertised the sale of Mr. Michael TAYLER's pew. The vestry gave an order to Richard RUFF, Church Warden to demand and receive of David HUGHS, executor of the estate of John ROBERTS, deceased, 925 pounds of tobacco.
An order to Thomas BIRCHFIELD, Church Warden, on Mrs. Susannah STOKES, executrix of John STOKES for 1745 pounds of tobacco.
Mr. BENNETT and John CLARK appointed to view the books of the parish now in the hands of Mr. Stephen WILKINSON.
26 May 1735: Thomas BIRCHFIELD was paid for mending pews and the churchyard gates.
1 February 1736: Summons issued for Mary BROWN, for William BOOZLEY for holding unlawful communication with each other; Jane NORVEL, John NORVEL and James RUTTER summoned for evidence against them.
Summons sent to Abraham CORD to appear and answer for contempt.
Thomas COMBEST was summoned to produce a certificate of his marriage.
Last Saturday in February, 1736: Abraham CORD appeared and "promised never to have any society with Elizabeth HARGAS, nor to admit her to his home nor on any premises belonging to him nor to frequent her company elsewhere."
Mary BROWN and William BOOZLEY "being likewise summoned appeared and promised to refrain all lawful practices.
The vestry summoned Thomas COMBEST, Godfrey VINE, Sarah BEDDO, Robert COLLINGS and Ann SYLBE to appear on Easter Monday next "to answer what shall be objected against them which paid summons are accordingly made out and directed to the church wardens . . ."

VESTRY PROCEEDINGS

11 April 1737, Easter Monday: Thomas COMBEST produced a certificate of marriage with Elizabeth THORNBERRY on 20 November 1734, rites performed by Elisha GATCHELL, Justice of the Peace in the Provence of Pennsylvania.
Robert COLLINGS being summoned, appeared and promised the vestry turn Anna SYLBY away & have no society with her in any respect. Orders given to Gregory FARMER, church warden, "To enquire whether Godfrey VINE and Sarah BEDDO cohabit together still."
6 June 1737: Then was William BOSSLEY (BOOZLEY), Mary BROWN, Robert COLLINGS and Ann SILBE (SYLBE) returned to court for not "separating and refraining from each others company according to promises made to the vestry."
5 July 1737: Godfrey VINE and Sarah BEDDO appeared but could not prove their marriage. The vestry allowed them until the last Saturday in July to procure a certificate.
Samuel F. GRIFFITH and David SISK agreed with the vestry to cover the vestry house and mend a hole in the closet.
4 October 1737: A certificate of marriage was produced of Godfrey VINE's marriage with Sarah BEDDO. They were married by Rev. James COX, minister of St. Paul's parish in Queen Anns County 14 February 1733.
25 February 1737: Joshua WOOD is appointed to hire a carpenter to mend the church, yard and gates.
Easter Monday, 3 April 1738: James TAYLER was paid for bread and wine for sacrament days.
2 May 1738: Agreed with William COOK to repair the church and new addition.
Then was Patrick KILMURRY and his wife summoned to inform the grand jury what they knew to be unlawfully actions between Abraham CORD and Elizabeth HARGAS.
1 August 1738: Summons sent to Thomas PHELPS and Rose wife and Mark FORD; and likewise another for William RICHARDS to appear and given to Isaac WOOD, church warden, to execute.
26 August 1738: "Thomas PHELPS and Mark FORD being summoned to appear at the vestry, did appear and both of them declared to the vestry that they have been married to her that is next called Rose PHELPS. SWIFT was first married unto her and she eloped from said SWIFT and after said PHELPS declares that he was married unto her the said Rose on the 28th of May 1710."
5 June 1739: Samuel PRICHARD paid for bread and wine.
7 October 1740: Notice given to elect vestryman in the room of Joshua WOOD, deceased.
16 October 1740: Summons sent for Samuel HOWELL, Robert BOWDEN, John SPURGEN, Jno. WOOD. (Reason not given.)
3 November 1740: Mary BAULKM appeared according to summons. "Robert BOWDEN appeared, was examined by the vestry and gave evidence concerning Mary BAULKAM, whereupon she was acquitted by the vestry."
2 December 1740: James PHILLIPS qualified as vestryman in the room of Roger MATTHEWS, deceased.
2 March 1740: Summons ordered for Lydda JOHNSON and James ROW and "sent to Captain COLE and offer evidence against the said ROW and JOHNSON."
5 January 1741: Summons ordered to "Thomas PAWMER to shew charges why he unlawfully cohabits with." (name not given)
2 February 1741: Daniel RUFF, church warden, excused as sick. Thomas PAWMER, being summoned, appeared.

VESTRY PROCEEDINGS

1 February 1742: Several books belonging to "this parochial library, which books were in the custody of the Rev. Stephen WILKINSON, minister to parrish, are or cannot be produced by the said gentleman and likewise the plantation he liveth on is gone mightily to decay." The vestry asked Mr. WILKINSON to appear to explain the condition of the Glebe and "the eldest vestrymen will wait on Mr. WILKINSON to take an act of this library belonging to the parish and view the plantation . . ."

11 April 1743: Summons to Samuel HUGHS, Thomas and Ann LITTON and John and Isaac LITTON and Elisabeth PRICHARD, James PHILLIPS, Col. Thomas WHITE, Maj. John HALL and Capt. Peregrine FRISBEE "went to wait on the Rev. Stephen WILKINSON, but he heard of their coming and went out of the way."

7 February 1743: Sherwood LEIGH (LEE) agreed to take the office of Sexton.
James PRICHARD appeared to his summons and refused to qualify as church warden of this parish.

20 February 1743: "Then came Capt. Skipworth COALE and alleged that he is joyned to the people called Quaker and that it is required by the vestry that he shall produce a certificate from the vestry then from Deercreek Meeting setting forth that he is joyned to the monthly meeting at Nottingham."
Vestry resolved to enter an action against the Reverend Stephen WILKINSON unless he produces the books belonging to this parish.
George HOLLINGSWORTH appeared to his summons and refused to qualify for church warden of this parish.

26 March 1744, Easter Monday: Elders of the vestry met and agreed to acquaint the governor of the problems with Rev. WILKSINSON and to request him "not to induct another minister disagreeable to the parishoners."

3 April 1744: "Sherwood LEIGH (LEE) brought two books, which said books were in the possession of Rev. Steven WILKINSON and now lodged in the chest with the other books."

2 October 1744: Rev. Hugh CARLILE produced induction from the Governor of Maryland.

7 May 1745: "Aquila HALL is to re-transcribe the register. (Both registers, old and the new one mentioned here are in the Hall of Records, Annapolis, Maryland. In his so re-transcribing, our assumption is that many original spellings of last names were changed to the spellings in use in 1745 by the same family. Throughout this book we have used original spellings whenever possible.)
Sherwood LEIGH (LEE) will be Sexton for the coming year.

26 June 1745: James STEWART to be Sexton for the coming year.

31 March 1746, Easter Monday: Summons for James CAIN and Ann SPRICER to appear.
Summons for John NORVIBAND and Mary JACKSON to appear.

6 May 1746: Samuel WEBB chosen church warden in the room of Edward MORGAN, who refused to serve.
Summons ordered for Moses, Thomas and Alexander SPENCER to appear as evidence against Dr. WAKEMAN and James TAYLOR.

3 June 1746: Summons for Henry O'NEAL and Sarah HENNEYSE to appear. (Henry O'NEAL appeared 5 August and was discharged by putting Sarah away.)

26 June 1746: Summons for Thomas LYTTLE (LITTLE) and Sarah HUGHS.
Summons for Abraham CORD and Elizabeth HARGUES to appear.

VESTRY PROCEEDINGS

3 November 1746: Thomas LITTLE and Abraham CORD appeared and were discharaged by putting away Sarah HUGHS and Elizabeth HARGUES.
20 April 1747, Easter Monday: Agreed with John HALL of Cranberry to keep the plate and linen belonging to the church clean for the year.
17 August 1747: Mr. Joseph CHEW refused to qualify himself being "a Quaker."
2 February 1747: Appeared Thomas BROWN, woodcutter, to his summons and promised to turn away Mary GORDON immediately.
12 April 1748: Appeared Peter WOOLF to his summons and was discharged, putting away his housekeeper.
3 May 1748: John PREBLE paid for wine.
6 July 1748: Summons issued for William NORVIL & Sarah CANTWELL.
14 October 1748: John MATHEWS, Hudson DAVIDGE, Michael GILBERT and Daniel RUFF chosen tobacco inspectors.
1 April 1748: Summons for John THOMAS and Elizabeth TOOLSON.
3 October 1749: Rev. Mr. Andrew LANDRUM produced an induction from his excellency, Samuel OGLE, Esq. Governor of Maryland. Michael GILBERT, Richard DALLAM, Daniel PRESTON inspectors.
1 May 1750: Agreed with Aquila HALL to carry a petition to the assembly . . . to build a church and chapel.
3 September 1750: Inspectors for Swan Creek chosen and Rock Run Warehouses, Michael GILBERT, Richard DALLAM, James GARRETTSON, and Samuel WEBB.
16 September 1750: Agreed that a new church should be built on land given by James PHILLIPS, Esq. to the dimensions given. Summons for Joseph JACKSON for unlawfully cohabitating with Ann COAL.
30 October 1750: Alexander HALL and Edward MORGAN "according to the trust reposed in them, agreed upon two acres of Mr. JENKINS and one of Mr. James LEE's, convenient for the parish and for wood and water and good burying ground."
"Then came Mr. John HALL of Cranberry and William BENNETT to undertake the building of church and chapple."
13 November 1750: Summons issued for John GIANT to appear for unlawful cohabitation with ____. (No name given.)
Summons issued to John THOMAS and Elizabeth TOOLSON.
8 April 1751: Abraham CORD appeared and was convicted for being drunk and was fined.
7 May 1751: "Summons issued to Joseph JACKSON for illicit cohabitating and affirmed he was married out and had no certificate nor proof thereof."
John THOMAS, Elizabeth TOWLSON (TOOLSON), John GIANT and Ann TOULSEN not found by the church warden.
30 March 1752: Benjamin CULVER paid for wine.
5 May 1752: Two deeds for land for the chapel from Mr. LEE and from John LUNN.
Summons Joseph JACKSON unlawful cohabitation with Ann COAL.
11 August 1752: Inspectors chosen: Richard DALLAM, Michael GILBERT, Richard JOHNSON and James PRESTON.
26 December 1752: Summons for Samuel HOWELL to appear; summons for Robert CARLILE to appear to testify for his Lordship against Samuel HOWELL.
4 September 1753: Inspectors chosen: Richard DALLAM, Michael GILBERT, Ephiram GROVER and George GARRETTSON.
First Tuesday in October 1753: William PRIGG to enclose the chapel.
5 February 1754: John PACA, Jr. to mend the door, etc.

VESTRY PROCEEDINGS

1754: "The vestry then proceeds to business and as this day was appointed for the sale of the chappel pews do value them as follows:" Pollard KEENE purchased No. 2 & No. 3; No. 3[sic] William BENNETT for himself and one other; No. 6 Ed MORGAN; The purchasers of the pews are to have eight months credit. The vestry agrees to pay John PACA Jr. to procure a sexton for the chapel.
26 August 1754: William FISHER paid for two bottles of wine.
10 September 1754: Inspectors chosen: Richard DALLAM, Michael GILBERT, Ephraim GOVA and George GARRETTSON.
2 December 1754: Resolved that Col. William YOUNG settle his accounts for the parish since his being sherrif.
12 October 1755: Maj. William DALLAM to send for three prayer books and one Bible.
First Tuesday in May, 1756: Thomas HAWKINS and Mary JONES appeared according to summons for unlawfully cohabitating together and said HAWKINS and JONES were admonished "by the vestry to quit their viccious courses and discharged."
Second Tuesday in June, 1756: Capt. John HALL agrees to "make burn and deliver on the place where the church is to be built bricks . . ."
27 July 1756: "The vestry proceeds to business and qualified according to act of assembly and made out a list of bachelors." James MATHEWS, Bennett NEAL, William OSBORN, Luke GRIFFITH, James KIMBALL, John KIMBALL, John PEACOCK, Garrett GARRETTSON, Robert STOKES, Phillip GOVER, Samuel HIGGENS, Robert M. GAY, Aq. NELLSON, Gervis GILBERT, Isaac WEBSTER, Aquilla JOHNS, Edward HORNIBY, William JENKINS, George BOTTS, John MOULTON, Benjamin NILLSON, William HUEBANDS [sic] (HUSBANDS?), Jr., John JOLLY, John HENSON, Henry RUFF, John BENNETT, John LOVE, William JOHNSON, Samuel WELLS, William ASHMORE, Samuel WALLICE, James BILLINGSLEY, Bennett NEAL, James ARMSTRONG, Amos HOLLIS, John GALLION, Isaac DUTTERWORTH and (?) MAXWELL son of David MAXWELL.
Agreed with William GARRETT to pay one half of the expense of digging walling and putting in a pump in a well at the chapel after the parish church is built.
9 August 1756: "The following bachelors certificate as exempt from the tax imposed by act of assembly viz. John KIMBALL, Aquilla NELLSON, Amos HOLLIS, and John GALLION and William ASHMORE having a certificate from Mr. LANDRUM that he was married before last vestry expt."
John WOOD produced his account for mending the church, which Maj. William DALLAM paid him.
8 September 1756: Inspectors chosen: Richard DALLAM, Michael GILBERT, Ephriam GROVER and George GARRETTSON.
11 April 1757, Easter Monday: First payment made to John HALL of Cranberry towards payment for the bricks for the new church. George GARRETTSON, former vestryman, is mentioned as deceased.
30 May 1757: Agrees with John DEVER son of Antill to pay him to lay the bricks.
27 June 1757: The bachelors above the age of 25, the following persons are liable to the said tax: James MATHEWS of S. Lower, William OSBORN of Susquahanna; Garret GARRISON (GARRETTSON), John PEACOCK, James KIMBAL, John KIMBAL all of Spes. L.; Phillip GOVER of Susquahanna Hundred, William HUSBANDS and James LEE, Jr. of Dear Creek; Isaac WEBSTER, Jr. of S. Lower; Henry RUFF of S. Upper; Samuel WALLACE of D. Creek; James BILLINGSLEY, Jr. of S. Upper; James ARMSTRONG and Robert M. GAY

VESTRY PROCEEDINGS

of S. Lower; John BENNETT and John GALLION; Samuel HIGGINSON of Susquahanna Hundred; George BOTTS and John MOULTON; John Tolly FORGEMAN of Deer Creek; John HANSON; John LOVE of S. Upper; William JOHNSON; MAXWELL son of David MAXWELL of Deer Creek; Henry WATERS of S. Lower and Michael WEBSTER, Jr. of S. Upper. James STEWART produced his account for which he had an order on David MC CULLOCK, sheriff.

11 July 1757: Took proposals of Benjamin CHEW and Aquila JOHNS and Benjamin CULVER fordoing the carpenterwork and to complete the church. John DEVER gives in his proposals for plastering.

18 July 1757: Summons issued for Rachel STOCKS to testify again, Sam SUTTON and Ruth CANTWELL to appear.
Summons for Morris DEXON (?) and Drusilla CHANDLEY to appear.
Agreed with Samuel WALLACE to build the church.

9th day (?) 1757: Samuel WALLACE offers William HOPKINS and Phillip GOVER his security for building the church.
Summons issued for John RICHARDSON and Lidia WANSAL to appear.
Summons issued for William PILE and Jane HUGHS to appear.
Bennett NEAL produced a certificate that he is not worth 100 pounds and not liable to pay the bachelor tax.
John LEVER gives Benjamin CULVUR (?) as his security.

6 September 1757: Michael GILBERT, Edward WARD, Ephriam GOVER and James TAYLOR named inspectors for Swan Town and Rock Creek warehouses.

28 November 1757: Richard REASON summoned to endeavor to acquit himself of a slanderous report of him concerning his daughter, who is also summoned.
Summons ordered for Nathan SMITH and Nathaniel LAZZEL and John JOHNS, also wife of Richard REASON to testify and also for George CHANEY.

26 June 1758: Batchelors liable to pay tax: James MATHIAS(?), William OSBORN, Garret GARRETTSON, John PEACOCK, James KIMBALL, Phillip GOVER, William HUSBANDS, James D. LEE, Isaac WEBSTER, Jr., Samuel WALLACE, James BILLINGSLEY, James ARMSTRONG, Richard JOHNS, Samuel HILL, John WEBSTER son of Isaac, John GALLION, George BOTTS, John AOULTON (?), John Jolly FORGEMAN, John Hanson FORGEMAN, John LOVE, William JOHNSON, Maxwell son of David MAXWELL, Michael WEBSTER, Jr.

16 October 1758: Summoned George SMITH and --- NORTON to appear.

19 June 1759: "The vestry proceeded to business and taxes the undermentioned as bachelors: William OSBORN, Garrett GARRETTSON, John PEACOCK, James KIMBLE, Philip GOVER, William HUSBANDS, Jr., James LEE, Jr., Isaac WEBSTER, Jr., Samuel WALLACE (WALLIS), James BILLINGSLEY, Jr., Jacob GILES, Jr., Richard JOHNS, James HILL, Joseph HILL, John Lee WEBSTER, John WORTHINGTON, John LOVE, Benjamin NELSON, James MATHEWS, Thomas HUSBANDS, John GALLION, John MOULTEN, William JOHNSON, David MAXWELL, Richard WEBSTER, Jr., James CRESWELL & Samuel WILSON."

6 July 1760: "Undermentioned persons taxed as bachelors." Same as list above except Jacob GILES, Jr. does not appear on the list and the following new people are added: George CLARKE, Josiah LYONS, William WOOD, Robert DUNN, John COOPER, Thomas COOPER, Stephen COOPER, John WILKINSON, David TATE, David MAXWELL, Joseph BROWNLEY, Michael WEBSTER, Jr., Joseph WILSON, James CRESWELL, Edward HANSON, Francis BILLINGSLEY, Richard KEENE, Richard DALLAM, Jr., Robert BRIERLY son of Robert.
Joseph CLANCY produced his account for sweeping and cleaning the chapel.

VESTRY PROCEEDINGS

The vestry chose Samuel HOWARD to officiate as registrar in room of Mr. Amos GARRETT, who declines serving.
21 October 1790: The vestry sold tobacco to Mr. Robert ADAIR.
2 December 1790: Notice given to Samuel WALLACE to finish the church. On 23 December he agreed to put springs to the sashes of the windows.
25 February 1761: Mr. James CHRISTIE, Jr. appointed to send for two "pulpot cloths, one cushin and 800 foot of flagg."
23 March 1761, Easter Monday: Frederick ASHMORE appointed sexton of the chapel over Deer Creek and as registrar.
7 July 1761: Undermentioned persons liable to pay the batchelors tax: The list is as the previous with the following exceptions: Garrett GARRETTSON, Joseph HILL, Stephen COOPER, John WILKINSON and Richard KEENE no longer appear. New entries are: Moses HILL, Nathaniel GILES, Charles WORTHINGTON, Jr., Robert DARBY, Samuel PERRIMAN, James FOSTER, William HILL & William MC CLURE. Mr. Robert PATTERSON's account paid "for numbering the pews doors of the church with paint allowed."
"The reg. is ordered to acquaint Dr. A. STENHOUSE to clear the old church away immediately according to former agreement."
13 July 1762: Bachelor's taxed same as previous list but the following no longer appear: William OSBORNE, Philip GOVER, Samuel WILSON, Robert DUNN, Nathaniel GILES, Robert BRIERLEY son of Robert, Robert DARBY, and Samuel PERRIMAN. New names on the list include: Dr. James SPAVOLD, Samuel GRIFFITH, Nathan NORTON, Jacob ALLEN, Edward WALLIS and James KENNEDAY.
29 June 1763: Bachelor tax list: William HUSBANDS, Thomas HUSBANDS, Thomas RIGBIE, John RIGBIE, John WORTHINGTON, Joseph WILLSON, Samuel WILLSON, Joseph HOPKINS, Jeremiah SHEREDINE, Josiah LYON, David CLARK, Joseph BROWNLY, William MC CLURE, John JOHNSTON, John LOVE, John COOPER, John Thomas COOPER, Nicholas COOPER, Natt. John GILES, John HUSBANDS, Richard JOHNS, Hosea JOHNS, James BILLINGSLY, John HALL son of Col., John Lee WEBSTER, Aq. PACA, John PEACOCK, John CLARK, Dr. James SPAVOLD, James KIMBLE, William HALL, Isaac HUMBLE, James MATHEWS, Samuel GRIFFITH, Samuel PERRIMAN, William FISHER, W. Richard DALLAM, Philip COAS son of William, George DAUGHTERY, John BRIARLY, Samuel SMITH, John BURK, James CANADA, Andrew WILLSON, John RUTH and David HANNER.
24 August 1763: Robert DUNN produced his account for cleaning the well at the chapel. William PRIGG produced his account for repairing the yard at the chapel and for makinga new "upping block."
6 September 1763: William HOPKINS, Edward WARD, Charles GILBERT and John GALLION appointed inspectors.
23 April 1764, Easter Monday: James STEWART sexton and Robert DUNN sexton at the chapel.
12 June 1764, Whitsun Tuesday: Summons for John TOKER to appear for unlawful cohabitation with a negro woman belonging to Capt. James PHILLIPS.
11 June 1765: Francis DEACON appointed sexton at chapel.
21 June 1766: Mr. Benjamin CULVER to build the vestry house. Capt. John HALL of Cranberry paid for keeping the church plate.
2 September 1766: Messers. (Garrett) GARRETTSON, William HOPKINS, Richard GARRETTSON and Thomas RENSHAW chosen as inspectors.
14 October 1766: Benjamin CULVER given order on high sherrif for tobacco per agreement. James STEWARD produced account for serving as sexton. William WEBB, Rev. Andrew LENDRUM and John FARMER all agree to pay fines for not attending meetings.

VESTRY PROCEEDINGS

11 November 1766: Summons issued for Saverell(?) HARDEN and Elizabeth PRICE to appear for unlawful cohabitation. Summons Henry THOMAS, Sr. for an evidence.
16 March 1767: Summons Peter HENLEN and Sarah COLLINS for unlawful cohabitation and likewise Benjamin CROSS; also for John CLARK for evidence.
Agrees to give John HENRY 14 shillings a day to carry a return to the governor regarding inspectors.
20 April 1767: Peter HELEN (HENLEN) and Sarah COLLINS appeared and "the vestry agreed upon proviso they would never cohabit together any more," they were discharged.
Mr. George PATTERSON will serve as sexton for the ensuing year.
Mr. William WEBB produced account for serving as sexton at the Chappel in 1759, for which "he made appear never was paid."
5 May 1767: Garrett GARRETTSON produces a certificate "from under John MATHEWS hand where said MATHEWS qualifies as inspector for 1767."
The sexton to layout the burying grounds and to receive 2/6 per each grave and to dig and attend the same.
8 September 1767: Garrett GARRETTSON and William HOPKINS as inspectors.
6 October 1767: Summons issued for Henry BEACH, etc. for unlawful cohabitation and summons Jane BEACH for evidence.
Tuesday, February 1768: Edward GARRITTSON and John HENRY nominated as inspectors for Swan Creek in room of Garrett GARRETTSON, deceased. Appoints George PATTERSON to settle vestry's account with Robert ADAIR, late sheriff.
John FARMER produced account for expenses at the "chapple".
23 February 1768: "Martha JOHNSON complains against her sister Elizabeth JOHNSON and Patrick BRANNON for unlawful cohabitation and summons issued for same."
3 May 1768: George PATTERSON produced account for serving as sexton and 25 shillings cash for going to Baltimore Town to settle vestry's account with Mr. Adair, late sheriff.
Micajah GREENFIELD account for keeping church plate, etc.
5 September 1768: Miss Sophia GARRETTSON produced a bond from vestey in Pa. currency and had an order on Richard DALLAM for tobacco. Richard GARRETTSON refuses to sign the note to Sophia GARRETTSON.
George REED produced account for mending & putting of glass in gallery windows.
Francis DEACON produced account for serving as sexton at chapel for two years.
29 November 1768: Benjamin G. CULBERT shall repair the church windows. Abraham GUYTON produces account for "toxing a ladder".
29 February 1769: Aquila HALL delivers account for 3 years of his sheriff's office as follows "viz. tobacco shipment on board of Capt. MC DOUGALL to Messers. STEWART and CAMPBELL 6398 pounds of tob. . . . and likewise the alter cloths and flag stone."
Miss Sophia GARRETTSON gives up the vestry's note payable to her.
23 March 1769: Samuel GRIFFITH produces account for serving as clerk. Capt. John HALL of Cranberry produced account for books and keep, etc. for church windows.
27 March 1769: Richard DALLAM produced account for 2 books, which he got for the vestry.
Rev. Mr. Andrew LANDRUM has undertaken the sexton's place for this year for a person who he is to mention to dress the church 3 times a year with green bows according to custom and to keep

VESTRY PROCEEDINGS

large fires when necessary, and the church to be clean and in proper order.

27 June 1769: Micajah GREENFIELD produces account for keeping church plate and sacrament expenses. Samuel GRIFFITH's account received for serving as clerk. Francis DEACON's account for washing the "cirplus," etc. Capt. John HALL of Cranberry account for making a ladle and chain for the use of the parish. Vestry sells the chimney in the old vestry house to Mr. Samuel BULL.

5 September 1769: Chooses Charles GILBERT and John GALLION inspectors for Swan Creek; Edward WARD and Richard WELLS inspectors for Rock Run.

5 March 1770: Summons Paul GADDISS and Margaret McCOOBS and Henry BEACH and Elizabeth DIXON and Morriss DIXON and Drewsilla CHANLEY for unlawful cohabitation.

21 May 1770: Paul GADDISS appears to summons and denies his "cohabiting with Margarett MC COOB." James ARMSTRONG was qualified as a witness and "said the widow MC COOB did appear very bukikey and it is said that she is with child. Likewise George STEWART being examined declares its the common report the said MC COOL[sic] is with child on which the vestry agrees to return them to court."
Henry BEACH and his wife appeared and declared that she had reason to believe he did unlawfully cohabit with Elizabeth DIXON "upon which said BEACH to appear at the next vestry and bring a certificate from under the hands of his neighbors that they have parted."
Edward MORGAN appointed sexton.

4 June 1770: Henry BEACH produces "a certificate by Samuel SMITH, Jane SMITH and Robert HAWKINS that Elizabeth DIXON has left his house and they do not think they cohabit together at present."
The vestry agrees that Paul GADDIS and Margarett MC CALL[sic] should be presented to the grand jury for cohabitation.

5 February 1771: Summons issued for Jacob COVENTRY, Hannah FINNEY, Richard BROWN, Joyner and Catherine SMALL, James KILPATRICK and Barbarah THATCHER, Anthony DURANT and Elizabeth PARR, all to appear for unlawful cohabitation.

15 April 1771: Complaint made against Henry BEACH and Elizabeth DIXON for cohabitation.

7 May 1771: Agrees with William COALE to repair the chapel. Francis DEACON produces his account as sexton and had an order on Dr. Alexander STANHOUSE.

6 September 1773: Samuel GRIFFITH produced account for serving as clerk and for sacramental expenses.

23 May 1774, Whitsunmonday[sic]: Capt. John MATHEWS "through his infirmities refused to serve as vestryman." The vestry agreed to build a "Brick Vestry house at St. George's Chapel. . . 24' long & 20' wide; 8' foundation to be made of stone, the walls to be a brick and a half thick and to be covered with cyprus shingles and to have a pine floor." Mr. Jeremiah SHEREDINE and Mr. Edmund BULL to agree with workmen to complete the above work. Benedict Edward HALL and Francis HOLLAND to employ some persons to do the roof.

18 October 1774: "Amos GARRETT, Esq. is to inquire whether the deed for the land where the chapel stands on has been legally recorded or not."

VESTRY PROCEEDINGS

James FISHER and Robert CHRISTIE, Jr., present accounts for sacramental expenses in 1772. William WILLIAMS paid for serving as sexton last year.
17 November 1774: Michael GILBERT appointed inspector for Swan Creek warehouse; Edward WARD, Sr. appointed inspector for Rock Creek warehouse on the Susquehanna.
Summoned Abraham TAYLOR and Martha WHAYLAND on suspicion of illegal cohabitation.
William PERKINS and Sarah DURBIN on notice given them by Mr. SHEREDINE "and being admonished by the Vestry agree to separate and to remove all cause for further suspicion."
Summons issued for Thomas WAMMAGHAM and Ann SOWARD (HOWARD?) to appear on suspicion of illegal cohabitation.
William HUFMAN produced his account for mending pews.
6 December 1774: Thomas WAMMAGHAM produced a certificate that he was married by John DAVIS to Ann DULANY 27 November 1774.
23 June 1775: Abraham TAYLOR and Martha WHAYLAND refused to appear.
Francis HOLLAND presented account for benches, and "had an order on Thomas MILLER, Esq. for same."
1 August 1775: Edmund BULL will furnish the parish with an Iron Ladle and Chain 8' long to be fixed at the church spring. John GARRETTSON to prepare 4 horse blocks and place them at each corner of the church yard. Samuel WEBB, Jr. to furnish 2 padlocks to lock the gate.
8 February 1776 at Harford Town: Edmund BULL gave account for making a pair of andirons and tongs and shovel.
11 September 1776: Joseph DAVIS produced account for expenses on the well in the chapel.
27 March 1780, Easter Monday: Francis DEACON delivered church plate, tablecloth and napkin to Mr. Edward HALL.
3 July 1780: Ordered that Col. Francis HOLLAND settle with John WATKINS for the rent of the Glebe.
4 June 1781: Dr. Jacob HALL chosen in room of Amos GARRETT who declined to qualify.
3 September 1782: James WOOD of the Glebe removed from being a tenant under WATKINS.
1 April 1782, Easter Monday: Church plate, etc. delivered to the care of Dr. Philip HENDERSON.
6 May 1782: Coll. Jonas C. HALL is desired to employ Samuel KIMBEL to survey the Glebe land. Samuel GRIFFITH and William SMITH are empowered to rent the Glebe land.
17 May 1784: Mr. COTTINGHAM presented account for serving as clerk and sexton.
21 June 1787: Gave order to Mathew SNOWDY(?) for repairs to the church. Allowed money to Mr. SNIDER per Sunday as organist.
19 July 1787: Mr. W. HALL appointed Treasurer and ordered to pay Captain BOYER for freight of the organ from Baltimore to Havre de Grace and pay Barry CAHILL's bill for work done to the organ and church windows.
7 February 1788: Treasurer ordered to pay balance due Mr. SNYDER organist. John DEBRULAR appointed sexton.
21 March 1788: Capt. Roger BOYCE appointed Treasurer.
17 April 1788: Benedict E. HALL appointed to represent parish at the convention at St. Paul's, Baltimore on 4th Tues., May next.
21 May 1791: Peter RODINHEISER appointed sexton. Settled with Dr. Jacob HALL for expenses for attending the convention.
6 April 1792: Subscription put in hands of William BOLSTER and Thomas MITCHEL for collection.

VESTRY PROCEEDINGS

9 April 1792: William HALL, vestryman mentioned as deceased.
6 May 1793: Gabriel CHRISTIE to attend convention as a lay member.
21 April 1794: Roger BOYCE to attend convention as a lay member.
5 January 1795: Rented Glebe to Amos CORD for one year.
4 April 1796: Appointed Rev. Mr. John ALLEN as Rector.
2 May 1796: William DALLAM to attend the convention held in Easton on Thursday the 19th instant. Mr. RUMSEY declined to serve as church warden.
5 September 1796: Distribution of the seats in the church: No. 1: John CARLILE, Roger BOYCE and Michael -----; No. 2: Messrs. ALLENS & Co. & Doct. J. HALL; No. 9. B. E. HALL; No. 11: John CHANNCEY; No. 29: Dr.Samuel GRIFFITH, L. GRIFFITH, Col. S.--; No. 30: Parker HALL, H. RUMSEY, Frisbey DORSEY, Benjamin TOWLAND and John DALLAM. No. 25: Aquila NELSON.

PEW HOLDERS OF ST. GEORGE'S PARISH
ca 1770

"The Distribution of the Seats in St. George's Church according to their Number in which according to a rule and agreement of the Vestry Respect. was had to Each mans Contribution or Number of taxes and had Either his Choice or Seat accordingly the most honourable Number given to the highest Number of taxes where they did not Chuse It otherwise."
{H-1}

No. 9: Colnl. John HALL; Francis HOLLAND.
No: 3: Capt. John HALL; ditto LALLY(SALLY?) for his Cranberry Plantation; Sarah WEAKEMAN.
No. 30: John HALL, Sr. the Esq.; Mr. James HEATH.
No. 31: Capt. James PHILLIPS; Mr. Edward HALL; Mr. Bennet MATHEWS.
No. 28: Capt. Aquilla HALL, Esq.; Jacob GILES for his wife; Colnl. Thomas WHITE.
No. 27: Capt. John MATHEWS, Esq., Leven MATHEWS; Peregreen PRISBEY, Amos GARRET.
No. 10: Widow RISTAU for son Samuel dito CHRISTY; Robert ADDAIR; James CHRISTY.
No. 11: Capt. John PACA for Black Wallnut; Widow PACA for her sons; Josep LUSBEY.
No. 12: Thomas TREDWAY; William HORTON; Thomas LITTLE; John HENERY; Greenberry DORSEY; Joseph PENTONY(?); Thomas HENDERSON.
No. 4: Major William DALLAM, his two sons Richard & Joseph & Doctor STENHOUSE; Robert PETTERSON.
No. 29: Martha GARRETSON, widow of George for her family; Luke GRIFFITH; Sam BUD.
No. 5: John LONEY; Anthony DREW.
No. 35: "for Strangers and Capts. of Ships &tc."
No. 6: James & William OSBURN; James BISSET; Richard WILLMOTH.
No. 34: Widow GRIFFITH for her son Samuel & Family; Benj. HENSON; John WOOD.
No. 2: Andrew LENDRUM for his family &tc.; Dr. Henry STEPHENSON; Dr. Ben CROCKET.
No. 7: George CHANCEY; Widow BISSET; James TAYLOR.
No. 33: James STEWARD; James THOMSON; James TAYLOR, Jr.
No. 18: Jacob & John HANSON; Wm. GREENFIELD
No. 19: Widow LISTER for her family; John DEAVER, Christopher SHEEPERD.
No. 13: Wm. DAUGHERTY; Robert, Sam, Wm., James & Stephen RYMBALLS(?); Michael Thomas TAYLOR.
No. 14: Widow RUFF now RICHARDSON for Ruffs & Richardsons; family Thomas BROWN, Jr.; James & Absolem BROWN; Nicholas BAKER; Thomas & Jacob CORD; THomas GILBERT; Jas. SAUNDERS.
No. 32: James John & Garret GARRETTSON.
No. 8: Edward GARRETTSON; Thomas BROWN, Sr.; James BROWN, son of Thomas.
No. 1: "The Rectors for the time being."
No. 17: Nathaniel SMITH; Arthur INGRAM; William JENKINS; George BRADFORD.
No. 20: Widows BRADFORD, OSBURN & EVERRET WEST(?)
No. 16: MITCHELS, Thomas, Sr. & Jr.; Edward William & KENT.
No. 15: Ben DAVIS; The JACKSONS; The CHENEYS; John ATKINSON;

Joseph GORDON.
No. 26: For overseers their wives & single taxes.
No. 25: Aquilla NELLSON; Ben CULVERT; Archibald JOHNSON; William HUGHS; Adam BURCHFIELD; William BURTON; Sam. PRICHARD.
No. 23: Richard MORRIS; Tim MURPHEY; Wm. ditto; John LOW; John & William OSBURN; Henry KNIGHT; Rubin PERKINS.
No. 24: Ford, John & James BARNS; James ALLEN; Thomas HENDERSON; Taylor, Robert CRUTE; Abraham ROBINSON; Widow ROBINSON; William ARNOLD; Henry GARLAND; Forgeson TANNER (?).
No. 21: Richard MONK; Francis SHODEY; Thomas BRISCO; Abraham SPRUSBANK.
No. 22: William PERRY; Sam. MC CARTY; Jacob & John COMBEST; Moses COLLENS.

Those that are omitted: If there be any are to be added to such Seats as are Lest frequented according to their contribution. Bro't from Old Book A, April 16, 1770.

{H-170} "A list of the Members of the Protestant Episcopal Church and of St. George's Parish March 13th 1800. Those marked thus + no parishioners."

+Michael GILBERT, Jr.
+John CARLILE, Dec'd.
+William BULL, discont'd
+William ALLEN & Co. no parish'r
Jacob HALL
+Joshua WOOD discont'd.
+Roger BOYCE
+Jacob FARWOOD Dec'd.
+Samuel GRIFFITH Dec'd
+Frisby DORSEY Dec'd
+Elijah DAVIS no par'r
+Alexander L. SMITH Dec'd
+William LOVEY/LONEY Dec'd
+Richard RUFF discont'd
+John DALLAM, left the Parish
Josias HALL
Winston SMITH
+George CHAUNCEY, Sr. Dec'd
+John B. COLE
+Roger MATTHEWS Dec'd
+James OSBORNE Dec'd
+Benedict Edward HALL discont'd
+Lewis GRIFFITH Absentee & Dec'd
+John CHAUNCEY, Dec'd
Aquila NELSON
+Parker HALL
+James MICHAEL
+Jacob GREENFIELD Dec'd
+Stephen KIMBLE Dec'd
+David CRANE Dec'd
Benedict HALL
John FORWOOD
Edward HALL
George CHAUNCEY
Benedict HENSON
Isaac PERRYMAN
+Roger BOYCE no par?

+Cyrus OSBORNE
Thomas SHAY
+James TAYLOR
+John HALL, Dec'd.
+Carvel MATTHEWS, Dec'd
+Paca SMITH no parish'r
+Ashbury TAYLOR
+Nathaniel HENDERSON Dec'd.
+William BEATTY, Dec'd.
+Ephraim ARNOLD
+John H. RUFF
Jacob BROWN
+John WOOD
+Francis L. PITT
+Michael STEWART Dec'd
+Henderson PIKE Dec'd
+Gab. CHRISTIE, Dec'd
Richard SAPPINGTON
Samuel JAY
William S. DALLAM
John NELSON
John JOLLEY
David E. PRICE
Walter Tolley HALL
+John MYERS
Jacob MICHAEL
Stephen CRANE
Henry VANSIDE
Henry DENNISON
+William HALL no par?
Thomas COURTNEY
William HOLLEY
William LAWDER
William OSBORNE
Thomas SHAY
Jacob Washington GILES
John N. GRIFFITH

John BUDD
Crispin CUNNINGHAM

William KNIGHT (near H. D. Grace)

OATHS

{H-173} "We whose names are underwritten do declare that we believe in the Christian Religion, March 25th 1799:

Vestrymen March 25th 1799

John ALLEN, Rector; Michael GILBERT, Jr.; Samuel GRIFFITH; John CARLILE; John CHAUNCY; George CHAUNCY; Jacob HALL.

May 6th, 1799

Frisby DORSEY; Benedict Edward HALL. Aquila NELSON & John B. COLE; Wardens. Paca SMITH, Roger MATHEWS. David CRANE & Carvel MATHEWS; Wardens. John B. COLE, William LOVEY; Joshua HOOD, W. S. DALLAM; Jacob FORWOOD; William SMITH; Aquila NELSON; Josias HALL; Isaac PERRYMAN; George CHAUNCEY; J. W. GILES; Edward GRIFFITH.

{H-174} "We the undersigned do swear that we do not hold ourselves bound to yield any allegiance or obedience to the King of Great Britain, his Heirs or Successors and that we will be true and faithful to the State of Maryland, and will to the utmost of our powers support, maintain and defend the freedom and the independence thereof and the Government as now established against all open Enemies, and secret and traiterous corrspiracies, and will use our utmost endeavours to disclose and make known to the Governor, or some one of the Judges or Justices thereof, all treasons or traiterous conspiracies attempts or combinations against this State or the Government thereof, which may come to our knowledge. So help us God!"

The above was signed by : VESTRYMEN: John CARLILE; Michael GILBERT, Jr.; John CHAUNCEY; Joshua WOOD, Samuel HUGHES; Benedict Edward HALL; James White HALL; William HALL; Samuel GRIFFITH; Greenberry DORSEY; James PHILLIPS. CHURCH WARDENS: John BROWN; BENNET MATHEWS; Paca SMITH. Francis DEACON, Register. George CHAUNCEY. (undated)

Same, dated April 17th, 1788: John Beedle HALL, Vestryman; Jacob FORWOOD, Church Warden; David CRANE, Church Warden; Carvil MATHEWS & John B. COLE, Church Wardens.

Same, dated August 5th 1790: George CHAUNCY, Vestryman; Parker HALL, Church Warden; Josias Carvil HALL.

Same, dated April 1, 1793: Fras. HOLLAND, Vestryman; Alexander Lawson SMITH, Vestryman. May 25th, 1805: J. W. GILES, Vestryman. December 26, 1805: Edward GRIFFITH. May 4th 1807: Benedict HALL. May 1st 1809: Edward HALL. July 2d 1810, R. W. HALL. 2d November 1812 David MCCLOSKEY, William P. PATTERSON, Hosea BARNES, John CHAUNCEY.

INDEX

ADAIR, Robert 109, 110
ADAMS, James 96
  John 96
  Mary 96
ADDAIR, Robert 114
ADKINS, John 30
ADKINSON, Ann 77
  Ann (SHEPHERD) 46
  John 30, 46
ADKISSON, Ann 50
AGON, Ellinor 83
AISHFORD, Mary (COX) 47
  Rachel 7
  Thomas 47
AISHLE, Elizabeth 7
  John 7
  William 7
AISHLEYS, Elizabeth 7
ALEXANDER, Elizabeth 88
  James 88
  Lydia 88
  Lydia (JONES) 88
  Rachel 88
ALGOOD, Lidia 6
ALLEN, Ann 9
  Elizabeth 25, 79
  Elizabeth (JONES) 79
  Isabel 32
  Jacob 109
  James 32, 67, 76, 115
  John 36, 116
  John, Rev. 113
  Joseph 25, 41, 45, 54, 56, 79
  Josias 73
  Margaret 25, 32, 68
  Mary 29, 30, 36, 41, 45, 48, 50, 56, 67, 73, 76
  Mordecai Hanby 76
  Susanna 29
  William 29, 30, 36, 41, 45, 48, 50, 56, 67, 73, 79, 115
  William Millin 76
  Zachariah 50, 79
  Zacharias 48
AMBOY, Mary 16
AMOS, Hannah (CLARK) 42
  James 42
  Robert 43
AMOSS, Hannah 43
  James 43
ANCHER, Alice (BATTS) 54
  Lawrence 54
ANDERSON, Charles 30, 35, 42, 52, 60
  Daniel 35
  Grace 35, 42, 52, 64
  Grace (PRESTON) 30

ANDERSON, Margaret 35, 52
  Martha 31
  Sarah 30
ANDREWS, Nathaniel 4
ANHOUSIN, Elizabeth 62
ANNUS, Ruth (KERSEY) 44
  William 44
ANSHOR, Ruth 67
ANTIL, Jane 55
AOULTON, John 108
ARMSTRONG, Elizabeth (BARNS) 78
  James 107, 108, 111
  Joshua 32, 78
  Margaret 53, 78
  Margaret (BARNS) 78
  Martha 71
  Mary 32, 46, 53
  Sarah 32
  Soloman 32, 78
  Solomon 46, 53, 78
ARNAL, Elizabeth 42, 56
  Johannah 42
  William 42, 56
ARNEL, Elizabeth 63
  Fanny 63
  William 63
ARNOLD, Comfort (COURTNEY) 82
  Elizabeth 25, 26, 35, 48, 68, 80
  Elizabeth (GILBERT) 35
  Ephraim 82, 115
  Johanna 75
  Joseph 80
  Martha 68
  Mary 29, 35
  Mrs. 13
  Sarah 48, 80
  Sarah (SMITH) 68, 69
  Thomas 25, 68, 69
  William 25, 26, 35, 48, 68, 69, 80, 82, 115
ARPIN, Ann (MACFARLOE) 49
  Francis 49
ASELWORTHY, Charles John 82
  Linnah 82
ASHFORD, Hannah 10
ASHMORE, Bridget (AYRES) 85
  Elizabeth 38, 57, 85
  Frederick 85, 109
  James 67
  John 85
  Magaret 50
  Margaret 57, 63, 67, 84, 85
  Rebecca 50
  Susannah 85
  Susannah (O'NEAL) 84
  Walter 50, 57, 63, 67, 84

ASHMORE, William 84, 85, 107
ASSEL, Nathaniel 80
  Sarah (JACKSON) 80
ASSELL, Martha 80
  Michael 80
  Nathaniel 80
  Sarah 80
ASWLWORTHY, Blanch 82
ATKINSON, John 114
AUCHARD, Sarah 87
AYRES, Abraham 61, 88
  Bridget 61, 85
  Elizabeth 88
  Mary 61
AYRS, Benjamin 63
  Mary 63
  Thomas 63
BADHAM, Richard 37
  Sarah 37
  Thomas 37
BAILEY, Aquilla 82
  Benedict 82
  Charles 52, 82
  Elizabeth 52
  Joseph 82, 86
  Margaret 86
  Sarah 52, 86
BAKER, Ann 4, 5
  Benjamin 75
  Christian 39
  Elizabeth 46
  Elizabeth (CANNON) 50
  George 85
  Hannah 39
  Joshua 85
  Joshua Wood 84
  Martha 69, 74, 75, 85
  Martha (WOOD) 66
  Mary 46, 67, 95
  Mary (CRAWFORD) 40
  Morris 39
  Nicholas 66, 69, 74, 75, 85, 114
  Nicols 95
  Providence 69
  Susannah 95
  Thomas 40, 46, 67
  William 50, 67
BALCH, Dorothy 24
  Hezekiah 24, 25
  James 24
  John 25
  Martha 24, 25
  Mary 24
  Thomas 24
BALE, Ann (PLUMMER) 17
  Anthony 17
  Ewrah 14
  Mr. 13

BALE, Mrs. 14
BALEY, Josias 82
BALLS, Rachel 33
BARKEY, Margaret 82
BARNES, Cassandra 80
  Elizabeth 89
  Ford 45
  Gregory Farmer 45
  Hosea 116
  Margaret 45
BARNS, Amos 92
  Anna 53
  Arrabella 80
  Avarilla 92
  Bennett 80
  Bethiah 70
  Bethiah (LONEY) 34
  Bethyah 41, 52, 64
  Bothya 83
  Cassiah 45
  Constance 45, 47, 55, 58, 67
  Constant 23, 24, 33
  Constant (WEST) 23
  Elisabeth 47
  Elizabeth 16, 33, 39, 47, 78, 89
  Elizabeth (MITCHEL) 92
  Ezekiel 78
  Foard 22
  Ford 16, 23, 27, 30, 33, 39, 53, 59, 69, 70, 74, 75, 80, 92, 115
  Grigory 92
  Hannah 30
  James 27, 33, 34, 41, 52, 53, 64, 70, 83, 115
  Jamima 78
  Jemimah 34
  Job 23, 24, 33, 45, 47, 55, 58, 63, 74, 78
  John 33, 34, 89, 115
  Joseph 16
  Margaret 23, 24, 27, 30, 33, 39, 53, 59, 69, 70, 74, 78
  Margaret (FARMER) 22
  Martha 69, 70
  Mary 64, 78
  Mary (CRAWFORD) 78
  R'th 92
  Rachel 41, 78, 92
  Richard 64, 80, 92
  Ruth 75, 80
  Ruth (GARRETT) 70
  Thomas 55
  William 21, 52
BARRETT, Edward Bedle 58
BARTLE, Margaret 48
  Mary 48, 59
BARTON, James 80

BARTON, Joanna 80
Lewis 80
BASHTEEN, Lidia (ALGOOD) 6
William 6
BASTEENE, Mary 6
William 6
BATTS, Alice 54
BAUCHAM, John 24
Mary 24
Nicholas 24
BAULCH, Ann 60
Elizabeth 60
James 60
John 49
Mary (CANNON) 49
BAULICK, Ann (GOODWIN) 50
James 50
BAULKAM, Mary 104
BAYLES, Abigal 96
Augustine 96, 97
Elizabeth 97
John Brown 97
Samuel 96
BAYLEY, Charles 44, 62, 71, 73
Cotteril 44
Henry 28
Joanna 27
John 22, 23, 27, 28, 38, 62
Joseph 73
Lucy 22, 23, 27, 28
Lucy Ann 46
Margaret 71
Mary 22, 48
Richard 60
Sarah 44, 62, 71, 73
BAYSHER, Elizabeth 43
Sarah 43
Thomas 43
BEACH, Henry 110, 111
Jane 110
BEARDY, Christian 30
BEASLEY, Elizabeth 25
BEATTY, William 115
BEAVER, Blanch (DULY) 64
Francis 64
Henry 26
John 26
Mary 26
Michael 26
William 26
William, Jr. 64
BEDDO, Sarah 103, 104
BEDDOE, John 26
Sarah (LITTEN) 26
BEDFORD, Sarah 6
BEECH, Elizabeth 70
Elizabeth Voss 24
Henry 62, 66, 70
Jane 66, 70

BEECH, Jane (GARVIN) 62
Thomas 66
BEECHAM, Ann (BURTON) 48
John 48
BEESLEY, Johannah 39
William 39
BEEZLEY, Elizabeth 36
BELCHER, John 10, 49
Mary 49
Ruth 16
BELL, Ann 53
BELLROES, Annah (THOMPSON) 20
Christopher 20
BELSHER, Ruth 59
BENNETT, (?) 103
Amelia 97
John 107, 108
Pamelia 97
Phillip 97
Victor 97
William 99, 106, 107
BENNINGTON, Constant 79
Elizabeth 79
Henry 30, 31, 37, 79
Job 79
John 37
Moses 30
Nehemiah 79
Sarah 31, 37
Sarah (HARRIS) 30
Thomas 30
William 31
BENTLEY, Elizabeth
 (BUTTER/BUTLER?) 50
William 50
BEVER, Sarah 46
BEVINGS, Thomas 6
BEVON, Elizabeth 3
John 2
Mary 1
Thomas 1, 2, 3
William 1
BICARD, Anna Mary 30
Christianah 30
Elizabeth 30
Henry 30
BIDDER, George 33
John 33
Joseph 33
Sarah 33
BIGNALL, Rebecca 47
BILLINGSBY, Sarah (LOVE) 66
BILLINGSLEY, James 107, 108
James, Jr. 107, 108
BILLINGSLY, James 109
James G. 99
Walter 99
BIRCHFIELD, Ann (CLARK) 48
James 41

BIRCHFIELD, Mary 41
  Robert 48
  Sarah 61
  Susannah 87
  Thomas 41, 61, 103
  Thomas, Jr. 61
BIRNEY, Robert 95
BISHOP, Avis 53
  Avis (GINKINS) 46
  Elizabeth 87, 89
  Evas 87
  Eviss 56
  Frances 87
  Hannah 89
  Jonathan 89
  Mary 89
  Prudence 89
  Rachel 89
  Roger 46, 53, 56, 87
  Samuel 87
  Sarah 56
BISIT, Ann (ADKINSON) 77
  David 77
BISSET, James 114
BISSETT, Ann 86
  David 86
BLACK, Elizabeth 53, 56
  Elizabeth (WILSON) 46
  James 53
  Peter 46, 53, 56
  Thomas 56
BLACKISTON, Avarilla
  (GARRETTSON) 95
  Elijah 95
BOIS, Elizabeth 59
  John 59
BOLSTER, William 99, 112
BOND, Alis 32
  Ann 65, 78
  Charles 61
  Elianer 61
  Elianor 53
  Elizabeth 68
  James 53
  John 53
  Susanna 61
BONNER, Arthur 92
  Christianh (INGRAM) 92
  John 92
  Martha 92
  Sarah 92
  William 92
BONNEY, Peter 20
BOORIN, Charles 4
  Mary 4, 5
  Sara 4
  William 4, 5
BOOTHBY, Edward 4
  Elizabeth 5

BOOZLEY, William 103, 104
BOREN, Mary 34
BORING, Mary 17
BOSSLEY, William 104
BOTTS, Abraham 54
  Avarilla 67
  George 32, 107, 108
  Isaac 58
  John 32, 44, 54, 58, 65, 67
  Mary 67
  Sarah 44, 54, 58, 65, 67
  Sarah (WOOD) 32
BOULTON, Ann (HIGGINSON) 60
  Charles 60
BOWDEN, Robert 104
BOWDEY, Mary 67
BOWEN, Edward 72
  Mary 72
  William 72
BOWING, John 22
BOYCE, Elizabeth 26, 27
  Hannah 26
  John 26, 27
  Johnson 27
  Mary 26
  Roger 99, 113, 115
  Roger, Capt. 112
BOYD, Abraham 55, 99
  Hester (BUTTERWORTH) 55
BOYER, (?), Capt. 112
BOYTON, Elizabeth (GENKINS) 61
  Jonathan 61
BRADALL, Edward 20
  Martha 20
  Mary 20
BRADFORD, Elizabeth 66
  George 114
BRADLEY, Ann 47, 88
  Elizabeth 47, 88
  Mary 47, 64
  Thomas 47
BRADY, Sarah (HILLIARD) 66
  Terrence 66
BRAGG, Hannah 23
  Sarah 23
BRANACAN, Phillip 6
  William 6
BRANDIGAN, Hugh 14
BRANICAN, Elizabeth 9
  Phillip 9
  Susannah 9
BRANNAGHAN, Hugh 15
  Phillip 15
  Susanna 15
  Susannah 15
BRANNAN, Phillip 5
  Susanna (THOMAS) 5
BRANNICAN, Edward 13
  Elizabeth 11

BRANNICAN, Phillip 11, 13
　Susan 13
　Susanna 11
BRANNON, Patrick 110
BRASHER, Elizabeth 77
　Peter 77
　Thomas 77
BRASHIER, Aquilla 65
　Elizabeth 32
　Jane 22, 23, 26, 33
　Richard 22
　Sarah 23, 32, 65, 72
　Thomas 32, 65, 72
　William 22, 23, 26, 32
BRASYEAR, John 6
　William 6
BRAYSHER, Elizabeth 37
　John 51
　Sarah 51
　Sarah (CONSTANCE) 37
　Thomas 37, 51
　William 37
BREADLEY, Jane 47
BREEDEN, Rebecca 87
BRIARLY, Eleazer 75
　Hugh 75
　Isabella 64
　John 109
　Rebecca 75
BRICE, Ali 87
　Barnet 87
　Elizabeth 65
　Elizabeth (ANHOUSIN) 62
　James 67, 73, 87
　John 87
　Margaret 87
　Mary 73, 87
　Mary (JOHNSON) 67
　Samuel 62, 73
　Thomas 73
　William 87
　Xtian 87
BRIERLEY, Robert 109
BRIERLY, Catharine 39
　Catherine 53
　Hugh 73
　John 39, 53, 73
　Margaret 64
　Mary 39, 65
　Rebecca 73
　Robert 64, 108
BRINDLEY, Constance 88
　Elizabeth 88
　Jane 88
　Mary 88
　Nathaniel 88
　Rachel (SPENCER) 88
　Sarah 88
BRISCO, Thomas 115

BRISCOE, Margaret 90
BRITTAIN, Ann 38
BROOKE, Clement 96
　Sarah 96
BROWN, Absolam 28, 29, 38, 40,
　46, 57, 60
　Absolem 79, 83, 114
　Absolom 9
　Absolum 90
　Amellia 56
　Ann 41, 53, 60
　Ann (CUTCHEN) 40
　Augustus 16, 24, 40, 41, 53,
　60
　Avarilla 90
　Avarilla (OSBORNE) 85
　Benjamin 102
　Blanch 1, 11, 35
　Catherine 90
　Eliza (MORGAN) 83
　Eliza. 91
　Elizabeth 13, 17, 24, 29, 31,
　62, 67, 81, 84
　Elizabeth (BROWN) 88
　Elizabeth (COURTNEY) 82
　Elizabeth (SICKELMORE) 13
　Frances 26
　Francis 11, 23
　Freeborn 72
　Gabriel 16, 34, 36, 53
　Gabril 24
　Garrald 66
　George 38, 40, 83
　Hannah 57, 81
　Hester 53
　Jacob 53
　James 2, 19, 20, 43, 73, 81,
　83, 88, 90, 94, 99, 114, 115
　John 13, 17, 24, 31, 36, 40,
　58, 62, 68, 71, 81, 84, 99,
　116
　Joseph 85, 90
　Margaret 14, 53, 83, 90
　Margaret (CONSTANCE) 62
　Margaret (HANSON) 79
　Mark (SKELTON) 14
　Martha 90
　Martin 67
　Mary 8, 9, 11, 13, 15, 17, 19,
　21, 28, 31, 36, 53, 57, 58,
　60, 62, 67, 81, 103
　Mary (CORD) 46
　Mary (KEAN) 34
　Peregrine 17
　Rebecca 79
　Richard 13, 29, 111
　Sam 13
　Samuel 1, 2, 8, 9, 11, 14, 15,
　17, 19, 28, 31, 53

BROWN, Sarah 31, 38, 40, 43, 52, 56, 58, 60, 62, 66, 72, 79, 81, 90, 94
  Sarah (JOHNSON) 73
  Sarah (SHEPARD) 29
  Susan 79
  Susana 93
  Susanna 68, 71, 81, 84
  Susanna (HIGGINSON) 60
  Thomas 8, 13, 31, 40, 43, 52, 56, 60, 62, 66, 68, 71, 72, 82, 84, 88, 94, 99, 106
  Thomas, Jr. 114
  Thomas, Sr. 114
  William 29, 60, 62, 90
  Zachriah 31
  Zackariah 21
BROWNE, Sarah 96
BROWNLEY, Arthur 67
  Joseph 108
  Margaret 67
  Thomas 67
BROWNLY, Joseph 109
BRUCEBANKS, Abraham 79, 83
  Ann 81
  Blanch 80
  Catherine 80
  Edward 80
  Frances 81
  Francis Og 80
  Martha 83
  Mary 80, 83
  Mary (JACKSON) 80
BRUSBANKS, Abram 90
  Jane 90
  Mary 90
BRYAN, Ann (VEARES) 10
  Daniel 10
BRYERLEY, Catharine 46
  John 46
  Robert 46
BUCHANNAH, Archible 99
BUCHANNAN, Archabel 11
  Mary 11
BUCHANNON, Archabel 12
  Mary (TREBBLE) 12
BUCHER, James 59
  Mary 59
BUCKANNA, Anne (ROBERT) 31
  Archibald, Jr. 31
  Archibald, Sr. 31
BUCKNAL, Blanch 45
  Blanch (BROWN) 35
  Elizabeth (GRIFFIS) 7
  Francis 35, 45
  James 45
  Judith 35
  Mary 43
  Thomas 7, 35

BUCKNALL, Blanch 62
  Francis 13, 62
  Mary 13
  Thomas 13
  William 62
BUCKNEL, Elizabeth (BURK) 12
  Tho. 12
BUD, Sam 114
BUDD, George 94
  John 115
  Martha 94
  Milcah (YOUNG) 94
  Samuel 94
  Sarah 94
BUILBERT, Elizabeth 13
BULL, Ann 84
  Edmund 95, 99, 111, 112
  Elizabeth 84
  Esther 95
  Isaac 84
  Jacob 95
  John 84, 95
  Mary 45, 95
  Rachel 95
  Richard 84
  Samuel 111
  Susana (LYEN) 95
  William 115
BULLOCK, Elizabeth 45
  James 26, 27, 45
  Mary 45
  Mary (JOB) 26
  Sarah 27
BUNN, Elizabeth 1
BUR, Mary 12
BURBIN, Avarilla 20
  John 20
BURCHFIELD, Adam 20, 25, 29, 34, 90, 115
  Ann 90
  Ann (NELSON) 90
  Aquila 56
  Elizabeth 20, 75
  Elizabeth (MACARLEY) 25
  Elizabeth (TURNER) 81
  Frances 25
  Hannah 65, 90
  Johannah (CANTWELL) 22
  John 29
  Joseph 34
  Mary 14, 20, 25, 29, 34, 38, 75, 90
  Mary (JOHNSON) 28
  Mary (WILSON) 14
  Prissilla 90
  Robert 14
  Sarah 56, 65, 75
  Sarah (GASH) 51

BURCHFIELD, Thomas 14, 15, 20, 22, 25, 28, 29, 34, 56, 75, 81, 99, 102
  Thomas, Jr. 51, 65
BURGEN, Ann 89
  Catherine 89
  Dennis 89
  Isaac 89
  James 89
  John 89
  Mary 89
  Thomas 89
BURIDGE, Frances 71
BURK, Easter (PINE) 10
  Elizabeth 12
  Henry 10
  John 109
BURNETT, Thomas 51
BURNEY, Jane 84
BURROUGH, Elizabeth 20, 24
  Richard 20, 24
  Sarah 24
BURROWS, Tho. 12
BURTHEL, Mary 1
BURTON, Ann 48
  Francis 70
  Jane 70
  John 69
  Mary 70
  Mary (HARGAS) 69
  William 70, 115
BUTCHER, Elizabeth (EASTWOOD) 63
  Elizabeth (ESTWOOD) 65
  James 63, 65
  Mary 65
BUTLER, Elizabeth 50
BUTLERS, Mary (BURTHEL) 1
  Thomas 1
BUTTER, Elizabeth 50
BUTTERAM, Ann (LYAL) 72
  Isaac 72
  Jacob 58
  Jane 58
  John 58, 72
BUTTERS, Frances 2
  Thomas 2
BUTTERWORTH, Benjamin 72
  Charity 62, 72
  Elizabeth 36, 72
  Esther 10
  Francis 19
  Hannah 19
  Hester 19, 55
  Hesther 19
  Isaac 10, 19, 31, 36, 43, 62, 72, 99, 107
  Isaac, Jr. 29
  Isaac, Sr. 29

BUTTERWORTH, Jane 31, 36, 62, 72
  Jane (WHEELER) 29, 72
  Jean 43
  Mary 19, 29, 31, 72
  Sarah 43
BUTTUM, Elizabeth 35
BYFOOT, Sarah 22
  Thomas 22
  William 22
CAHELL, Mary 9
CAHILL, Barry 112
CAIN, Ann (SPICER) 73
  James 73, 105
CAMBELL, Ann 49
  James 49
  John 49
CAMMEL, Ann 73
  Ann (JOHNSON) 44
  John 44, 73
CAMPBEL, Ann 62
  John 62
  Phebe 62
CAMPBELL, (?) 110
CANADA, James 109
CANNADAY, John 35
  Mary (ARNOLD) 35
  Rachel 35
CANNON, Ann 34
  Charity 36
  Elizabeth 35, 50
  Frances (JOHNSON) 36
  Hannah 36
  James 34
  John 34
  Mary 36, 49
  Mary (BOREN) 34
  Rachel 35
  Robert 35
  Sarah 34, 35
  Sophia (JOHNSON) 35
  William 1, 36
  William (WILLING) 1
CANTWELL, Adam 63
  Blanch (JACKSON) 71
  Edward 5, 7, 8, 9, 21, 28, 29, 34, 38, 48, 55, 56, 61, 71
  Elizabeth (M'KIM) 85
  Francis 49
  Hannah 34
  Joan 8, 9
  Joan (CHATTUM) 5
  Johanna 83
  Johannah 22, 44, 48
  John 38, 44, 49, 56, 63
  Luce 7
  Lucian 8
  Lucy 7, 38, 61
  Mary 28, 44, 56, 63

CANTWELL, Nicholas 85
  Ruth 55, 79, 108
  Sarah 28, 29, 34, 38, 55, 61, 106
CAPLE, Mary 10, 11
  Thomas 10
CARLIEL, William 6
CARLILE, Hugh Rev. 105
  Hugh, Rev. 77
  John 99, 113, 115, 116
  Robert 106
CARLISLE, Elizabeth 84
  John 99
CARLISS, Ann 35
CARRAGAN, Alice 46
CARRINGTON, Alce 39
CARROLL, Catharine 43
  Catherine 58
  Edward 43
  Katharine 43
  Mary 43
  Mary (RENSHAW) 14
  Mordicai 43
  Peter 14
CARSON, Elizabeth 78
CARVIL, Avarilla 21
  Mary 17
CASELTINE, Ailse 96
  John 96
  Mary 96
CASSADY, James 43
  Mary 43
CASSIDY, Cathrine 81
  Elinor 81
  Simon 81
CASTLY, Mary 9
CAVE, James 40
CAWTHREY, Isabel (ALLEN) 32
  John 32
CHACE, Thomas, Rev. 92
CHAMBLEY, John 13
  Margery (CHEEK) 13
CHANCEY, George 99, 114
  Sarah 81
CHANCY, George 10, 14, 48, 58, 70, 74
  James 14, 74
  Mary 70
  Sarah 14, 48
  Susan 74
  Susanna 58
  Susannah 48, 70
CHANDLEY, Drusilla 108
CHANEY, George 12, 108
  Ruth 81
CHANLEY, Drewsilla 111
CHANNCEY, John 113
CHATHAM, Francis 31
  Henry 31

CHATHAM, Mary 31
CHATTAM, Edmund 34
  Francis 34
  Henry 34
  Mary 34
CHATTO, Jane 53
CHATTUM, Joan 5
CHAUNCEY, George 115, 116
  George, Sr. 115
  John 99, 115, 116
CHAUNCY, George 43, 99, 116
  John 99, 116
  Susannah (OGG) 43
CHEAPMAN, Hannah (MARKUM) 7
  John 7
CHEEK, Margery 13
CHEETAM, Elizabeth 4
  Francis 4
CHENEY, (?) 114
CHERN, John 3
  Wilks 3
CHEW, Benjamin 108
  Elizabeth 77
  Joseph 106
CHISNAL, Thomas 15
CHISNALD, Elinor 16
  John 16
CHISNALL, Elinor 15
  John 15
CHITCHING, Ann 16
CHRISTIE, Charles 77, 86, 96
  Charles James 86
  Cordelia 86, 87, 97
  Cordelia (STOKES) 77
  Gab. 115
  Gabriel 96, 97, 112
  Gabriell Charles 77
  James, Jr. 109
  John 99
  Priscilla 97
  Priscilla (HALL) 96
  Robert, Jr. 111
CHRISTY, James 114
CHUSTEE, Gabriel 99
CLAARK, Ann 48
CLANCY, Joseph 108
CLARK, Ann 34, 70
  Annaple 62
  David 109
  Elizabeth 16, 20, 34, 40, 42, 49
  Elizabeth (CLARK) 15
  Elizabeth (DRAPER) 17
  Elizabeth (SMITHSON) 42
  Frances 20, 42
  George 39, 42
  Hannah 22, 42, 50, 56, 62, 73, 94
  Hester 42

CLARK, John 15, 17, 20, 50, 56,
  62, 73, 94, 99, 103, 109, 110
  Margaret 34, 50
  Martha 16
  Mary 14, 26, 42, 50, 75, 83
  Matthew 34
  Robert 18, 20, 22, 26, 32, 39,
   42, 70, 99
  Sarah 32, 42, 73
  Sillina 39, 70
  Sillinah 20, 32
  Sillinah (SMITH) 18, 42
  Silvana 26
  Sophia (LESTER) 94
  Syllina 42
  William 32, 42
CLARKE, George 108
CLEGG, Ann 69
COAL, Ann 106
  Mary 33
COALE, Skipworth 105
  William 111
COAS, Philip 109
  William 109
COB, Margaret 34
COBB, Charity 18
  Frances 34
  James 14, 18, 19, 67
  Joseph 67
  Margaret 18, 67
  Mary (POGE) 67
  Presilla 34
  Rebecca 18, 19
  Rebecca (ERNSTON) 14
  Ruth 67
COCKEY, Joshua 21
COLE, (?) Capt. 104
  Casandra 69
  Comfort 57, 82
  Elizabeth 44, 82
  Ephraim 82
  George 36, 49
  Henry 49
  James 44, 82
  Jane 82
  Jane (POLOKE) 82
  John 64
  John B. 99, 115, 116
  Margaret 64
  Martha 49
  Martha (LITTEN) 36
  Mary 64, 69
  Phillip 53, 64
  Sarah 53
  Sarah (GILES) 47
  Skipwith 64
  Skipwith, Capt. 64
  Skipworth 69, 99
  Thomas 44

COLE, William 47, 53, 64
COLEMAN, Mary 11
COLIT, Anne 15
  Catharine 15
  Michael 16
  Samuel 15
COLLENS, Moses 115
COLLET, Daniel 26
  John 15
  Ruth 26
COLLIER, Mary 39
COLLINGS, Ann 38, 68
  Francis 38
  George 68
  Jemima (JOY) 55
  Moses 38
  Robert 55, 68, 103, 104
COLLINS, Ann 25, 43, 44, 53
  Cassandra 83
  Ephraim 83
  Francis 25, 43, 44, 53
  Geres 43
  Hannah 53
  Jacob 83
  Johanna (CANTWELL) 83
  John 83
  Mary 83
  Moses 83
  Patience (POWELL) 83
  Samuel 83
  Sarah 26, 44, 83, 95, 110
  Sarah Powel 83
  Silence 25
  Susanna 83
  William 83
COLLYER, Ann 8
COLMAN, Elizabeth 11
COLSON, Benjamin 8
COLSTON, Henry 67
  John 50, 67
  Rebecca 50, 67
COMBEST, Abigell 6
  Annah Lury 18
  Cassandra 74, 95
  Elisabeth 52
  Elizabeth 57, 62
  Elizabeth (GILBERT) 95
  Ettie 95
  Israel 71, 94
  Jacob 21, 69, 71, 74, 95, 115
  John 1, 3, 7, 18, 62, 67, 95,
   115
  Josiah 52
  Ketturah 1
  Keziah 57
  Martha 7, 21, 71
  Mary 3, 67, 71, 74
  Mary (BOWDEY) 67
  Mary (SOLAVAN) 69

COMBEST, Sarah 1, 16, 33
  Sarah (COLLINS) 95
  Susannah (PERRYMAN) 94
  Thomas 52, 57, 62, 67, 95,
    103, 104
COMPTON, Joseph 14
  Margaret 21
  William 14
CONNOLLY, Alice 89
  Ann 89
  Barnaby 89
  Catherine 89
  Eleanor 89
  Mary 89
  Rosannah 89
  Sarah 89
CONSTANCE, Elizabeth 45
  John 45
  Margaret 62
  Sarah 37
  Susanna 45
  Susannah 54
CONSTANT, John 37
  Susannah 37
  William 37
CONSTANTE, Margaret 37
  Susanah 37
COOB, Christian 33
COOCK, Sarah (GARRETT) 15
  William 15
COOK, Ann 51
  Ann (BRUCEBANKS) 81
  Elizabeth 27, 82
  Hannah 62
  James 51
  Jeremiah 27, 81
  John 1, 27, 33, 39, 45, 51
  Martha 51
  Mary 27
  Presilla 33
  Richard 27
  Robert 39
  Sarah 21, 27, 32, 33, 39, 40,
    45, 82
  Sarah (WEST) 27
  William 1, 21, 27, 32, 40, 104
  William Minor 40
COOLEY, Alice 47
  Edward 47, 55, 56, 71
  Elizabeth 47, 55, 56, 71
  John 47
  Mary 71
  Rachel 56
  Warner 55
COOPER, Alce 24
  Alce (GILL) 23
  Alice 42
  John 23, 24, 42, 108, 109
  John Thomas 109

COOPER, Nicholas 109
  Priscilla 24
  Prisilla 24
  Samuel 33
  Sarah 33
  Stephen 42, 108, 109
  Thomas 42, 108
COPELAND, George 99
  John 99
CORD, Abraham 7, 23, 29, 30,
    40, 41, 103, 104, 105, 106
  Amos 56, 94, 113
  Aquila 94
  Ashberry 65
  Elizabeth (COOK) 82
  Greenberry 94
  Hannah 5, 10, 13, 15, 17, 18,
    19, 52, 82, 94
  Hannah (MATHEWS) 1
  Hannah (MATTHEWS) 2
  Isaac 15, 29, 40, 52
  Jacob 17, 82, 114
  James 40
  Luhannah 47
  Martha 43
  Mary 19, 41, 43, 46, 47, 56,
    65
  Mary (PRITCHARD) 41
  Mary (WILLIAMS) 32
  Phebe 41
  Rebecca 23, 29, 30
  Rebeccah 40
  Roger 13, 82
  Ruth 23, 30, 32
  Sarah 5
  Stinchcomb 29
  Susanna 15, 18, 82
  Susannah (KIMBEL) 94
  Thomas 1, 2, 5, 7, 10, 13, 15,
    17, 18, 19, 32, 41, 47, 56,
    65, 114
CORTNEY, Abigale 48
  Rowland 48
COSLE, James 3
  Margaret 3
  Mary 3
  William 3
COSLEY, Mary 61
  Mary (ELLIS) 14
  William 14
COSTLEY, Elinor (CHISNALD) 16
  Elizabeth 16
  James 16
  Mary 16
COSTLY, Alce 29
  James 29
  John 29
  Margaret 29
  Mary 9, 29

COSTLY, Susanna 29
  Thomas 29
  William 29
COTRALL, Deborah 46
  Elizabeth 21
  Isabella 46
  John 21
  Sarah 21
COTTAIN, William 22
COTTAM, William 22
COTTERILL, Sarah 21
COTTINGHAM, (?) 112
COTTREL, Elizabeth 4
  John 4
COURTNEY, Abigail 41
  Abigal 58
  Comfort 63, 82
  Comfort (COLE) 57
  Elizabeth 63, 71, 82
  Frances 63, 71
  Frances (GREENFIELD) 58
  Francis 67
  Hannah (COOK) 62
  John 58, 63, 67, 71
  Jonas 57, 63, 82
  Rachel 63
  Robert 41, 58, 62
  Rowland 41
  Thomas 82, 115
  William 67
COVENTRY, Jacob 111
COWDERY, Mary 28
COWEN, Elizabeth 55
  Elizabeth (BOND) 68
  Elizabeth (WOOD) 74
  Hannah 74
  John 54, 61, 68, 74
  Martha 64
  Susanna 54
  William 74
COWIN, John 63
  Mary 61
  Sarah 61
  Susanna 63
COWING, Edward 25
  Elias 27
  Elizabeth 20
  John 17, 20, 23, 25, 27
  Martha 20
  Sarah 17
  Susanna 20, 22, 23, 25, 27
  Susanna (TEAGUE) 17
  Thomas 22
  William 23
COWLING, Aaron 99
COWLY, Sarah 97
  Thomas 97
COX, James, Rev. 104
  Mary 47

CRABTREE, Ann 34
  Mary 32, 39
  Thomas 39
CRAFFORD, Elias 11
  Elizabeth 11
  James 11
CRAFOOT, Geenet 14
  James 14
CRAMPTON, Mary (CASTLY/COSTLY?) 9
CRAMTON, Joseph 9
CRANE, David 99, 115, 116
  Stephen 115
CRAWFOOT, James 40, 57
  Rachel 57
  Sarah 40, 57
CRAWFORD, Frances 18
  Francis 18
  Hannah 27, 31
  James 18, 24, 27, 31, 54, 66
  John 18
  Josias 66
  Katherine 18
  Mary 40, 78
  Mordica 31
  Rebecca 54
  Ruth 54
  Sarah 24, 27, 31, 54, 66
CRAWLEY, Elizabeth 25, 43
  John 25, 43
CRAYTON, John 74
  Martha 74
  Patrick 74
CREGG, Robert 63
CREICHTON, Mary 88
  William 88
CRESWELL, Agness 92
  Catherine 86
  Elizabeth 92
  James 86, 108
  Robert 86
  Samuel 92
CRISUP, Daniel 29
  Hannah (JOHNSON) 29
  Thomas 29
CROCKET, Ben, Dr. 114
  Esther 65
  Jane 61
  Jean 65
  Joseph 61, 65
  Mary 61
  Samuel 65
CROCKETT, Benjamin 77
  Elizabeth (CHEW) 77
  Esther 61
  Gilbert 77
  John 77
  Samuel 61
CROMPTON, David 11

CROMPTON, Joseph 11
  Liddia 10
  Margaret 10, 11
CROMTON, Joseph 10
CROMWELL, Anna Maria 55
  John Giles 55
  Oliver 55
CRONEY, Elizabeth (CARSON) 78
  Paul 78
CRONY, William 78
CROOK, Ann 40
  Mary 40
  Sarah 88
CROSS, Benjamin 110
  James 93
  John 61
  Samuel 92, 93
  Sarah 61, 69
  Susanah 93
  Susannah (PRESBURY) 92
  Thomas 66
CROW, Grace (DENSON) 69
  Hannah 57, 63, 68
  James 16, 57, 63, 68, 69
  John 21, 41, 47, 53, 60, 63, 72
  Judith 47, 53, 60, 72
  Judith (MAGEE) 41
  Mansfield 72
  Margaret 47
  Margaret (COMPTON) 21
  Mary 16, 68
  Thomas 60, 72
CRUTCHLEY, Lydia 67
CRUTE, Cordelia 92
  Francis 92
  Rachel 92
  Rachel (BARNS) 92
  Rebecca 92
  Richard 92
  Robert 92, 115
  Sarah 92
  Taylor 115
CULBERT, Benjamin G. 110
CULLEN, Elizabeth 48
CULLINGS, Catherine 35
  Thomas 34
CULVER, Benjamin 99, 106, 108, 109
CULVERT, Ben 115
  Benjamin 99
CULVUR, Benjamin 108
CUNNINGHAM, Crispin 115
CUTCHEN, Ann 40
  Elizabeth 49
DALLAM, Ann 61
  Ann (MATHEWS) 77
  Elizabeth 71
  Frances 61, 94

DALLAM, Francess 94
  John 113, 115
  John Josias 94
  Joseph 114
  Josias Middlemore 94
  Josias William 99
  Richard 61, 94, 99, 106, 107, 110, 114
  Richard, Jr. 108
  Samuel 61
  Sarah (SMITH) 94
  W. Richard 109
  W. S. 116
  William 61, 77, 99, 107, 113
  William S. 115
  William, Maj. 114
DANDE, Jane 17
  Mary 17
  Mary (FOX) 16
  Ralph 16, 17
DANIEL, Edward 15
DARBY, Robert 109
DAUGH, Bridget 15
  Elizabeth 15
  Owen 15
DAUGHARTY, Margaret 82
DAUGHERTY, Eleanor 84
  Elianor 68
  Mary 68, 73, 84
  Ufan 84
  William 68, 73, 84, 114
DAUGHTERY, George 109
DAVIDG, Elizabeth 62
  Hudson 62
  Susannah 62
DAVIDGE, Hudson 106
  Sarah 93
DAVIS, Ben 114
  Benjamin 28, 81
  Charles 60
  David 47, 88
  Easther (FUGAT) 12
  Elianor 67
  Elijah 115
  Elizabeth 28, 81, 90
  Elizabeth (DOOLEY) 88
  Henry 47, 57, 60, 67
  Jane 57
  John 12, 81, 90, 112
  John, Rev. 97
  Joseph 112
  Mary 57, 81, 87
  Richard 90
  Sarah 47, 57, 60, 89
  William 90
DAWKINS, Elizabeth 46
  Jane 54
  Jane (THORNTON) 40
  Joan 46

DAWKINS, Mary 67
  Richard 40, 46, 54, 56, 67
DAWLEY, Blanch 33
  Rachel 33
  William 33
DAY, Elizabeth 13
  John 93
  Mary 93
  Philliszana 93
DEACON, Francis 109, 110, 111,
    112, 116
  Frank 99
DEAN, Hugh, Rev. 77
DEANS, Hugh, Rev. 93, 94
DEATH, Edward 8
  Randal 8
DEAVER, Ann 47, 77
  Ann (BOND) 78
  Antil 21, 26, 30, 32, 37, 47,
    55, 68
  Antill 102
  Daniel 75
  David 75
  Deborah 61
  Deborah (HARTLEY) 46
  Elizabeth 16, 37
  Hannah 16, 17, 19, 21, 66
  John 16, 17, 19, 32, 39, 66,
    77, 78, 87, 114
  Kesiah 19
  Martha 55, 68
  Mary 17, 30, 39, 40, 66, 75,
    87
  Nathan 87
  Perina (GREENFIELD) 66
  Richard 40, 73, 75
  Richard, Jr. 37
  Samuel 17
  Sarah 21, 26, 30, 32, 37, 40,
    47, 55, 68
  Sarah (PRITCHARD) 37
  Stephen 46
  Susannah (BIRCHFIELD) 87
  Thomas 17, 46, 61, 77, 79
  William 87
DEBRULAR, Anthony 30
  Elizabeth 30
  Frances 74
  Frances (BURIDGE) 71
  John 30, 71, 74, 112
  Mary 30
  Sarah 74
DEBRULER, John 10
  Mary 51
  Mary (DRUNKARD) 10
DEE, Elinor 27
  Phillip 27
DEFORGE, Elizabeth 1
  Knowell 1

DEMASTERS, Anthony 13
  Catherine 13
DEMOSE, Catherine 32
  Charles 32
  James 32
  Lewis 32
  Pine 32
  Thomas 32
DENHAM, Edward 28, 29, 31
  Mary (GERISH) 29
  Middleton 28
DENNIS, Alice (CARRAGAN) 46
  Elisha 46
  Rozannah 29
  Samuel 46
DENNISON, Henry 115
DENSON, Abigal 44
  Barthia 35
  Elizabeth 57
  Elizabeth (COWEN) 55
  Grace 69
  John 55, 57, 60
  Margaret 35, 60
  Mary 44, 50
  Sarah 55, 57
  William 35, 44, 60
DEPOST, Martha (ANDERSON) 31
  Martin 1, 31
  Presilla 31
  Tammeson (HOLT/HOFF) 1
DERUMPLE, Middleton 27
  Robert 27
DEVER, Aneil 99
  Antill 107
  Benjamin 43, 59
  Deborah 55
  Elizabeth 79
  James 79
  John 55, 79, 107, 108
  Margaret 51, 60
  Mary 43, 55
  Micajah 79
  Prianah 79
  Richard 43, 51, 99
  Richard, Jr. 58, 60
  Sarah 51, 58, 102
  Thomas 55
  Ufan 79
  William 79
DEW, Elizabeth 37
DEWLEY, Blanch (JONES) 35
  Elizabeth 35
  Margaret 43
  Rachel 35
  William 35
DEXON, Morris 108
DICKSON, Mary 81
DINNING, John 86
  Mary 86

DINNING, Oliver 86
DIXON, Elizabeth 111
　Johannah 85
　Margaret (PECKOO) 85
　Morriss 111
　Peter 85
DOCKARTY, George 59
　Mary (BARTLE) 59
　William 59
DONAVIN, Daniel 80
　Hannah 80
　Margaret 80
　William 80
DONAWIN, Daniel 75, 76
　Johanna 76
　Johanna (ARNOLD) 75
　Philip 76
DONIVIN, Jacob 80
DONNAVIN, Thomas 80
DONOWIN, Mary 19
　Thomas 19
　Timothy 19
DOOLEY, Blanch 82
　Elizabeth 88
　Mary 82
DORSESY, Frisbey 113
DORSET, Frisby 115
DORSEY, Benedict 86
　Frances 86, 91
　Frisby 86, 99, 116
　Greenberry 86, 91, 99, 114, 116
　Mary 86
　Sally Frisby 91
DOWLEY, Elizabeth 18
　John 18
　William 18
DOWNS, Elizabeth 68
　Guilielmus 61
　Guiolmus 68
　Gulielmus (GOODEN) 58
　Mary 39, 61
　Thomas 58, 61, 68
DOYLE, Mary 59
DRAPER, Abigal 24, 36
　Abigle 19
　Anthony 19
　Bethiah 27
　Digbey 25
　Elizabeth 17
　Frances 25
　John 19, 24, 36, 71
　John, Jr. 45, 53, 57, 64
　Jonathan 36
　Lawrence 19, 25, 27
　Leorance 99
　Martha 36
　Mary 19, 24, 25, 27, 53, 55, 57, 64, 71

DRAPER, Mary (REES) 45
　Rachel 53
　Susanna 19
　Thomas 24, 36
　Thomas Symmons 57
　William 64
DREPER, Elizabeth 15
　Lawrence 16
　Lawrence, Capt. 15
　Mary (DREW) 16
DREW, Ann 81, 92
　Anthony 2, 4, 6, 8, 14, 29, 81, 92, 99, 114
　Drusilla 48
　Frances 71, 77
　Francis 29
　George 6, 29, 48, 49, 52, 81, 99, 102, 103
　Hannah 48, 81
　Hannah (LISBY) 29
　Henry 81
　James 81, 103
　Johannah 52
　Johannah (PHILLIPS) 49
　Margaret 22
　Margaret (BROWN) 14
　Mary 16, 81, 92
　Mary Ann 29
　Maryanne 8
　Sarah 8, 41, 92
　Susanna 2
　Susannah 52
DRUNKARD, James 12
　Mary 10
DRUNKCOORD, James 6
　Mary (GREENFIELD) 6
DUDNEY, Jane (LEAK) 13
　Mary 13
　Roger 13
DULANY, Ann 112
　Daniel 88
　Elizabeth (BRADLEY) 88
DULEY, Aquila 47
　Blanch 47
　Blanch (JONES) 25
　William 25, 47
DULY, Blanch 30, 64
　Elizabeth 30
　William 30, 64
DUN, Christen 60
　John 60
　Martha 60
　Mary 60
DUNAHUE, Elizabeth 61
　Elizabeth (THOMPSON) 45
　Gilbert 61
　Roger 45, 61
DUNAVIN, Frances 62
　Sarah 62

DUNAVIN, Thomas 62
DUNAWIN, Amey 48
  Jellen 1
  Thomas 48
DUNN, Bridgett 73
  Christian 36, 46
  Dennis 73
  Elizabeth 73
  Jenit 36
  John 36, 46
  Robert 46, 85, 99, 108, 109
  Sarah (PRITCHARD) 85
  Sarah (WAKEMAN) 85
  William 36
DUNNAWAY, Frances (HALL) 34
  Thomas 34
DURANT, Anthony 111
DURBAIN, John 99
DURBAN, John, Jr. 62
  Mary (HAWKINS) 62
DURBIN, Ann (MITCHEL) 75
  Avarilla 22, 23, 24, 38, 40,
    51, 60, 65, 75, 91
  Daniel 24, 65, 75, 91
  Elianor 70
  Elizabeth 20, 46
  Hannah 60
  John 20, 22, 23, 24, 38, 40,
    51, 60, 65, 70, 75, 91
  John, Jr. 65
  Mary 51, 65, 91
  Mary (JOHNS) 91
  Ralph 70
  Samuel 91
  Sarah 38, 86, 112
  Thomas 23
  William 38, 91
EAGAN, Barnett 63
  Elianor 63
  Elizabeth 43
  Hugh 63
  James 43, 63
  Katharine 48, 51, 63
  Margaret 48
  Rachel 63
  Richard 43, 48, 51, 63
EASTWOOD, Elizabeth 63
EAVES, George 16
  Mary (COSTLEY) 16
EDMONS, Thomas 11
EDUNDS, Mary 11
EDWARDSON, John 11
ELIOT, Faithey 61
  John 61
  Keren (JOHNSON) 64
  Mary 28
  Unity 61
  William 64
ELLET, Judith 15

ELLET, Mary 15
  Sarah 15
  Thomas 15
ELLETS, Elizabeth 87
  Kern 87
  Rachel 87
  Samuel 87
  William 87
ELLIOT, Caran 70
  John 70
  Keren 65
  Pearcy 65
  Sarah 40
  Unity 70
  William 65, 70
ELLIS, Elizabeth 11
  Mary 8, 12, 14
ELSTON, Elizabeth (PARKER) 33
  Robert 33
EMMERSON, Mary (BUR) 12
  Tobias 12, 14
EMSON, Ann 21
  Elizabeth 19
  James 18
  James, Jr. 20
  Rachel 18, 23
  Rebecca 18, 19
ENGLAND, Elizabeth 57
  Jemima 23
  Joseph 23
  Margaret 23
ENNIS, John 58
  Ruth 58
  William 58
ERNSTON, Rebecca 14
ESTWOOD, Elizabeth 65
EVANS, Edward 25, 37
  Elizabeth 26
  Evan Rev. 102
  Hannah 25
  James 28
  John 28
  Mary 28, 31
  Rachel 25, 37
  Rachel (JOHNSON) 25
EVERET, Benjamin 83
  Cassandra 83
  John 83
  Margaret 83
  Thomas 83
  William 83
EVERETT, John 86, 99
  Martha 86
EVERIST, Elizabeth 98
EVERITT, Ann 90, 95
  James 90
  John 90
  Margaret (PRICE) 74
  Martha 90

EVERITT, Thomas 74
EVES, Elizabeth 18
  George 18
  Mary 18
EWINS, Elizabeth 14
FAIRBOURN, Jane 66
FARLEY, John 50
  Mary (WEEKS) 50
FARLOW, Elizabeth 48
  Elizabeth (LYTTLE) 46
  Mary 48
  Thomas 46, 48
FARMER, Elisabeth 49, 55
  Elizabeth 17, 38, 70
  Elizabeth (ROSS) 66
  Gregory 9, 16, 17, 19, 23, 64, 99, 104
  Grigory 18, 20, 21, 23, 69
  Hannah 16, 33, 59
  John 16, 47, 49, 55, 59, 64, 67, 99, 109, 110
  Margaret 22, 52
  Margarit 16
  Martha 19, 57
  Mary 57, 62, 67, 69
  Mary (WOOD) 55
  Peter 18, 55, 57, 62, 67, 69
  Rachel (EMSON) 23
  Samuel 21
  Sarah 16, 17, 18, 19, 21, 23, 55, 67, 74, 89
  Sarah (HEWS) 9
  Sophia 49, 55, 59, 64, 67
  Sophia (JONES) 47
  Thomas 20, 66, 70
FARWOOD, Jacob 115
FAUKNER, Thomas 8
FEELER, Sarah 43
  Thomas 43
FELL, Anna 98
FENICK, Thomas 7
FENIX, Mary 13
  William 13
FENN, Henry 7
  Jane 7
  Thomas 7
FERRIL, Mary 12
FIELD, Ann 65
  Catharine 37, 65
  Catharine (HOGG) 32
  Jo. 37
  John 32, 37, 65
FIELDS, Elizabeth 28
FINCHECOME, Mary 19
FINNEY, Hannah 111
FISHER, Amelia 86
  Amelia (WHITACRE) 85
  Elizabeth 68
  Elizabeth (GOODWIN) 68

FISHER, James 99, 111
  Semmelua 3
  Stephen 68
  Thomas 85, 86
  William 99, 107, 109
  William Hitchcock 86
FITSPATRICK, Charles 66
  Jane (FAIRBOURN) 66
FLANAGAN, Charles 43
  Cormack 43
  Edward 43, 63
  Eleonor 63
  John 43
  Katherine 43
  Mary 43, 63
FLEEHARTEE, Hannah (PENICK) 45
  John 45
FLOOD, Jane (FRENCH) 37
  Mary 37
  William 37
FORD, Benjamin 79
  Darkis 79
  David 79
  John 79, 91
  Mark 104
  Rachel 91
  Sarah 91
  Sarah (MURPHY) 79
FORESIGHT, Joseph 35, 55
  Mary 35, 55
  Mary (MARSHALL) 35
  Prudence 55
FORGEMAN, John Hanson 108
  John Jolly 108
  John Tolly 108
FORWARD, Constance Elizabeth 95
  Faithful (WEBB) 94
  Faithfull 95
  Jacob 94, 95
  Jane 95
FORWOOD, Faithful 97
  Jacob 97, 99, 116
  Jane 98
  John 97, 115
  Martha (JARRITT) 97
FOSTER, Ann 29
  Annabell 87
  Benedict 87
  James 29, 109
  Margaret 87
  Mary 29, 34
  Susannah 87
  William 29
FOWLER, Charlotte 97
  Frances 97
  James 9, 39, 54, 55
  Joshua 5, 9, 39
  Margaret 39, 54, 55
  Mary 9, 53, 54, 58, 65, 82

FOWLER, Samuel 52, 53, 58, 65, 97
  Sarah 11, 52, 53, 81
  Sarah (MACCARTY) 52
  William 55
FOX, Margaret 65
  Mary 16, 65
FREEBORN, Priscilla 45
FREEBOURN, Elizabeth 9
FREELAND, George 18
  Mary 14, 18, 19
  Perdine 18
  Sarah 18, 19
  Stephen 14, 18, 19
FREEMAN, Elizabeth 33, 40
  Elizabeth (PIKE) 33
  Francis 33, 40
  John 40
  Mary 33
FREEZLAND, George 8
  John 9
  Sarah 8, 9
  Stephen 8, 9
FRELAND, George 14
  Mary 14
  Stephen 14
FRENCH, Elizabeth 28
  Jane 37
  Michael 28
  Nathaniel 28
FRETWELL, Ann (PALMER) 35
  Thomas 35
FRISBEE, Peregrine 105
FRISBY, Frances 15
  Mary 75
  Mary (HOLLAND) 59
  Peregrine 75
  Peregrine, Capt. 59
  R.Peregrine 99
  Sarah 75
  Thomas 15, 75
FRITZBY, Frances 64
  Mary 64
  Peregrine 64
FUGAT, Easther 12
FULLAR, Jane (JOHNSON) 41
  William 41
FULTON, Ann (MATHEW) 78
  Francis 78
FURAT, Ann 1
  John 1
  Peter 1
FURNIVAL, Richard 99, 102
FUTT, Senea 87
GADDIS, Jane 85
GADDISS, Paul 111
GAILEY, Margaret (OSBORN) 82
GALHAMPTON, Catherine 38
  Elizabeth 38, 39, 42, 54, 65

GALHAMPTON, Elizabeth (HILL) 38
  Jane 42
  John 38
  Mary 38, 39
  Sarah 54
  Thomas 38, 39, 42, 54, 65
GALLION, Elizabeth 33, 40, 42, 65, 94
  Elizabeth (ARNOLD) 80
  Elizabeth (EVANS) 26
  Fanny 64
  Gregory 87
  Hannah 40
  Jacob 42, 66, 80, 94
  James 33, 42, 51, 64, 66, 71, 85, 94
  John 10, 14, 17, 23, 25, 26, 33, 40, 65, 87, 94, 99, 108, 109, 111
  Joseph 23, 33, 40, 87
  Kezia 51
  Margaret 69
  Martha 40, 51, 70, 72
  Martha (JOHNSON) 39
  Mary 17, 23, 25, 59, 69
  Mary (HANSON) 94
  Mary (YOUNG) 42
  Phebe 42, 51, 64, 66, 70, 71
  Pheby (JOHNSON) 33
  Priscilla 85
  Rachel 42
  Rachel (MARIARTY) 85
  Samuel 17
  Sarah 25, 72, 81, 87
  Sarah (AUCHARD) 87
  Sinai 59
  Soloman 72
  Solomon 17, 39, 40, 51, 70
  Sophia 80
  Thomas 14, 17, 42, 59, 69, 80
  William 71, 87
GALLOWAY, Elizabeth 79
  Rebecca 79
  Samuel 79
GAMBELL, Abraham 3
  Giddeon 3
  Rebecca 3
GARLAND, Bethia 34
  Bethiah (OGG) 28
  Bethyah 44, 61, 66
  Catherine 85
  Elizabeth 15, 17
  Francis 66
  Henry 15, 15, 17, 69
  James 34, 85
  Jane (GADDIS) 85
  Lidia 17
  Lydia 15
  Sarah 15, 17

GARLAND, Sarah (HERRINGTON) 69
  Susannah 61
  William 15, 28, 34, 44, 61, 66
GARMER, Sarah 20
GARNET, Mary 71
GARRET, Amos 77, 114
  Henry 99
GARRETSON, Avarilla (HANSON) 77
  Catherine 78
  Edward 77
  Elizabeth 77
  Frances 78
  Freeborn 78
  Garrett 77
  George 76, 114
  Goldsmith 76
  James 78
  Martha 76, 78, 114
  Mary 78
  Mary Goldsmith 76
  Priscilla (NELLSON) 78
  Richard 78
  Sophia 78
GARRETT, Amos 77, 99, 109, 112
  Amos, Esq. 111
  Amoss 23, 71, 72
  Arrabella 23, 31, 54
  Bennet 31, 55
  Bennett 23, 34, 54, 58, 66, 72, 77
  Cassandra 77
  Elizabeth 28, 60, 72
  Frances 77
  Frances (DREW) 71, 77
  Hannah 45, 72
  Henry 29, 32, 34, 40, 45, 60, 72
  Isaac 32, 72
  John 40, 72
  Martha 58
  Martha (PRESBURY) 55
  Mary 32, 34, 40, 41, 45, 60, 72
  Mary (BUTTERWORTH) 29
  Milcah 77
  Richard 14, 72
  Ruth 31, 70
  Sarah 15, 60, 72
  William 107
GARRETTSON, Acarilla 94, 95
  Aquila 84
  Avarilla 84, 85, 91, 93
  Benjamin 85
  Bennett 90
  Catherine 75, 90
  Catherine (Nelson) 73
  Cordelia 84
  Edward 29, 84, 85, 91, 93, 94, 114

GARRETTSON, Eliza. 90, 91
  Elizabeth 17, 19, 20, 22, 29, 74, 75, 91, 95
  Frances 83
  Frances Goldsmith 96
  Freborne 17
  Freeborn 90
  Freebourn 74
  Freenettah 91
  Frenetah 73
  Garret 108, 114
  Garrett 17, 19, 20, 22, 29, 50, 73, 75, 91, 93, 99, 107, 109, 110
  George 73, 74, 75, 83, 90, 93, 94, 95, 96, 98, 99, 106, 107
  George (Mrs.) 91
  Goldsmith 96
  James 17, 73, 75, 90, 91, 106, 114
  John 17, 66, 90, 99, 112
  Martha 73, 74, 75, 83, 93, 94, 95, 96, 98
  Martha (PRESBURY) 93
  Martha (TODD) 73
  Mary 19
  Mary Goldsmith 95
  Priscilla 84
  Prissila 91
  Richard 84, 90, 91, 99, 109, 110
  Ruthen 93
  Sarah 17, 84, 90, 91
  Sarah (MERRYARTER) 66
  Semelia 20, 69
  Sophia 17, 110
  Susannah 93
  Susannah (ROBINSON) 91
  Thomas 90
GARRISON, Elizabeth (FREEBOURN) 9
  Garret 9, 107
  Garrett 9, 99
  George 9, 99
  James A. 99
  John 99
  Richard 99
GARRITT, Bennett 99
GARRITTSON, Edward 110
  James A. 99
GARVIN, Jane 62
GASH, Blanch 25, 41
  Hannah 20, 22, 24, 25
  Hannah (GILBERT) 18
  Johannah 35, 36, 41
  Mary 22, 24, 25
  Michael 35
  Sarah 20, 51
  Tho. 22

GASH, Thomas 18, 20, 24, 25, 35, 41
GATCHELL, Elisha 104
GAY, Robert M. 107
GAYLOR, John 99
GENKINS, Elizabeth 61
 Francis 45, 56, 64
 Margaret 70
 Mary 45, 56, 64
 Mathew 61
 Rachel 56, 61, 70
 Sarah 56
 William 56, 61, 70
GERISH, Mary 28, 29
 Stephen 28
GIANT, John 106
GIBBERD, Nem 7
 Nern 7
 Sarah 7
 Sarah (BEDFORD) 6
 Thomas 6, 7
 Thomas, Jr. 7
GIBBINS, Mary 52
 Sarah 52
 Thomas 52
GIBSON, Frances 33
 Francis 33
 James 33
 Mary 12
 Mary (GOLDSMITH) 9
 Robert 9, 12
GILBERT, Anthony 24
 Aquilla 27
 Arabella 62
 Benjamin 32
 Charles 20, 26, 71, 93, 99, 109, 111
 Elisabeth 57
 Elizabeth 32, 52, 63, 65, 69, 70, 82, 95
 Elizabeth (COLE) 44
 Elizabeth (HAWKINS) 71
 Elizabeth (PRESTON) 47
 Frances 92
 Garvace 62, 65
 Garvis 26, 27, 32, 36
 Gervace 47, 57
 Gervace, Jr. 52, 57
 Gervis 107
 Hannah 18, 26, 62, 82
 James 82
 Jarvace 69
 Jarvis 14, 16, 18, 20, 99
 Johanna 18
 John 24
 John Webster 51
 Margaret 18, 52, 89
 Martha 33, 51, 57, 69, 92, 93, 94

GILBERT, Martha (WEBSTER) 37
 Martin Tayler 59, 93, 94
 Mary 20, 26, 27, 32, 57, 62, 70, 92, 93
 Mary (FOWLER) 82
 Mary (TAYLER) 57
 Micah 42
 Michael 18, 26, 33, 36, 42, 57, 69, 70, 82, 99, 106, 107, 108, 112
 Michael, Jr. 115, 116
 Preston 69
 Rachel 26, 82
 Rebecca 24
 Ruth 44
 Samuel 37, 51, 69, 99
 Sarah 36, 42, 65
 Sarah (BEDFORD) 6
 Sarah (PRESTON) 33
 Solomon 14
 Susanna 82
 Thomas 6, 7, 18, 44, 63, 82, 114
 Tomas 92
 William 69, 82, 99
GILBIRD, Garvis 42
 Martha 40
 Mary 40, 42
 Samuel 40
GILES, Anna (FELL) 98
 Aquila 97
 Aquilla 93
 Edward 93
 Eliza. 93
 Elizabeth 97
 Hannah 32, 41, 92
 Hester 51
 J. W. 116
 Jacob 32, 41, 93, 97, 98, 114
 Jacob Washington 98, 115
 Jacob, Jr. 108
 James 93, 98, 99
 Johanna 98
 John 32, 43, 51, 62
 Nathaniel 92, 98, 109
 Natt. John 109
 Sarah 47, 51, 62
 Sarah (BUTTERWORTH) 43
 Sarah (HAMMOND) 92
 Susanna 98
 Thomas 93
 William Axtel 97
GILIES, Johannah 93
GILL, Alce 23
GILLBART, Elizabeth 15
 Thomas 15
GILLUM, Ralph 2
 Sarah 2
GILSE, Eliza 97

GINKINS, Avis 46
Francis 39
Margaret 10
Mary 46
Mary (DOWNS) 39
Rachel 39, 46
Sarah 38, 39
William 39, 46
GISSARD, Sarah 79
GLASPIN, Sarah (LOWRY) 37
William 37
GLASS, Elizabeth 88
Judith 88
Thomas 88
GLOVER, Tho. 9
GOBY, Susanna 23
GODLEY, Rev. Mr. 94
GOLDSMITH, Martha 13
Mary 9
GOODEN, Gulielmus 58
GOODIN, John 51, 52
Margaret 51, 52
William 51
GOODING, Hannah 71
Jacob 71
Mary 71
GOODWIN, Alexander Philip 66
Ann 50, 87
Benjamin 68, 70, 87
Elanor 56
Eleanor 86
Elizabeth 46, 56, 68, 87
Hannah 70, 87
Hannah (URGHWUART) 68
Isaac 87
James 87
John 66, 87
Joseph 87
Margaret 66
Rebecca 87
Rebecca (BREEDEN) 87
Sam 87
Samuel 46, 87
Thomas 87
William 46, 56, 70
GORDEN, Daniel 35
James 81
Mary (WEST) 35
Ruth 81
GORDON, Daniel 78
James 81
John 78
Joseph 81, 114
Mary 45, 78, 81, 106
Richard 45
Ruth (CHANEY) 81
Sarah 45
GOULDSMITH, Martha 1
GOVA, Ephraim 107

GOVER, Elizabeth 63
Ephraim 63
Ephriam 99, 108
Philip 109
Phillip 107, 108
GRADDE, Edmund 1
Jellen (DUNAWIN) 1
GRAFTON, Ann 50
GRANT, David 79
Elizabeth (MORRIS) 79
James 79
GRAVES, Catharine 38
Sarah (BEVER) 46
William 38, 46
GRAY, Allen 72
Elizabeth 97
George 97
Henry 35
James 97
Jane 35
John 97
Judith 35
Mary Ann 97
Thomas Henderson 97
GRAYDON, Mary (AYRES) 61
William 61
GREENFIELD, Charrott 97
Elizabeth 32, 43, 52
Elizabeth (EVERIST) 98
Frances 58, 97
Harriott 97
Henry Austin 98
Jacob 98, 115
Jane 6
John 2, 3
Joseph 98
Martha 98
Mary 2, 6
Micais 11
Micajah 11, 43, 99, 110, 111
Perina 66
Poly 98
Purify 52, 79
Rachel 5, 6, 7, 8, 10, 11
Richard 99
Rowland 97
Sarah 2
Thomas 2, 3, 5, 6, 7, 8, 10, 11
Thomas Truman 97
William 5, 6, 32, 43, 52, 114
GREGORY, Edmund 52
Rachel 52
GRENFIELD, Jane 2
Thomas 2
GRIFFIN, Luke 99
GRIFFIS, Elizabeth 7
GRIFFITH, (?) 99
Alice 49

GRIFFITH, Ann 68
  Avarilla 72, 96
  Avarillah 96
  Avarillah Mariah 96
  Blanch (HALL) 90
  Catherine 92, 93, 94, 95, 96
  Charlotte 95
  Edward 116
  Elizabeth 10, 12, 59, 66, 92
  Frances 95
  Freenettah 92, 93, 94, 95, 96
  Freenettah (GARRETTSON) 91
  George 92, 93
  Isaac 69
  Jane 71
  Jane (REES) 69
  John 66, 94, 95
  John Hall 96
  John N. 115
  L. 113
  Lewes 49
  Lewis 49, 59, 94, 115
  Luke 90, 92, 93, 94, 95, 96,
    97, 107, 114
  Martha 94, 97
  Martha (PRESBURY) 96
  Mary 44, 56, 59, 68, 69, 72,
    86, 93, 96
  Mary (JOHNSON) 59
  Prescilla 72
  Richard 69, 71
  Sam 56
  Samuel 44, 56, 59, 66, 69, 72,
    91, 92, 93, 94, 95, 96, 97,
    99, 109, 110, 111, 112, 114,
    115, 116
  Samuel F. 104
  Samuel Goldsmith 96
  Samuel, Dr. 113
  Sarah 44, 91, 96
  Thomas 49
GROOM, Jemima 92
  Moses 102
GROVER, Ephiram 106
  Ephriam 107
  Mariah 80
GUILBER, Hannah (ASHFORD) 10
  Thomas 10
GUILBERT, Elizabeth 10
  Hannah 13
  Thomas 13
GUYTON, Abraham 110
GWIN, Elizabeth 47
  Mary 38
  Rachel 38
  Sarah 38, 47, 53
  Sarah (GINKINS) 38
  Thomas 38
  William 38, 47, 53

GYLES, Hannah 51
  Jacob 51
  John 52
  Nathaniel 51, 52
  Sarah 52
HAAS, Samuel 99
HAIL, Ann 71
  Henry 66, 71
  Mary 66, 71
  Thomas 66
HAILL, Henry 64
  Mary (BRADLEY) 64
HALE, Patrick 14
HALL, (?) 102
  (?), Dr. 100
  Alexander 106
  Amy 8, 11, 15
  Ann 19
  Anne (HOLLIS) 1
  Aquila 4, 48, 67, 72, 76, 96,
    99, 102, 105, 106, 110
  Aquila, Capt. 96
  Aquilla 22, 30
  Aquilla Beadle 98
  Aquilla, Capt., Esq. 114
  Avarilla 77
  Avarilla (CARVIL) 21
  Avarilla Jane 98
  B. E. 113
  Barthia 74, 76, 98
  Barthiah (STANSBURY) 73
  Benedict 95, 100, 115, 116
  Benedict E. 112
  Benedict Edward 72, 99, 111,
    115, 116
  Berthia 90
  Bethia 84, 93
  Blanch 50, 62, 72, 90
  Bothya 77
  Charlotte 76
  Cordelia 83, 93
  Cordelia (HOLLAND) 75
  Cordelia Knight 97
  Cordelia Night 98
  Edward 2, 10, 21, 50, 74, 83,
    95, 97, 98, 100, 102, 103,
    112, 114, 115, 116
  Edward, Col. 100
  Eliza. 90, 95
  Elizabeth 77, 84
  Frances 15, 34
  Hannah 63, 67, 72, 73, 93, 96
  Hannah (JOHNS) 48
  Henry 16
  Hetta 98
  Hetty 97
  J. W. 100
  J., Dr. 113
  Jacob 115, 116

HALL, Jacob, Dr. 112
James 100
James W. 100
James White 76, 97, 116
Jaocb 100
Johanna 48
Johannah 30, 48
Johannah (PHILLIPS) 22
John 1, 2, 4, 5, 6, 8, 9, 11, 14, 15, 21, 30, 63, 67, 71, 72, 73, 74, 75, 76, 77, 83, 84, 90, 91, 93, 95, 98, 100, 105, 106, 107, 109, 115
John B. 98, 100
John Beadle 97, 98
John Bedle 76
John Beedle 116
John Biedle 100
John, Capt. 2, 96, 96, 109, 110, 111, 114
John, Col. 96, 100, 109, 114
John, Esq. 9, 10, 13, 20
John, Jr. 48, 100
John, Maj. 63
John, Sr. 100
John, Sr., Esq. 114
Jonas C., Col. 100, 112
Josiah 63, 100
Josias 76, 98, 100, 115, 116
Josias Carvil 73, 100, 116
Louisa Elizabeth 98
Martha 4, 9, 13, 14, 21, 30, 48, 73, 76, 91, 93, 95
Martha (BRADALL) 20
Martha (GARRETTSON) 98
Martha (GOULDSMITH) 1
Martha Matilda 98
Mary 8, 62, 63, 76, 84
Mary Clarissa 98
Parker 13, 50, 62, 72, 90, 93, 100, 113, 115, 116
Priscilla 77, 96
R. W. 116
Sara 2
Sarah 83, 97, 98
Sarah (HALL) 97
Sarah (PHILLIPS) 83
Sophia 14, 73, 94, 95, 96
Sophia (WHITE) 76
Sophia White 97
Susanna 71
Susanna (MARSHALL) 67
Susannah 86
Thomas 76, 100
W. 112
Walter Tolley 115
William 75, 76, 100, 109, 112, 115, 116
William, Jr. 100

HAMBELTON, Jno., Rev. 77
HAMBEY, Jeremiah 60
Martha 60
William 60
HAMBLETON, Ann 47
Rebecca 49, 56
Rebecca (BIGNALL) 47
Robert 47, 49, 56
Thomas 56
HAMBY, Alce (MONDAY) 35
Alice 44, 52
Elizabeth 17, 22, 23, 34, 69
Frances 69
Francis 17, 22, 24, 35, 40
Francis, Jr. 44
Jane 44
Martha 24, 38, 40
Martha (SIMPSON) 23
Mary 17, 35
Mary (SYMPSON) 50, 69
Samuel 17, 50, 52, 69
Sarah 69
Thomas 38
William 17, 23, 24, 38, 40
HAMMOND, Sarah 92
HANAN, Hannah 81
James 81
HANBY, Jane 86
HANDSON, Benjamin 28
Hollis 28
Sarah 28
HANNAN, Margaret 81
William 81
HANNER, David 109
HANNES, Elizabeth 3
Elizabeth (KELLE) 3
Elizabeth (KELLY) 4
Michael 3
Miles 1, 3, 4
Thomas 1
HANNIS, Miles 21
HANSON, Avarilla 44, 77, 90
Benjamin 44, 52, 71, 85, 90, 93, 94, 95
Eliza. 93, 95
Elizabeth 80, 85, 90, 93, 94
Hollis 74, 85
Jacob 28, 32, 44, 48, 60, 67, 72, 74, 81, 114
John 14, 69, 71, 72, 73, 74, 80, 85, 100, 108, 114
Luke 94
Margaret 44, 67, 72, 79, 81
Margaret (HUGHES) 60
Margarett 74
Martha 67
Mary 60, 81, 85, 94
Rebecca 32, 44, 48, 60, 74
Rebecca (MILES) 28

HANSON, Samelia 80
  Samuel 74, 85
  Sarah 44, 48, 52, 67, 79, 80, 85
  Semelia 71, 73, 74
  Semelia (GARRETTSON) 69
  Sibbel 28
  Sophia 80
  Thomas 14, 15, 28, 31
HARAGUS, Ruth 46
HARDEMAN, Hannah 16
HARDEN, Saverell 110
HARGAS, Aquilla 49
  Elisabeth 103
  Elizabeth 49, 56, 104
  Mary 69
  Stephen 56
HARGESS, Eliza 34
  Elizabeth 34
  Thomas 34
  William 34
HARGUES, Elizabeth 27, 105, 106
  Mary 27
  Thomas 27
HARGUS, Elizabeth 46
HARLEY, John 50
  Mary (WEEKS) 50
HARMAN, Hannah (JACKSON) 80
  James 80
HARPER, Samuel 72
  Sarah (MACCAREE) 72
HARPLE, Edward 4
HARRIS, Edward 22
  Frances 22
HARRRIS, Sarah 30
HARTLEY, Deborah 46
HARTSHORN, Elizabeth 4
  George 1
  Mary 1
HARVEY, Evans 44
  Michael 44
  Sarah 44
  William 44
HASEELWOOD, John 4
  William 3
HASELWOOD, Henry 4
HAWKINGS, Elizabeth 67
HAWKINS, Ann 18, 24, 26, 33, 40, 54
  Ann (TREBLE/PREBLE?) 17
  Anna 50
  Elizabeth 24, 38, 45, 49, 54, 64, 71, 74, 75
  Elizabeth (FARMER) 38
  Gregory Farmer 45
  James 39
  John 18, 19, 22, 26, 34, 39, 49, 56, 67
  John, Jr. 22, 26

HAWKINS, Joseph 34
  Ludia (CRUTCHLEY) 67
  Martha 75
  Mary 24, 54, 62
  Mary (WELLS) 67
  Rachel 56
  Rebecca 22, 26, 34, 39, 49, 56
  Rebecca (EMSON) 19
  Robert 17, 18, 24, 33, 40, 67, 111
  Robert, Jr. 67
  Samuel 74
  Sarah 33, 38
  Thomas 17, 38, 45, 54, 64, 67, 74, 75, 107
  William 33
HAYS, Ann 42
  Edmund, Jr. 55
  Elizabeth 32, 55
  Grace 32, 42, 49
  John 32, 42, 49, 55
  Martha 55
  Mary 32, 55
  Mary (CRABTREE) 32
HEATH, James 86, 100, 114
  Susannah (HALL) 86
HEDG, Henry 6
  Mary (PARKER) 6
HEDGE, Clemency 11
  Henry 6, 11, 14, 31
  Mary 11, 14, 31
  Mary (PARKER) 6
HELEN, Peter 110
HELL, Henry 16
HENDERSON, Cordelia 91
  Francis 91
  Hannah (HOLLANDSWORTH) 91
  Nathaniel 115
  Philip, Dr. 100, 112
  Thomas 114, 115
  Thomas Frisby 91
HENDLEN, Mary (LEEK) 80
  Peter 80
HENERY, John 114
HENISSEE, Elizabeth Vois 47
HENLEN, Peter 110
HENLEY, Mary (WILD) 87
  Peter 87
  Sarah 87
HENNEYSE, Sarah 105
HENRY, John 110
HENSON, Benedict 115
  Benj. 114
  Edward 32
  John 107
HERRINGTON, Abraham 25
  Ann 31
  Hannah 25, 31, 48
  Hannah (JOHNSON) 25

HERRINGTON, Isaac 31
　Jacob 25, 31, 47
　Johannah 47
　Mary 25
　Sarah 47, 48, 64, 65, 69
　Thomas 47
HERRITT, Catharine 47
HEWLINGS, Mary 84
HEWS, Sarah 9
HICKSON, Hannah 44
　Hester 44
　Jane 44, 48
　Joseph 44
HIGGENS, Samuel 107
HIGGINSON, Ann 60
　John 59
　Susanna 60
HIGINSON, Samuel 108
HILL, Alexander 33, 47, 61, 67
　Anna 61
　Elizabeth 38
　Elizabeth (HOPKINS) 92
　James 108
　Joseph 108, 109
　Mary 47, 61, 67
　Mary (REDMAN) 33
　Moses 109
　Samuel 92, 108
　William 47
HILLIARD, Sarah 66
　Ssuanna 62
　Susanna (WEST) 55
　Thomas 55, 62
HOAKS, John 102
HODGE, Henry 11
　Mary 11
HODSKEN, Catherine (CARROLL) 58
　Joseph 58
HOFF, Tammeson 1
HOGG, Catharine 32
　Margaret 36
HOLBROKE, John Rev. 102
HOLLADAY, James 22
　Sarah 22
HOLLAND, (?) 102, 103
　Cordelia 74, 75
　Cordelia (NIGHT) 71
　Frances 64, 74
　Frances Utie 50
　Francis 20, 22, 48, 50, 64, 71, 74, 75, 100, 111, 112, 114
　Francis Utie 96
　Francis, Capt. 96
　Francis, Col. 112
　Fras. 116
　Hannah 96
　John 58, 62, 96
　Mary 22, 59

HOLLAND, Sarah 62
　Sarah (WILABEE) 58
　Susanna 20, 22, 50, 64
　Utee 48
HOLLANDSWORTH, Ann 28
　George 55, 91
　Hannah 91
　Hannah (NELSON) 55
　James 28
HOLLEY, William 115
HOLLICE, Mary 9
　Sarah 9
　William 9
HOLLIDAY, James 22, 23
　Robert 22
　Sarah (MOTTON) 22
HOLLINGSWORTH, Ann 18, 20, 25, 70
　Ann (CHITCHING) 16
　Enock 69
　George 18, 70, 100, 105
　James 16, 18, 20, 25, 62
　John 66, 102
　Keziah (HOLLIS) 64
　Mary (DEAVER) 66
　Sarah 70
　Thomas 25, 64
HOLLINS, Jonathan 6
HOLLINSWORTH, John 69
　Mary 69
HOLLIS, Amos 51, 86, 107
　Amoss 90
　Ann 27, 32, 51, 66, 81
　Ann (RHODES) 22
　Anna 51, 62
　Anne 1
　Avarilla 9, 30, 90
　Catharine 51
　Cathrine 81
　Clark 5, 9, 22, 32, 81, 86
　Frances 81
　Hannah 81
　James 81
　Kezia 27
　Keziah 64
　Martha 90
　Martha (EVERETT) 86
　Mary 9, 10, 12, 66, 81
　Rachel 81
　Sarah 12, 86
　Sarah (GALLION) 81
　William 3, 5, 6, 9, 10, 12, 22, 27, 32, 51, 62, 66, 81, 86, 100
HOLT, Tammeson 1
HOOD, Joshua 116
HOOPER, Isabel 5
HOPKINS, Charles 67
　Elizabeth 92

HOPKINS, Joseph 109
  Rachel 67
  William 67, 108, 109, 110
HORNER, Cassasndra 69
  Grace 66, 69
  Grace (ANDERSON) 64
  Sarah 66
  Thomas 64, 66, 69
HORNIBY, Edward 107
HORSEMAN, (?) 31
HORTON, Edward Wakeman 85
  Elizabeth (WAKEMAN/PRITCHARD) 85
  William 85, 100, 114
HOSSEY, Danaiel 44
  Elizabeth 44
  Isaac 44
  Rachel 44
HOUSTEN, Alexander 20
HOW, Christopher 19
  Else 90
  Mary (LESTER) 90
  Rebecca 19
  Sarah 19
  William 90
HOWARD, Ann 112
  John 1, 2
  Samuel 100, 109
  Thomas 1
HOWEL, Aquila 45
  Daniel 45
  Frenetta 45
  Job 45
  Mordica 45
  Phebe 45
  Priscilla (freeborn) 45
  Samuel 45
HOWELL, Asenath 86
  Avarilla 86
  Mordecai 86
  Samuel 86, 100, 104, 106
  Sarah (DURBIN) 86
HUFMAN, William 112
HUGHES, Margaret 60
  Samuel 100, 116
HUGHS, Ann (EVERITT) 95
  Catherine (NOBLE) 72
  David 103
  Eleanor 27
  Elizabeth 21, 22, 25, 27, 64, 69, 73
  Elizabeth (CRAWLEY) 25, 43
  Elizabeth (NORRIS) 61
  Esther 21
  Everitt 95
  Felix 72
  Grace 43
  Gwain 43

HUGHS, Jane 20, 22, 23, 24, 34, 69, 108
  Jane (SHEPARD) 30
  Jane (WATKINS) 16
  John 20, 21, 61, 64, 69, 73, 95
  John Hall 71, 95
  Jonathan 30, 34
  Margaret 20, 72
  Mary 24, 73
  Rowland 22
  Samuel 16, 20, 22, 23, 24, 105
  Sarah 23, 34, 71, 105, 106
  Scott 95
  Thomas 64, 72
  William 21, 22, 25, 27, 43, 100, 115
HULL, David 3
  Joseph 3
HUMBLE, Isaac 109
HUMPHREY, John 100
  John Rev. 102
HUNTER, Bradberry 29
  James 32
  Joseph 23
  Mary 23, 29, 32, 36
  Owen 36
  William 23, 29, 32, 36, 100, 103
HUSBANDS, John 109
  Thomas 108, 109
  William 100, 107, 108, 109
  William, Jr. 100, 108
INGRAM, Ann 63, 68, 82
  Arthuer 82
  Arthur 63, 68, 82, 114
  Christian 92
  Hannah 82
  Margaret 82
  Mary 68
  Sarah 63
  William 82
IRELAND, J., Rev. 97
  John, Rev. 98
JACKSON, (?) 114
  Abraham 6
  Blanch 26, 71
  Catharine 21, 27, 31, 66
  Catherine 34, 66
  Cathrine 81
  Eliza 79
  Elizabeth 1, 30, 34, 37, 48
  Elizabeth (DEBRULAR) 30
  Ephraim 81
  Hannah 7, 20, 30, 49, 80, 81
  Henry 10
  Isabel (HOOPER) 5
  James 31, 54
  Jno. 31

JACKSON, John 1, 4, 17, 21, 23,
  27, 34, 49, 54, 66, 81
 Joseph 26, 106
 Judith 1, 3
 Juleon 21
 Julon 34
 Katharine 23, 49, 54
 Katherine 17
 Margaret 21, 27, 66, 90
 Margaret (SUTTON) 84
 Mary 12, 22, 23, 26, 31, 34,
  43, 67, 79, 105
 Mary (KEMBAL) 9
 Moses 34, 84
 Robert 5, 6
 Samuel 3, 4, 7, 12, 17, 34
 Sara (MATHEWS) 4
 Sarah 7, 12, 13, 34, 80
 Sarah (MATHEWS) 3
 Simeon 1, 3, 4, 22, 26, 30,
  31, 34, 84
 Simon 43
 Thomas 1, 4, 9, 30, 34, 37,
  48, 102
 William 37, 67
JAMES, Constance 57, 61
 Edward 57
 Elizabeth 28
 John 61
 Michael 28, 57, 60
 William 28, 61
JARMAN, Lewis 3
JARRITT, Martha 97
JAY, Samuel 115
JEFF, Elizabeth (AISHLEYS) 7
 Margaret 7
 Ruth (MARTHEWS) 1
 William 1, 6, 7
JENKINS, (?) 106
 Elizabeth 33
 Francis 100
 Hannah 83
 J. Francis 100
 Mary (CLARK) 83
 Rachel 33
 Rachel (BALLS) 33
 Richard 44
 Samuel 100
 Sarah 37
 William 33, 37, 83, 107, 114
 William, Jr. 100
JEWELL, Mary 93
 William 93
JINKENS, John 91
 Mary 91
 William 91
JOB, Mary 26
JOHNS, Ann 91
 Aquila 108

JOHNS, Aquilla 107
 Hannah 48
 Hosea 109
 John 108
 Mary 91
 Richard 91, 108, 109
 William 39
JOHNSON, Abraham 65
 Alce 36, 58
 Alexander 54
 Alice 48, 59
 Alice (MORE) 12
 Alis (BOND) 32
 Ann 31, 44, 88
 Ann (BRADLEY) 88
 Ann (TOD) 15
 Archibald 115
 Aron 2
 Barnett 36
 Cathrine 83
 Charity 18
 Daniel 6, 7, 18
 Dann 70
 Elijah 88
 Elizabeth 31, 54, 70, 110
 Ephraim 88
 Frances 18, 22, 36
 Hannah 18, 25, 29, 54
 Hannah (MITCHEL) 41
 Henry 31, 49
 Isaac 31, 36
 Isabel 29
 Jacob 2, 12, 59
 James 70
 James Isham 53
 Jane 41, 49, 54
 Jeremiah 36, 61
 John 1, 2, 41, 44, 48, 52, 54,
  58, 59, 71
 Joseph 15, 23, 25, 31, 36, 39,
  46, 48, 53, 61, 62, 66, 88,
  100
 Keren 24, 64
 Levina 70
 Lidia 71
 Lydda 104
 Lydia 65
 Margaret 65
 Martha 23, 25, 36, 39, 46, 53,
  61, 62, 66, 88, 110
 Mary 17, 24, 28, 46, 49, 52,
  59, 67, 70, 71
 Mary (CLARK) 75
 Moses 2
 Pheby 33
 Rachel 17, 18, 25, 44
 Rail 40
 Richard 106
 Robert 70

JOHNSON, Ruth 1
  Samuel 70
  Sara 7
  Sarah 33, 48, 59, 61, 62, 71, 73
  Sophia 18, 35
  Thomas 17, 23, 24, 32, 36, 44, 48, 52, 58, 59, 71, 75, 88, 100
  William 32, 39, 107, 108
JOHNSTON, Ann 83
  Cathrine 83
  Jean 83
  John 109
  Mary 83
  Samuel 83
  Sarah 83
JOLLEY, John 100, 115
JOLLY, John 107
JONES, Abraham 87
  Ann 45
  Apa. 35
  Aquila 65, 72, 73, 78
  Avarilla 35
  Benjamin 34, 37
  Blanch 25, 35
  Cadd. 12
  Cadwalder 53
  Cadwalladar 9
  Cadwalladay 35
  Cadwallady 8
  Caldwall 12
  Cassandra 39, 82
  Charles 9, 34, 53, 68, 72
  Cordelia 44
  Elisabeth 37
  Elizabeth 37, 53, 72, 73, 79, 82, 87
  Elizabeth (BRICE) 65
  Elizabeth (LINLEY) 63
  Frances 35, 53, 68
  Frances (COBB) 34
  Francis 68
  George 63
  Hannah 57, 87
  Humphry 26
  Immanuel 44, 45
  Isaac 87
  Jacob 37, 87
  John 1, 90
  Jonathan 52, 54, 57, 61, 64, 67, 82, 100
  Judith 61
  Lydia 88
  Margaret 10, 57
  Margaret (FARMER) 52
  Margaret (JACKSON) 90
  Martha 54, 57, 64, 67, 82
  Martha (LOVEILL) 1

JONES, Mary 9, 26, 31, 35, 39, 47, 50, 54, 61, 65, 78, 107
  Mary (DOOLEY) 82
  Mary (ELLIS) 8
  Mary (POOL) 12
  Mary (POWEL) 35
  Prissilla 82
  Rebecca 68
  Sarah 45, 58, 82
  Sarah (LEEK) 44
  Sophia 47
  Stephen 37
  Theophilus 53
  Thomas 13, 35, 39, 47, 61, 64, 68, 82, 87
  William 37, 87
JOY, Jemima 55
JUDD, Daniel 52, 55, 59, 64
  Joshua 64
  Sarah 55, 59, 64
  Sarah (FOWLER) 52
  William 55
KACKARTE, (?) (WOOLSHER) 10
KEAN, Ann 17
  Mary 17, 34, 47
  Timothy 17
KEEN, Emelia 58
  Emilla 61
  Hannah 22
  Henry 58, 61
  Henry William 58
  Mary 16, 22, 39
  Timothy 22, 39
KEEN(E), Pollard 100
KEENE, Amelia 84
  Anne 83
  Charles 84
  Edmund Lake 84
  Elizabeth 83
  John 83
  Latitia 83
  Mary 84
  Mary (MOONE) 14
  Parthenia 84
  Pollard 84, 107
  Richard 109
  Samuel Young 83
  Susannah 83
  Timothy 14
  Violetta 84
  Young 84
KELLE, Elizabeth 3
KELLEY, Elianor 73
  Elizabeth 73
  John 73
KELLY, Alce (LOW) 65
  Charles 78
  Cornelious 65
  Elizabeth 4

KELLY, Prissilla 78
　Rachel 78
　Sarah 78
KEMBAL, Elizabeth 11
　Elizabeth (GUILBERT) 10
　Giles 11
　Hannah 26, 27, 31
　Hannah (JACKSON) 20
　James 31
　John 11
　John, Jr. 10
　John, Sr. 12
　Mary 9
　Robert 20
　Rowland 20, 26, 27, 31
　Samuel 27
　Sarah 26, 69
　Susanna 69
　William 31
KEMBALL, Mary 19
　William 19
KEMBEL, Hannah 33
　Rowland 33, 100
KEMBLE, Hannah 56
　Robert 68
　Rowland 56
　Sarah 68
　Stephen 56
KEMP, Johannah 18
　Richard 48
KENDALL, Elizabeth 79
　Isaac 79
　Martha 79
　Mary 79
KENLY, Daniel 68
　Frances (WELLS) 68
　William 68
KENNEDAY, James 109
KENT, Edward William 114
KERSEY, Ruth 44
KILMURRY, Patrick 104
KILPATRICK, James 111
KIMBAL, Hannah 74
　James 107
　John 107
　Robert 74
　Sarah 74
KIMBALL, Ann 78
　Bothya 78
　Frances 79
　Giles 80
　Hannah 43, 78
　James 78, 107, 108
　Jamima 78
　Jamima (BARNS) 78
　John 80, 107
　Margaret (DAUGHARTY/BARKEY) 82
　Martha 79
　Mary 80, 82

KIMBALL, Rachel 78
　Robert 80
　Roland 79
　Rowland 43
　Sabra 80
　Samuel 78
　Sarah 80
　Sarah (HANSON) 79
　Sophia 81
　Stephen 43, 82
　Susanna 80
　William 79
KIMBEL, John 33
　Margaret 84
　Samuel 112
　Stephen 84
　Susannah 94
KIMBLE, George 84
　Hannah 44, 50, 63
　James 100, 108, 109
　John 44
　Josiah 68
　Robert 50, 63
　Rowland 44
　Samuel 100
　Sarah 63
　Sarah (TAYLER) 50
　Sophia 63
　Stephen 115
KIMBLES, John 7
KININGTON, Hannah (TREGO) 1
　Thomas 1
KINSBY, Mary (WOOD) 14
　Robert 14
KNIGHT, Ann 92
　David 25
　Elizabeth 20, 26, 92
　Henry 115
　Light 19, 26, 92
　Mary 92
　Rachel 92
　Rachel (RUSE) 92
　Sarah 54, 92
　Susanna 20, 23, 25
　Susanna (SIMPSON) 19
　Thomas 19, 20, 23, 25, 26, 92, 102
　William 92, 115
L'SHODY, Francis 84
　Laurana 84
　Mary 84
LAMBETH, Elizabeth 53
LANCASTER, Pamela 97
LANDRUM, Andrew, Rev. 106, 110
LARRIFSEE, John 50
　Mary (DENSON) 50
LARRISSEE, Mary 59
LAWDER, William 115
LAWRASSEY, Mary 33

LAWRASSEY, Sarah 33
LAZELL, Sarah 90
LAZZEL, Nathaniel 108
LEAK, Jane 13
LEE, (?) 106
  Alce 55
  Alice (NORRIS) 39
  Corbin 100
  Eleanor 40
  Elianor 47, 69
  Eliner (TEMPLE) 33
  Elizabeth 37, 47, 48, 52, 53, 60, 69, 72, 85
  Elizabeth (ASHMORE) 38
  Elizabeth (SHELDS) 7
  James 47, 48, 60, 72, 88, 103, 106, 107
  James D. 108
  James, Jr. 108
  Jane 49, 57
  Jane (HICKSON) 48
  Joannah 49
  John 33, 39, 40, 48, 49, 57, 90
  Joseph 38
  Margaret 76
  Mary 36, 37, 57, 58, 60, 90
  Parker 88
  Priscilla 88
  Samuel 88
  Sarah 90
  Seaborn 90
  Sheerwood 40, 43, 47, 69
  Sherwood 33, 105
  Thomas 7
  William 72
LEEK, Abraham 43, 44
  Grace 43
  Mary 44, 80
  Sarah 43, 44
LEIGH, Sherwood 105
LENDRUM, Andrew 114
  Andrew, Rev. 76, 84, 90, 91, 92, 93, 94, 95, 109
  James 85
  Jane 95
  Jane (BURNEY) 84
  Lucinda 84
  Mary 85
  Robert Burney 84
LESHODY, Francis 81
  Myhannah 81
  Susana 81
LESTER, Alce 59, 67, 70
  Alce (LEE) 55
  Alice 81
  Ann 18, 19, 20, 22
  Charlotta 81

LESTER, George 19, 55, 59, 67, 70, 81, 100
  Martha 16
  Martha Pain Norriss 67
  Mary 22, 69, 70, 90
  Norris 81
  Parker 16
  Peter 18, 19, 20, 22, 38
  Sarah 59, 81
  Sophia 81, 94
  William 81
LEVER, John 108
LEWIS, Ann 70
  James 52
  John 43, 52, 70
  Margaret 52, 57
  Margaret (DEWLEY) 43
  Margaret (HUGHS) 72
  Samuel 55, 57, 72
  Sarah 57
  Sarah (MARSHALL) 55
LINDSEY, Edmund 25
  Elizabeth (BEASLEY) 25
LINLEY, Elizabeth 63
LINZEY, Edmond 36
  Elizabeth (BEEZLEY) 36
  John 36
LIPER, Edgar 15
  Elizabeth (PRICHET) 15
LIPPER, Elizabeth 28
LIPPINS, Thomas 57
LISBY, Hannah 29
LISTER, (?) 114
LITLE, Frances 31
LITTEN, Ann 39, 47, 62
  Anna 60
  Elizabeth 39, 40
  James 62
  Martha 36
  Mary 45
  Samuel 47
  Sarah 26
  Thomas 39, 47, 60, 62
LITTLE, Ann 60, 91
  Avarilla 55, 60, 63
  Avarilla (OZBOURN) 53
  Catherine (ROBERTSON) 91
  Elizabeth 31
  George 63, 91
  James 31
  Mary (SHEPARD) 34
  Rosanna 31
  Thomas 34, 53, 55, 60, 63, 105, 106, 112
  William 55
LITTON, Ann 17, 23, 24, 34, 105
  Elizabeth 17
  Hannah 23
  Isaac 24, 105

LITTON, John 24, 105
　Martha 19
　Mary 23
　Michael 34
　Sarah 19
　Thomas 17, 23, 24, 34, 105
LOADER, Richard 40
　Sarah (ELLIOT) 40
LOCKARD, Christian (TIPPINS) 60
　John 60
LOFTON, Ann 3
　Elinor 21
　Elizabeth 8, 10, 21
　Isabell 3
　Mary 21
　Rachel 21
　Sarah 21
　Thomas 3, 21
　William 3, 5, 8, 10
LONE, Jean 12
　William 12
LONEY, Arrabella 15
　Bethiah 34
　John 15, 55, 57, 60, 69, 100, 114
　Sarah 57, 60, 69
　Sarah (DENSON) 55
　Stephen 69
　William 15, 57, 100, 115
LONY, Arabella 15
　Margaret 15
　William 15
LORESON, Elenor 4
LORRESON, Elinor 4
LOUGH, Temperance (PICKETT) 14
　William 14
LOVE, Arrabella (WALSTON) 10
　John 107, 108, 109
　Robert 36, 48, 58
　Ruth 58
　Sarah 36, 48, 58, 66
　Tamar 36
　William 10, 36
LOVEILL, Martha 1
LOVEY, William 115, 116
LOW, Abraham 19, 55
　Alce 65
　Elizabeth 81
　James 19
　John 55, 115
　Kissiah 81
　Ralph 55
　Rebecca 19
　Ruth 55
　Samuel 19
　Thomas 19
　William 19
LOWRY, Edward 37
　Sarah 37

LOWRY, Sarah (JENKINS) 37
LUMBARD, George 50
LUNN, John 106
LUSBEY, Josep 1114
LUSBY, Joseph 100
　Milcah 77
LYAL, Ann 55, 72
　Ann (MUTURE) 35
　Elisabeth (FARMER) 55
　Elizabeth 66
　John 35, 55, 66
　Thomas 35
LYALL, Ann 26
　John 26
　Margaret 81
　Thomas 26
LYEN, Susana 95
LYLEY, James 50
　Margaret (PAINTER) 50
LYNCH, James 36, 40
　Margaret 36
　Mary 36
　Mary (LEE) 36
LYNSEY, Mary 60
LYON, Eliza. (BROWN) 91
　Elizabeth 92
　John 92
　Josiah 91, 92, 109
LYONS, Josiah 108
LYTTLE, Elizabeth 46
　Thomas 105
M'CABE, Barnett 86
　Catherine 86
　Eleanor (GOODWIN) 86
　Elizabeth 86
　John 86
M'COLLOCH, Jane 89
M'CULLOCH, Janet 89
　John 89
　William 89
M'KIM, Elizabeth 85
M'MAHAN, Benjamin 85
　Lucretia 85
　Thomas 85
MAC CARTHY, Samuel 60
　Sarah 60
MAC CARTNEY, Jane (SMITH) 61
　William 61
MAC CLOUD, Ann 57
　Ruth 57
　Ruth (CRAWFORD) 54
　William 54, 57
MAC DANIEL, Elinor 55
　John 55
　Mary 16
MACARLEY, Elizabeth 25
MACARTY, Sarah (MORRIS) 17
MACCARTY, Daniel 17, 21
　Mary 21

MACCARTY, Samuel 21, 63, 68
  Sarah 21, 35, 52, 63, 68
  William 63
MACCLOUD, William 62
MACCOMUS, Alexander 24
  Ann 18, 24, 31, 66
  Hannah 72
  Hannah (DEAVER) 66
  John 18, 24, 31, 59, 66, 72
  John, Jr. 54
  Mary 18, 24
  William 66, 72
MACCRAREE, Sarah 72
MACDANIEL, Ann 58
  James 58
  Sarah (JONES) 58
MACFARLOE, Ann 49
MACGOMERY, Elizabeth 65
  Mary (BRIERLY) 65
  William 65
MACKAN, Elizabeth (CULLEN) 48
  Owen 48
MACKARTE, Daniel 10
MACKELROY, Archabald 21
  Francis 21
  John 21
  Rachel 21
MACKENNEY, Jane 50
  Martha 50
MACKENNY, Jane 63
  Martha 65
MACMAHON, Rachel 42
MACURAHON, Arthur 26
  Rachel (GILBERT) 26
MAGEE, Judith 41
MANING, Elizabeth (SMITH) 38
  Richard 38
MANSFIELD, Catherine 97
MARCY, Ann (COLLYER) 8
  Jonathan 8
MARIARTY, Rachel 85
MARKUM, Hannah 7
MARSHALL, Mary 30, 35
  Mary (WELLS) 19
  Sarah 55
  Susanna 30, 67
  William 19
MARTHEWS, Ruth 1
MARTIN, Lodowick 2
MARYFIELD, Elizabeth 10
MASEWELL, Anna 53
MASON, Elizabeth 37, 80
  John 37
  Joseph 80
  Maria 80
  Mariah (GROVER) 80
MASTERS, Anthony 13
  John 13
  Margaret (JONES) 10

MASTERS, Mary 22
  Thomas 10
MATHESON, John 79
MATHEW, Ann 78
MATHEWS, Ann 40, 59, 66, 67,
  71, 77, 95
  Anna (MASEWELL) 53
  Aquila 41, 66, 77
  Bennet 100, 114, 116
  Bennett 64, 90
  Carvel 116
  Carvil 116
  Cassandra 59, 66
  Elizabeth 31, 40, 41, 54, 64,
   66
  Elizabeth (GARRETT) 28
  Emelia 31
  Hannah 1, 11, 15, 77
  Jacob Forwood 98
  James 28, 94, 95, 100, 107,
   108, 109
  James Maxwell 59
  Jane (FORWOOD) 98
  John 17, 53, 59, 66, 67, 71,
   77, 90, 95, 98, 100, 106, 110
  John Day 93
  John, Capt. 111
  John, Capt., Esq. 114
  Josiah 98
  Leven 54, 91, 93, 95, 100, 114
  Levin 84
  Mary 15, 19, 20, 77, 91, 95,
   98
  Mary (CARVIL) 17
  Mary (DAY) 93
  Mary (HEWLINGS) 84
  Milcah 90
  Milcah (LUSBY) 77
  Rebecca 67
  Roger 14, 15, 17, 19, 20, 28,
   31, 40, 41, 54, 64, 66, 77,
   100, 103, 116
  Sara 4
  Sarah 3, 95
  Sophia (HALL) 94
MATHIAS, James 108
MATHISON, Alexander 79
  Sarah (MORRIS) 79
MATTHEWS, Carvel 115
  Carvil 100
  Hannah 2
  Roger 100, 104, 115
MAXWELL, (?) 107
  David 107, 108
  Maxwell 108
  Philixana 14
MC CALL, Margarett 111
MC CARTY, Sam. 115
MC CLOSKEY, David 116

MC CLURE, William 109
MC COOBS, Margaret 111
MC CULLOCK, David 108
MC DOUGALL, (?), Capt. 110
MC GAY, Hugh 94
  James 94
  John 91
  Robert 91, 94
  Sarah 91, 94
  William 94
MEADS, Martha 41
MEGAY, George 81
  Robert 81
  Sarah (LESTER) 81
MERRIARTER, Edward 52
  Sarah (HANSON) 52
MERRIKEN, Elizabeth (EWINS) 14
  Joshua 14
MERRYARTER, Sarah 66
MICHAEL, Barbary (RISSARD) 79
  George 79
  Jacob 115
  James 115
MICHE, Richard 54
MICHEL, Ann 54
  Elizabeth 54
MIDDLEMORE, Frances 40
  Francis 40
  Josias 40
  Josias, Dr. 77
MIDDLETON, Jane (PERRY) 68
  Thomas 68
MIFFINA, Henry 100
MILES, Charles 1, 30, 34
  Edward 52
  Elisabeth 52
  Elizabeth 30, 34, 43
  Elizabeth (DAVIS) 28
  Evan 1, 3, 6, 8, 28, 30, 34, 43, 52
  Even 3
  John 3, 39
  Margaret 3
  Martha 10
  Mary 5, 40
  Rebecca 6, 8, 28
  Thomas 19, 43
  William 8
MILLAN, Henry 103
MILLEN, Henry 20
  Mary (NORRIS) 20
MILLER, Adam 38
  Hannah 36, 38, 45
  Henry 100
  Thomas, Esq. 112
  William 36, 38, 45
MILLIN, Henry 55
MILLINER, Ann 32
MILS, John 15

MITCHEL, Ann 18, 22, 25, 27, 35, 75, 91
  Avarilla 74
  Edward 27, 91
  Elizabeth 63, 68, 74, 91, 92
  Elizabeth (WILLIAMS) 41
  Hannah 18, 31
  Hannah (OSBORN) 68
  John 74
  Kent 25
  Martha 91
  Mary 91
  Richard 15, 41, 63, 68, 74, 100
  Sarah 91
  Sarah (OSBORN) 91
  Susanna 25
  Thomas 18, 22, 25, 27, 35, 68, 112
  Thomas, Jr. 68, 114
  Thomas, Sr. 114
  William 35, 91
MITCHELL, Elisabeth 45
  Elizabeth 82
  Gabriel 82
  Hannah 82
  James 82
  Kent 68, 82
  Mary 45, 86
  Richard 45
  Sarah 82
  Sophia 82
  Susanna 82
  Thomas 103
  William 82
MOATON, Mathew 14
MOLTON, Ann 11, 23
  John 23
  Mathew 11, 23
  Matthew 25
  Sarah 11
MONDAY, Alce 35
  Arthur 34, 46, 50
  Christopher 50
  Edward 80
  Elizabeth 46, 50
  Elizabeth (HAMBY) 34
  Hannah 80
  Henry 41, 43, 45, 58
  James 58
  John 43
  Katharine 46
  Sarah 41, 45
  Susanna 41, 45, 58
MONK, Agnes 79
  Mary 79
  Richard 79, 115
MOONE, Mary 14
MOOR, Elizabeth 34

MOORE, Samuel 87
  Senea (FUTT) 87
MORE, Agnus (TAYLOR) 40
  Alice 12
  Henry 40
MORGAN, Abraham 83
  Charles 27, 89
  Constance (BARNS) 67
  Edward 46, 56, 65, 83, 89,
    100, 105, 106, 107, 111
  Elisabeth (WALKER) 50
  Eliza 83
  Elizabeth 60, 65, 88
  Elizabeth (SMITH) 5, 6
  George 5, 6, 27
  Hannah 89
  James 33, 50, 60, 83, 87, 103
  Jane (BRASHIER) 33
  Johanna 27
  John 2
  John Permenta 60
  Joseph 67, 89
  Margaret (POGUE) 89
  Martha 46, 83
  Mary 2, 33, 83
  Mary (DAVIS) 87
  Prementer 87
  Rachel 27, 89
  Robert 83, 100
  Samuel 56, 100
  Sara 2
  Sarah 46, 56, 65, 83, 87, 89
  William 83, 100
MORON, Catharine 73
  Edward 73
  Elizabeth 73
MORPHEW, Cathurinah 28
  Honour 28
  John 28, 30
  Mary 28
  Mary (ELIOT) 28
  Rachel 28
  Timothy 28
  William 28
MORRIS, Edmond 69
  Edward 79
  Elizabeth 2, 12, 20, 69, 79
  Elizabeth (JACKSON) 1
  Henry 19
  John 79
  Mary 12, 19, 31, 63, 69, 79
  Michal 79
  Richard 20, 58, 63, 69, 79,
    115
  Sara 4
  Sarah 4, 17, 63, 79
  Susanna 12
  Thomas 1, 2, 4, 12, 19, 20, 79
  Wilborn William 31

MORRISS, Edmund 51
  Elizabeth 51
  John 58
  Mary 51, 58
  Mary (DEBRULER) 51
  Mary (MURPHY) 35, 44
  Richard 44
  Thomas 35
MOTTON, Sarah 22
MOTTS, Maryan 9
MOULTEN, John 108
MOULTON, John 107, 108
MOUNTEGUE, Agnus 10
MOURN, Edward 53
  Elizabeth (LAMBETH) 53
MUCKLEDUROY, Rachel 31
MULAIN, Edward 71
  Margaret 71
  Mary 71
MUNDAY, Henry 35
  John 35
  Susanna (TEMPLE) 35
  Thomas 35
MURDAGH, Daniel 64, 73
  James 64
  Martha (COWEN) 64
MURDAUGH, Daniel 68, 73, 74
  Martha 68, 73, 74
  Sarah 68
  Susanna 74
MURDOCH, Christian 89
  James 89
  Mary 89
  William 89
MURFFY, Darcas 16
  Edward 16
  John 16
MURPHEW, Darkas 28
MURPHEY, Catherine 88
  Eliza. 93
  Elizabeth 74, 75
  Mary 74, 88
  Sarah 58, 93
  Tim 115
  Timothy 74, 75, 93
  William 75, 88, 115
MURPHY, Benjamin 59
  Dianah 79
  Dorcass 58
  Elizabeth 79, 90
  Joab 79
  John 74
  Joseph 90
  Martha 90
  Mary 35, 44
  Sarah 79
  Sarah (GISSARD) 79
  Timothy 79, 90
  Ufan 79

MURPHY, William 79
MURRY, Elizabeth 28
  George 28
  James 28
  Mary 28
  Rachel 28
MUTRAN, Ann 29
  John 29
MUTURE, Ann 35
MYERS, John 115
NASAM, Thomas 40
NEAL, Bennett 107, 108
NELLSON, Aq. 107
  Aquilla 81, 115
  John 81
  Priscilla 78
  Sarah (CHANCEY) 81
NELSON, Ann 90
  Aquila 113, 115, 116
  Benjamin 108
  Catherine 73
  Francis 32
  Hannah 55
  John 32, 115
  Precilla 32
NEWLAND, Frances (SMITH) 74
  Thomas 74
NEWMAN, Ann 70
  Thomas 70
NEWSOM, Catherine 20
  Hellen 19
  John 19, 20
  Mary 19
  Mary (FINCHECOME/STINCHCOMBE?) 19
  Thomas 19, 20
NEWSUM, John 1
  Susanna 2, 3
  Thomas 1, 2, 3
NICHOLA, Alexander 55
  Ann 55
  Phebe 55
NICHOLAS, Ann 58
NICHOLS, John 10
  Thomas 10
NIGHT, Cordelia 71
  Elizabeth 72
NILLSON, Benjamin 107
NOAH, Martha (MEADS) 41
  Mary 41
  Richard 41
NOBLE, Catherine 72
  Mary 78
NOEL, Lewis 12
  Mary (FERRIL) 12
NORRIS, Alice 39
  Elizabeth 14, 61
  Ells 15
  Mary 11, 20

NORRIS, Sarah 11, 15
  Susannah 102
  Thomas 14
  William 11, 15, 20
NORTON, Elizabeth (CLARK) 40
  Nathan 109
  William 40
NORVEL, James 63
  Jane 103
  John 56, 63, 103
  Mary 56, 63
NORVELL, Jane 61
  John 48, 52
  Mary 52
  Mary (BAYLEY) 48
  Sarah 52
NORVIBAND, John 105
NORVIL, Hannah 70
  John 70
  Mary 70
  William 106
O'HERD, Ann 78
O'NEAL, Daniel 84
  Henry 105
  Susannah 84
OACHISSON, Elizabeth 64
OBRYAN, Bridget 15
  Charles 15
  Daniel 15
  Margaret 15
  Terence 15
OCHISSON, Elizabeth 58
  Johannah 58
  Joseph 58
OGG, Bethiah 28
  Caturinah 28
  Francis 28, 41, 100
  Stockett 41
  Susannah 43
OGLE, Samuel 106
OGLESBY, Daniel 22, 38
  David 38
  Elisha 22, 38
  Margaret 38
  Martha 22, 38
  Mary 22
  Richard 38
  Ruth 22
  Subrid 38
  William 38
OLEE, John 20
ORR, Ann 85
  Hugh 85
  James 85
  Martha 85
  Mary 85
ORRISS, Richard 51
OSBORN, Ann 81
  Ann (BISSETT) 86

OSBORN, Avarilla 15, 19, 22,
  23, 66
 Avarilla (HOLLIS) 30
 Benja 80
 Benjamin 1, 25, 26, 31, 33,
  86, 91
 Bennett 92
 Catharine 31, 34
 Catherine 66
 Cathurinah (RHOADES) 28
 Cyrus 80
 Elizabeth 86, 92
 Elizabeth (SIMPSON) 91
 Frances 34
 Francis 91
 Hannah 26, 68, 81
 Jacob 81
 James 15, 30, 31, 69, 72, 80,
  81, 100
 Jane 72, 80
 Jane (HUGHS) 69
 John 81
 Josias 72
 Margaret 26, 31, 82
 Margaret (LYALL) 81
 Martha 80
 Mary 3, 30, 80, 81, 91
 Mary Clark 22
 Sarah 25, 26, 31, 33, 81, 91
 Sarah (FOWLER) 81
 Sary 91
 Susanna 26, 81
 Thomas 3, 33, 91, 92
 William 1, 3, 7, 10, 15, 19,
  22, 23, 25, 28, 30, 31, 34,
  66, 80, 81, 86, 91, 107, 108
 William, Sr. 12
OSBORNE, Avarilla 85
 Cyrus 100, 115
 James 115
 William 100, 109, 115
OSBOURN, Benjamin 100
 James 11, 12
 Katharine 54
 Margaret 12
 Martha 54
 William 54
OSBOURNE, William 100
OSBURN, Cyrus 96
 James 114
 John 115
 Susannah (ROBINSON) 96
 William 114, 115
OZBORN, Benjamin 59
 John 59
 Sarah 59
OZBOURN, Avarilla 53
 Benjamin 43, 52
 Jacob 52

OZBOURN, Sarah 43, 52
 Susannah 48
 William 100
OZBURN, Katharine 43
 Mary Ann 43
 William 43
PACA, Aq. 109
 Aquila 5, 8, 25, 40, 72, 76,
  100
 Aquila, Jr. 100
 Frances 25
 James 76
 John 25, 76, 77, 93, 107
 John Stokes 77
 John, Capt. 97, 114
 John, Jr. 100, 106
 Margaret (LEE) 76
 Margaret 77
 Martha 8, 40, 93
 Martha (PHILLIPS) 5
 Mary 8
 Prescilla 64
 Rachel 40
 Susanna 97
PAINTER, Edward 55
 Margaret 50
PALMER, Ann 35
PARIS, Elizabeth 72
 Joshua 72
PARKER, Clemensi 4
 Clemensy 4
 Elizabeth 33
 Isabella 6
 Isabella (SMITH) 5
 James 26
 John 4, 6, 10
 John, Sr. 5, 12
 Joseph 6
 Junio 10
 Mary 6
 Samuel 4
 William 4, 5
PARKS, Dorothy 10, 13
 Edward 10, 13
 Mary 10
 Philip 16
 Robert 13
PARR, Elizabeth 111
PARRISH, Alexander 53
 Jane (CHATTO) 53
PARTRIDGE, Katharine 50
PATTERSON, Cynthia 66
 George 74, 100, 110
 Jane 61, 66, 73, 74
 John 73
 Robert 61, 66, 73, 74, 100,
  109
 Sarah 61
 William P. 116

PAWMER, Comfort 58
  Elizabeth 58
  John 58
  Thomas 104
PEACA, Aquila 5
  Mary 5
PEACOCK, Frances 48
  John 48, 107, 108, 109
PEARSON, Ann 89
  Enoch 89
  Thomas 89
PECA, Aquila 40
  Martha 40
  Rachel 40
PECKOO, Margaret 85
PENICK, Hannah 45
PENTONY, Joseph 114
PERKINS, Adam 68
  Avarilla 68, 86
  Aventen 68
  Benjamin 41
  Elisabeth 52
  Elisha 2, 21, 44
  Elizabellaw 82
  Elizabeth 19, 21, 23, 38, 59, 86
  Elizabeth (CUTCHEN) 49
  Hannah 36, 75
  Isaac 58, 68
  Isabel 38
  John 19, 38
  Joseph 36
  Margaret 59
  Margaret (SHERRIL) 21
  Margery 44
  Martha 7
  Martha (MILES) 10
  Mary 2, 23, 36, 41, 60, 68
  Mary (LEE) 58
  Mary (SHEERWILL) 60
  Mary (WALTERS) 68
  Rachel 36, 59, 86
  Reuben 86
  Richard 2, 5, 7, 16, 41, 68, 86
  Richard, Jr. 49, 52
  Richard, Sr. 60
  Robert Biggin 52
  Ruben 23, 75
  Rubin 115
  Sarah 5
  Stephen John 49
  William 2, 10, 11, 19, 23, 38, 49, 59, 68, 86, 112
PERREIR, Gilbert 4
PERRERILL, Daniel 3
  Sarah 3
PERRIMAN, Samuel 109
PERRY, Elizabellaw (PERKINS) 82

PERRY, Elizalla 82
  James 82
  Jane 68
  Mary 82
  Rachel 82
  Sarah 27
  Sarah (MACCARTY) 35
  William 27, 35, 82, 115
PERRYMAN, Elizabeth 71
  Isaac 115, 116
  Martha (ARMSTRONG) 71
  Mary 71
  Roger 71
  Susannah 94
PETTERSON, Robert 114
PEW, Matthew 100
PHELPS, Avinton 31
  Rachel (MUCKLEDUROY) 31
  Rose 104
  Thomas 104
PHENIX, Bridget 13
  William 13
PHILLIP, James 100
PHILLIPS, Bethiah 8, 16
  Cordelia 73
  James 8, 16, 18, 19, 54, 57, 62, 67, 73, 75, 76, 77, 93, 94, 100, 104, 105, 106, 116
  James, Capt. 109, 114
  James, Col. 22
  Johannah 19, 22, 49, 67
  Johannah (KEMP) 18
  Martha 5, 94
  Martha (PACA) 93
  Mary 75, 76
  Rebecca Knight 77
  Sarah 57, 62, 67, 73, 75, 76, 77, 83
  Sarah (KNIGHT) 54
  Susanna 19, 76
  Susannah 73
PICKETT, Temperance 14
PIKE, Elizabeth 33
  Henderson 115
PILE, William 108
PILGRIM, Amos 42, 53
  Mary 42
  Rachel 42, 53
  Rachel (MACMAHON) 42
  Thomas 53
PINE, Easter 10
PITT, Francis L. 115
PITTCOCK, Elizabeth 12
PLUMMER, Ann 17
POAG, Elizabeth 41
  John 41
  Sarah 41
POGE, Ann 50
  Daniel 55

POGE, George 56
  Jane (ANTIL) 55
  John 50, 56, 65
  Mary 67
  Sarah 50, 56, 65
  William 65
POGNE, John 25
  Joseph 25
  Mary 25
  Sarah 25
POGUE, Ann 88, 89
  Hannah 89
  John 89
  Joseph 89
  Margaret 89
  Sarah 89
  Sarah (FARMER) 89
  Susannah 89
POLOKE, Ann 82
  Daniel 82
  Jane 82
POLSON, Andrew 47
  Ann 47
  Cornelious 47
POOL, Mary 12
PORTER, Aaron 63, 68
  Ann 68
  Jane 68
  Jane (MACKENNY) 63
  John 68
  John, Rev. 95
  Thomas 68
POTEE, Mary 89
POTEET, Joan 42
  William 42
POULSON, Ann 24
  Ann (EMSON) 21
  Cornelious 24
  Cornelius 21
  Rebecca 24
POWEL, Hannah Peninah Winnifred 30
  John 27, 30
  Mary 35
  Philis 27
  Phillis 30
  Richard 18
POWELL, Elioanah 27
  Patience 83
POWLSON, Ann 22
  Cornelious 22
  Elizabeth 22
PRAICE, Griffin 29
PREBBELL, Ann 1
  John 3, 4
  Mary 1
  Sara 7
  Thomas 1, 3, 4, 7
PREBBLE, Ann 27

PREBBLE, Elizabeth 5
  John 27
  Mary 5, 9
  Sarah 9
  Thomas 5, 9
PREBLE, Ann 17, 24
  John 24, 106
  Mary 27
  Sarah 24
  Thomas 24
PRECHAR, Mary 7
PRECHAT, William 5, 7
PRESBURY, James 13
  Martha 55, 93, 96
  Martha (GOLDSMITH) 13
  Martha (HALL) 91
  Susannah 92
  William Robinson 91
PRESTON, Ann 58, 65, 69, 71, 73, 75, 76, 77, 78, 87
  Ann (GRAFTON) 50
  Anna 84
  Barnett 76
  Bernard 84, 88
  Clemency 88
  Corbin 87
  Daniel 50, 58, 65, 69, 73, 75, 76, 77, 78, 87, 106
  Elizabeth 47, 61
  Grace 30
  Grafton 73
  Hannah 66, 86
  James 39, 42, 48, 61, 66, 71, 75, 88, 100, 106
  John 71
  Margaret 58
  Martin 88
  Mary 84, 88
  Mary (GARNET) 71
  Sarah 33, 42, 48, 61, 65, 66, 71, 75, 77, 84
  Sarah (PUTTEET) 39
  Sarah (RUFF) 84
  William 78
PRIBBLE, Ann 59
  Anna 51
  Anne 37
  James 59
  John 37, 51, 59
  Mary 88
  Sarah 57
  Sophia 37
  Stephen 51
PRICE, David E. 115
  Elizabeth 110
  Marcy 29
  Margaret 74
  Mariah 29
  Martha 64

PRICE, Martha (SPENCER) 30
Mary 29, 30
Sarah (CROSS) 69
Thomas 30, 64, 69
PRICHARD, Daniel 62
Elisabeth 105
Elizabeth 52, 58, 60, 62
Isabella 62
James 52, 58, 60, 62, 100
Margaret 52
Obadiah 100
Obediah 58, 60, 62, 102
Reuben 62
Sam. 115
Samuel 62, 100, 104
PRICHAT, William 2
PRICHET, Elizabeth 15
William 15
PRICHETT, Margett 14
Samuel 14
PRIGDON, Alexander 100
PRIGG, Edward 83
Martha (MORGAN) 83
Mary 83
Sarah 83
William 83, 106, 109
PRISBEY, Peregreen 114
PRITCHARD, Ann 70, 83
Avarilla 57
Charles 76
Charles Anderson 72
Christina 37
Elizabeth 10, 47, 57, 69, 70, 78, 85
Elizabeth (DURBIN) 46
Elizabeth (LITTEN) 40
Ezibella 76
Hannah 37
Henry 37
Isabel 72
Isabella 54, 56
Isabella (COTRALL) 46
James 16, 46, 57, 69, 76, 105
John 54
Joseph 41
Mary 41, 76
Maryan 10
Obadiah 47
Obediah 16, 30, 40, 56, 70
Samuel 46, 47, 54, 56, 72, 76
Sarah 37, 78
Thomas 76
William 10
PRITCHET, Elizabeth 8
Margaret 21
Maryan 8
Obediah 21
Sarah 21
William 8

PRITCHETT, Obediah 14, 100
PRITON, John 59
PUSHIN, John 100
PUTTEE, Mary 61
PUTTEET, Isabel 54
Jane 54, 57
Joan 59
Joan (STEWART) 39
John 42
Mary 59
Sarah 39
William 39, 54, 59
PYCRAFT, Sarah 34
Thomas 34
RALSTONE, Elizabeth 89, 89
Gavin 89
RAMSEY, Ann 6
Charles 2, 8, 14, 37, 71
Charly 6
Christian 64
Elianor 64
Elizabeth 2, 8, 14, 71, 83
Elizabeth (DEW) 37
John 64, 83
Mary 2, 71
Sarah 71
Thomas 2
William 37, 71, 83
RANSHAW, Abraham 59
Anna 59
Frances 43
Frances (CLARK) 42
Jane 43
Thomas 42, 43, 59
REA, Hugh 79
Margaret 79
Rachel 79
William 79
READ, Annes 70
Eliza (JACKSON) 79
John 70, 79
Mary 70
REASIN, Alice 80
James 82
Mary 82
Mary (DICKSON) 81
Mathew 81, 82
Richard 80
Thomas 80
REASON, Richard 108
Sarah 80
REDDELL, Eleanor (DAUGHERTY) 84
John 84
Sarah 84
REDMAN, Ann (BELL) 53
Christopher 53
Mary 33
REECE, Mary 57
Mary (DRAPER) 55

REECE, Sarah 57
　Solomon 55
　Solomon, Jr. 57
REED, George 110
REES, Abraham 72
　Daniel 72
　Elizabeth (NIGHT) 72
　Jane 69
　Mary 45, 70
　Soloman 70
REESE, Ann 78
　Ann (O'HERD) 78
　Elizabeth 78
　Hannah 78
　Mary 46, 78
　Rachel 78
　William 78
REEVES, Ann 87
　Eleanor 87
　Emanuel 87
　George 87
　John 87
　Margaret 87
　Mary 87
RELPH, Henry 13
RENSHAW, Abraham 50, 66, 74
　Alice Hannah 49
　Ann 66, 67, 74
　Anna (HAWKINS) 50
　Casandra 70
　Cassandra 70
　Elizabeth 70, 85
　Elizabeth (WELS) 67
　Frances 85
　James 85
　John 45, 49, 66, 67, 70, 89
　Joseph 67, 70, 74
　Mary 14, 49, 67, 70
　Mary (BISHOP) 89
　Mary (LITTEN) 45
　Robert 85
　Selina 85
　Thomas 85, 109
　William 85
RESON, Martha 80
REVES, Ann 4
　Elizabeth 79
　Josias 79
　Latisha 79
REWARK, Ann 38
　Patrick 38
　Ruth 38
　Sarah 38
REYLEY, Elizabeth 63
　Francis 63
　Joseph 63
RHOADES, Ann 76
　Cathurinah 28
　Henry 76

RHODES, Ann 22, 39, 44, 49, 58, 69
　Anna 63
　Catharine 44
　George Lester 63
　Henry 39, 44, 46, 49, 58, 63, 69
　John 60, 69
　Katharine 46
　Margaret (ALLEN) 68
　Martha 49
　Mary 39, 60
　Sarah 58, 63
　William 60
RICE, Ann 70
　Elianor 70
　Elizabeth 36, 42, 49, 61
　Elizabeth (BUTTUM) 35
　John 49
　Mary 61
　William 35, 36, 42, 49, 61, 70
RICHARDS, Jeremiah 56
　Mary 56
　Samuel 56
　William 56, 104
RICHARDSON, (?) 114
　Ann 10
　Delia 89
　Elizabeth 89
　James 85
　John 108
　Mark 12
　Marks 3
　Mary (RUFF) 85
　Samuel 89
　Sarah 89
　Sarah (DAVIS) 89
　Susanna 11
RIDDELL, Charlotte 97
　Jessie 97
　William 97
RIDDLE, Andrew 58, 63
　Ann 63
　Ann (NICHOLAS) 58
　Elisabeth 63
RIGBEE, Ann 76
　Cassandra 76
　Nathaniel 76
RIGBEY, Nathan, Col. 100
RIGBIE, Cassandra 69
　Elizabeth 67
　James 67
　John 109
　Nathan 67, 69
　Nathan, Col. 69
　Thomas 109
RIGDEN, Elizabeth 36
　George 36
　Stephen 36

RIGDON, Alexander 67
  Ann 32, 49, 59, 67, 70, 88, 89
  Baker 89
  Charles 14
  Elizabeth 14, 15, 22, 26, 32, 45, 59, 64, 65, 70, 90
  Elizabeth (OACHISSON) 64
  Enock 26
  George 14, 15, 22, 26, 32, 55, 59, 70, 88
  George, Jr. 49, 55, 64
  James 88
  John 22, 64, 65, 70, 90
  Margaret 89
  Mary 88, 89
  Mary (PRIBBLE) 88
  Ruth 89
  Sarah 55, 64
  Sarah (THOMPSON) 49
  Thomas 67
  Thomas Baker 22
  William 22, 70, 88, 90
RILEY, Francis 70
  John 70
  Ruth 70
RILLE, Daniel 6
RIMSON, Richard 2
RISSARD, Barbary 79
RISTAU, Samuel 114
ROACH, John 29
  Rozannah (DENNIS) 29
  William 29
ROBERT, Anne 31
  John 102
ROBERTS, John 12, 103
  Mary (JACKSON) 12
  Robert 10
  Stephen 28
ROBERTSON, Catherine 91
ROBINSON, Abraham 71, 115
  Anne 84
  Blanch 21
  Cathrine 81
  Daniel 84, 91, 93
  Mary 84
  Sarah 21, 24, 60
  Sarah (COMBEST) 16, 33
  Sarah (SIMPSON) 71
  Susana (BROWN) 93
  Susannah 84, 91, 96
  Susannah (BROWN) 84
  Thomas 81
  William 16, 21, 24, 33, 81
RODINHEISER, Peter 112
ROE, James 59
ROGERS, Mary 15
ROSS, Elizabeth 66
  Elizabeth (LEE) 52
  George, Rev. 84

ROSS, Rebecca (WOOD) 34
  Samuel 34, 52
  Thomas 34
ROUSE, Ann 54
  Ann (ADKISSON) 50
  Elizabeth 51
  Elizabeth (PERRYMAN) 71
  John 71
  Zachariah 50, 51
  Zachary 54
ROW, James 60, 104
  Lydia 60
  Stephen 60
RUARK, Ann 48
  Ann (CARLISS) 35
  Patrick 35, 48
RUFF, (?) 114
  Daniel 62, 72, 100, 104, 106
  Daniel III 15
  Elizabeth 72
  Elizabeth (WEBSTER) 62
  Hannah 20
  Hannah (PRESTON) 86
  Henry 30, 86, 107
  John 17
  John H. 115
  Mary 22, 27, 85, 88
  Richard 14, 15, 17, 19, 20, 22, 27, 30, 37, 85, 100, 103, 115
  Sarah 14, 15, 17, 19, 20, 22, 27, 30, 84, 86
RULEY, Elizabeth 68
  Francis 68
  Sarah 68
RUMMAGE, David 78
  Elizabeth 78
  George 78
  Margaret 78
  Mary (NOBLE) 78
RUMSEY, (?) 113
  H. 113
  John 100
RUPH, John 18
  Richard 18
  Sarah 18
RUSEER, Rachel 92
RUSH, John 18
  Richard 18
  Sarah 18
RUSSEL, Elizabeth 26
  Frances 26
  Francis 11
  Mary 10, 11
  Mary (BORING) 17
  Mary (CAHELL) 9
  Sarah 26
  Tho. 9
  Thomas 10, 11, 17

RUTH, Catherine 97
  John 109
  Joseph 97
RUTTER, James 103
RYCRAFT, Sarah (PRESTON) 33
  Thomas 33
RYLEY, Elizabeth (ENGLAND) 57
  Francis 57
  John 67
  Ruth (ANSHOR) 67
RYMBALLS, James 114
  Robert 114
  Sam 114
  Stephen 114
  William 114
SANDERS, Christian 32
  Christian (BEARDY) 30
  Edward 30, 32
  Mary 30
SAPPINGTON, Richard 115
SAUNDERS, Elizabeth 81
  Frances 81
  James 81
  Jas. 114
  Sarah 81
  William 81
SAVERY, Ann (REVES) 4
  John 4, 7
SAVORY, Anne 8, 11
  Diane 11
  John 8, 11, 43, 46
  Mary 46
  Mary (BUCKNAL) 43
  William 46
SCARLET, James 68
  Mary 71
  Ruth 63, 68, 71
  Ruth (BELSHER) 59
  Stephen 59, 63, 68, 71
  Thomas 63
SCOTT, Ann (WHEELER) 65
  James 65
  Mary (KEAN) 47
  Richard 47
SEALY, Emanuel 13
  Sarah 14
SEAMER, Elizabeth 21
  Sophia 21
SEAMORE, Elizabeth 31
  Thomas 31
SHAW, Elizabeth 39
SHAY, Thomas 115
SHEELD, Elizabeth (BUNN) 1
  John 1
SHEEPERD, Christopher 114
SHEERWILL, Mary 60
  William, Sr. 60
SHELDS, Elizabeth 7
  John 6

SHEPARD, Bridget 14
  Christopher 14, 41
  Jane 30
  Jane (TAYLOR) 28
  Rowland 14, 28, 30
  Sarah 29
  Sarah (DREW) 41
SHEPERD, Bridget 38
  Rowland 38
SHEPHARD, Bridget 11
  Christopher 11
  Elizabeth 11
  George 11
  Rowland 11
SHEPHEARD, Mary 11
SHEPHERD, Ann 46
  Christopher 44, 51
  Constance 48
  James 51
  John 48
  Mariana 51
  Rowland 100
  Sarah 44, 51
  Susanna 44
SHEPPARD, Ann 35
  Elizabeth 35
  John 35
  Mary 34, 35
  Rachel 35
  Sarah 35
SHEREDINE, Jeremiah 100, 109, 111
SHERRIL, Margaret 21
SHODEY, Francis 115
SHYE, Elizabeth 13
  Sarah 13
  Thomas 13
SICKLEMORE, Elizabeth 13
SILBE, Ann 104
SIMPSON, Ann 13
  Anne 27
  Avarilla 70
  Elianor 24
  Elizabeth 13, 21, 24, 33, 74, 91
  Gilbert 25
  Hannah 24
  Jonathan 13
  Martha 23
  Mary 21, 24, 25, 27, 33
  Mary (SMITH) 25
  Mathew 13
  Nathaniel 74
  Richard 24, 74
  Ruben 70
  Sarah 33, 71
  Sarah Collins 18
  Susan 13
  Susanna 18, 19

SIMPSON, Thomas 13, 24, 25, 27, 33
William 13, 21, 24, 33, 70
SIMSON, Elizabeth 2, 4
Jonathan 5
Richard 4, 5
Susanna 2
Thomas 2
William 2
SINCLER, James 69
Mary (LESTER) 69
SINKIN, Thomas 31
SINKLER, Elisabeth 49
James 49
William 49
SISK, David 104
SITHS, Mary 14
SKELTON, Mark 14
SKY, Elizabeth (MARYFIELD) 10
Thomas 10
SMALL, Catherine 111
Joyner 111
SMITH, Abraham 33
Adam 89
Alexander L. 100, 115
Alexander Lawson 116
Alizanah 90
Ann 33, 42
Anne 42, 57
Anne (SIMPSON) 27
Benjamin 11, 12
Blanch (DOOLEY) 82
Cassandra 76
Elizabeth 5, 6, 8, 38, 43, 50, 57, 66, 69, 76, 80, 90, 97
Elizabeth (GALLION) 42
Elizabeth (GILES) 97
Elizabeth (WEBSTER) 80
Emanuel 7, 12
Emanuell 4
Frances 74, 97
Francis 8
George 1, 5, 6, 12, 28, 108
Grace 66
Hannah 6, 12, 48, 69, 80
Isaac 33
Isabella 5
Jacob 47, 100
Jacob Giles 97
Jane 61, 111
John 14, 16, 33, 47, 89
Josiah 43
Martha 4
Mary 7, 16, 25, 28, 33, 47, 48, 64, 80, 89
Mary (HEDGE) 14
Nathan 76, 82, 108
Nathaniel 28, 80, 90, 119
Paca 97, 115, 116

SMITH, Prescilla (PACA) 64
Priscilla 71
Samuel 27, 42, 43, 50, 57, 66, 69, 109, 110
Sarah 27, 68, 69, 76, 94
Sarah (HOLLIS) 12
Selina 8
Shellina 6
Sillinah 18, 42
Susanna (PACA) 97
Susanna (STOKES) 71
Susannah 95
William 1, 28, 39, 48, 51, 64, 76, 82, 90, 95, 97, 100, 103, 112, 116
Winston 95, 97, 115
Winstone 64, 71, 76, 100
SMITHERS, Blanch (WELLS) 8
Richard 8
SMITHES, Philixana (MAXWELL) 14
Richard 14
SMITHS, Blanch 14
George 14
John 14
Philizana 14
Richard 14
SMITHSON, Elizabeth 42
Sarah 48
SNELSON, Abraham 28, 30, 54
Margaret 44, 54, 62
Margaret (HOGG) 36
Rachel 30, 44
William 30, 36, 44, 54, 62
SNIDER, (?) 112
SNOWDY, Mathew 112
SNYDER, (?) 112
SOLOMON, Jean 12
SOLOVAN, Mary 69
SOWARD, Ann 112
SPAIN, Beaver 54
Beven 45
Bever 48
Elizabeth 48, 54
Elizabeth (RIGDON) 45
Joshua 54
Thomas 48
SPAVOLD, James, Dr. 109
SPEGLE, Deborah (COTRALL) 46
John Cole 46, 51, 63
Mary Cole 63
Rebecca 51, 63
Thomas Cole 51
SPENCER, Alexander 53, 105
Ann 88
Ann (POGUE) 88
Charity 49, 88
Christian 29, 38
Christian (COOB) 33
Elizabeth 88

SPENCER, Elizabeth (LEE) 53
John 88, 97
Margaret 88
Martha 30, 97
Moses 105
Rachel 49, 88
Richard 97
Sarah 88
Thomas 105
William 88
Zachariah 88
Zackariah 33, 38, 49
SPICER, Ann 73
SPINKS, Sarah 25
SPRICER, Ann 105
SPRUSBANK, Abraham 115
SPURGEN, John 104
STANHOUSE, Alexander, Dr. 111
STANLEY, Ann 39
John 39
Richard 39
STANSBURY, Barthiah 73
Jane 90
STAPLETON, Alice 50, 88
Edward 50, 87
Hannah 87
Joseph 87
Joshua 87
Margaret 88
Rachel 50, 87
Sarah 88
Sarah (CROOK) 88
Thomas 88
STEAVENSON, George 92
Rachel (CRUTE) 92
William 92
STEELE, John 14
Mary (CLARK) 14
STENHOUSE, (?), Dr. 114
A., Dr. 109
Alexander, Dr. 87
Cordelia (CHRISTIE) 87
STEPHENS, John 46
STEPHENSON, Henry, Dr. 114
STERLING, James, Rev. 94
STEUART, George 87
Margaret 87
Thomas 87
STEVENS, Susannah 102
STEVENSON, Rachel 93
William 93
STEWARD, James 109, 114
STEWART, (?) 110
Ann 84
Bennett 97
Charles 71
Elizabeth 97
George 111
STEWART, James 66, 71, 84, 97, 101, 105, 108, 109
Jane 71
Joan 39
Margaret 84, 85
Mary 71, 84
Mary (WOOD) 66
Michael 115
Mitchel 101
Mitchell 84
Susanna 97
STIGINGS, Mary (MASTERS) 22
William 22
STINCHCOMBE, Mary 19
STOCKS, Rachel 108
STOKES, Cordelia 49, 77
Elizabeth 48
Frances 15
George 49
Humphrey Wells 15
Humphry Wells 36
John 15, 101, 103
Mary 15, 36
Rebecca 83
Rebecca (YOUNG) 77
Robert 36, 77, 83, 107
Robert Young 83
Robert Young, Esq. 96
Sarah (BROOKE) 96
Susanna 71
Susanna Maria 15
Susannah 15, 49, 103
Susannah Maria 15
William 101
William Young 96
STONE, Constance 61
Henry 61
STORY, Ann (BRITTAIN) 38
Charles 38
Jesper 90
Joshua 90
Margaret (BRISCOE) 90
STREET, Sarah 54
Sarah (FEELER) 43
Thomas 43, 54
STRINGER, John 39
Mary (COLLIER) 39
SULIVAN, Hanah 95
SULLIVAN, Nathaniel 95
SUTTEN, Ann 95
Hannah 94
Margaret 90
Robert 94
Samuel 90, 94, 95
Sarah 94, 95
Sarah (LAZELL) 90
SUTTON, Ann 42, 44
Jeremiah 42, 44
John 42

SUTTON, Joseph 44
  Margaret 84
  Mary 41, 79
  Robert 41
  Ruth (CANTWELL) 79
  Sam 108
  Samuel 41, 79
SWAIN, David M. 83
  Hannah 83
  Jonathan M. 83
  Mary (DREW) 92
  Nathan 92
  Thomas M. 83
SWAN, Edward 10, 12, 15
  Elizabeth (GRIFFITH) 10, 12
  Frances 15
SWIFT, (?) 104
  Elizabeth 25, 31
  Elizabeth (WHITEAKER) 24
  Flower 24, 25, 31
  Margaret 31
  Thomas 25
SWILLAWIN, Ann (MILLINER) 32
  John 32
  Mary 32
  Owen 32
SWILLEVANT, Dorothy (TAYLOR) 7
  Owen 7
SYLBE, Ann 103, 104
SYLBY, Ann 40, 50
  Anna 104
  Anne 43
  Caleb 50
  James 40
  John 40, 43, 50
  Martha 43
SYMMONS, Mary 46
SYMONS, Elianor 46
  Samuel 46
SYMPSON, Ann 41
  Anna 59
  Avarilla (PERKINS) 68
  Elizabeth 41, 54
  John 54
  Joshua 57
  Martha 53
  Mary 41, 50, 53, 57, 69
  Mary (LARRISSEE) 59
  Samuel 41
  Sarah 55
  Thomas 41, 53, 55, 57, 59
  William 41, 54, 59, 68
TALBOT, Charles 15
  Elizabeth (WOOD) 15
TANNER, Forgeson 115
TANSEY, Alexander 8
  Elizabeth 8
  Rebecca 8
TATE, David 108

TAYLER, Abraham 56
  Agnus Mountaine 50
  Ann 56
  Ann (HAWKINS) 54
  Benjamin 54, 56
  Hannah 56
  James 41, 46, 50, 104
  John 56
  Lawrence 46
  Luranah 41
  Mary 41, 46, 50, 57
  Michael 56, 103
  Sarah 50
TAYLOR, Abraham 63, 68, 80, 92, 112
  Agnes 15, 21
  Agnus 11, 13, 17, 40
  Agnus (MOUNTEGUE) 10
  Amasa 80
  Ann 29, 61, 66
  Aquila 86
  Aquilla 80
  Asa 80
  Ashbury 115
  Dorothy 7
  Elizabeth 39, 86
  Elizabeth (WHITEAKER) 33
  Francis 33, 39
  George 61
  Grace 33
  Hannah 63, 68, 86
  Henrietta 80
  James 15, 33, 34, 53, 65, 70, 80, 85, 91, 101, 105, 108, 114, 115
  James, Jr. 114
  Jane 28, 66, 92
  Jane (HANBY) 86
  Jeremiah 80
  Laama 91
  Larranc 5
  Law 13
  Lawrance 68
  Lawrence 10, 11, 13, 15, 17, 31, 33
  Lawrrant 4
  Lorance 21
  Margaret 29
  Mary 11, 13, 33, 53, 65, 70, 86
  Mary (FOSTER) 34
  Mary (MILES) 5
  Mary (MITCHELL) 86
  Mary (RUFF) 85
  Michael 29, 86
  Michael Thomas 114
  Rachel 39
  Robert 61, 66, 80
  Sarah 21, 91

TAYLOR, Sarah (KIMBALL) 80
Stephen 80
Thomas 29, 63, 86, 92
William 13
TEAG, Katherine 12
TEAGUE, Susanna 17
TEMPLE, Elenor (LORESON) 4
Eliner 33
Elinor (LORRESON) 4
Michael 35
Susanna 5, 35
Thomas 4, 5, 14
THARP, Catherine (CULLINGS) 35
Edward 35
THATCHER, Barbarah 111
THODES, Thomas 68
THOMAS, Ann 78
Charles 78
Daniel 14
David 13, 19, 39
Elizabeth (WHEELAR) 39
Hannah 13, 14, 19
Henry 13, 57, 64
Henry, Sr. 110
Jane 64
Jane (PUTTEET) 57
John 22, 27, 41, 43, 64, 106
Joseph 27, 41
Mary 22, 27, 43
Moses 22
Nathan 41
Sarah 41
Susanna 5
William 78
THOMPSON, Alexander 48, 49
Andrew 42, 58, 60, 70
Andrew, Jr. 51
Ann 89
Annah 20
Edward 92, 93
Elizabeth 36, 42, 45, 51, 58, 70, 89
Ellinor (AGON) 83
Hannah 58, 89
James 36, 65, 83
Jarvis 89
Jemima (GROOM) 92
Jemimah 93
John 40, 61, 65, 83, 89
Margaret 89
Margaret (GILBERT) 89
Martha 93
Mary 65
Mary (POTEE) 89
Mary (PUTTEE) 61
Matthew 58
Rachel 83
Sarah 42, 49, 89
Sarah (SMITHSON) 48

THOMPSON, Thomas 49, 83
THOMSON, James 114
THORNBERRY, Elizabeth 104
THORNBURY, Bethyah 47
Elizabeth 47
THORNTON, Jane 40
THORP, Catherine (CULLINGS) 35
Edward 35
THURSTON, Frances (GIBSON) 33
George 33
Thomas 18
TIBBS, William, Rev. 18
TIPPER, Elizabeth 28
TIPPINS, Christian 60
Thomas 57
TOD, Ann 15
James 14
TODD, Martha 73
TOKER, John 109
TOLLEY, Edward Carvil 76, 101
Martha (HALL) 76
Walter 76
TOLLY, John 101
TOMMAS, Hannah 14
TOMPSON, Andrew 39
Elizabeth (SHAW) 39
TOMSON, Aquila 32
Elizabeth (GILBERT) 32
James 32
John 16
Margaret 32
TOOLSON, Elizabeth 106
TOULSEN, Ann 106
TOWLAND, Benjamin 113
TOWLSON, Elizabeth 106
TOY, Francess (DALLAM) 94
Joseph 94
TREADWAY, (?) (PARKER) 12
Elizabeth 76
Moses 76
Richard 12
Thomas 76
TREBBLE, Mary 12
Thomas 12
TREBLE, Ann 17
TREDAWAY, Mary 16
Richard 13
Thomas 16
TREDWAY, Aaron 71
Chrispin 52
Elizabeth 71
Elizabeth (OSBORN) 86
Jane 22, 45
John 46, 86, 91, 93
Martha 45, 51
Martin 65
Mary 46, 51, 52, 65
Mary (BULL) 45
Milcah 86

TREDWAY, Richard 45, 51
  Sarah 93
  Sarah (GRIFFITH) 91
  Thomas 45, 46, 51, 52, 65, 71, 114
  William 51
TREELL, Bethena 1
  Samuel 1
TREGO, Hannah 1
TRIBLE, Thomas 13, 14
TUCHSTONE, Richard 33
  Sarah (JOHNSON) 33
TUCKER, Catherine 66
  Jacob 34
  Katharine (PARTRIDGE) 50
  Lewis 50, 66
  Margaret 47, 53
  Margaret (COB) 34
  Seaborn 47, 53
  Seborn 34
  Susannah 47
  William 50
TURNER, Elizabeth 81
TWEEL, Samuel 6
URGHQUART, Hannah 68
URGHVART, Alexander 37, 45, 46
  Ann 37
  Elizabeth 37, 45
  Hannah 37
  John 37
  Mary 37
  Mary (REESE) 46
  Rachel 37
  Sarah 37
  William 45
UTIE, George 2, 3
  Mary 3
  Susanna 2
VANSICKLE, Henry 101
VANSIDE, Henry 115
VANSUCKER, Henry 101
VATOR, Mary 53
  William 53
VEAL, Ann 39, 55
  Christian 39, 55
  Christian (SPENCER) 29
  Daniel 29, 39, 55
  Elizabeth 29
  Hannah 29
  Mary 55
  Rachel 55
VEARES, Ann 10
VERMIEL, Mary 58
  Oliver 58
VERNON, Mary 64
  Oliver 64
VERNUEL, John 58
VERNUM, Abraham 70
  Mary 70

VERNUM, Mary (BROWN) 53
  Oliver 53, 70
VINE, Godfred 49
  Godfrey 49, 103, 104
  Sarah 49
VINER, Elizabeth 10
  Henry 74
  Jane 74
VINEY, Godfrey 60
  John 60
  Sarah 60
VISSAGE, Hannah 78
  Jacob 78
  James 78
  Jane 78
  Thomas 78
WABLINGTON, William 12
WAINWRIGHT, Susanna (RICHARDSON) 11
  Thomas 11
WAIT, James 55
  Mary 54, 55
  Samuel 54, 55
WAKEMAN, (?) Dr. 105
  Edward, Dr. 77
  Elizabeth 85
WALKER, Ann 45
  Eleanor 87
  Elisabeth 50
  Elizabeth 33, 45, 49, 87
  Jane 87
  John 33, 44
  Mary 33, 68, 87
  Thomas 68
  William 33, 49
WALLACE, Samuel 107, 108, 109
WALLICE, Samuel 107
WALLIS, Cassandra 57
  Edward 109
  John 57
  Mary 57
  Samuel 57
WALLOX, Elizabeth 36
  Elizabeth (JONES) 37
  John 36, 37
WALSTON, Arrabella 10
  John 12
  Sarah 19
WALSTONE, Arabella 5
  John 5
  Margaret 5
  Sarah 5
WALTERS, Margaret 53
  Mary 53, 68
  Mary (JONES) 50
  William 50, 53
WAMMAGHAM, Ann (DULANY) 112
  Thomas 112
WANSAL, Lidia 108

WARD, Ann (HALL) 19
  Edward 86, 93, 101, 108, 109, 111
  Edward, Sr. 112
  Elianor 61
  George 19
  Jane 61
  John 23, 93
  Jonathan 19
  Mary 16, 23
  Mary (GRIFFITH) 86
  Samuel 86
  Sarah (WALSTON) 19
  Stephen 16
  Susanna (GOBY) 23
WARREN, Thomas 49, 101
WATERS, Ann (ALLEN) 9
  Henry 88, 101, 108
  Robert 9
WATKINS, Elizabeth 79
  Jane 16
  John 48, 51, 79, 91, 112
  Margaret 48, 51, 79
  Purifie 91
  Purify (GREENFIELD) 79
  Susanna 79
  Thomas 48
  William 51, 91
WATSON, Abraham 10
  Margaret (GINKINS) 10
WATTERS, Godfrey 88
  Henry 88
  Mary (RUFF) 88
WEAKEMAN, Sarah 114
WEBB, Elizabeth (LEE) 85
  Faithfull 70, 94
  Jane 66, 85
  Margaret 85
  Samuel 66, 70, 85, 101, 102, 103, 105, 106
  Samuel, Jr. 101, 112
  Sarah 85
  William 85, 101, 109, 110
WEBSTER, Alizanah 71
  Elizabeth 23, 24, 36, 51, 62, 69, 71, 72, 80, 88
  Elizabeth (DALLAM) 71
  Hannah 17, 20, 24, 36, 72
  Hannah (GILBERT) 62
  Hannah (WOOD) 88
  Isaac 24, 29, 31, 39, 47, 107
  Isaac, Jr. 107, 108
  James 20, 36
  John 17, 19, 20, 36, 39, 71, 88, 108
  John Lee 108, 109
  John, Jr. 16, 22, 23, 62
  Margaret 24, 29, 31, 39, 47, 69

WEBSTER, Margaret (STEWART) 85
  Martha 23, 37
  Mary 19, 22, 23, 29, 36, 51
  Mary (MAC DANIEL) 16
  Michael 22, 23, 24, 36, 51, 69, 72
  Michael, Jr. 108
  Plisannah 17
  Richard 72
  Richard Dallam 71
  Richard, Jr. 108
  Samuel 71, 72, 88
  Susannah 47
WEEKS, Mary 50
WEEL, Samuel 6
WELCH, Ann (HOLLANDSWORTH) 28
  John 28, 50
WELLS, Benjamin 8
  Blanch 8, 12
  Cassandra 25
  Elisabeth 52
  Elizabeth 25, 37, 47, 63, 67
  Frances 25, 68
  George 8, 12, 15, 19
  George, Col. 1, 3
  James 52
  Mary 19, 25, 67
  Parker 47
  Richard 25, 37, 47, 52, 63, 101, 111
  Richard, Jr. 101
  Samuel 107
  Sarah 37
  Susannah 37
  William 63, 101
WEND, Mary 3
WESCOMB, Samuel 45
  Sarah 45
WEST, Ann (PRITCHARD) 83
  Constant 23
  Constantia 11
  Daniel 23
  David 73
  Elinor 78
  Enock 21
  Isaac 82
  Jacob 78
  James 82
  Joannah 53
  Johanna 38, 75
  Johannah 35, 45, 75
  Johannah (GASH) 36
  John 16, 48, 49, 53, 73, 75, 78, 82
  Jonathan 17, 75, 78, 81
  Margaret 49, 73
  Martha 78
  Mary 18, 35
  Michael 75

WEST, Moses 21
Precilla 16
Prisilla 30
Robert 11, 16, 17, 18, 21, 25, 45, 75, 81
Robert Jr. 35, 36, 38
Robert, Jr. 45, 53
Ruth 78
Sara 11
Sarah 11, 17, 18, 21, 23, 27, 53, 75
Sarah (SPINKS) 25
Sophia (KIMBALL) 81
Susanna 21, 55, 73, 78, 82
Susannah 49, 53
Susannah (OZBOURN) 48
Thomas 38, 83, 93
William 78
William, Rev. 97
William, Rev. Mr. 95
WESTCOMB, Samuel 66
Sarah 66
WESTCOMBE, Hannah 42
Samuel 41, 42, 56
Sarah 42, 51, 56
Sarah (THOMAS) 41
Tryal 56
WESTER, Samuel 85
WESTERLY, Sibil 16
WESTREY, Jean 11
Michael 11
Solomon 11
WESTRY, Jean (SOLOMON) 12
Micael 12
WESTWOOD, Elijah 50
Mary 50
William 50
WEYMAN, Robert 102
WHAYLAND, Martha 112
WHEELAR, Benjamin 40
Elizabeth 39
Sarah 40
Thomas 40
WHEELER, Ann 32, 65, 72
Ann (BOND) 65
Benjamin 32, 64
Elizabeth 32, 66, 89
Hannah 65
Jane 29, 72
Josias 89
Leonard 32, 65, 72
Martha 54
Mary 38, 59
Sarah 32, 46, 54, 59, 65
Susannah 89
Thomas 32, 46, 54, 59, 65, 72, 89
WHINERY, Thomas 52
WHITACRE, Amelia 85

WHITACRE, Catharine 39
Charles 39, 101
Frances 46
Mary 39
Peter 46, 85
WHITAKER, Abraham 55
Charles 46, 58, 62
Isaac 46
Mary 46, 55, 58
WHITE, Ann 42
Ann (BAKER) 4, 5
Ann (WILKINSON) 39
Elizabeth 41
Francis 39, 42
James 34
John 34
Presilla (COBB) 34
Sarah Charlotta 56
Sophia 36, 41, 56, 66, 76
Thomas 36, 41, 42, 101, 105
Thomas, Col. 114
Thomas, Maj. 56, 66
William 4, 5
William, Rev. 96
WHITEAKER, Ann 21
Blanch 30
Catharine 18
Catherine 19
Charity 19
Charles 19, 20, 23, 26, 30, 55, 69
Elizabeth 16, 19, 21, 24, 32, 33
Elizabeth (EMSON) 19
Empson 24
Frances 30, 35
Frances (BROWN) 26
James 21, 26
John 16, 21, 23, 69
John, Sr. 21
Luraney 20
Mark 16, 18, 19, 21, 24, 32
Mary 20, 23, 26, 30, 69
Mary (KEMBALL) 19
Peter 21, 23, 26, 30, 35
Thomas 16
WHITECAR, Charles 101
WHITEHEAD, Abiezer Francis 2
Francis 2
WHITEKER, Ann 102
WHITHEAD, Dannelana 3
Francis 3
WHITLATCH, Charles 86
Elizabeth 86
John 86
Mary 86
Rachel 86
Sarah 86
William 86

WHITTACAR, Katherine (TEAG) 12
  Mark 12
WHITTECAR, Abraham 9
  Catharine 9
  Charles 8
  Elizabeth 8
  John 8, 9
  Katharine 8
  Ruth 8
  Sarah 8
WILABEE, Sarah 58
WILBORN, Ann (CRABTREE) 34
  William 34
WILBOURN, Ann 41, 43, 51
  Edward 38
  James 51
  Jane 41
  Margaret 38, 41
  Martha 41
  Thomas 38, 41
  William 41, 43, 51
WILD, Jonathan 57
  Mary 87
  Sarah (PRIBBLE) 57
WILDAY, Edward 14
WILES, Jonathan 60
  Mary 60
  Sarah 60
WILKINSON, Ann 39, 46
  Isabella 54
  John 108, 109
  Ruth 46, 54
  Stephen 103
  Stephen Rev. 105
  Stephen, Rev. 46, 54, 70, 76
WILKISSON, John 40
  Ruth 40
  Stephen, Rev. 40
  Thomas 40
WILL, William 109
WILLIAMS, Ann 38
  Ann (DU??) 92
  Charles 61
  Daniel 32
  David 32
  Edward 92
  Elisabeth 38
  Elizabeth 41
  Henry 102
  Jane 32
  John 38, 44, 50, 66, 70, 92
  Judith (JONES) 61
  Lucy 49
  Lucy Ann (BAYLEY) 46
  Margaret 66, 70
  Margaret (CLARK) 50
  Martha 92
  Mary 13, 32, 38, 92
  Mary (WHEELER) 38

WILLIAMS, Morriss 38, 92
  Moses 49
  Paul 32
  Peter 50
  Thomas 38
  William 46, 49, 54, 55, 111
WILLIAMSON, Elizabeth (BOIS) 59
  Hannah 27
  Sarah 27, 56
  Thomas 27, 56, 59
WILLING, Mary 1
WILLMOTH, Richard 114
WILLMOTT, Richard 101
WILLSON, Andrew 109
  Joseph 109
  Samuel 109
WILSON, Benjamin 64
  Elizabeth 46
  Hannah 52, 61, 68
  Hannah (FARMER) 33
  Hezakiah 27
  Jane 27, 44
  John 33, 38, 44, 56, 61, 64
  Joseph 33, 52, 61, 68, 108
  Margaret 38
  Martha 61
  Mary 14, 38, 44, 56, 61, 64,
    68
  Moses 56, 61
  Rebecca 39
  Samuel 39, 108, 109
  Sarah 27, 39, 44
WINWRIGHT, Ann (RICHARDSON) 10
  John 10
WISE, Margaret (OSBOURN) 12
  William 12
WISEMAN, Henry 24, 62
  Jane (GARVIN) 62
WITHERINGTON, Charles 101
WOLLOX, Elizabeth 65
  Elizabeth (YATES) 65
  John 65
WOOD, Alce 66
  Benjamin 57
  Elizabeth 15, 23, 24, 27, 32,
    42, 45, 52, 57, 65, 69, 74,
    93
  Elizabeth (BRADFORD) 66
  Elizabeth (PITTCOCK) 12
  Hannah 12, 32, 50, 69, 88
  Isaac 6, 8, 23, 24, 27, 32,
    42, 45, 52, 57, 65, 69, 101,
    104
  James 45, 112
  John 54, 66, 93, 95, 96, 104,
    114, 115
  Joshua 6, 8, 12, 22, 23, 29,
    30, 32, 41, 50, 54, 63, 65,
    95, 101, 104, 115, 116

WOOD, Martha 22, 23, 29, 32, 66
  Mary 8, 14, 22, 50, 54, 55, 63, 66, 93
  Mary (GARRETT) 41
  Moses 65
  Prisilla 31
  Prisilla (WEST) 30
  Rebecca 34, 93
  Sara 12
  Sarah 32, 63, 93, 95, 96
  Sarah (DAVIDGE) 93
  Sophia 42
  Stephen 41, 63
  Susannah 93
  William 52, 108
WOODCOK, Mary (AMBOY) 16
  William 16
WOODEY, Hannah 68
  John 68
  Mary 68
  Robert 68
WOODS, Aaron 11
  Joshua 11
  Moses 11
WOODY, Elianor 60
  John 60
  Mary (LYNSEY) 60
WOOLF, Peter 106
WOOLSHER, (?) 10
WORSTLEY, John, Rev. 96
WORTHINGTON, Anna 60
  Charles 60, 101
  Charles, Jr. 109
  Elizabeth 60
  John 60, 108, 109

WORTHINGTON, Sarah 60
YATES, Catharine (HERRITT) 47
  Elizabeth 29, 65
  John 29, 31
  Joseph 28, 31, 42, 47
  Mary 28, 42
  Mary (COWDERY) 28
  Mary (EVANS) 31
  Robert 28
  Susanna 28, 47
  Thomas 29
  William 29
YESTWOOD, Elizabeth 44, 45, 52, 57, 62
  Hannah 45
  James 45
  Mary 45, 62
  Michael 44, 45, 52, 57, 62
YORK, Elizabeth 12
  William 12
YOUNG, Margaret 95
  Mary 42
  Milcah 94
  Rebecca 77
  Robert 95
  Sarah 95
  Sarah (MATHEWS) 95
  William 77, 107
YOUNGBLOOD, Henry Miles 33
  John 46
  John Miles 17, 33, 37, 46
  Mary 17, 37, 46
  Mary (COAL) 33
  Thomas 17

Other Heritage Books by Martha and Bill Reamy:

*Erie County, New York Obituaries as Found in the Files of
The Buffalo and Erie County Historical Society*

*Genealogical Abstracts from Biographical and
Genealogical History of the State of Delaware
Volumes 1 and 2*

History and Roster of Maryland Volunteers, War of 1861–1865, Index

Immigrant Ancestors of Marylanders, as Found in Local Histories

Pioneer Families of Orange County, New York

*Records of St. Paul's Parish, [Baltimore, Maryland]
Volumes 1 and 2*

St. George's Parish Register [Harford County, Maryland], 1689–1793

St. James' Parish Registers, 1787–1815

St. Thomas' Parish Register, 1732–1850

The Index of Scharf's History of Baltimore City and County [Maryland]

Other Heritage Books by Martha Reamy

*1860 Census Baltimore City: Volume 1, 1st and 2nd Wards
(Fells Point and Canton Waterfront Areas)*

Abstracts of Carroll County Newspapers, 1831–1846
Marlene Bates and Martha Reamy

*Abstracts of South Central Pennsylvania Newspapers
Volume 2, 1791–1795*

Early Church Records of Chester County, Pennsylvania, Volume 2
Martha Reamy and Charlotte Meldrum

Early Families of Otsego County, New York, Volume 1

www.ingramcontent.com/pod-product-compliance
Lightning Source LLC
Chambersburg PA
CBHW051101160426
43193CB00010B/1268